The publisher gratefully acknowledges the generous

ontribution to this book provided by the Philip E. Lilienthal

ian Studies Endowment Fund of the University of California

Press Foundation, which is supported by a major gift from

Sally Lilienthal.

A

Philip E. Lilienthal

■   ■

B O O K

Erotic Grotesque Nonsense

ASIA PACIFIC MODERN

Takashi Fujitani, Series Editor

Erotic Grotesque Nonsense

The Mass Culture of Japanese Modern Times

MIRIAM SILVERBERG

University of California Press

BERKELEY   LOS ANGELES   LONDON

Thank you to Duke University Press for permission to publish material from "Constructing a New Cultural History of Prewar Japan," in *Japan in the World*, edited by Masao Miyoshi and H. D. Harootunian (1991), and to the University of California Press for permission to publish new versions of "The Modern Girl as Militant," in *Recreating Japanese Women, 1600–1945*, edited by Gail Bernstein (1991), and "The Café Waitress Serving Modern Japan," in *Mirror of Modernity: Invented Traditions of Modern Japan*, edited by Stephen Vlastos (1998).

University of California Press
Berkeley and Los Angeles, California

University of California Press, Ltd.
London, England

Library of Congress Cataloging-in-Publication Data

Silverberg, Miriam Rom. 1951–
    Erotic grotesque nonsense : the mass culture of Japanese modern times / by Miriam Silverberg.
        p.   cm.—(Asia Pacific modern : I) (Philip E. Lilienthal Asian studies)
    Includes bibliographical references and index.
    ISBN 978-0-520-22273-1 (cloth : alk. paper)
    1. Popular culture—Japan—History—20th century.   2. Japan—Civilization—1912–1926.   3. Japan—Civilization—1926–1945.
I. Title.

DS822.4.S63   2007
306.095209041—dc22   2006027326

Manufactured in the United States of America
15   14   13   12   11   10   09   08
10   9   8   7   6   5   4   3   2

Printed on Ecobook 50 containing a minimum 50% post-consumer waste, processed chlorine free. The balance contains virgin pulp, including 25% Forest Stewardship Council Certified for no old growth tree cutting, processed either TCF or ECF. The sheet is acid-free and meets the minimum requirements of ANSI/NISO Z39.48–1992 (R 1997) (Permanence of Paper).

To Ryan (as promised)
For my Mother, June Naomi Rom Silverberg
and in memory of Fujita Shōzō

Contents

Illustrations

FROM *ERO* TO EMPIRE

THE HOUSEHOLD BECOMES MODERN LIFE

ASAKUSA EROTICISM

DOWN-AND-OUT GROTESQUERIE

MODERN NONSENSE

By Way of a Preface:
Defining *Erotic Grotesque Nonsense*

Beginning in the earliest years of the 1930s, the Japanese mass media told the imperial subjects who were its audience that this was a time of "erotic grotesque nonsense." The words became the shorthand *ero guro nansensu* in a successful attempt, it would appear, to match what was considered the upbeat tempo of the era. While the intensification of pace in such new public places as cafés and the boulevards of the so-called Modern Girls may have been one breathless response to the calls for speedup by Japanese industry, it was at the same time expressive of more liberatory energies. But just as the call to arms took hold during the decade preceding Pearl Harbor, the three-part phrase was quickly and has forever since been taken for granted. The phrasing *ero guro nansensu* has been the means to make sense of a culture represented as decadent—a culture ostensibly eager to celebrate the degradation wrought by sensual pleasures while ignoring the pleas of party politics and the unharnessed militancy in the streets.

I agree that yes, the early 1930s—as well as the years immediately preceding the invasion of Manchuria in 1931, up through the years following the attack on Pearl Harbor—were a time of erotic, grotesque nonsense, and not only because the print and visual media in Japan chose to repeat those terms. This was true, not because these were erotic (meaning pornographic, without here debating the nuances of that term), grotesque (viewed as malformed or unnaturally unseemly), or even nonsensically silly (and thus meaningless) years. I have my own definitions for the erotic, grotesque, and the nonsensical following from my reading of the language of the Japanese mass media of what I call "Japan's Modern Years." In the segments that follow, *erotic* connotes an energized, colorful vitality. *Grotesquerie* is culture resulting from such deprivation as that endured by the homeless and by beggars. Finally, *nonsense* makes a great deal of sense, as the filmmaker

Itami Mansaku pointed out for us. The boisterousness of popular vaudeville can, and in modern Japan did, challenge relationships of domination of one class, culture, or nation-state by an other.

In sum, in Japan from the 1920s into the 1940s, *ero guro nansensu* was expressive of the vitality of the culture of the time. This was a culture which in no small part included fantasies, language, and gestures sold and created by "consumer subjects," including those rendered down and out by the vicissitudes of capitalism. It is my hope that my montage will show that so-called "nonsense" was no aside, but rather was in fact expressive of a politics that was quite cognizant of the power play involved in the attempts of cultures to colonize.

What follows is one version of a history that continues to be told at the same time it is lost to us, while still, and even more so, the noise of the drum-roll surrounds all of us.

Los Angeles
September 11, 2005

Acknowledgments

I would like to acknowledge all who have given me support for far too many years. I am grateful to the generations of graduate students for their enthusiasm and their delicacy in asking after "the book." I especially wish to thank Michael Baskett, Elyssa Faison, Hiromi Mizuno, Michiko Takeuchi, and Greg Vanderbilt. Thank you also to the other students: Todd Henry, Naomi Ginoza, Serk-bae Suh, Kristine Dennehy, David Eason, Haeng-ja Chung, Ann-Marie Davis, Shinn Nakamura, Yeunjee Song, Helen Lee, Marvin Sterling, Hajime Imamasa, Rumi Yasutake, Eiichiro Azuma, Sung Choi, and Yuki Terazawa.

Thanks also to my relatives who waited in bewilderment: Joe, Gail, and Katie Silverberg, Sybil Hexter, Fern and Louis Guthman, Sindy Levine, and Helen Hopps. To my close readers: Sande Cohen, Fred Notehelfer, Martin Krieger, Tetsuo Najita, Jamie Quinn, Sue-Ellen Case, Seiji Lippit, Esha De, Susan Foster, Joyce Appleby, Ken Pomerantz, Kano Masanao, Michael Bourdaghs, Harryette Mullen, Walter Lew, Tsurumi Shunsuke, Jim Fujii, Mariko Tamanoi, Norma Field, Valerie Matsumoto, and Tak Fujitani. To my kin, friends, and colleagues: Fujita Haruko, Gail Bernstein, Susan Griswold, Sondra Hale, Michelle Tanebaum, Mizusawa Tsutomu, Anne Allison, Saito Yoko, Suranjan De, Fumiko Nishino-Friedewald, Muriel McClendon, Jan Reiff, the Monday Night Group, the Birthday Girls, the Got to Stop Meeting Group, Madonna Hettinger, Maria Lymberis, Hosokawa Shuhei, Hayden White, Suh Kyung-sik, Janet Gershon, Tani Barlow, Margaret Brose, Nora Barziv, Masao Miyoshi, Dorinne Kondo, Alice Wexler, Ryusawa Takeshi, my staff at the UCLA Center for the Study of Women, Fujime Yuki, Sharon Traweek, Jonathan Hall, Ken Wissoker, Toshi Saneyoshi, Herman Ooms, my colleagues at the Stanford Humanities Center, MJ Manocchio, Yoshimi Shunya, Henry Smith, Saul Friedlander, Harry Harootunian,

Karen Brodkin, Belli Fiori, Kano Masanao, the Colonialism and Modernity Group at the University of California Humanities Research Institute, Ann Notehelfer, Nishikawa Yuko, Song Youn-ok, Debora Silverman, Nora Barziv, Mariko Bird, Anne Walthall, Rick and Helen Werner, Aaron Seligman, Wayne, Scapino, and Fiorello Fisher, Nakagawa Shigemi, Rin Shukumi, Stephanie Quinn, John Dower, Nimura Kazuo, Norma Field, Mushiga Munehiro, Helen Sanematsu, Amy Richlin, Fujita Yuichi, Jeffrey Prager, Don and Toshiko McCallum, Noah Guthman, Lissa Wadewitz, Lisa Yoneyama, Howard Feinstein, Hans and Claire Rogger, Jose Peregrino, Stacy Yamaoka, Buster Silverberg, Janet Gershon, Lillian Wang, Okamoto Naoko, Margaret Freiwald, the staff at International House, Mary Yeager, Yasumidokoro, Gene Tobin, Chungmoo Choi, and so many others. I am grateful for the memories of Agha Shahid Ali, Ishido Kiyotomo, and Sata Ineko.

My deep appreciation goes out also to the *Asahi Shinbun* archive, the *Ie no Hikari* archive, the *Shufu no Tomo* library, and the Kawakita Memorial Film Institute. This book was made possible by funding from the Guggenheim Foundation and the National Endowment for the Humanities, the support of the Stanford Humanities Center and the UCLA Center for Japanese Studies, and the generosity of the UCLA Office of the Dean of Social Sciences and the UCLA Department of History.

Many thanks also to audiences at the University of Chicago, Duke University, Ritsumeikan University, University of California, Santa Cruz, The Southern California Japan Seminar, and Stanford University for listening and responding to my thoughts.

I would very much like to thank my editor, Sheila Levine, for waiting, and to acknowledge the conscientious efforts of my tireless copy editor, Erika Büky. Many, many thanks also to Mary Severance and Danette Davis of UC Press. This book was completed thanks to the tireless labor of Jennie Vu and to Jesse Engel, Chelsea Szendi Schieder, and Kelvin Teng—who more than kept his promise to stay until the very end.

And finally, there is an end: and again, thank you to Wayne for seeing this through to the end, more than twice.

Introduction

On May 14, 1932, Charlie Chaplin arrived in Japan. The following evening the prime minister of Japan was assassinated by members of the armed forces. These two events were not coincidental: Naval Lieutenant Koga Kiyoshi, abetted by a group of naval cadres, army officers, and civilians, had originally intended to mount their attack at a reception for Chaplin planned by Prime Minister Inukai Tsuyoshi. These activists, eager to ingest a nativist Yamato spirit into politics, recognized the charged political nature of mass culture, as the court testimony of the ringleader revealed: Chaplin was to be murdered, in order to facilitate both war with the United States and domestic anxiety. This was to lead to revolution—they used the term "restoration"—in the name of the emperor. Ultimately, the right-wing zealots appear to have decided that the assassination of members of the Japanese ruling classes, including the party politicians and capitalists who would inevitably attend a reception in Chaplin's honor, would suffice.[1]

Charlie Chaplin (who at the time of the attack was attending sumo with the prime minister's son) may have been saved only because of last-minute scheduling problems that delayed public announcement of the date of his welcoming reception. After inspecting the scene of the killing and following an obligatory statement of sympathy to the press, Chaplin went on to partake of cultural offerings already essentialized for non-Japanese consumers as ultimately, unreachably Japanese. At the top of his list were tempura, geisha, and kabuki. He also visited what this book will call Japanese sites of the modern: he strolled down the boulevard of Ginza, the ostensible play space of the Japanese Modern Girl; he was entertained by café waitresses at the fanciest café in Ginza; he was a central icon of an eroticized movie culture and he visited Asakusa, the playground on the eastern edge of Tokyo serving gustatory, sensual, and visual pleasures to all classes.

Chaplin also made a field trip to a rather different modern social space—a prison built in 1930. We do not know whether he made comparative note of the architectural principles of surveillance informing Kosuge Prison—which featured a central clock tower looking down on a grid—with those of other prisons he had observed but he is on record as having inquired as to the number of sex offenders incarcerated. Chaplin explained that wherever he traveled, he liked to determine the number of sex offenders. This, he said, was the key to national character. Was Chaplin being ironic? In other words, did he really care about sex crimes, or was he more concerned about the discipline meted out by the state through the modern prison—a site that he would take on four years later in *Modern Times*? In other words, when he expressed concern with national character, was the unsaid his interest in the creation of new mores from below, the suppression of the same from above, or both? Chaplin's account of this visit to Japan (in an ironic reworking of his would-be assassins' preoccupation with the Yamato spirit) refers to a "virus of Western civilization" about to extinguish the Japanese people's appreciation for the simple moments in life. I cannot agree with this assessment, nor could the cultural commentators of modern Japan to whom I defer in this book. However, Chaplin did see beyond his tempura to the grotesquerie of the early 1930s, and he took due note of the "smog of Western enterprise": "I saw food rotting, goods piled high while people wandered hungrily about them, millions of unemployed and their services going to waste."[2]

While the moment of Charlie Chaplin's trip to Japan and the assassination of Inukai mark the end of any semblance of party government in our textbook histories of modern Japan, my intellectual history of the culture of a self-consciously modern Japan tells a different narrative. I view the politics of culture and the culture of politics from a perspective that emphasizes two aspects of cultural continuity: the continuity of the political power of mass culture and the political continuity of a constitutional structure giving ultimate power to the emperor. However, the political landscape after 1932 exhibited both such continuity and a shift in the political order. The shift is revealed in "The Fall of the Political Parties March," a parody of the 1929 hit song "Tokyo March." The original hit had celebrated the beat of the urban culture of Tokyo. In it, Saijō Yaso's march tempo referred to the rhythms of jazz, the pleasures of sipping on café liqueurs, and the "rush hour" motions of subway and bus. In contrast, Maruyama Tetsuo's tongue-in-cheek rendition displaced the reference to the willow trees of Ginza past with a nostalgic longing for party politics. And rather than suggesting that the addressee accompany the singer to the cinema, or "flee on the Odakyū train line," the parodic verse suggested that the now-outmoded parliamentarians of the two major parties, "unable to receive bribes" or to "hug geisha," should instead "flee to Manchuria." At least the lyricist referring to carpetbagging apparently felt little longing for party government now that the military, the bureaucracy, and the financial world clearly dominated a prime minister backed by neither cabinet nor party. My guess is that there was much support for the new words, for this was a populace that had stayed away from the polls during their ostensible chance at political representation during the 1920s. As more than one historian has pointed out, the parties had no mass base. Moreover, the new power of the military, alluded to in the "The Fall of the Political Parties March" and abetted by dissatisfaction with the dire conditions wrought by the depression, was to intensify in tandem with the events we associate with pre–Pacific War politics: the Manchurian Incident of 1931, the establishment of the puppet state of Manchuria the following year, the failed coup of February 1936, the outbreak of war with China in 1937, the economic and political mobilization for war, and the bombing of Pearl Harbor in 1941.[3]

This process of change and the awareness of the Japanese populace regarding this transformation are expressed in the changing keywords of two decades. By 1926 *modan* (modern), meaning "(modishly) of the present," was sufficiently prevalent to give rise to the transitive verb *modaru* ("to modern"). By 1933 even children were using the word *hijōji* (state of emergency) as a gloss on the moment as the military circulated its "emergency announcements." In 1937 the populace was "spiritually mobilized" for the war against China, and in 1938, the State Mobilization Law extended control into the realm of material resources on the "home front." (Messages such as "Protect the home front" also appeared on the screen before the beginning of all movies.) In 1938 Prime Minister Konoe proclaimed a "new order in Asia." Two years later, in 1940, Japanese imperial subjects were warning each other not to "miss the bus," in support of the eagerness of some leaders to emulate the Nazi model of domestic centralized control through a single party along with the Nazi method of Blitzkrieg invasions of neighboring nations. By 1942, a year after the beginning of the "Greater East Asian War," the award-winning motto "We shall not desire—until we win" (inspired by a newspaper contest to create a proverb that exemplified the establishment of a wartime mentality), signaled the end of consumer culture. But not until 1944 did references defaming "devilish Americans and British" for their war atrocities first appear in the press.

Although this book takes account of the institutional changes implied by these expressions, changes that have been ably documented by historians, it is much more about such popular shifts in sentiment as the sentiment illustrated by the parody of the "Tokyo March," produced during the liminal moment of the early 1930s. Just how liminal that moment may have been will be investigated through the examination of writings about mass culture and writings circulated within that cultural formation. It has been my intention, in other words, to think about mobilization differently from historians who have documented the state ordinances, programs, and implementations of policy from the 1930s into the 1940s. I am concerned with what I consider to be a popular mobilization that offered an alternative to the state ideology of the 1920s, 1930s, and 1940s, albeit one positioned from within capitalist structures of domination.[4]

I call the men, women, and children of these Japanese modern years of the 1920s and the 1930s consumer-subjects in order to express the double-edged nature of Japanese mass culture during that era. The consumer was both a subject of the emperor and a subject with agency, acting as autonomously as the imperial system would allow. Japanese women and men were both privy to a network of pleasures offered within mass culture and subject to an increasingly tight web of state controls on freedom of expression and consumption. And when considering them as imperial subjects, we must also recognize that not only was the imperial reign said to span countless generations, it also covered the contemporaneous geographic terrain of empire.

My understanding (and vision) of Japanese culture in this period is that the principle of montage was central to popular consciousness. The cultural articulations of the Japanese consumer-subjects constantly juxtaposed distinct ideas and entities in such sites as magazine layouts, theater costumes, and language, because culture was seen as fragmented in time and space. The active and often sophisticated process of moving between pieces chosen from various cultures within and outside Japan is presented in the following segments of this book as "code-switching." I also argue that the modern years, from the early 1920s to the early 1940s, were informed by a "documentary" impulse. This was encouraged by the mass media, which constantly demanded new montages to fan and feed the desires of the consuming Japanese subject. The documentary impulse of the Japanese modern years cannot be disassociated from this capitalist process.

Charlie Chaplin's visit to Japan did coincide with the end of party government, but it also occurred at the time when the phrase—a phrase that was itself a montage—"erotic grotesque nonsense" was gaining widest currency. Now, as scholars in Japan extend their exploration of Japanese culture to include a "wartime modernism," the rise of erotic grotesque nonsense in the early 1930s is usually deemed to be the decadent pivot between an era of "modernism" and the years of "fascism." Yet the concept of erotic grotesque nonsense has not been seriously interrogated on its own terms, maybe because it has been seen only as decadent. This book both extends the moment of erotic grotesque nonsense beyond the usual one- or two-year frame of reference and examines each of its constitutive parts in order to consider how the consciousness of the "modern" was not fleeting but spanned the eras usually associated with the modern (the mid-1920s), with the erotic as pornographic (1930–1931), and with the emergency era of war first with China and then with the United States (from the 1930s and 1940s). In my view this moment was not an apolitical prelude or interlude but an intense expression of cultural phenomena with profound political implications. I see this moment as lasting from roughly 1923 until 1938, but with repercussions lasting into the 1940s. In other words, while Japan scholars have come to accept the notion of a fifteen-year war stretching from the Japanese invasion of Manchuria until the moment of unconditional surrender, the following pages delineate a different fifteen-year period, one that of course intersects with war and empire in its closing years. My history of Japanese modern culture begins in 1923 following the Great Earthquake (eight years before the invasion of Manchuria) and concludes approximately seven years before the end of the Pacific War. I also argue, however, that aspects of the culture of erotic grotesque nonsense (so akin to the cultural milieu of Chaplin's *Modern Times*) continued into the Pacific War because the consumer-subjects of the patriarchal Japanese family-state did not want to let go of the modern.[5]

For more than a decade, the documents from the modern years have directed me into the street, the café, the household, the movie theater, and the working-class alleyways that were the sites of the erotic grotesque nonsense examined herein. In this book each site is a segment contributing to recalling the montage that was Japanese modern mass-culture. These sites of Japanese modern culture are examined in juxtaposition as parts 2 and 3 of this book: (1) the Modern Girl on the streets (but really in the imagination of the media); (2) the café waitress working to fulfill the desires of others but rarely able to meet her own; (3) the movie magazine selling fantasy; (4) the modern housewife, within the modern family, within the modern magazine; and (5) Asakusa as a modern site of desperation and of liberatory energies. Asakusa was the honky-tonk exemplification of erotic grotesque nonsense. Therefore, this eroticized modern playground for nightlife and daytime adventures merits its own section as part 3 of this book. The space of Asakusa is treated in three parts—a montage within montage—as a place offering eroticized, sensual pleasures, and as a site of social practices of a down-and-out (which is to say "grotesque") social order. Thirdly, I treat Asakusa as a place of producing political "nonsense" in a popular theater critically attuned to the surrounding eroticism and grotesquerie.

Here are a few brief notes on methodology. One of my goals in the following pages is to illuminate the modern practices of the 1920s and 1930s by focusing on their representation in the mass media and, to a lesser extent, in the words of social critics and of the bureaucracy. For those who demand an account of the reader's response to the media representations, my response is that the producers of modern Japanese culture *were* consumers: all were privy to the imagery being circulated. In other words, production presumes consumption, and vice versa. It has never been possible to document the actual response of the café waitress reading *Shufu no Tomo* or the housewife examining the pictures in *Shūkan Asahi* or the white-collar worker turning the pages of *Kingu* because of the way consciousness is layered from the time of original reception through its reformulations in memory. Instead I attempt to provide close textual readings that can give a good idea of how meaning was produced and circulated. I also attempt to go beyond the extant literature on the cultural history of the period by thinking carefully about the meaning of *ero guro nansensu*, subjecting each of the three parts of the phrase to revision. The appropriation of the method of montage is in such a way central to my approach, just as I think the montage was central to the mass media and to the consumer-subject consciousness of the modern years.

To capture some of the sense of fragmentation and dynamism of Japanese modern culture, I have tried to make use of the principle of montage in two ways in structuring this book. I have employed montage at the level of the organization of chapters, which I call segments. Each segment takes on one aspect of Japanese modern culture, but I do not presume to come up with an all-encompassing vision of culture in its entirety, nor do I expect my readers to engage in such totalizing. Like the spectators imagined by Sergei Eisenstein, discussed in part 1 herein, readers are expected to produce their own partial meanings with the understanding that a montage is never univocal and that a history covering "all" of a time or place is never possible, especially when dealing with a time racked by class, cultural, and gendered tensions. The segments juxtapose aspects of the years when *modan* and *ero guro nansensu* were used to talk about the everyday, and the reader should consider incongruities (such as the distinctions among the idealized female as autonomous, promiscuous Modern Girl, as submissive café waitress, and as ingenious housewife) or the choice of (not necessarily between) samurai figure and Rudolph Valentino in the dreamworld of the cinema.

Secondly, I employ my form of montage by italicizing the loanwords that were incorporated from English and transliterated into Japanese. These were central to the vernacular of the modern Japanese years. For example, the English word "modern" was rendered as *modan* in Japanese and *modan gaaru* was the transliteration for "modern girl." Whenever I have found a loanword, I have italicized it, while retaining the English spelling in order to give a sense of the degree to which English was embedded and reshaped in conversational Japanese of the modern years. For example, when I use the word "modern" in italics, this is my reference to the word *modan* that had become part of the Japanese language by the mid-1920s.

Finally, regarding my methodology, to those who would believe in the sanctity of the archive and the ensuing authority of the historian, I can with honesty say that my reading of primary documents can in no way begin to be called comprehensive. With modesty, as an historian who adheres to the importance of interpretive writing, especially when dealing with questions of consciousness offered up by what we have come (unwisely) to differentiate as "intellectual" and "cultural" history, I can share my excitement at reading both theater memoirs (written during and after the modern years) and select scripts from the modern years. My excitement was based on material that, like Kon Wajirō's Modernology writings, countered the stereotype of the mimetic tendency of the Japanese to borrow Western culture. Secondly, like the humor in *Friends of the Movies*, my reading challenged the still widely accepted thesis that a consumer culture was displaced by a decadent, pornographic, escapist hedonism on the eve of fascism. Thirdly, my reading confirmed my findings of the colonial within the modern, as embedded in *Friend of the Housewife*.

In a sense, my treatment of the Japanese articulations of the *modern* picks up where my study of Nakano Shigeharu ended. In the conclusion to that book, I called Nakano a "modern Marxist" who critiqued a modern, mass commodity culture in which class had become embedded, a capitalist society guilty of "organizing an empire abroad and social forms at home." I stressed what Marilyn Ivy has termed the "coeval" nature of Japanese modernity within a global modernity and conceptualized the Japanese Marxist culture of the 1920s and 1930s as an integral part of Taishō culture. I also pointed out that within this diversified cultural space it was not considered strange for a revolutionary actress to dance the Charleston; mass culture could not be separated from Marxist culture. This book is much more about the woman dancing the Charleston than it is about Marxist revolution, for it positions women in motion at the center and looks at everyday phenomena termed *modern* that were not considered revolutionary but could definitely be seen as threatening.[6]

Japanese modern culture can be configured in many other ways. Another montage, for example, might incorporate the modern into the colonial or undertake an analysis of films, children's literature, or detective novels. A new generation of Japan scholars is already doing exciting work to contribute to such interpretation. They have opened up the field of history of Japan in unprecedented ways. My apologies to them for the absence of their work herein. This book has been much too long in coming. At one point during the process of writing this book I determined that I had to draw a line—to close the door to the archive all the while knowing there were new citations to be written.[7] Thus, I ask the reader to approach this work of history in light of these very important absences, and with an awareness that many journals, genres, institutions, and political questions surrounding or informing the culture of Japan from the 1920s into the 1940s remain to be studied. When I began my investigations, many of my sources, such as popular movie magazines, had not been studied by scholars investigating the intellectual history of the modern years. This is one reason why this project has always felt like a preliminary reconnaissance of archives and issues. If it can be of aid to others interested in similar projects, I will be pleased.

While much still needs to be studied, I can now conclude that the cultural order of modern Japan of the 1920s and 1930s was marked by enormous energy, the urge to create, and acerbic challenges to the status quo. Through mass-media imagery it is possible to begin to gain a vision of the relationship between movies and Japanese modernity, a vision that makes room for Hollywood fantasy, for unprecedented and often eroticized gestures, for working-class spectatorship, for colonial voyeurism, and for the onset of a Nazi-inspired control of film culture. The documentary impulse of the era has provided us with an archive of that legacy that can be used to challenge the contemporary will to forget in Japan and the will to remain ignorant in the United States. This will to ignorance is evident in the *New York Times* review of *Shall We Dance?* on July 6, 1997, which stated: "The Japanese movie 'Shall We Dance?' suggests how a people intimidated by modern life can learn to let go." My study attempts to document a "modern life" defined not by intimidation but by innovation and experimentation. The will to forget was more than evident a year later when the producer of the film *Pride* (the film about General Tōjō Hideki that represents the Japanese as the saviors of their Asian brethren) told his audience at the Brisbane International

Film Festival that he was delighted to be able to offer them the accurate version of history. The audience was at least unresponsive, possibly skeptical, and no doubt in part critical. I have researched and written this book in large part with such a non-Japanese audience in mind, and so if my writing serves to shake up Western notions of Japanese quietude and of pre-1945 cultural isolation, I will be more than pleased. But, I also hope that the cultural imagery already familiar to readers in Japan will appear in a different, more contestatory light at a time when an oppositional mobilization of cultural expression is almost absent and when revisionist voices are overpowering even that opposition.

I would like to admit that I have had a personal agenda in pursuing this project. My attempt to theorize the Japanese appropriation of non-Japanese items and images and gestures not as an "Americanization" but as a historical process specific to Japan has undoubtedly offered me one way to theorize my own conscious and unconscious history of code-switching from English to Japanese and back again, and of transcoding aspects of Japanese and American cultures as an American child in Japan and as an American adult in the American academy. The juxtapositions I offer come from my own experiences of signs, signals, and traces in my own history. I hope that they will also give meaning to the history of others.

PART I

Japanese Modern Times

Japanese Modern within Modernity

I place the years of "erotic grotesque nonsense" within the global modern culture of the 1920s and 1930s, and I position the Japanese modern culture of those decades within a Japanese modernity stretching from the state-sponsored modernization policies of the Meiji era into the late twentieth century. In distinguishing between *modern* and *postmodern*, and among *modernism, modernization,* and *modernity,* I agree in part with John Frow's distinctions. For Frow, *modernism* refers to "a bundle of cultural practices, some of them adversarial"; *modernization* is "an economic process with social and cultural implications"; and *modernity,* overlapping with the modernization process, is "a philosophical category designating the temporality of the post-traditional world." Frow's definition of *modernism* corresponds to *seikatsu,* the all-pervasive Japanese term of the 1920s and 1930s, since both were concerned with the everyday. (*Seikatsu* originally meant "life" or "livelihood," but as will be seen, by the 1930s it would be associated with the everyday necessities and luxuries of clothing, food, and domicile.) His *modernization,* emphasizing the economic process, had its counterpart in such processes as the rationalization encouraged by the introduction of Taylorism into Japan during the 1920s and 1930s, which in the 1940s merged with a Nazi-inspired rationalization policy.[1] Third, the Japanese word *kindai* implies the presentist temporality emphasized in Frow's *modernity.* To these terms I add a fourth, the Japanese word *modan* (written as *modern* from hereon or as *"modan"* when emphasizing pronounciation), which, like Frow's modernization, presumes a post-traditional world not bound by national boundaries or timeless customs but informed by the open-endedness and dynamism of capitalism.[2]

In Japan, Minami Hiroshi and his associates have been most active in writing the history of what Minami terms *modanizumu.* Although I eschew the term, my focus is roughly equivalent to one aspect of Minami's

"modernism." This pioneer in modern Japanese cultural history sees different types of Japanese "modernism" and has also broken it into two aspects:
its rationalist, technocratic side, and the side characterized by the "liberation
by mores" brought in by Western, particularly American, movies. It is the
latter definition that I see informing Japanese modern culture. Minami's
work is more historicist than the other works on Japanese modernism, such
as the lavishly illustrated *Nagoya no Modanizumu* (The modernism of
Nagoya). Although this picture book, which features images of art deco fur-
niture and of such household items as "noritake art deco," does capture one
aspect of the material culture of the era, what most often characterized the
writings on the modern in Japan during the era of erotic grotesque nonsense
was the emphasis on the mores shaping material culture—mores that encompassed a culture of play. There was of course some discussion of technology, rationalization and industry, but in no way could it compete with
the discussions of food, cafés, parks, and boulevards.[3]

Although *kindai* was often used interchangeably with *modern (modan)*
by the 1930s, *modern* was more closely associated with the new, urban practices that are the subject of this book. Moreover, the term *kindai* has its own
history. For example, Arahata Kanson and Ōsugi Sakae, the editors of the
anarchosocialist journal *Kindai Shisō* (Modern thought), which appeared
from 1912 to 1916, were not explicit in defining the implications of this title.
Arahata's recollection of their decision to break out of the embattled position of the Japanese left, following the sensationalized trial and execution
of the anarchist Kōtoku Shūsui (convicted, along with eleven colleagues, of
plotting to kill the emperor), gives a sense of why he and Ōsugi were interested in the here and now. Rather than "waiting for the moment" when
they could reactivate the social movement, the two young men had determined that they would "make that moment." Each issue of *Kindai Shisō*
would thus have the same woodblock print image of a bare-chested worker,
arms stretched wide, breaking loose from his chains, with the words "Modern Thought" printed below it. The image and title always appeared above
a brief inspirational piece. For example, the cover for the February 1913
issue, titled "The Creation of Morals," offered an agenda for making the
modern present: those who deemed "dangerous" would create new morals
and therefore push history forward.[4]

If the *kindai* of *Kindai Shisō* implied morals and liberation of the mind,
the "modern" of the magazine *Kindai Seikatsu* (Modern life) connoted
modern mores enacted within a material culture. Here the operative term
was *seikatsu*, whose materialist connotations were well in place before the
1920s. As early as March 1914, an article in the journal *Seikatsu* had called

for the "renovation" of clothing, food, and living quarters in order to counter the "fossilization of contemporary daily life," thus associating this trilogy with *seikatsu* in a way that would repeat itself in the 1920s and 1930s. But the everyday could also be linked with play. The association of *seikatsu* both with capitalist production and with leisure-time consumption is evident in the special (Tokyo Taishō) "Exposition Issue" of *Seikatsu* that appeared the following month. The exhibition was mapped out building by building and product by product, the products associated with their sites of origin. Osaka contributed celluloid materials, for example, while Nagoya showcased watches and violins. And it was not merely the production of things but their mass production that was to be celebrated. The appended guide to "New Tokyo" dedicated a great deal of space to Tokyo's "pleasures," outlining, for example, the varied forms of theater and gustatory experiences available to the consumer, while warning that the livelier the eatery and the greater the number of clogs lined up in the entranceway, the worse the food. And thus when "modern life" was discussed in the first issue of the magazine *Kindai Seikatsu* in 1929, the phenomenon was associated mostly with urban pleasures, and the sensation of speed was added to the enjoyment of women, movies, and food. All that remained was the displacement of the term *kindai* by the loanword *modan*.[5]

By the late 1920s, innumerable discussions sought to associate the word "*modan*" with material culture. In a 1928 roundtable discussion labeled "A Chat about Modern Life," a group of women and men gathered to discuss the new mood in daily life *(seikatsu kibun)* after the devastating earthquake of September 1, 1923. These left-wing critics agreed that the source of the *modan* was America, and that Americanization was taking place in both Europe and in Japan. Although they agreed that the absence of a national tradition in the United States had led to the superficial, ephemeral quality of modern life, they could not answer Murayama Tomoyoshi's query: "If the cause of the *modern* was in America, what was the source of the modern in *America?*" Ōya Sōichi's essay indicting Japanese modern life *(modan raifu)* as superficial—lacking content and history, emotion, morals, and ideals, and artificially superimposed on a Japanese "real culture"—still remains largely unquestioned today. This book challenges this premise, as did Murayama Tomoyoshi when he answered his own question: "The source is in America because America is the world's largest capitalist country." Murayama also made a historical distinction between capitalist Japan and capitalist America. Japanese society, he said, had until recently been defined by an ephemeral quality, but now there was a sense that things were being constructed. The new, modern material culture did not disappear so quickly.[6]

The two decades of the *modan* years—framed by the devastating Tokyo earthquake of 1923 and the immediate aftermath of Pearl Harbor—emerged from within a modern project of Japanese state-building that had been buoyed by Enlightenment ideology and European technology since the end of the nineteenth century. But it is important to maintain distinctions specific to Japan. For example, this modernity corresponds only in part to Matei Calinescu's notion of two conflicting modernities. The modernity of the Meiji state was indeed a product of scientific and technological progress, of an industrial revolution, and of "sweeping economic and social changes" brought about by capitalism. In this sense Japanese modernity corresponds to Calinescu's first, "bourgeois" modernity. But because the capitalist order in Japan was imposed largely from above and without, Calinescu's second, "cultural" modernity, a modernity defined by "radical antibourgeois attitudes," is much less relevant in Japan than in Europe. When cultural radicals from within the Japanese Proletarian Arts Movement indicted a Japanese bourgeois order, it was economic oppression based on class differences, rather than a Japanese bourgeois sensibility, that was usually the object of attack. The sensibility of the newly rich Japanese bourgeoisie, open to new modes of living, stands in contrast to that of the European bourgeoisie, whose highly ritualized, privatized domestic sphere was rejected by avant-garde artists, intellectuals, and other rebels.[7]

The discourse on the modern bears resemblance to David Harvey's eloquent synthetic interpretation of modernity and modernism, but again there are differences. His explication of the contrast between modernity in Europe and in America helps in refining my definition of Japanese modern. For example, his recognition of the absence in the United States of "traditionalist (feudal and aristocrat) resistance, and the parallel popular acceptance," resulting in an avant-garde possessing much less political force than its European counterpart, may indeed apply to Japan also. However, it does not explain why the American version of modernity, often termed "Americanism" in the Japanese press, gained currency; after all, the American individualist, liberal ideology that welcomed and incorporated change was very different from the family ideology, buttressed by laws, codes, and, if need be, brute violence, that constituted the cultural politics of the Japanese imperial system.[8]

Most of the "material practices" that Harvey identifies as "catalysts" for modernity—the machines, new transport and communications systems, buildings, and bridges—were evident in Japan by the 1920s. So was the instability that accompanied innovation and social change. Consider, for example, the implications of the demographic shift during the modern years.

Working from census figures, Minami Hiroshi reports how by 1930 one out of every four Japanese subjects was an urban resident and how the population in the major cities of Tokyo had increased by more than one third. Rural areas saw only a 6 percent increase in population within a decade. Minami's conclusion that there was a "preservation of rural practices, everyday lifestyle, and modes of thought" follows from his emphasis on the fact that the overwhelming majority of the populace was employed as either peasant or service worker in small family style industrial and commercial enterprises still in their premodern form. While Minami's historical narrative of "major fluctuation from country to city and from farmer to urban laborer" should not be disputed, I am not ready to conclude that the similarity in scale and kinship (or fictive kinship) practices presumes a continuity in modes of thought and practice. I would like to challenge this supposition for two reasons. First, workers moved constantly from rural to urban cultural spaces and back again during the modern years. Workers who joined the small-scale enterprises mentioned by Minami would return to the countryside to maintain family ties, to choose marriage partners, and, when the urban economy failed them (as it failed so many during the depression), to gain a modicum of financial security. This does not mean that the relationships of the workers within their family units in the country were identical to the family ties within the family-seized urban enterprises. This is not the place to construct a history of shifting consciousness and practices of the peasant turned worker. Moreover, what follows is not a social history which could catalogue the belongings of women and men who traveled from urban areas back to rural communities. I do believe however that the movement of belongings such as magazines and the latest fashions was one way whereby the modern was brought into the countryside. Therefore, I ask the reader to imagine the likelihood that these new urbanites did indeed transport these objects along with the fantasies that were associated with this material culture from city to countryside, thereby transporting modern culture.[9]

My second reason for challenging what I see as the overemphasis of the impact of rural community on urban culture lies in the national aspect of mass culture in Japan during that era, especially the culture celebrated in the mass magazines. While Minami has emphasized the end of the monopoly of Tokyo culture on the nation after the earthquake of 1923, and Jeffrey Hanes has discussed the segmented, class-differentiated market of mass culture in Osaka, my emphasis is on the crossing of class and regional boundaries implied by the marketing and movement of magazines and movies (even if some audiences saw the latter only in the form of movie stills presented in the pages of magazines). The magazine *Ie no Hikari* (Light of the household), a mouthpiece for the agrarian cooperative movement, was found in rural homes from 1925 onward. But the fact that its publishers issued a separate version for urban audiences indicates that urban culture was more than a transfer of rural practices into the cities. Moreover, the version of the magazine aimed at the countryside contained articles revealing the intense draw of modern culture among rural youth. (Proscriptive literature, after all, can indirectly be descriptive.) And it is too simple to presume that magazines aimed at the new urban middle class were consumed only by the white-collar worker and his family. As Tsurumi Shunsuke, citing Katō Shūichi, informs us, during the 1920s, 1930s, and 1940s, "the president of a company and the janitor would both read the magazine *Kingu* (King), which sold a million copies." Café waitresses identified with modern culture, including the Hollywood movies featured so prominently in *Shufu no Tomo* (Friend of the housewife). As for the café waitresses, while their customers might be nouveau riche, they were most certainly working-class girls. And these working-class girls bought the same mass magazines from vendors who came into the café. These working-class girls tended to have provincial or rural origins, and we must presume that when they went home to visit or to relocate they took their magazines and their presumptions about Hollywood with them. This is not to say that different classes all read modern culture in the same way; nor can I here compare its reception by workers and by middle-class women and men. To do so would work against my acknowledgment of social instability. I am pointing to the continuity and the ubiquity of the discourse on the modern, both of which destabilized official ideology.[10]

In modern Japan there was also the more abstract but widely shared emphasis on "the fleeting" that Harvey borrows from Baudelaire. The earthquake of 1923 signified a break with the past and with traditions, including those created by the modern state. Officially, time might be measured in terms of imperial reigns, but numerous documents attest that people divided their lives into pre- and post-earthquake segments. I do not, however, see in Japanese modern culture the other Baudelairean concept discussed by Harvey: an eternal notion of humankind. Of course, official ideology, encapsulated in the "Imperial Rescript on Education" that yoked the Japanese subject to empire through family and ancestry, was premised on the idea of a timeless, seamless filial piety. The state's modernization project was modeled in part on the notion of an eternal order expressed in Confucian family relationships. But in the Japanese mass media, the "fascination with speed and motion" was ubiquitous—the word *tempo* beat a constant, contrapuntal rhythm to the cadences of official documents. Like the Euro-American counterparts Harvey discusses, Japanese modern culture was international and often propagandist in its socialist allegiance. A Japanese constructivism emerged alongside socialist realism. The image of modernism put forth by Raymond Williams is also apposite: he places it among the "greatest changes ever seen in the media of cultural production." The media he lists, "photography, cinema, radio, and television," also made their mark on Japanese culture in the modern years. In Japan this was most definitely the dawn of the era of mechanical reproduction.[11]

Despite these comparisons with European culture, when I refer to Japanese modern (which is how I retranslate the word *modan*, to mark it as a distinctly Japanese phenomenon), Western aesthetic (or cultural) modernism falls out of the picture. This is not because the avant-garde movements listed by Williams were not present in Japan during the 1920s and 1930s. In fact, futurism, surrealism, and dadaism all found expression alongside constructivism in journals produced by Japanese intellectuals who either had personal contact with the "antibourgeois" artists in Europe or were emotional kin to the artists Williams called "emigrés." Moreover, the popular press adopted the fractured aesthetic of modernism exemplified by the montage. I fully recognize that the modernist poetry of the 1920s and the illustrated articles about modern family life in the Japanese illustrated press emerged from within the same political, cultural, and intellectual moment and can be said to have partaken of the same discourse about new practices and unprecedented social relationships. Here, however, I am curious to know what *modern* meant in the mass culture of the era, a mass culture that concerned itself with material culture. My goal is to gain insight into the politics of a cultural autonomy and of its relationship to political mobilization from the 1920s into the 1940s in Japan.[12]

The avant-garde artist and playwright Murayama Tomoyoshi, who introduced constructivism into Japan, offered a commentary on the modern that illustrates the importance of the domestic everyday realm. His treatise on Constructivism reveals a crucial point of overlap between the modernist avant-garde and the consumer of the modern: a concern for *seikatsu*, a daily life made up of both repeated practice and popular innovations. Murayama contended that *seikatsu* was the primary problem for the present and that the "priests of art" were preventing the creation of a new everyday. This constructivist saw art in the quotidian arrangement of objects in a room: "When you try to put a *typewriter* or a sewing *machine* in a room, the housewife comes over and says, 'Please do not place such a thing there. That will destroy the harmony of my room.' She says that postcards, stamps, pipes, tickets, chamber pot, umbrella, *towels,* chairs, bedding, *handkerchiefs, neckties*—no matter how trifling the object—are all unartistic."[13]

Murayama's equation of the housewife—whom I see as an agent of everyday modern culture—with an obstructionist "priest of art" is questionable. But his desire for a newly created daily life was consistent with my view of Japanese modern culture. The point for Murayama and others was that the new mores were post-earthquake and therefore post-traditional. The present and the future were open-ended: they were there for the making.

The most compelling of unprecedented *fūzoku* (the much-used word for mores) were new bodily gestures. The gestures, including new ways of encoding and decoding language, were unquestionably linked to the movies—mostly American movies, as Minami has pointed out. It was not uncommon for the media to note that the Japanese were less animated than their Western contemporaries. What interests me, however, is not a literal reading of that statement but rather the fact that such comparisons were being made. There is evidence that new movements and expressions were coming into use. The gestures articulated in cinema, and the references to the need for gestures, contributed to what I term the "documentary impulse" of the Japanese modern years. As late as 1942, even after the state cooptation of the film industry through such propaganda as the "culture movie," the power of film gesture was still acknowledged in a work entitled *Eiga Hyōgen Keishiki* (Film, expression, formation). More than anything, film was a human means of expression, as "language, sounds, and molding were a human means of expression." Murayama had been even more direct. In 1936, he had commented on new gestures made apparent by the technology of film. Using the term *zesuchaa* (gesture), he lauded the speed of speech in the talkie. ("Tempo," along with newness—being in the "vanguard"—was one of the most lauded traits of the modern years.) Dialogue and gestures could be placed in counterpoint, and an expressiveness in both gesture and language, hitherto lacking in Japanese actors because of the absence of such emotion in everyday life, was to be aspired to. While Murayama did not talk explicitly about the Japanese movie audience, let us turn to these women, men, and children who were living the modern life.[14]

PLACING THE CONSUMER-SUBJECT WITHIN MASS CULTURE

The Japanese New Year's game of *sugoroku*, a board game resembling Parcheesi, was an appropriate giveaway in the mass-marketing wars of prewar Japan, for the boldly colored mazes well expressed the experience of the urban consumer-subject from the eve of World War I into the era of Japan's advance into China two decades later. The fortunes of the players lurched

forward and pulled back as did the Japanese economy after the unprecedented boom during World War I. Commentators called the war a "gift from
heaven," and indeed the urbanization and industrialization of the economy,
as Japan moved into the armaments markets vacated by the European powers, were so intense that more secular assessments seemed inadequate. Between 1914 and 1919, the number of workers in factories employing five or
more workers rose from 948,000 to over 1.7 million, and by 1920, 18.1 percent of the populace was living in urban areas. (This figure was to rise to 24.1
percent by 1930.) As a result of the expansion of heavy industry, especially
the shipbuilding and steel industries, the expansion of the textile industry
(by the end of the war, Japan was second only to England in the production
of cotton), and the new trade relationships with Europe, the United States,
and Asian nations, Japan was also transformed from a debtor into a creditor
nation. The first downturn ending the postwar boom, which resulted from
the extension of credit by banking institutions, came in 1920. The economy
recovered by 1922 but was again decimated by the earthquake of 1923. A reconstruction boom that began in 1924 was brought to an end by the financial crisis of 1927, compounded by the worldwide depression two years later.
This downturn was attended by the drop in silk and rice prices that devas-
tated the rural sector by 1931, exacerbating a depression that would last
until 1934. Between 1934 and 1936, as a result of military spending accompanied by a reflationary policy, there was another upswing, and by 1937
there was virtually full employment.[15]

The white-collar, nouveau riche class of salaried workers, bureaucrats,
and teachers, which first emerged during the Russo-Japanese War and
which constituted 7 to 8 percent of the population by 1920, was hard hit by
the 1923 earthquake. However, the rise in the cost of living during the early
1920s was offset by the reconstruction boom of 1924, and the white-collar
salaryman generally had a good life during the 1920s. A college graduate
who received the average salary of eighty yen per month, supplemented by
a bonus worth four months of pay, could easily afford new accessible consumer items such as ready-made clothing, radios, phonographs, cameras,
and electric irons: a made-to-wear suit jacket cost ten yen, and rent
amounted to twenty yen per month. With one yen he could go to the
movies and enjoy a dinner of grilled eel along with a bottle of sake before
taking the train home to his suburban "culture house." His fortunes were
not totally secure, however. Salaries and raises were fixed during the 1920s,
and by the end of the decade many of the new urban consumers were casu-
alties of "enterprise rationalization" who faced unemployment. The popularity of the Ozu movie of 1929, *Daigaku wa Deta keredo* (I graduated from

college, but . . .) and the 1928 *Kaishain Seikatsu* (Life of an office worker), featuring a salaryman who is fired on the day he receives his bonus, attest to the precariousness of the new good life.[16]

What is important about this history is that this consumer culture was not restricted to the middle class. Small shopkeepers and factory workers were also consumers, as Ishikawa Hiroyoshi has shown. He sets forth three socially distinct geographic spheres: the *shitamachi* (usually translated as "downtown") region of self-employed craftsmen and tenement slums; the *yamanote*, the upper- and middle-class neighborhood of bureaucrats, military employees, teachers, and office workers; and "the other side of the [Sumida] River," where workers in small-scale factories joined rickshaw drivers, cart-pullers, rag-pickers, and day laborers in the lower reaches of urban society. There was a leap in the standard of living between 1919 and 1922: real wages rose, and the level of consumption increased 160 percent. (Housing expenditures rose from 10.3 percent to 16.3 percent, and clothing expenditures rose from 9.7 percent to 15.5 percent.) After 1922, desires were refocused from housing and food to what Ishikawa terms "social, cultural desires." Using surveys from the 1920s and 1930s, Ishikawa documents the new recreations of the skilled laborer, who enjoyed such forms of leisure as sports, travel, and reading from the early 1920s onward.[17]

The extensive research by Minami Hiroshi and his associates yields a series of links within mass culture that create a dual meaning for the term *taishū* (mass). In these writings, *mass* refers both to the techniques of mass production, distribution, and consumption and to the producers and consumers thereof. More important, these sources reveal (possibly unintentionally) how the use of the term served to gloss over the relationship of class to mass culture. A close reading of that history also reveals links between the state (embodied in the emperor) and cultural production. It is clear that the mass-produced material culture of housing and clothing, newspapers, books, magazines, movies, records, and spectacles (including nightlife), state ideology, and policy presumed and produced a consumer-subject; all were intricately interconnected.

After World War I, both consumption and production were rationalized, as department stores offered household goods, clothing, and "mass cafeterias" that became sites of new family leisure activity. By 1919, the major emporiums of Shirokiya, Matsuya, Takashimaya, and Sogō were catering to urban customers and provincial gawkers; they were followed by Marubutsu and Daimaru in 1920 and Isetan in 1922. By April 1923, a nationwide consumer organization had been started, and the following year Mitsukoshi customers were asked to vote on whether the pre-earthquake practice of removing shoes at the entrance should be abandoned. Shopping by monthly installments, most mass-produced clothing and the new forms of housing were undoubtedly accessible only to white-collar consumers, who constituted less than 10 percent of the populace. Moreover, hotel toll roads encouraging tourism, the private railway lines linking passengers to amusement parks, the all-girl Takarazuka theater and music review, and the department stores placed conveniently at railway terminal points provided a nationwide network of consumer activities for the more prosperous on set incomes. There was also the no less obvious network of highly commodified print and broadcasting media, including the movies, that reached beyond the new nuclear family of the new white collar-worker, the "salaryman." Even if consumer objects were not attainable, all consumer-subjects had access to department stores and cinema spectacles. Even more significant must have been the immediate accessibility of the pictures of commodities in the ubiquitous print media. In other words, the consumption of images of objects rather than the objects themselves was central to Japanese modern culture.[18]

By the 1920s, print culture was almost universally available: readers were notified of new publications by advertisements in newspapers, magazines, and one-yen books. The school system had provided a broad literate readership by the end of the nineteenth century, and the fanfare surrounding both the Sino-Japanese and the Russo-Japanese wars had primed the population's desire for news. Yet there was a double edge to the power of the press, for, just as it advertised for the state, it could also spread news of unrest, as during the rice riots of 1918, when news of the "North Coast Women's Uprising" pushed many into the streets. Newspaper circulation, which had been 1,630,000 in 1905, soared to 6,250,000 by 1924 (reaching one household out of six), and by 1931 the population of 65 million purchased 10 million copies because of the marketing ploys offering new forms of entertainment. Advice columns written by noted women authors, along with religion and agriculture columns, sold newspapers. Comic-strip heroes such as Maggie and Jiggs (in Japanese) sold news magazines. The adventures of Lazy Daddy, a character who first entertained working-class readers of the *Hōchi Shimbun* in November 1923, testify to the links among media. For years, this well-meaning, bespectacled, rotund figure, respectably clad in kimono and kimono jacket, would confront such modern innovations as radio broadcasting and the unemployment line. Lazy Daddy's popularity ran to thirty-three volumes of cartoons and a theatrical production.[19]

By the early 1900s magazines had become part of the mass media, and over 180 magazines were produced for such carefully segmented audiences as elementary-school boys and bourgeois housewives. By the late 1920s, these specialized publications vied for market space with the "all-round" magazines *(sōgō zasshi)*, featuring fiction and roundtable discussions by professional journalists and critics. *Kingu*, modeled after the *Saturday Evening Post*, sold 740,000 copies on its first printing in 1925, after an unprecedented ad campaign. The premier issue included a free *sugoroku* game. Within a year, sales reached one million copies. Between 1918 and 1932, the number of periodicals registered with the state more than tripled, from 3,123 to 11,118. And during the *enpon* (one-yen book) wars, publishers, taking their cue from the Harvard Classics, packaged multivolume editions of literature and other types of books. This system obligated the consumer to buy the entire set, and the authors amassed overnight fortunes that were immediately spent on fancy villas or trips abroad.

Advertising for material culture had begun as early as 1907, when the Mitsukoshi department store invited leading artists and writers to form a "Group on Trends" to advertise variations on clothing fads. By World War I, the advertising industry had become institutionalized by such groups as the Advertising Study Group at Waseda University (organized in 1916), and by trade publications such as *Jitsugyō Sekai* (Business world), which introduced Scott's *Psychology of Advertising*, *Kōkoku Zasshi* (Advertising magazine), and *Kōkoku Kenkyū Zasshi* (Advertising studies magazine) in 1916 and 1917.[20]

Movies were a potent medium for marketing. Encouraged by the popularity of documentary films of Russo-Japanese War heroism, an indigenous film industry had been established around 1907. By 1926, there were 1,056 movie theaters showing Japanese and Western films—one theater for every sixty thousand viewers, including militant factory workers who on more than one occasion experienced employer lockouts on returning from group outings to the movies. Kikuchi Kan's novel *Tōkyō Kōshinkyoku* (Tokyo march), originally serialized in *Kingu* from June 1928 through October 1929, was made into a film by the Nikkatsu film studio. The film was then advertised with photographic ads in major magazines and with the hit song "Tokyo March." Another crossover was the popularization, through both plays and movies, of the new genre of popular songs *(ryūkōka)*, beginning with "The Song of Kachūsha," the theme song sung by Matsui Sumako for the 1914 Imperial Theater production of Tolstoy's *Resurrection*. These songs challenged the ideology of Confucian family cohesion and Japanese behavior celebrated in official texts, with such lyrics as "My wife has a moustache" and a tirade against "my old lady" who cooks only *korokke* (a new Japanese variation on the Western croquette).[21]

These popular songs also advertised the urban cafés where the new music could be heard. Cafés are mentioned in virtually all accounts of the mass culture of this period. By 1933, when forty thousand cafés were operating nationwide, state regulations were instituted to control these drinking places. This did not curb their popularity.

Another link in the media network was provided by radio broadcasting. From the outset, in March 1925, it was controlled through NHK, a state monopoly, but it was nevertheless connected to mass culture, for newspapers spread the new notion of *rajio kibun* (radio frame of mind). The radio broadcast of folk ballads was a version of the reworked folk traditions found in mass magazines, samurai epics, and the movies of the cult idol Matsunosuke, whose swashbuckling antics glamorized the premodern era. The radio audience, which numbered 3,500 homes in 1922 and 24,500 the following year, also listened to Western music and to such programs as *Oto de Kaita Manga* (Cartoons drawn with sounds). The "cartoons" went by such titles as "Spring at the Department Store" and featured representations of cultural shift, as in the account of the Japanese couple visiting Hollywood who meet Charlie Chaplin, suffer at the hands of a pickpocket, and are kept awake by a dance troupe rehearsing in the adjacent hotel room.

One mass medium would often promote another. For example, department stores featured art and photography exhibits; magazines like *Fujin no Tomo* (Woman's friend) sponsored concerts and exhibits. By the early 1930s, photographers had organized into working groups to produce such magazines as *Fuoto Taimusu* (Photo times) and *Kōga* (an avant-garde journal featuring montage). Photographers were also responsible for organizing such events as a traveling photo exhibition from Germany in 1931, which featured 870 prints, including works by László Moholy-Nagy. The separation between state and consumer culture was not always delineated in these spectacles. For example, as early as 1907, items in an art exhibit sponsored by the Ministry of Education provided the motifs for Mitsukoshi's annual ad campaign.[22]

A peculiarity of the culture presented to the consumer-subject, and one of the reasons I have determined that these consumers may not merely be called *consumers*, but must be identified as imperial subjects at the same time, is that all these forms of mass culture, at the same time as they were vying for profit in the marketplace, were censored. Japanese consumers were always simultaneously imperial subjects (needless to say, consumers are never only consumers—the term always masks differences).

The press was the most autonomous of the mass media, as revealed both by the ambiguities in the control system and by successful attempts to resist censorship. Home Ministry bureaucrats could suspend the publication of journals, ban the circulation of specific editions, and mandate the deletion of passages from books and magazines prior to publication. Journal editors circumvented these controls through such ploys as distributing a journal before submitting it for censorship, submitting self-censored copies to state officials and then rewriting the contents before printing, using pseudonyms, and using Xs and Os or blank type in place of words or passages that would undoubtedly be flagged by the censors. Newspapers were also subject to an unpredictable system of prepublication warnings that was ignored by the leading publishers, who either circulated banned editions before receiving official warning or ignored the warnings altogether. Most spectacular of spectacles, and those that best illustrated the ambiguity of the relationship of the subject to consumption and the tension between state and mass-produced consumer culture, were the expositions that were organized in the name of industry and nationhood. The well-advertised and highly organized Tokyo Taishō Exposition of 1914 featured booths staffed by geisha (solicited from throughout the city), the nation's first escalator, such new commodities as the gas-heated bathtub, heater, and range (presented by the Tokyo gas company), and exhibits of the colonized territories of Taiwan and Korea. Eight years later, the Tokyo Peace Exposition introduced an airplane on pontoons and celebrated the empire by adding a "Hall of the South Pacific" to the tableaux of the other colonial holdings in the Taiwan and Korea halls. A third exposition was Tokyo's municipal celebration to commemorate the end of post-earthquake reconstruction in 1930.[23]

Radio censorship was imposed through station officials who telephoned summaries of programs to state officials prior to broadcast, by written instructions sent to the radio stations regarding permissible content, and by NHK inspectors, who activated circuit breakers to cut off broadcasts when commercial advertising was illegally inserted or, less often, when political misstatements were made. There were relatively few muzzlings for overtly political reasons, undoubtedly because political discussion was banned from the airwaves. State sensitivity to form as well as content is reflected in regulations stipulating the broadcaster's tone of voice ("coldly neutral") and the supposed prohibition of the terms "extremely" and "absolutely" with regard to any topic whatsoever. Such songs as the notorious "Wasurecha Iyayo" (I don't want you to forget me now), from 1936, were banned because of the erotic style of singing. However, as a genre of songs with similar plaintive refrains caused the period to be dubbed the "era of 'please, please' [ne ne] songs," such controls apparently had only limited effect.[24]

Movies were censored earlier and more thoroughly than songs through the Home Ministry's regulations, which mandated state inspection of all movies before screening. Films undermining public peace, manners and morals, or health could be banned, cut, returned for revision, recommended for withdrawal, or restricted to limited viewing. Films were not allowed to express any criticism of the political system, including any form of anti-militarist sentiment, or any reference to class or other group conflict (including gang warfare). They were also forbidden to threaten the belief in the Japanese people as a nation, "damage goodwill in foreign affairs," or show how to commit or conceal a crime. Movies such as the Keystone Kops films were banned because they undermined respect for the police. Under the morals category, cruelty and ugliness (including the depiction of bloody battle scenes and physical deformity) were banned, as were scenes depicting extramarital sex, "kissing, dancing, embracing, nudity, flirting, sexual innuendo, pleasure-seeking," and "other." Also to be cut were "items related to the ruin of work," scenes hindering education (for example, by challenging the authority of teachers), and those directly challenging the family-state ideology. Anything that ran "counter to the customs of a virtuous home" was forbidden, as were allusions or references to the imperial family. Makers of feature films could not show the imperial regalia or any member of the imperial household, including past emperors; nor could they film any images suggesting the imperial chrysanthemum, including samurai crests: thus flower crests of twelve to twenty-five petals could be filmed only if they were clearly distinct from the imperial emblem. Documentary footage of the emperor was also subject to close scrutiny. The imperial household was to be presented accurately, with the stylized manner of speech of its members intact, but no shots of the exhaust from the cars of imperial bodyguards could be shown.[25]

By the 1910s, nonetheless, the imperial institution was inserted into the marketplace of mass culture. This development was in sharp contrast to the cultural terms of the preceding Meiji era, when, as Carol Gluck has so fully documented, popular culture was mobilized in order to familiarize newly naturalized subjects with the emperor, and, as Takashi Fujitani has illustrated, new cultural traditions inserted the emperor and the nation into popular memory. One example of how commodity culture appeared to take charge came with the enthronement of the second modern emperor in November 1915. This event was commemorated by the highly advertised marketing of items imprinted with chrysanthemum and paulownia patterns by the Mitsukoshi department store and numerous ads for other commodities "to commemorate the enthronement." The ceremonies surrounding this ritual were used both to familiarize the male populace with Western clothing and to sell domestic silk products in the latest colors, which represented the vivid shades of imperial pageantry. (The following year, the discerning consumer was urged to buy earth tones. The rhetoric of fashion, encouraging the ever-shifting desires of consumers, had been established.) The media campaign to promote the future Shōwa emperor as "the young prince" was instituted in March 1921, when he was sent on an extensively photographed six-month world tour in preparation for his regency, which was to commence in November of that year. The photos in newspapers and magazines inserted the new emperor into mass culture as a glamorous male to appeal to female readers.[26]

To what extent was the dashing crown prince being commodified to peddle commodities? Or alternatively, to what extent was the media a medium for the state? Did it serve to illustrate the ideologically freighted "Imperial Rescript on Education," which was recited by every schoolchild? This text opened with the injunction, "Know ye, our subjects," and celebrated the ancestry of the imperial throne as the basis for filial behavior, respect for the constitution, observance of the law, and "courageous" service to the state in order to "guard and maintain the prosperity of our Imperial Throne coeval with heaven and earth." Close reading of texts from the era can begin to offer answers. For example, mass magazines from the 1920s and 1930s, such as *Shufu no Tomo* (Friend of the housewife), beloved by both working- and middle-class women, and the more bourgeois *Shūkan Asahi* (Weekly Asahi), reveal a shift toward the consumer side of the consumer-subject formulation, emphasizing a modern subject's agency by offering articles on new mores and items to be consumed. Here, then, is an example of Carol Gluck's discussion of the disjunction between *ideology* and *experience*, although, for the modern years, I would rephrase this cultural and historical phenomenon as the disjunction between ideology and practice.[27]

The montage form is also central to my approach, just as I think the montage was central to the mass media and to the consumer-subject consciousness of the modern years.

EROTIC GROTESQUE NONSENSE AS MONTAGE

The words *ero guro nansensu* were and are still used to characterize the first few years of the 1930s in Japan, especially the year 1930. The term has been associated with a kaleidoscope of sites and motions, as encapsulated by Kawabata Yasunari in 1930: "*Eroticism*, and *Nonsense*, and *Speed*, and *Humor* like social commentary cartoons, and *Jazz Songs* and Women's legs."[28] I have taken the liberty of extending the term to cover the mid 1920s into the early 1940s.

The political theorist of Japanese modernity Maruyama Masao recognized the significance of related transformations in Tokyo following the 1923 earthquake. These were "the beginning of radio-broadcasting (1925); the proliferation of *baa* (bars), *kafuee* (cafés), *kissaten* (tearooms); the rapid growth of street buses and suburban railways; the beginning of the subway system (1927); the growth of department stores and modern business offices" that emerged to take hold of, to recreate, and to create anew cultural practices of the everyday order. To this list of elements of the growth of what he termed "mass society" Maruyama added mass literature, mass-produced journalism (including advertising), the culture houses "with red roofs and small gardens in which white-collar workers dreamed of enjoying 'my happy, though cramped, home,'" and Modern Girls *(moga)*, along with Modern Boys *(mobo)*. According to Maruyama, within this setting, well-to-do parents of college students feared two temptations for youth of the era. They could either indulge in "eroticism, grotesqueness, and absurdities" as *moga* and *mobo* aimlessly strolling down Ginza, or they could become serious versions of "Marx Boys" and "Engels Girls" making leftist revolution. For Maruyama the two options were diametrically opposed. Youth, especially bourgeois youth, could become "pink"—indulgent in sexual pleasures (the preferred choice of their parents)—or they could be "red"—adherents of "dangerous thought."[29]

I agree with Maruyama that this was the moment of the emergence of modern Japanese mass society. In fact, "mass" *(taishō)* was a key word of the era, used both by those who deemed to attach to it a Marxist connation celebrating proletarian praxis and by those who profited from a consumer culture that could offer images, if not objects, to the masses. However, my treatment of the media catchphrase *ero guro nansensu* differs from that of Maruyama, because it is my conclusion that the connotation of lasciviousness does not suffice. Granted, the term *ero* was ubiquitous in the popular media of the era, and was often attached to discussions of sexual promiscuity and to the configuration of the female (and sometimes the male) body. This does at one level appear to be an instance of an injunction to speak incessantly about difference and desire.[30] However, *ero* could and can be used in a much broader sense, alluding to a variety of sensual gratifications, physical expressiveness, and the affirmation of social intimacy. I examine *ero* in both these meanings. The other two constitutive terms must be treated with equal respect, although the meanings and significance of the terms *guro* and *nansensu* were rarely given in the mass media. While *guro*, short for grotesque, was associated with the malformed or obscenely criminal, my interpretation of Japanese modern culture treats the grotesque in a different light, associating it with the social inequities and ensuing social practices of those living within a consumer culture defined by the economic hardships of the depression.

My treatment of *nansensu* is even more revisionist, for rather than simply treating it as a reflection of the appeal of slapstick comedy, as did the few sources that bothered to define the term at the time, I associate it with a political, ironic humor that took on such themes as the transformations wrought by a modernity dominated by Euro-American mores. In sum, the erotic, the grotesque, and the nonsensical must be treated separately and in conjunction, especially for any interpretation of the "high modern" moment of the late 1920s and early 1930s. To aid in this interpretation I turn to the form that was used to document culture in motion in modern Japan: the montage. My appropriation of the term code-switching, in conjunction with the aid of the montage, connotes agency and movement.[31]

Both intellectuals and consumer-subjects in the different social strata saw a society being made from below, from within, and from without. In the archives from the modern years, the metaphor of construction emerges not only in the visual arts, but also in such terms as *fabrication* and *building*. (The related term *seikatsu* connoted the fabricated nature of everyday life, but the montage best expressed the concept of constructing new times.)

Sergei Eisenstein, the Soviet filmmaker whose work is most closely associated with montage, once termed montage "the operation of juxtaposing two signifying elements." He juxtaposed the "archaism" of kabuki, which he termed the product of "feudal thinking" that had survived political change, with the "montage thinking" of the late 1920s, which reflected the differentiations in political economy and consciousness wrought by capitalism. In his essay "The Cinematographic Principle and the Ideogram," he argued that "the principle of montage can be identified as the basic element of Japanese representational culture," by separating out the identifiable units of a series of Chinese characters and by viewing the process of their combination as "cinematographic exposition." He went on to describe poetry as "hieroglyphics transposed into phrases." I do not adhere to his outdated notion that Japanese behavior by the late 1920s had its basis in "feudal remnants." Nor does Eisenstein's romanticization of written culture interest me. Rather, it is the new print culture that I see as the main site of montage, although similar juxtapositions are also evident in other media, including film and popular theater. Thus, like Eisenstein, although for different reasons, I have adopted montage as a heuristic means of understanding the Japanese culture of that era. Moreover, like Eisenstein, I view the spectator—or consumer-subject—as the producer of meaning. (The montage, in other words, was also a heuristic device for the Japanese consumer of culture.) To quote Eisenstein: "It is precisely the *montage* principle, as distinguished from that of *representation*, which obliges spectators themselves to *create*, and the montage principle, by this means, achieves that great power of inner creative excitement in the *spectator* which distinguishes an emotionally exciting work from one that stops without going further than giving information or recording events."[32]

I presuppose that montage in print culture and on the street generated an energy among the Japanese consumer-subjects of the modern years. My use of the term, which was listed in a leading Japanese dictionary in 1934 as *montaaju*—where it was associated with the terms *assemble* and *combine*—is formal, theoretical, and political. I am consciously using *montage* in the following sense, as defined in *Webster's New World Dictionary.* "The art or process of making a composite picture by bringing together into a single composition a number of different pictures or parts of pictures and arranging these, as by superimposing one on another, so that they form a blended whole while remaining distinct." I am, in other words, concerned with the tension between the "blended whole" and the superimposed images which remain "distinct," rather than with blatant incongruity.[33]

The photomontage was a self-consciously modern aesthetic form employed by avant-garde artists, documentary photographers, and the producers of advertisements in Western and Eastern Europe, the United States, and Japan from the 1920s into the 1940s, and montage reception theories since the 1930s have emphasized the principle of rupture implied by the form. According to Harvey, the montage was about simultaneity and the tension between the ephemeral and the acknowledged "potency" of current conditions. Walter Benjamin had made the same point about the dialectics of montage: because "the image's ideational elements remain[ed] unreconciled," they interrupted "the context" into which they were inserted. Ernst Bloch, the theorist of the nonsynchronous, valorized disjuncture and fragmentation in montage, relating montage to "anticipatory consciousness."[34]

The Japanese photography critics featured in the avant-garde journal *Kōga* in 1932 and 1933 were historians and critics in their own right, not mimics of the works of Hannah Hoch, John Heartfield, and other European artists. But their agenda was to discuss what Horino Masao, writing in *Kōga*, called the "social nature of photomontage" and of photography as a documentary medium that could be a "record of the era and a report of daily life." Horino noted that the sensibility of photomontage was marked by a modern *"tempo"* and termed it the most progressive work open to photographers because it could give active results to individual photographs. Another critic, Hara Hiroma, attributed the popularity of newspaper photographs and news magazines to modern limitations on daily life: readers had neither the time nor the physical wherewithal to read at a more leisurely pace.[35]

More recently, historians of the montage have referred to a practice of "combination, repetition, and overlap" evoking a sense of "narrative breakdown" and the acceleration of the "unfolding of time" experienced by modern citizens well aware of historic rupture, radical realignments of power, and the way in which the viewer of the montage is compelled to rethink the relations between objects in order to reestablish a hierarchy of meaning. According to Maud Lavin, who offers a two-part typology, montage should be, first, an individual work composed of the juxtaposition of fragments; and second, an organized system dependent on the juxtaposition of parts. This definition allows us to see the magazine or the newspaper as montage. Two illustrated magazines of the Japanese modern years, *Shūkan Asahi*, a middlebrow source of entertainment, and *Asahi Gurafu* (Asahi graph) both illustrated three forms of montage: actual photomontages on a page, made up of juxtaposed fragments, organized around a theme; the juxtaposition of multiple photomontages within an issue; and the juxtaposition of one issue with other issues of the magazine and with the leading newspaper produced by the same company. For an illustration of the first two forms, see the pair of photomontages picturing the intensity of modern desire in *Asahi Gurafu* in June 1928: "Daydream of a Modern Girl" and "Daydream of a Salaryman" (figures 2 and 3).[36]

The idea of "montage in motion" expresses the choices and interpretations made by Japanese consumers of film, fashion, food, and other consumer items that could be coded as Western but were decoded and reencoded as *modern*. In other words, this culture of montage in motion entailed a transcoding process that enabled the consumer to maintain a sense of indigenous identity while both moving within and creating a montage of foreign gestures, objects, and words. I use the word *transcoding* in the sense provided by Tzvetan Todorov, who has concluded that "the intercultural is constitutive of the cultural" and that a "culture is constituted by a constant effort of translation" or "transcoding" by social subgroups within a society, defined by criteria such as age, sex, and place of origin. Although I agree with Todorov that cultures are not organic unities but assemblages or "composites of fragments of diverse origins," I have also adopted the linguistic concept of "code-switching," which refers to such transcoding as shifting between languages and inserting words from one language into a discourse in another.[37]

Although my primary interests here are not specifically linguistic, the metaphor of code-switching is helpful because it emphasizes agency and flexibility while challenging the idea of cultural "borrowing" and replacing it with the idea of cultural strategizing. In other words, like Eisenstein's spectators, who make meaning, the individuals discussed by contemporary linguists "create their own language from the options around them." As they switch between languages, inserted words from one language become embedded in another. In the words of one linguist, "Every loan starts off life as a code-switch." The speaker creates context using code-switching along with intonation, rhythm, gesture, and posture. As with the montage, which is always multivalent, code-switching involves ambiguity, an ambiguity that can be used strategically by a speaker who wants to maintain more than one social identity.[38]

In "Code-Switching and the Politics of Language," Monica Heller talks about agency in terms of the way "language practices are bound up in the creation, exercise, maintenance or change of relations of power." Citing Pierre Bourdieu, she says that code-switching is political because it is a form of "symbolic capital" that gives individuals access to additional symbolic and material resources. By borrowing Heller's argument, I conclude that the Japanese speaker, writer, artist, and consumer-subject made use of a "socially agreed upon matrix of contextualization cues and conventions used by speakers to alert addressees, in the course of ongoing interaction, to the social and situational context of the conversation." And, just as important, the audience or recipient of the shifting cues was capable of interpreting them. I am not considering here the relationship of two discrete semiotic systems; it is not a matter, for example, of an American culture being inserted into a Japanese culture. Rather, I focus on the complex, constant movement of words, items, and narratives appropriated by different groups in Japan. There was not one system constituting Japanese modern language or culture; there were many, including the rules of the ever-changing grammar of fashion, cooking, and other aspects of everyday life to which commentators on the moment were acutely attuned. Thus, according to my use of *code-switching*, the insertion of an English-language word into a sentence of Japanese words was a strategy as relevant as the juxtaposition of contemporary costume with clothing marked as premodern, or the placement in a woman's magazine of a recipe of European origin next to a New Year's ritual unquestionably identified as Japanese. In fact, this strategy was so prevalent that I have chosen to italicize all uses of English language words, as is explained in my introduction above.[39]

Discussion of transcoding and code-switching gives me a way to talk about the movement of culture, but it does not allow me to fully characterize the culture itself. And this task is of immediate concern, for the notion of a culture organized around borrowing from the West, the view prevalent in the cultural histories of the era, does not allow for the significance of agency informed by indigenous history. I leave the reader with one caveat to Todorov's notion of a "complex" culture premised on the process of integration by a dominant culture and resulting in the discovery of multiplicity: a capitalist mass culture both propagated and challenged by the dominant ideology of the state. There was multiplicity within the culture in addition to that brought in from outside. I am most concerned with movement within and between those cultural formations.

Because I believe the political to be inseparable from the cultural, I attempt to foreground relationships of power and to keep in mind direct and indirect challenges to structures of domination, including ideological structures. All too often the study of mass culture is seen as frivolous. However, culture, especially under censorship, is not to be taken lightly, as the Marxist philosopher Tosaka Jun explained to his Japanese readership in 1936. In an article explaining why the policing of mores was equivalent to the policing of thought, Tosaka argued that the tightening control over films, cafés, dance halls, and musical revues passed as paternalistic protection of public morals but was in fact a cover for the suppression of freedom of thought. If the commingling of men with women were really threatening, for example, pleasure quarters would not be protected by the state. The discourse over improving public morals was tantamount to a mother-in-law's pretense of goodwill toward a bride she wished to control. Nor should concern over a *gesture* or clothing be taken simply as concern for public morals. Tosaka illustrated the politics of everyday mores by noting how the obligatory short haircut for middle-school students might have been intended to monitor their everyday life, but when the same regulation was applied to students at vocational schools and universities, it served a different purpose. Rather than preventing juvenile delinquency, it now constituted control over students' thought. In closing, Tosaka was scathing in his indictment of the fascist attention to the everyday. The "*fascists* of the world," he said (making no distinction between Japan and the outside world), were "dealers in manners." These "dealers in public morals" even wanted to "make clothing into strange uniforms." By the same token, it was simple for them to "put thought in strange uniforms." Tosaka summed up his position as follows:

"Thought appears as mores and mores symbolize thought." Tosaka also explained why mores were the target of state control. His reasoning was but one illustration of my finding that a sense of discontinuity was important to Japanese *modern* culture. It was the very newness of such mores as going to *dance halls*, he explained, and not the dancing or any ensuing interactions, that was so threatening.[40]

JAPANESE MODERN CULTURE AS POLITICS

My focus on the cultural as political in some ways complements Andrew Gordon's discussion of the Japanese "dispute culture" of the 1920s, although Gordon makes clear that he has focused on the overtly political aspect of this culture. By cultural, I mean that this book, in contrast, focuses on the political meanings of language, symbols, images, and gestures as historical practices generally not seen as political. In this sense, there is also some overlap with Sheldon Garon's concern for the "daily life improvement campaigns" and other official Japanese attempts at rationalizing everyday life. However, unlike Garon, I am not concerned with the repressive nature of what he terms the state's "moral suasion." While I recognize the escalating presence of such state programs from the 1920s into the 1940s, my position is that reference to new forms of everyday practice could be liberatory as well as controlling: that the media and other modern play spaces introduced options to consumer-subjects, and they give us a record of those options. For example, although Garon rightfully points to the influence of *Ie no Hikari*, as a source circulating tips on household management sanctioned by the state to one million households, a close reading of the magazine of the rural cooperative movement reveals another side to its treatment of modernity. The 1934 montage from *Ie no Hikari* that Garon uses to illustrate the rationalization policies of the state, featuring a communal clock, communal cooking, and a kitchen designed to be highly functional, along with the new, efficient clothing for farm women in the name of the "renovation of everyday life," does bespeak a controlling organization. But articles in *Ie no Hikari* also directly and indirectly point to the draw of modern culture in the countryside. As late as 1939, an article advocating spiritual mobilization in the countryside revealed the continued attraction of neon signs and cafés by expressing an editorial antipathy to these modern institutions. By the same token, the references to the tragic fate of young women who went to the big cities to work as café waitresses tell us that not all rural women were accepting the state-sanctioned version of modern life as the ideal existence.[41]

As I have indicated above, I place the politics of the modern years within the confines of an "emperor system." I thereby part ways with some American historians who have criticized this term (coined by Japanese historians) as outmoded, while agreeing with them on other aspects of their political analysis. Like Gordon, I acknowledge the significance of an emperor-centered constitution and I see continuity in adherence to emperor and empire from the early twentieth century into the 1940s. And I am also interested in the politics of protest, but protest most clearly expressed in irony, parody, and the documentation of new everyday practices within mass culture. My study therefore encompasses the middle and working classes, whose members were the consumer-subjects of this culture. Garon, more than Gordon, has been critical of the emperor system as an analytical rubric. I agree that a study of allegiance to the emperor, or of attempts to inculcate such a connection, does not suffice in illuminating the politics of the era— indeed, this book is an attempt to show a very alternative view. But if Garon is against a systemic view of the emperor's place, he has also provided a succinct summary of the institutions mediating that power: "The national school system, the military, a network of State Shinto shrines, and numerous hierarchically organized associations."[42]

Kamishima Jirō's definition is to the point: "The Emperor system *(tennōsei)* refers to a political system centered on the Emperor as *symbol.*" In other words, I agree that ultimately almost all activity was constrained by the power of the emperor, although modern culture was never totally suppressed. As documented in these pages, and by Carol Gluck in her study of Meiji ideology, there was a range of ideological positions in Japan. However, the power of the family-state ideology established during the Meiji era persisted through the Pacific War (and in modified form afterward), and it must be taken into account to understand the modern years and their end. By the 1920s, the imperial national monuments had been put in place and the ceremonial style made familiar. As Takashi Fujitani eloquently argues, the Meiji project of disciplining was complete, and by the modern years there was a new "viewers' code of behavior" dictated by the mass media. Fujitani and others make clear that the emperor system was consistently about gender and about family, and, because this gender ideology coincided with the modern years, we must relate the official ideology to the mass-based ideas about masculinity, femininity, and family without imposing a simplistic binary opposition between state and an opposing mass society. Other examinations of the layering of gender ideology are provided by Japanese women in the anthology of autobiographical essays edited by Kano Mikiyo, *Josei to Tennōsei* (Women and the emperor system). The book contains such quotidian detail as one woman's reminiscence that for her the entire emperor system was embodied in the power held by her father.[43]

Of course there are other primary sources for investigating the ideology of the emperor system during the modern years. One morals textbook from 1928, aimed at higher school boys in 1928, taught that all were born unequal, yet that humankind was related not only materially but also spiritually. A similar textbook for girls, on which I draw in the pages to follow, set forth categories and precepts absent from the book for boys and equally absent from the discourse on the modern. The girls were taught not only their wifely place but also the importance of a *minzokuteki bunka* (culture of the people), the unity of the emperor and his subjects, and the existence of the imperial household and the state as one big family. Here is a popularized version of the ambiguous term *minzoku*, which, as Tessa Morris-Suzuki has pointed out, was premised on the identity of nation-state and ethnos but interpreted in various ways. Although she is referring to more recent times, her words hold true for the Japanese *modern* culture of the 1920s and 1930s: "Dimensions of identity, besides, do not stack neatly inside one another like Russian matrioshka dolls, but (even in the most integrated societies) overlap and jostle against one another, so that the sense of self is created and recreated out of a constant struggle to draw the many dimensions of identity together in actions of everyday life." She concludes that, as a result, culture "is an always incomplete effort to pull together the edges of conflicting definitions of identity." In an era when the montage was a dominant way of looking at the world, there may have been less of an effort "to pull the edges together." Thus what concerns me is the disjuncture between the state ideology on ethnic, gender, and family identity and the messages disseminated by the mass media during the 1920s and 1930s.[44]

Late in the 1930s, even as celebrations of indigenous, expansionist culture increased in the illustrated press, the same press was sending forth ideological messages that could not be reconciled with Fujita Shōzō's eloquent analysis of society under the emperor system. According to Fujita, there were no boundaries, or *kejime:* "The principle of the Japanese Emperor system is that in human society the natural world and the public world are not in opposition, the state is not in public opposition to the family, the village, or the provincial organization, public allegiance is not in opposition to private sentiment, and the total and the singular are not placed in public opposition. Without such boundaries, the distinction between origins and results is not clarified, and somehow the whole is stuck together."[45] That such organicism was the ideal but not always the reality is expressed graphically by the following graffiti found by authorities in 1940: "The Japanese revere this guy called the Emperor, but why do they? Such an Emperor should be beaten to death, roasted, and eaten dipped in soy sauce." Even if we accept the carnivorous sentiment as a mere expression of strong feelings, the sanity of the author is called into question by his pledge to put such a plan into action with the aid of one thousand followers. Nonetheless, the documentation of this and similar diatribes illustrates how the ideology of the emperor system was not fully hegemonic. It is difficult to imagine the Japanese consumer-subject imagining the emperor as god when we read the words from graffiti found in 1939 which stated that there was no difference between a vagrant and the emperor or the declaration of the 45-year-old man arrested the following year: the culprit had declared that the emperor was only doing what he did because of his annual income of three million yen. These words are consistent with "Kill the dumb Emperor," and "Her Majesty the Empress is a lecher."(Statements of lèse-majesté culled from Thought Police documentation by John Dower.)[46]

By the same token, at the very moment when the image of the imperial family was being invoked in the mass media, discourse within the media was articulating protest against the system if not active resistance. Invocations of imperial grandeur and challenges to imperial authority often appeared in the same media. By the early 1940s the emperor system, although not necessarily its ideological component, won out with readers and with film, cabaret, and theater spectators and audiences mentioned and implied herein. My conclusions come from the voluminous documentation provided within the mass culture of the Japanese modern years.

THE DOCUMENTARY IMPULSE

During the Japanese modern years, the media made use of essays, cartoons, surveys, and fiction. Moreover, photojournalism opened up a new vision of how Japanese women and men—from the slums and working class and up through the extended imperial family—synthesized the relationship between a Japan differentiated via history, region, gender, and culture and a West "out there." Through the media, we are enabled to move outside of the common approach which examines borrowing from the West or speaks of a double life allowing Japanese consumer-subjects to switch back and forth between white collar and kimono. The Japanese intellectuals of the time, whose work is herein studied in the context of five modern sites, were sensitive to the processes of the adaptation and creation of shared symbols, affects, attitudes, and gestures. Their acute awareness of code-switching liberates the reader from easy binary suppositions (and oppositions) related to a dynamic West meeting a passively active East. These social and cultural critics working in journalism participated in and encouraged the documentary impulse of the Japanese modern years: they made the new familiar.

The documents I refer to as the product of "the documentary impulse" include both official documentation of so-called facts and the "human" dimension of documentation discussed by William Stott. Stott saw a human document as "thoroughly personal," aiming to move its audience but at the same time providing information regarding "public events and social customs." Stott considered what he called the "documentary movement" of the United States a product of the Great Depression. The Japanese documents constituting modern culture were in part a product of similar economic hard times, but they also spoke of a new luxury in everyday life, as documented in such illustrated media as the weekly *Shūkan Asahi* and in much of *Shufu no Tomo*. Therein, photographs documented the "facts" of new customs but also blurred fictional and factual representation in stories and advertisements. Popular reportage resulting from the documentary impulse code-switched among bounded images and between the contrasting fonts of primary sources such as flyers and letters; it encompassed such proletarian literature as Tokunaga Sunao's novel *City without Sun,* documenting the Kyōdō printers' strike of 1926. Film critics told stories about Hollywood, blending documentary and fantasy. Even reports by the bureaucrat Kusama Yasoo, who reported on the down-and-out homeless during the depression years in Japan, used vernacular. Such are the documents I make most use of in my interpretation of reportage after the fact.[47]

When Murayama Tomoyoshi talked about construction, he was articulating the consciousness of many who documented the era: they worked from the idea not of rebuilding but of building anew. This was the approach that also informed the ideology of the Soviet artists of the 1920s with whom Murayama identified. In his argument that mass culture was the suppressed otherness of modernism and that there was a dialectical relationship between the European avant-garde and mass culture, Andreas Huyssen has called for an examination of how mass culture reworked the changing relationship between the human body and the object world. This was also a project in Japan. As inhabitants of an intellectual world dominated by Marxist conceptions of society, Japanese authors documented the fetishization of commodities under capitalism, but they also made place for practice in the form of constructed gestures, self-ornamentation, decoration of domestic space, and movement through urban play spaces in their critique of Japanese commodity culture as the site where the human body engaged with the object world. The Japanese intellectuals documenting modernity recognized that within contemporary consumer culture a struggle over meaning, symbols, and images was taking place. Their writing reveals to us the choices open to Japanese consumer-subjects in the construction of modern culture, and the overlap between John Frow's definition of modernism— "a bundle of cultural practices, some of them adversarial"—and the Japanese neologism *modan*.[48]

The names of two Japanese intellectuals who worked to document the finest of detail in their concern for social change recur in the following pages. Both Kon Wajirō (1888–1973) and Gonda Yasunosuke (1887–1951) substituted an emphasis on consumption for the productivist ethos of the Meiji state. Moreover, their sensitivity to differences in class, culture, and gender and their rejection of the idea of seamless cultural traditions express the Japanese modern sensitivity to such distinctions. Like the prescriptive approach of mass magazines, their work recording historic shifts such as changes in language, body language, and self-fashioning through clothing and material surroundings offers a way of accessing codes of behavior.[49]

After the earthquake, Kon walked through Tokyo, sensing that there were new artifacts and unprecedented processes that he must watch closely. His first response to the devastation of September 1, 1923, that killed over 100,000, injured more than 500,000, destroyed almost 700,000 dwellings, and led to the hunting down, torture, and execution of over six thousand Koreans residing in Japan, was to examine the barracks *(barakku)* or temporary structures that had sprung up and to organize the "Society for Barrack Decoration."[50]

Kon had to have known about the "Korean Hunt," yet he did not acknowledge the colonial, racist underside to the modern when he praised opportunities for cultural innovation. He could not have been ignorant of the carnage, for the post-earthquake fires had been equally cruel to the working-class inhabitants of the neighborhoods he studied. Thousands of prostitutes and laborers who lived in densely built, conjoined, wood tenement houses had met their deaths. The vigilante groups had set up checkpoints where suspected "incendiary Koreans" had their cultural and linguistic skills tested. By September 2, no Korean in the Tokyo area was safe from the vigilantes or from police officials, who were recording and disseminating the totally unfounded rumors that Koreans were throwing bombs and poisoning wells. Reports that the rumors had been false did not stop the carnage when police were given the right to round up and "protect" Koreans while guiding vigilante groups. It has been documented that the vigilantes were armed with swords, clubs, bamboo spears, fire axes, long-bladed hoes, bush hammers, scythes, and saws, and that they engaged in brutal acts of torture that will not be elaborated here. Moreover, rather than receiving asylum from this violence, Koreans were forcibly marched into internment centers, where they were trapped and killed by police. Kon may not have known that the internment centers were not safe, but he should have figured out, through a reading of the mass media, that as late as mid-September the state ordered that rumors of violence by Koreans continue to circulate through the press, while documentation of Japanese involvement in the violence was banned.[51]

Kon did not relate colonial connections and popular racism to the post-earthquake violence. However, he did address the plight of the working class when, in 1924, he was engaged to draw up plans for the Tokyo Imperial University Settlement House in Honjo. He also published a report on the Korean farmhouse under the auspices of the colonial government. In other words, his modern, colonial scientific skills were taken to Korea (the modern in the colonial), but Korean mores in Japan (the colonial in the modern) were not at issue. Instead, by the spring of 1925, Kon had begun his collaboration with the designer Yoshida Kenkichi on the series of investigations of urban life that would come to be known under the rubric of modernology. Kon distinguished modemology from anthropology and from folklore studies because he was not concerned with primitive people. The object of his study was the everyday practice *(seikatsu)* of the cultured people of the present, and therefore he labeled it "cultural modernology," as opposed to "primitive anthropology."[52]

Kon aimed to relate traditions to fads and to newly constructed practices through the study of objects related to human actions, housing, and clothing. None of these phenomena could be seen in isolation; all were to be studied in motion. For example, Kon wanted to study human actions in terms of a series of such constructs *(kōsei)* as the various speeds of walking in the city, the motions of the construction worker, the positions of farmer and fisherman at work and at rest, and the motions of crowds at festivals and at the corner of a café. One of his many illustrative sketches was a comparative statistical breakdown of the percentage of Western versus indigenous clothing worn by males and females on Ginza in the early summer of 1925. Kon pointed to the interaction of coded differences but the pages of drawings and analyses worked against a simple dichotomy between East and West. It was not merely that the bowler hat, or the cloche, or the high heels, or the overcoat denoted difference. The differences on each side of the divide separating Occident from Orient were too numerous—there were too many variations of the wearing of neckties or topcoats and too many variations on the Japanese woman's hairstyle accompanying her kimono.[53]

Kon's focus on the options open to the consumer-subject in terms of choice of place, space, object, and motion is evident in his survey of the practices of people picnicking—the term is *pikunikku*—in suburban Inokashira Park during the cherry-blossom viewing season. A series of tableaus is documented tersely. For example, three children "stare at a cluster of three soldiers": eight boy scouts are "seen with leftovers from a cookout," and "someone reads a *Bible*." But in his brief summation of the scenarios, Kon noted a cultural switch: although most of the picnic foods consumed were customary, *doughnuts* had appeared recently. He also marked a more significant difference: because the picnickers had all come out for the shared purpose of cherry-blossom viewing, people of different classes were mingling in the park.[54]

The working-class landscape of Honjo-Fukagawa was as meaningful to the modernologist as the middle-class-oriented Ginza: "The houses are small, the clothes-drying poles many and high, and these rise by each house in counterpoint to the factory chimneys." Kon's concern with working-class culture was most evident in a companion piece to his study of Ginza, "Collection of Information in a Slum Neighborhood." Therein, he emphasized that the neighborhood had expanded to cover the entire region east of the Sumida River. He also conjectured that this expansion might date back to the earthquake. Kon warned his readers to be careful in viewing and assessing "the mores of the contemporary poor," which were so different from those of "the contemporary cultured person." For example, large, fancy shops might line the street, but as soon as one entered an alleyway "the nests of the *seikatsu* of the poor extend before one." The modernologist was blunt: "Differences in mores emerge as historical traditions from differences in the natural environment," but these differences were also the result of "the difference between rich and poor." One outcome of this premise was a detailed graphing of gender-differentiated items desired by women and by men in Honjō-Fukagawa, that were priced and displayed in the local stores. Kon made clear that distinctions must be made when studying the slum neighborhoods of industrial regions: he pointed to differences among the mores of construction workers, cart coolies, factory hands, and peddlers. He made sure to distinguish between the flophouses catering to the homeless day laborers and the households of the workers who commuted to nearby factories while their wives took in work at home. One finding that in fact denied difference was Kon's conclusion that laborers made no distinction between Japanese and Western clothing; utility was all that mattered. In conclusion, Kon said, that he wanted further study of differences: how were buttons buttoned? In what places were clothes torn? Clothing was to be shown on site, moving freely, as an expression of the human body in one class, in one place.[55]

Kon also related objects to class, to place, and to practice in his survey of behavior in the department store. By observing the interactions at the counters offering high-class wares to those who could afford to pay, the modernologist could be privy to the behavior of the upper-class customer that was ordinarily exhibited in the privacy of his or her home. At another counter, it was as though the lid had been removed from a middle-class household, as consumer-subjects anxiously compared samples of silk patterns. Showcase wares were presumably to be treated with the respect owed ancient artifacts in a museum. But although the department store was supposed to be a place where items were freely bought and sold, the middle-class customers were anxious, pushing—striving, Kon explained, to imitate the upper class. In the bargain basement, the struggle was intense.[56]

In "Survey of Things in a New Household," Kon captured objects in their class context from another angle when he asked what happens to things in differing regions and classes when they are actually used, and under what conditions are they used after the initial pleasure of buying or making an item. Kon claimed that his stance was different from that of an architect. He worked through the home room by room, documenting every item, like an archaeologist surveying the partitions of a tomb. He expressed respect as well as a somewhat concealed contempt for the commodities he had studied on site. If one continued to buy one thing after another, whatever one wanted, he asked, what happened to all of these objects when they were no longer found to be of use? His discussions accompanying his sketches and survey data can be read as a critique of capitalism informed by a knowledge of Marxism. For example, his contention that he wanted to leave a record of things, and the uses they were put to at the site of their consumption, and not as a place where they were exchanged, was a gloss on Marx's distinction between exchange and use value.[57]

Like Michel de Certeau, Kon was most concerned with an urban text written by walkers in the city, and like de Certeau (who applauded Charlie Chaplin because he "multiplies the possibilities of his cane: he does other things with the same thing") he viewed the multiplicity of practices, even in suicide, as resulting from a series of choices. However, such choices were not placed within an analysis of the emperor system, or of any other system.[58]

Like Kon, Gonda Yasunosuke, the bureaucratic expert on leisure activities, had his perceptions profoundly altered by the earthquake. Through the study of "living social facts," he believed, one could gain an understanding of the "construction" of play. To that end, his study of popular play, begun before the earthquake and continuing into the 1930s, encompassed movie-going, leisure activities in the provinces, and the subcultures of traveling entertainers as expressions of practice generated from below.[59]

Even before the earthquake Gonda had written that "popular play" or "people's recreation" *(minshū goraku)* was an integral part of modern life. It had entered the language in such declarations as "Honey, I'm going out for a little popular play" *(oi kimi, boku wa chotto, minshū goraku ni itte kuru karane)*. When Kon used the term *minshū*, or people, he was not referring to undifferentiated masses but primarily to a proletariat wanting for both money and free time and desiring their own pleasures. After the earthquake, Gonda tracked the appearance of objects placed throughout the city by men and women creating new lives as they drank their first cups of sake sold near their barracks lodgings. According to Gonda, there had been a week of "absence of play" immediately after the earthquake, followed by two weeks of "shrinking from play" and two weeks of a "fervent longing." Play was then meted out by the authorities, as though it were rice, for the next four weeks, until the people finally reached a stage of "pleasurable play" based on their own autonomous, self-motivated actions.[60]

Gonda had no delusions about the manipulative dimensions of a technologically advanced capitalist consumer culture. Fads, he contended, went beyond the cosmetics and other items carried around by women: even the intellectual world was being commodified in a "race toward thought." Gonda decried that the meaning of things was determined not by the fulfillment of a genuine desire (for there could be no genuine satisfaction from things) but rather from the ability to purchase an object: the process of buying made life meaningful. To satisfy such created desire among consumer-subjects, imitations upon imitations were being constructed. In words sounding very much like a gloss on Marx's theory of commodity fetishism, Gonda proclaimed that people do not determine things. In his words, "there are things," and then people appear. He angrily proclaimed, "Hats are not made for people's heads; heads are stuffed into hats."[61]

Like Kon, Gonda saw the present as "modern," and in his scathing attack on the *modan* he indicted the "modern practices" of the street. These he identified with modern European practices by equating the European bourgeois way of life with the *seikatsu* of both the *boulevard* and the *Strasse*. Cafés, bars, restaurants, movie theaters, and dance halls were merely extensions of this street life, which could not flourish in the "house" or the "household." Not only was this new form of culture alienated from the domestic realm. Gonda further concluded that these practices of the street were "constructed in their purest form by a type of people who had no relationship to everyday practice of labor or of production." Proletarian play was to be admired; bourgeois play was not.[62]

There was a utopian aspect to his close reading of mass culture as working-class culture. In an essay privileging the importance of a historicized everyday practice over an unchanging "national character," Gonda pointed out how quotidian items—sushi and sake, for example—were transformed into objects for consumption by the mere appendage of the honorific prefix *o*. In other words, although *sushi* was food, *osushi* was not merely a polite way of signifying the same thing, as was usually presumed. Rather, *osushi* signified a different item, a different practice within the realm of play. It was the new "proletarianization" of play via the massification of play within the city that was Gonda's concern. Even *benshi* (stars in their own right who explicated the dialogue and actions for eager moviegoers) and workers on their fifteen-minute breaks were organizing baseball teams. Gonda's "On Workers' Play" documented how play for the worker was not a matter of killing time but an expression of everyday practice as choice. Gonda charted what workers chose to read and whether they went to cafés on Sunday; he determined that more working women than men chose to go to the movies, and he concluded that men and women workers considered the consumption of cigarettes and sweets as forms of play. He contended that class differences were crucial, but national differences in terms of a dichotomy between East and West were not as important.[63]

Gonda's refusal to categorize play into non-Japanese and Japanese components is illustrated by his approach to the movies. He stated that while popular play would not ultimately come from the West, the construction of an indigenous popular play had to be premised upon an understanding of the Western music accompanying Mack Sennett and D. W. Griffith productions. His brief narrative of the history of cinema in Japan looked at what had drawn Japanese audiences to the movies. His conclusion: Japanese audiences had grown used to Western ways, but Chaplin and Fatty had had their day by 1923. The Western heroes Charlie Chaplin and Fatty Arbuckle had been displaced by dramatic features (*ninjō mono*), a newer fad that could be either Japanese or Western. In other words, Western faces had become but faces in a process of transcoding or code-switching between Japanese and non-Japanese movies. In fact even a child who did not know the name of the prime minister could easily identify both Charlie Chaplin and the sword-wielding idol Matsunosuke. Gonda reported interviewing girls and boys who could reel off dozens of names of both Japanese and Western movie idols.[64]

Gonda's views on modern culture could not easily accommodate the ethnocentric ideology propounded by the state. Even as late as 1935, in a corporatist treatise called "The Destruction of Popular Play and the Preparation of National Play," he did not subscribe to an essentialist ideology of "Japanese-ness." Instead, adhering to a principle of transcoding then very evident in the popular press, he called for a new Japanese rural culture based on movies, Western music, and dancing. It is his acceptance of Western music that is of significance here. For even as he was reformulating his earlier premises, Gonda did not turn to a dichotomy eliminating the West from the Japanese cultural experience. He retained his belief that culture was constructed from newly reformulated indigenous traditions of play and could be revitalized through the introduction of select aspects of Western (and now Japanese urban) culture, such as movies and *dancing* into rural play. Gonda's concern to link urban and rural culture further illustrates that modern culture (or more often, the desire for a modern culture) was not confined to the cities.[65]

Gonda's call for a hybrid modern culture gradually gave way to a vision of a seamless society. By 1935 the category of class had been displaced by the "general masses." And by 1941, he turned away from "popular play" to focus on state-organized "national play" *(kokumin goraku)*. Gonda's subjects, who had been "the people," were now "the people of the nation." He had become, without question, an advocate of a massive *tenkō*, or a cultural turn to the celebration of indigenous tradition, a trend which by this time was firmly entrenched in the mass press. By the 1940s, he was deferring to Nazi policy by expounding on such topics as "The Nazi Society for Strength through Joy" and "The Nazi Characteristics of the National Welfare Movement." Within a decade, his numerous books and essays had shifted from a language marking differences between social classes to one dominated by such words as *kokumin seikatsu*, "a nationalized people's everyday."[66]

One might say Gonda's turn was emblematic of the turn of Japanese culture away from what I shall call Japanese modern times. This was a moment celebrating universal yet differentiated emerging practices, but Gonda, like so many others, turned to the forced representation of a unitary national culture outside of time. Nonetheless, the places and practices of Japanese modern life had been put on record, and we can now return to the modern encoded in the references to the erotic and to the grotesque and to the culture that passed as nonsense. Do not be deceived by my use of Chaplin's title. This is not a history of derivative borrowings. In the commentary on and of the modern in Japan discussed in the first part of this book I have found a history of enormous creativity, fantasy, and political energy. In order to slow down the tempo sufficiently to differentiate the new from what passed as traditional, and in the hope that the reader will gain some sense of the tone, the humor, and the willed transgressions of the time, the second and third parts of my discussion of the modern in Japan stop at five sites of Japanese modern times, including Asakusa Park, the place where the erotic, the grotesque, and the nonsensical were in closest alliance.

PART II

Japanese Modern Sites

1 The Modern Girl as Militant

(Movement on the Streets)

Where can you folks clearly say that there is a typical
Modern Girl?

Kataoka Teppei

Let's get naked and while we're at it work our damnedest.

Hayashi Fumiko

The Modern Girl makes only a brief appearance in our histories of prewar
Japan. She is a glittering, decadent, middle-class consumer who, through her
clothing, smoking and drinking, flaunts tradition in the urban playgrounds
of the late 1920s. Arm in arm with her male equivalent, the *mobo* (Modern
Boy), and fleshed out in the Western flapper's garb of the roaring twenties,
she engages in *ginbura* (Ginza-cruising). Yet by merely equating the Japanese Modern Girl with the flapper we do her a disservice, for the Modern
Girl was not on a Western trajectory. Moreover, during the modern years
when this female, a creation of the mass media, titillated her Japanese audience, she was not easily defined. Who was this Modern Girl? What made her
do what she did? These two questions, raised by the Japanese Modern Girl's
contemporaries, are also the two problems posed in this part of my montage
of Japanese erotic grotesque nonsense.[1]

The Modern Girl was a highly commodified cultural construct crafted by
journalists who debated her identity during the tumultuous decade of cultural and social change following the great earthquake of 1923. By asking
first of all who she was, I am concerned more with the representation of the
Modern Girl as the most predominant Japanese cultural heroine of the era
than with the actual beliefs or practices of the young women of that era.
Therefore I do not call the heroine by her nickname, *moga*, for to do so would
be to deny her the full respect that is her due. (For, as will be shown, the café
waitress was identified with new leisure activities at the same time that the
housewives of the new era were expected to execute a newly rationalized series of domestic practices while waiting at home for the café waitress's be-
sotted customer, but it was the Modern Girl who was made most emblematic of the female eroticism with which the press was obsessed.)

As for what made her do what she did, the question has been appropriated from the title of the hit movie of 1930, *Nani ga Kanojo wo sō Sasetaka* (What Made Her Do What She Did?), a film that happened to be a "tendency" or left-wing movie. In this saga of an orphan turned criminal, based on a play by Fujimori Seikichi, the heroine withstood varied forms of servitude, including domestic labor for a lecherous government official, before taking her revenge by setting fire to a Christian institution for wayward girls. According to Fujimori's stage directions, published in 1927, at this moment the curtain was to fall on the electrically lit query, "What made her do what she did?" floating above the flames. The movie audience, which included members of the new salaried middle class, off-duty groups of geisha, and working men and women, who had crowded into Asakusa—the honky tonk nightlife neighborhood of Tokyo documented by Gonda Yasunosuke— to watch the show, had to formulate their own answers to this question. The historian must do the same when asking why the Modern Girl moved so vigorously through the closing years of the 1920s. To answer this question, the Modern Girl must be made a part of the political economy and socio-cultural transformations of her time.[2]

IDENTIFYING THE MODERN GIRL

Kitazawa Shūichi established the character of the Modern Girl as apolitical but militantly autonomous in his article "Modern Girl" (*"Modan Gaaru"*). She was neither an advocate of expanded rights for women nor a suffragette; nevertheless she had no intention of being a slave to men. The self-respecting Modern Girl had liberated herself from age-old traditions and conventions, and now, suddenly, without any argument or explanation, she had stepped out onto the same starting line with men in order to walk beside them. Kitazawa saw a reconstruction of gender accompanying this reordering of power, but he did not bemoan the fact that woman was becoming more like man both spiritually and physically, for what woman had lost in grace she had gained in a newfound animation.[3]

Nii Itaru, who is usually given credit for coining the term *modan gaaru*, followed with his "Contours of the Modern Girl" in a 1925 issue of another women's magazine, *Fujin Kōron* (Ladies' review). He provided a character sketch of someone who, like Kitazawa's Modern Girl, was highly animated. She was also "brightly breezy" and shockingly fond of the double entendre and other erotic come-hithers. One young woman, for example, after a single meeting with the author, had sent him a note that read, "I am lonely all alone today. Please come visit." Nii reported that he did not know how to interpret this message, but he was convinced that all contemporary young women were in the process of changing for the sake of "liberation and freedom of expression." Nii admitted that the contemporary young Japanese woman was aggressive and erotic, but was she in fact like her European counterpart, the modern young woman, whom he likened to a bouncing ball of reason, will, and emotion, thrown at full force? And was the anarchistic Modern Girl a creature to be lauded as the proletarian emblem of revolutionary possibility, or should she be reviled as one final expression of a decaying class, owing to her origins in the wealthier strata of society? Nii offered his readers choices, but he would not take a stand.[4]

Nii's ambiguity set the tone for Japanese mass journalism. From 1925 until the early 1930s, writers attempted to flesh out the contours provided by Nii in such print media as the cartoon series about an aggressive Modern Girl and a passive Modern Boy titled *Mogako and Moborō*, sensational newspaper articles, advice columns, and special issues of popular magazines aimed at both men and women. While ambiguity remained, a composite picture of a Modern Girl does emerge from a select reading of articles written by journalists and feminist critics of the 1920s and 1930s. Moreover, circulation statistics for the mass press indicate the power of the Modern Girl to travel nationwide. Those selling the Modern Girl took advantage of the national network that had been in existence since the turn of the century. For example, the circulation of *Ie no Hikari*, the journal of the agricultural cooperative movement that would be found in more than half of Japanese rural households and in the colonies by 1941, had a circulation of 105,000 by 1931, when the discourse of erotic grotesque nonsense was at its height; this grew to one million copies by 1935.[5]

Who was she? First and foremost, the Modern Girl was defined by her body, specifically by her short hair and long, straight legs. In a brief disquisition titled simply "Woman's Legs," the proletarian writer Kataoka Teppei argued that although other eras of Japanese history had been graced by sightly legs, the legs of the Modern Girl were a product of the ability of the human spirit to shape the human form; her legs symbolized the Modern Girl's growing ability to create a new life for women. The author ended his polemic with a hortatory appreciation of the Modern Girl in motion: "Onward! Dance! Legs! Legs! Legs!"[6]

Discussion of fashion is always talk about the female body, as another article, "Studies on the Modern Girl," made blatantly clear. In the course of his attempt to define the Modern Girl, Kiyosawa Kiyoshi illustrated this premise by emphasizing the significance of the Modern Girl's protruding buttocks. He noted that the traditional function of the sash or obi ("to hide the behind") had been abandoned by the Modern Girl, who wore her obi high. This preoccupation with the clothing of the Modern Girl also confirms Rosalind Coward's thesis that "women's bodies, and the messages which clothes can add, are the repository of the social definitions of sexuality." According to Kataoka Teppei, the Modern Girl's simple hairstyle was the outcome of a strategic decision to facilitate violent hugging, and her boldly colored and patterned clothing expressed her attraction to the fleshly vitality exuded by the Westerner. This Modern Girl went after the physical pleasures of love *(ren'ai)*, which meant that she sought "fleshly" stimuli in *flirtation*, an activity that had spread from the United States to England, France, and Japan. (The author code-switched twice, bracketing "flirtation" in English after he had transliterated it into *katakana*, the Japanese syllabary reserved for imported terms.) The Modern Girl was flirting, the author explained, when she went for a shoulder or a hand in a crowded train, and then pulled back protesting with a polite "Oh, excuse me—it was just that it was oh so crowded," when her motions were met with anger. This mixed message was also projected in dance halls and theaters, where the licentious Modern Girl went after men's physical rather than spiritual beauty.[7]

The Modern Girl was *ero* personified. For Kataoka, as for other male writers, to talk about the Modern Girl's body and clothing, and thereby her sexuality, was to underscore her promiscuity. In contrast, the feminist journalist and critic Kitamura Kaneko, in an essay called "Strange Chastity," defended the Modern Girl, pointing out the obvious double standard in the public outcry at women's indiscretions. For a woman to have played around with a man was considered bad, but if there were women who had transgressed with men, there must have been men who had played around with women. Kitamura refused to define the Modern Girl as sexual transgressor. Like Kiyosawa, who saw women as moving closer to men spiritually and physically, and like Kataoka, who celebrated new, separate cultures for men and women and claimed that gender distinctions were based on the differing attitudes toward love held by men and women, she accepted that what it meant to be feminine and what it meant to be masculine were being called into question.[8]

The intimate relationship between efforts to conceptualize the Modern Girl and the cultural reconstruction of gender is made clear in a section of Kiyosawa's essay "Man's Education and Woman's Education." According to the author, gender differentiation in Japan during the 1920s began at birth, as baby girls were put into red kimono and baby boys were swaddled in kimono decorated with images of the mythical peach-boy Momotarō. At age six or seven, the boy child was reprimanded for the unmanly behavior of crying with the rebuke "What is this—and you a boy . . . " By the time the boy and girl were adults, they had been educated for entirely different societies; they were like two races separated by a broad river, living according to differing moral standards. Kiyosawa gave the Modern Girl's resolution to this predicament: let the boy and girl start at the same place.

Although the bold gestures of the Modern Girl crossed gender boundaries, they were, according to her creators, unquestionably female. Her cultural identity, however, was less certain. Nii had begged the issue in his "Contours of the Modern Girl," when he claimed that European ways had been integrated into daily life in Japan while simultaneously refusing to equate the Modern Girl with her Japanese sisters. Kiyosawa also separated the Modern Girls of Europe and the United States from the Japanese Modern Girl. Whereas both sets of Modern Girls stood "in the vanguard of a changing age in order to battle old customs," the author feared that this had not actually been the original goal of the Japanese version. Her short hair might not in fact be an emblem of resistance, but the "mark of decadence" of a woman still content to live by the actions and decisions of men.[9]

Was the Japanese Modern Girl Japanese? Europeanized? Cosmopolitan? To the artist Kishida Ryūsei, who defined the short-haired Modern Girl by her body, clothing, and rapid gait on Ginza, she was all of the above. Kishida's formulation was consistent with Kon Wajirō's findings that only 1 percent of women wore Western clothing. He noted that while the Modern Girl appeared for the most part in Japanese-style clothing, the face of this beauty, originally that of a Japanese female, had been harmonized to become, in a most natural fashion, a Western-style face. But the Modern Girl was not indulging in the forced Europeanization of an earlier era. Kishida concluded that, instead, she was part of a process whereby "all material civilization would . . . inevitably Europeanize Japan." Japan was not to lose its identity; only after it had been thoroughly Europeanized could Japanese culture become non-European.[10]

An alternative resolution to the ambiguity in the cultural identity of the Modern Girl was embodied in Naomi, the polymorphously perverse heroine of Tanizaki Jun'ichirō's fictional *Chijin no Ai* (A fool's love), whose exploits were serialized in the *Ōsaka Asahi Shinbun* and *Josei* in 1924 and 1925. In the story, a nondescript young engineer becomes obsessed by the body and costuming of his child bride, whom he has rescued from her labors as a café waitress. As Naomi's body and desires mature, he is overwhelmed by her sexuality and both confused and enticed by her constantly shifting persona, which challenges fixed notions of gender and culture.[11]

Naomi's bold transgressions across gender and culture boundaries identify her as a Modern Girl and illustrate Coward's explication of how social definitions of both female and male sexuality are projected onto women's bodies, whereas men are "neutral." Naomi's play with the confines of gender identity, expressed by cross-dressing, is transformed into a power play involving the final shift in a mistress-slave relationship. By the end of the story, the heroine has adopted male language to challenge the authority of her former mentor. In response, her husband's speech does not become feminized, in a role reversal, but rather infantilized: he responds to her demands that he do whatever she desires of him with the acquiescent, monosyllabic grunt of a domesticated male child.[12]

Naomi's chief desire is to act and look Western, an aspiration at first encouraged by her mentor, who calls his Mary Pickford look-alike protégée a *Yankee Girl*. Although her upward mobility into ballroom society of the ostensibly genteel dance hall challenges class distinctions, and her affectation of male speech threatens the narrator, her appearance as a Westerner who is not Western (captured in the ambiguity of her untraceable name, "Naomi," which appears Eurasian but may not be) is her most militant statement. Naomi's identification with Pickford, Gloria Swanson, and Pola Negri remains titillating only as long as the hero is attracted to the *haikara* (fashionable and Western-influenced) lifestyle, which is epitomized in the "culture house" chosen by the young couple for its Western architecture and because it is furnished with imported goods aimed at a *"simple life."* In the end, however, the hero is drawn back to a "pure" Japanese-style house and to traditional notions of marriage and family. The ballroom dancing scenes prove to be battle sites of East-West confrontation, Naomi appears as an unrecognizable apparition in whiteface, and the author's real concern turns out to be his discomfort with anything that "smells" Western and therefore threatens the authentic Japanese family. Tanizaki projected this fear onto a Modern Girl who in fact wins out over the hero's desire to return to tradition.[13]

While journalists grappled with the Modern Girl's purported sexual activity, her gender identity, and her cultural identification, like Tanizaki, they were almost unanimous in proclaiming her unquestionable autonomy. Charges of promiscuity leveled against the Modern Girl, according to Kitamura, stemmed from the new, public nature of women's activity. She summed up these charges in a composite sketch:

> She went for a walk with a man in Nara Park; I spotted a glimpse of her at a Dōtonbori café; she was kicking up her heels at the dance hall; I discovered her going into the movies. When I watched her walking she

was moving her left and right legs one after the other; I saw her yawning and decided she was tired out from waiting for a man; she'd decorated her hat with a flower—I wonder who she got it from. She sneezed, she must be run down from being with a man; etc.; etc.; etc.; etc.; etc.; etc.; etc.[14]

Kitamura noted that whereas sins are committed in the dark, the so-called disgraceful conduct of the Modern Girl was conducted in broad daylight. The Japanese woman was no longer secluded in the confines of the household but was out in the open, working and playing alongside men. This was her real transgression: she would not accept the division of labor that had placed her in the home.[15]

The trumpeted promiscuity of the Modern Girl who moved from man to man, was thus but one aspect of her self-sufficiency. She appeared to be a free agent without ties of filiation, affect, or obligation to lover, father, mother, husband, or children—in a striking counterpoint to the state ideology of family documented in the Civil Code and in the ethics texts taught in the schools. According to one critic, the Modern Girl had not simply abandoned motherhood: she was anti-motherhood. Even Hiratsuka Raichō, the feminist theorist of the World War I era, agreed. Although she portrayed the Modern Girl as the daughter of the New Woman and as someone who had the power to create the future through her thought, emotion, action, and everyday life, Raichō did not imagine the Modern Girl having any daughters of her own.[16]

The autonomy of the Modern Girl who "strutted down the street" en route to and from work derived from her economic self-sufficiency. Kataoka surmised that the term *Modern Girl* had originated as a substitute for the vague label of "that sort of woman" that had been attached to the urban working women employed by stores and businesses after World War I. Kitamura warned that "it would be problematic to mistake the short skirts and the ability to endure chilled legs as the be-all and end-all of the Modern Girl," because the work and the morals of this "new working woman" differed from those of the "old household woman." According to Kitamura, the Modern Girl's financial independence positioned her beyond the reach of state and family: "Since the old morals have been broken and new morals have not yet come about and new standards of chastity have not been established, working women, in their system of thought, are a nomadic people. Nomadic people have neither laws nor national borders. All they can do is move as their convictions move them."[17]

When Kon Wajirō took on the study of the Modern Girl, his focus was the way she moved in urban space. Another modernologist, Koike Tomihisa, focused on the body, clothing, and autonomy of the Modern Girl in "The *Moga* Walking *Course* through the Maru *Building*," published in the journal *Moderunologio*. This brief study, which aimed to answer the philosophical question "What is a Modern Girl?" offered a complex typology of Modern Girls; nine examples of the Modern Girls moved through urban space. Only the first of the nine examples of Modern Girls, the "*moga* type," had a rendezvous with a male. The others—the rich young woman outfitted in a vivid orange, the type dressed in kimono, the full-bodied Modern Girl wearing a hat decorated with a tulip, the office worker, the schoolgirl, the Modern Girl in purple dress and purple stockings rushing away from friends, the "schoolteacher *moga*," and the housewife (?!) in *modern* kimono outfit with stylish parasol—had all created their own "walking *courses*." The author provided a sketch for each figure and a map of the chosen route for each. While he did express an interest in body language (the fourteen- or fifteen-year-old school girl in the green raincoat, for example, is swinging a package in a lively fashion), it was the movement of the Modern Girls to, from, and into the various shops in this most modern of office buildings, that intrigued him. The shopping and window-shopping he made note of; the freedom to look and to buy in public were implied.[18]

Although Tanizaki's Naomi also remains a consumer whose appetite for moving pictures and carefully chosen foreign and domestic order-in delicacies is matched only by her desire for a large assortment of male companions, the Modern Girl, according to many accounts, was not merely a passive consumer of middle-class culture, for she was depicted as producing goods, services, and new habits. She thereby differed from the so-called New Woman of the previous era, who had exhibited resistance to outmoded traditions but had offered no new model for an everyday life. The cerebral New Woman had been romantic rather than realistic; she had wielded ideals, not economics; she had imitated male habits instead of attempting to create a separately bounded life for women. In contrast, the Modern Girl was more interested in shaping the materiality of everyday existence. It cannot be emphasized too much that the Modern Girl was not "just looking," to employ Rachel Bowlby's evocative term for the commodified woman who is at the same time a customer in a newly rationalized consumer culture. While most accounts pictured her as a street-smart flaneuse, looking over men and store windows on Ginza, some recognized that her everyday was as much shaped by production as it was by consumption. Such authors agreed that this self-sufficient successor to the New Woman was definitely in the vanguard of the new modern age—the post-earthquake era of economic, social, and cultural reconstruction. There was also a general consensus that this "free-living and free-thinking" Modern Girl was making history in part because she was making her own money.[19]

There were, of course, dissenters, like the Marxist feminist Yamakawa Kikue. In "Modern Girls, Modern Boys," Yamakawa depicted the Modern Girl as a passive figure who lay supine on a beach and afterwards strolled through town, still clad in her bathing suit. Although she disagreed with the right-wing press reports that the Modern Girl and Modern Boy (who could be found Ginza-cruising or at the movies or theater) were part of a communist conspiracy to weaken the children of the privileged through dissipation, she concurred with the notion that the behavior of these girls, who painted themselves in bright colors and walked half-naked beside boys in kettle-shaped hats and flared pants, was reminiscent of the antics of the "degenerate customs and the ephemeral epicureanism" of functionaries in the closing years of the feudal era in Japan. Their lack of interest in anything but sensual pleasures signified a ruling class in decline. Here was another indictment of the eroticism of the Modern Girl.[20]

Yamakawa's prurient definition, which was consistent with the inability of early-twentieth-century Marxism to come to terms with questions of gender or sexuality, ignored the ambiguities and contradictions present in representations of the Japanese-but-Western Modern Girl. In contrast, other writers did attempt to reconcile images of gleeful consumerism and sexual play with the identity of the Modern Girl as a wage-earner who, having abandoned confining tradition, exhibited strains of resistance. These writers resorted to a twofold definition, determining that there were Modern Girls, and then there were *real* Modern Girls. According to Kiyosawa, the real Modern Girl lived outside Japan, whereas the Japanese Modern Girl was a colorful but apolitical and anti-intellectual imitation. In "One Hundred Percent *Moga*," Oya Soichi offered three versions of the Modern Girl. The first was crafty, manipulative, and intellectualizing. She was free to go out, even to sleep out, and maintained no boundaries between friends and lovers. She was a consumer, not a producer; she was like a mannequin. The second type was group-oriented, productive, and possessed of a self-consciousness. But only the third girl was "one hundred percent *moga*." She was identified as the daughter of heroic leftist activists who had been imprisoned countless times; she thus had no sense of family other than the police, the jails, and the streets. Liberated from the traditions of so-called female morality, she articulated the authentic language, gestures, and ideology of the new era.[21]

Hiratsuka Raichō's idealized version of the heroine appeared in the essay "The Modern Girl as She Should Be." According to Raichō, there were two versions of this heroine. The first was a young woman with the time and money to fashion herself a brightly colored ensemble of Western clothing with matching hat for frequenting the cafés on Ginza. This seemingly liberated woman, however, was not free. She was the object of men's physical desires, and, while she might appear upbeat, she was in fact depressed. The real Modern Girl, in contrast, had a social conscience. Although Hiratsuka could not find such a Modern Girl in Japan in the 1920s, she predicted that such women would appear not from among the "fashion slaves" but from within the ranks of working and laboring proletarian women who had organized as "social women." The model for such a modern woman was Takamure Itsue, the anarchist feminist.[22]

In sum, the discourse on the Modern Girl was more about imagining a new Japanese woman than about documenting social change. For this reason, as Kataoka Teppei admitted, despite repeated themes, there was no clearly defined image:

> When we say the Modern Girl exists in our era we are not in particular referring to individuals named Miss So-and-so-*ko* or Mrs. Such-and-such-*e*. Rather, we are talking about the fact that somehow, from the midst of the lives of all sorts of women of our era, we can feel the air of a new era, different from that of yesterday. That's right; where can you folks clearly say there is a typical *Modern Girl*? That is to say that the Modern Girl is but a term that abstractly alludes to one new flavor sensed from the air of the life of all women in society.[23]

The Modern Girl resisted definition, but this did not mean that pundits did not keep trying to confine her. In the January 1928 issue of *Shinchō* (New tide), although the members of a roundtable discussion on various facets of modern life agreed to talk about urbanization and new forms of "articulation, expression, language, gestures, writing, and clothing," they could not set aside the topic of the Modern Girl: they were obsessed by the desire to enclose her in one all-encompassing definition. These critics determined the following about the *moga:* (1) she was not hysterical; (2) she used direct language; (3) she had a direct, aggressive sexuality—she checked to see whether a man was compatible; (4) she scoffed at chastity—changing men, for her, was like putting on a clean white shirt; (5) she could be poor, for clothing was now inexpensive; (6) she was liberated from the double fetters of class and gender; (7) she was an anarchist; (8) she accosted men when she needed train fare; (9) she had freedom of expression, which she got from the movies; and finally, in an indirect commentary on the autonomy of this persona, they pronounced that her presumed counterpart, the *mobo,* was a "zero."[24]

The women writers of *Nyonin Geijutsu* (Women's arts), the journal for and by women that appeared with rare exception from July 1928 through June 1932, did not use the term "Modern Girl," but their unabashed celebration of female creativity, sexuality, and autonomy was a potent contribution to the process of representing and thereby defining the Modern Girl and her eroticism in a positive light. The magazine, advertised by well-heeled live mannequins at major shopping intersections, was premised on the shrewd analysis that media manipulation of women could be subverted through mass marketing of a self-consciously glossy journal produced by women cultural revolutionaries.

The tone of the journal was set on June 20, 1928, the day before the first issue appeared, when the leading women thinkers of the day, some in kimono and some in Western dress, seated themselves at the *Rainbow Grill* in Ueno and invited the press to photograph them. (The women, conscious of the power of self-representation, had adopted the Japanese male tradition of launching political and intellectual projects in semiprivate environs but had chosen a more modern and less sex-specific site than a geisha house.) The agenda for the new magazine was set in the inaugural issue in a manifesto by Yamakawa Kikue titled "An Examination of Feminism." Yamakawa placed women's culture in the context of economic advances and women's demands for equality in suffrage, education, and work. These demands for autonomy constituted yet another rephrasing of the discourse on the Modern Girl's creation of her own separate and unprecedented daily life by a woman who was representing herself as a producer of culture.[25]

The writers for *Nyonin Geijutsu* denied boundaries erected in our histories (and in those of their own Japanese political culture) by proving that women on the left could unite to construct a multifaceted critique of woman's place. Such writers as Sata Ineko, whose sympathies lay with the Japanese Communist Party, and the non-Communist but avowedly Marxist Yamakawa Kikue joined with the anarchist Yagi Akiko and numerous other female (and a few male) writers, poets, and critics to demand a cultural space in which women would not be treated like the live mannequins who had just appeared on Ginza. (In an article about these women, who were placed in department store show windows as if they were themselves for sale, Yagi called this new job the most extreme example of the commodification of a human being as an item for sale.)[26]

Nyonin Geijutsu used the weapons of the numerous magazines produced for mass circulation during the late 1920s—pictures and photographs, fiction, theoretical essays, and roundtable discussions—and drew on both indigenous and foreign sources to champion women's liberation. Unlike male intellectuals, who were nervous about the cultural identity of the Modern Girl, these writers made no attempt to distinguish "authentic Japanese" experience from imitations of the West. In addition to articles on Edo life and on domestic politics, the journal included writings by such thinkers as Alexandra Kollontai (whose works were causing a great sensation in Japan owing to rumors that they advocated free love), Katherine Mansfield, Bronislaw Malinowski, and Langston Hughes.[27]

The writers for *Nyonin Geijutsu* talked about more than just art and theory. The women's magazines of the 1920s featured articles on love and romance, and so too did *Nyonin Geijutsu*, in a series of pieces published in its earliest issues. One representative discussion was the "Roundtable Discussion of Other Angles on Love." The fourteen women participants in the event, which was subtitled "Feelings and Sensations of Jealousy; Chastity and Love, Adulterous Love; The Eternal Nature of Love; Love in a Three-sided Affair and in a Multi-sided Affair; Sexual Desire and Love," were tough, cynical, and, like the Modern Girl represented in the media, realistic. The political activist Kamichika Ichiko questioned whether strong feelings leading to a marriage based on love could last fifty years into the marriage. Love was well and good, she noted, if one had the time, but she was busy with her family and her work; there was no time for the cultivation of love. Another discussant claimed that only unrequited love was eternal.[28]

Unlike the imagined Modern Girl, the modern women on the panel were confronting actual issues of bonding, relating, and reproducing. Significantly, in the process of defining the militant as a Modern Girl, these women, like so many of the women who appeared in *Nyonin Geijutsu* as either writers or the subjects of articles, defined themselves as out in public as workers. They openly expressed their feelings about both love and work. Although they may have eschewed the label "Modern Girl," the sentiment that women should move out of the household and into the streets was familiar to the readers of *Nyonin Geijutsu*. An example is available in the large-print ad promoting a nationwide contest for the best lyrics for a "Women's March" in 1929. The title of the song might recall the "Tokyo March" of the same year, but it was clear that the editors were looking for a differently coded shift in sentiment. Theirs was a militant call to women of all classes to move forward, into the streets: "Women have already kicked off their heavy shackles and escaped from the dungeons of their darkened hearts. What lies before us now is for us to pour into the streets like rain in a sun-shower. What is left is the deafening roar of the factories, the tips of the spires of thought attacking the heavens. Lining up with all peoples we move forward into the world of all living things. Friends, at times like these we need a song that will sing, exhort, exalt, and push forward for us."[29]

The image of a Modern Girl on the road was also publicized in "Letters from a Trip to Kyushu," coauthored by Yagi Akiko and Hayashi Fumiko (the latter's *Hōrōki* [Tale of wandering], the sensational "diary" of the travels of a working woman spurred by desire, was currently being serialized in *Nyonin Geijutsu*). The travelogue opened with Yagi's expression of concern over Hayashi's drinking. Hayashi, in turn, boasted of the romance and whiskey she had enjoyed with a "tall, modern" fan in Nagoya, and of her behavior toward the soldier on the train whom she had pinched so as to terminate moves that were not fast enough. This document about wine, men, and song—an update of *Tōkaidō Hizakurige*, the Edo classic about the picaresque antics of two déclassé warriors—produced by two women writers on the road, proved that adventure was not gender-bound. In other words, Hayashi Fumiko, the lusty author-heroine of *Tale of Wandering*, who was busy punctuating her autobiographical account of a down-and-out woman drifter with such fragments as a lyrical reference to dancing naked women, was not an idiosyncratic anomaly. The Modern Girl's protest, expressed through sensuality and mobility, could be communal, like the trip taken by the two modern women.[30]

But *Nyonin Geijutsu* was not all about art, love, and exploration. Class consciousness made itself increasingly evident as articles on women factory workers, and especially on labor in the Soviet Union, increased in later issues. For the last six months that *Nyonin Geijutsu* appeared, the magazine contained a series on the notorious Tōyō muslin strike of 1930. This strike also produced fictional heroines, in a series of short stories published by Sata Ineko in 1931, a year after Sata had stood in support outside the factory walls, listening to the sound of the strike drums. Her four-part narrative, which appeared in diverse sources in the mass media, recounted violence both among the young women workers and between the women and the hired thugs of the "justice corps." Sata's documentary fiction also presented a montage of propaganda produced by both sides, including letters appealing to the power of patriarchy, addressed to the women's fathers and brothers from the factory management.[31]

Like Tanizaki's *Chijin no Ai* and Hayashi Fumiko's montage-like *Tale of Wandering*, which juxtaposed poetry with autobiography and superimposed autobiography onto fiction, Sata's stories presented the militant as a Modern Girl guilty of transgressing in both spoken language and body language. In her stories, class struggle, rather than the definition of a modern

culture, is at stake when the teenage activists refuse to stay in their designated place as obedient workers. These young women take to the streets, but
not to dance, shop, or strut to work. Instead, they brawl with an enthusiasm
equal to that of their male cohorts. They code-switch, using the rough male
word for "I," *ore*, to refer to themselves; they threaten to smash dishes; and
they wrestle—literally—over issues of ideology. The fighting and the new
way of talking are modern gestures. And while these young women do express sexual desires, like the Modern Girls in the media, by taking time to
flirt with male coworkers, this is clearly a secondary pastime. Flirtation is a
pleasurable diversion from their abiding concern—their desire is that they
be allowed to continue to produce. Above all, they want to work.

What emerges from the varied commentary on the Modern Girl is that
men and women writers for the popular press believed that this cultural
heroine was defining her own options and her own sexuality (along with the
sexuality of the *mobo*). This modern young woman transgressed boundaries of class, gender, and culture. Her resistance was usually not organized,
but nevertheless it was political: as observers like Kiyosawa acknowledged,
as distinct from her predecessors in the Japanese women's movement, the
Modern Girl, "like the grand waves of the Pacific Ocean," drew those
around her into her activity. She had neither a leader nor an organization,
but hers was the first nationally based movement of women; hers was the
first voice of woman's resistance.[32]

The Modern Girl, in other words, was militant. The only article in *Nyonin Geijutsu* with the term "Modern Girl" in its title is one that hints at this
equation of women's transgressions across class, sex, and culture lines with
political action. The heroine of this brief commentary, "The Modern Girl in
Jail," is imprisoned for soliciting funds for an after-hours school for working girls. When she is placed in a cell with other women, her "crime" is not
distinguished from their petty criminal acts. They are all, the article concludes, political prisoners.[33]

Although interviews with survivors of the Tōyō muslin strike indicate
that the street fighting did not last long, because the girls could not hold out
against the strength of the state-backed company, the image of the strikers
as street-fighting women has persisted. The same cannot be said for the
Modern Girl. The unattached, militant woman who publicly expressed her
desires for sex and for work in public places, thereby challenging the assumption that she belonged in the home, has vanished. An interrogation of
what modern young working women did—along with an inquiry into what
they were expected to do—contributes to an explanation of both the ap-

pearance and the disappearance of this pugnacious and lustful multifaceted heroine.[34]

In order to begin to explain why this Modern Girl did what she did, *when* she did, we must associate her representation with a history of Japanese women of the 1920s and 1930s that sees women as consumers, producers, legal subjects, and political activists. The Modern Girl appeared during a historical juncture when Japanese women were acting in all of these capacities.[35]

Talk about the Modern Girl's clothed (and disrobed) body cannot be divorced from documented social change in women's material culture during the 1920s. Magazine articles devoted to sewing Western-style clothes, for example, suggest a shift toward non-Japanese dress. The magazine *Shufu no Tomo* (its reassuring title translates as *Friend of the Housewife*) which was aimed at the housebound married woman, had run its first series on making Western clothing in 1917, and by 1923 such articles as "How to Make a Convenient House-Dress" were promoting Western attire as a stylish commodity. Nevertheless, the daughter of the poet Hagiwara Sakutarō recalled how neighborhood housewives had jeered, "Modern Girl!" when her mother—inspired by the author Uno Chiyo—first appeared in Western clothing in 1927. It would appear that many were not as quick to accept new fashions as they were to make use of a new media label.[36]

The social history of the affective lives of actual young Japanese women during the 1920s is even more difficult to recount. Were young women in fact as animated and promiscuous as they appeared in the claims of Nii and others who suggested that the Modern Girl's gestures mirrored movie imagery? To what extent did the bravado of the women intellectuals in *Nyonin Geijutsu* reflect the assertive attitudes toward sex and the opposite sex reported in the media? One recorded exchange between a man and a woman on a commuter train in 1930 provides an illustration of brazen behavior that matches the accusations of critics who caught (or lauded) the Modern Girl accosting helpless men: a woman of about thirty riding on a train was accused, by a well-dressed stranger, of acting shamelessly for a wife and of threatening the national good, because her permanent wave was "no good" and her powder too thick. The woman's reaction was immediate and relentless. "Excuse me, but how do you know whether or not I'm someone's wife?" she retorted. She then demanded his business card, threatened to visit his house that very day, and followed him off the train when he attempted to retreat.[37]

As noted by the witness to this incident, the woman was undoubtedly en route to the Marubiru, the office building in the financial district of Tokyo famous for its female clerical workers in Western dress. Beginning in 1923, these workers, the subjects of Kon's examination of the *moga's* walking *course*, could have their hair permed at Japan's first beauty parlor. According to contemporary sources, by 1924 women constituted 3,500 of the 30,000 white-collar workers commuting to the Marunouchi district. By the second half of the 1920s, approximately 8,200 women were employed at secretarial and service jobs in Japan's urban centers.[38]

During the 1920s, at the same time that the Modern Girl was being defined, journalists and state officials were surveying working women *(shokugyō fujin)*. A comparison of the six categories used in the 1924 "Survey regarding Working Women," one of the many surveys released by the Tokyo Social Affairs Bureau, with the categories used in "A Modern Girl Mental Test," published in *Fujokai* (Woman's world), reveals that the discourse on the Modern Girl and the response to the working woman were part of the same social and economic history. Whereas the six headings used by the Tokyo officials were teachers, typists, office workers, storekeepers, nurses, and telephone operators, the "Mental Test" had also included bus conductors, café waitresses, and urban women producers of services who could not be classified as middle-class and who came from working-class backgrounds. Although the term *shokugyō fujin* was usually used to distinguish white-collar women employees from their sisters in the factories, the meaning of "working woman" remained ambiguous. As late as 1932, a commentator who had read several works on the "working woman problem" in order to put the café waitress in a sociological perspective still could not find a concept to fit the label. Kon Wajirō's typology of the working woman in his 1929 *New Edition of the Guide to Greater Tokyo* also illustrated the blurring of class distinctions when he included in his list women bus conductors, chauffeurs, company representatives, journalists, office workers, shop clerks, and *gasoline girls,* women who handed out advertisements and matchbooks, *elevator girls* (newly being paid), and the *mannequins,* who had first appeared in 1928 and were now found even in the provinces.[39]

A living counterpart to the imaginary Modern Girl emerges from these various surveys. She is a single or married Japanese woman wage-earner who was forced into paid employment by financial need following the end of the economic boom of the World War I years. The omnipresent working-class café waitress in novels and stories of the late 1920s and early 1930s therefore represents the Modern Girl's true identity better than the figure of an aimless, mindless consumer frequently found in our history textbooks.[40]

The representation of the Modern Girl as free from family obligations had an actual social corollary. The struggle of Tanizaki's hero to redefine his marriage with Naomi occurred at a time when scholars and state officials, in response to the emergence of the "small" nuclear family, were actively considering the reconstitution of the modern Japanese family. Commentators on the Modern Girl have all ignored the fact that the discourse on this threatening woman reached its height just when the government was debating revision of the Civil Code, having recognized that the "law ignoring women," as Oku Mumeo had called it, was not working. Inasmuch as the denial of civic responsibility to women had been premised not on biological determinism but on a notion of the woman's proper place within the family, changes in family life resulting from women's newly expanded economic roles appeared to call for an institutionalized ideological shift. By 1924, faced with the rise of wife-initiated divorce in urban Japan, pundits were lamenting the destruction of the family. By 1925, proposals challenging key provisions of the Civil Code, which in 1898 had granted full power to the male head of the household, were under active consideration by the Rinji Hōsei Shingikai, a special investigative committee established in 1919 to revise the family provisions of the Meiji Civil Code. Women's competence was acknowledged in the proposed changes that would seemingly eliminate the requirement of parental consent to a marriage, make divorce easier for women, expand the parental rights of women, and grant women the right to manage their own property.[41]

The notoriety of the Modern Girl thus corresponded historically with a change in state policy on women's position within the family. An equally important historical conjuncture was the simultaneous appearance of the ostensibly apolitical Modern Girl and of political groups for women. The displacement of the term "husband-wife quarrel" *(fūfugenka)* by the more evocative "household struggle" *(katei sōgi)* around this time indicates the extent to which family reality belied state ideology in the 1920s and corroborates Sharon Nolte's suggestion that various interrelated political "configurations" during the interwar years might have served "to form a collective impression of rising politicization among women."[42]

Increasingly, there was political mobilization of women by women. Numerous militant feminist organizations emerged during the 1920s after the establishment of the liberal Shin Fujin Kyōkai (New Woman's Association) in 1919 and Sekirankai (the Red Wave Society), the first Japanese socialist woman's organization, in 1921. In 1922, the ban on women attending political meetings was lifted. The Fusen Kakutoku Dōmei (League for Women's Suffrage) was well established by 1925, and, as a result of the establishment of left-wing political parties following the promulgation of universal male suffrage in that year, auxiliary women's associations, such as the Kantō Women's Federation of the Labor-Farmer Party, came into being. Women were also active in both the radical and moderate wings of the labor movement; in the tenancy movement; in the Fujin Shōhi Kumiai Kyōkai (Organization of Women's Consumer Unions), established in 1928; and in such professional organizations as the Taipisuto Kyōkai (Association of Typists), the Shokugyō Fujinsha (Society of Working Women), which published its own journal, *Shokugyō Fujin* (Working woman); and the *Mannequin Club*, organized by Yamano Chieko in 1929, six years after the opening of her beauty parlor in the Marunouchi Building. By April 1922, the Advertising Corps of the Federation of Café Waitresses had sent union members into the streets of Osaka. More than twenty young waitresses traveled through the streets of Osaka in five automobiles, paying visits to major newspapers, handing out more than twenty thousand flyers calling for solidarity. Waving their banners, they quoted the opening words of Hiratsuka Raichō's feminist manifesto, reminding their audience that "in the beginning woman was the sun" and calling for women of the world to unite.[43]

The struggle of working women was as multifaceted as the Modern Girl's many guises, and women's political engagement during the 1920s also took numerous forms. It encompassed the journalistic endeavors of activist leaders such as Yamakawa and Hiratsuka, the organization of lectures, the lobbying of state officials, the formation of study groups dedicated to women's issues, the establishment of schools to educate proletarian women, and the use of leaflets and tea parties to influence politics. Women workers also took organized action over such issues as the woman worker's freedom to leave her dormitory to go into the streets. By the end of 1928, 12,010 women had joined the labor movement; women had been solely responsible for twenty-one labor actions and had participated in 138 of the 397 labor struggles of the year. The Tōyō muslin strike of 1930 was one of 329 instances of labor strife in which women were active participants. The Florida Dance Hall strike of the same year, one of the thirty-eight strikes organized solely by women in 1930, illustrates how class conflict took place not only on the factory floor, but also in the play spaces where working women served consumers.[44]

WHAT MADE THE MODERN GIRL DO WHAT SHE DID?

The Modern Girl is rescued from her free-floating and depoliticized state when her willful image is placed alongside the history of working, militant Japanese women. Then the obsessive contouring of the Modern Girl as promiscuous and apolitical (and, later, as apolitical and nonworking) can be understood as a means of displacing the very real militancy of Japanese women (just as the real labor of the American woman during the 1920s was denied by the trivializing of the work of the glamorized flapper). But whereas the American woman worker by the mid-1920s had allowed herself to be depoliticized by a new consumerism, the modern Japanese woman of the 1920s was truly militant. Her militancy was articulated through the adoption of new fashions, through labor in new arenas, and through political activity that consciously challenged social, economic, and political structures and relationships. The Japanese state's response encompassed attempts to revise the Civil Code, consideration of universal suffrage, organization and expansion of groups such as the Fujin Dōshikai (Women's Alliance) and the nationwide network of *shojokai* (associations of young girls), censorship, and imprisonment of leaders. The media responded by producing the Modern Girl.[45]

Yet the Modern Girl must have represented even more, for the determination that talk about the Modern Girl displaced serious concern about the radical nature of women's activity does not fully account for her multivalence. Why was she both Japanese *and* Western, intellectual *and* worker, deviant *and* admirable? This code-switching within the discourse raises such queries. One answer is suggested by Natalie Davis in "Women on Top," where she argues that the "unruly woman" in early-modern Europe, who whored, tricked, and traded, served both to reinforce social structure and to incite women to militant action in public and in private. The culturally constructed figure of the Japanese Modern Girl certainly did both. Like the disorderly woman on top, the Modern Girl as multivalent symbol questioned relations of order and subordination and at the same time, through her cultural gender play and promiscuity, served "to explore the character of sexuality" and of gender while also suggesting that order be preserved.[46]

Of course, the Japanese Modern Girl is no more a copy of her premodern European sister than she is of her kinetic American contemporaries, but the term *namaiki*, meaning cheeky, bold, or brazen, which recurs in Sata Ineko's prewar writings and which she would much later use in mock-critical reference to herself during interviews, is a powerful analogue to the notion of woman as "disorderly." The connotations of this word are not violent, but they are certainly aggressive and transgressive: the person who is *namaiki*, like the Modern Girl, dares to take liberties. The symbol of a *na-maiki*, uppity Modern Girl, who crossed boundaries of gender, class, and sexual mores, may indeed have spoken to those who demanded expanded social, economic, and sexual liberation for both women and men. In this sense, she was admirable. But, conversely, the Modern Girl did what she did because woman's new place in public as worker, intellectual, and political ac-tivist threatened the patriarchal family and its ideological support, the def-erential woman who was presented in state ideology as the *ryōsai kenbo* (good wife and wise mother). Inflected in this fashion, the Modern Girl was a threat. Finally, the Modern Girl, who was both Japanese and Western—or possibly neither—played with the principle of cultural or national differ-ence. Seen in this way, she highlighted the controversy over the adoption of non-Japanese customs in everyday life and called into question the essen-tialism (as opposed to the European physiological determinism) that sub-ordinated the Japanese woman to the Japanese man. This thesis was indeed offered by the feminist Kitamura, who claimed that "labor struggle, tenancy struggle, household struggle, and struggle between man and woman" were inevitable and had recently been joined to a new battle: "a struggle over good conduct" that pitted Japanese against Western behavior and used the Modern Girl to work out the struggle.[47]

This, then, is the significance of the Japanese Modern Girl in the broad-est context of pre–Pacific War Japanese history. The Modern Girl stood as the vital symbol of overwhelming "modern" or non-Japanese change insti-gated by both women and men during an era of economic crisis and social unrest. She stood for change at a time when state authority was attempting to reestablish authority and stability and thus inverted the role of the good wife and wise mother. The ideal Meiji woman of the late 1800s had served as a "repository of the past," standing for tradition while men were en-couraged to radically change their way of politics and culture. In contrast, the Modern Girl served critics who wanted to preserve rather than chal-lenge traditions during a time of sweeping cultural change. The fact that these were male critics is brought into relief by the fact that the women writers of *Nyonin Geijutsu* did not bother to mull over the national identity or cultural specificity of the Modern Girl.[48]

The Modern Girl as un-Japanese and therefore criminal was the real sub-text to such headlines as "Modern Girls Swept Out of Ministry of Rail-roads," and "Conquering the *Moga* and *Mobo*." In 1925, a "vanguard *moga*" in short hair and Western clothing was tried for murdering a delin-quent foreigner with whom she had been consorting. The case, which received sensational press coverage, illustrated both sexual and cultural transgression. This story and others like it served a dual function: they registered unease with non-Japanese customs and at the same time denied the political activity of Japanese women. The Modern Girl's crime, in other words, was packaged as a culturally colored crime of passion; it was not a politically motivated thought crime. Thus, a father in the 1920s could beg his leftist son to "become a *Modern Boy* or even a *Modern Girl*" (!) as long as he did not "go red."[49]

One of the most graphic examples of the Modern Girl as cultural transgressor, and one that signaled an end to her prominence, was presented in a series of ink drawings constituting a history of Japanese mores in different years of the modern era, published in the pages of *Chūō Kōron* (Central review) in 1932. In the first image, in a reference to Meiji society, two women in kimono gossip under a parasol, and men in Western military garb drive behind them in a horse and carriage. The following five sketches (with only one small exception) elaborate on a demure figure in kimono. Only in the image standing for 1932, does one of the four figures wear Western dress; a second reclines decadently on a chaise lounge, and a third sits with her legs spread and her elbows exposed. It is, however, the illustration accompanying the title of this piece that best reveals the intensity with which tradition was being defended. Alongside the painterly calligraphy of the title is a woman in kimono sheathed in fur; above her head is a large gun, pointed at the characters for "modern traditions."[50]

The Modern Girl stood for a contemporary woman, but, like Tanizaki's Naomi, she also represented threats to tradition, just as the good wife and wise mother had stood for the endurance of tradition: To talk about the Modern Girl was to talk about women on the street, militant and otherwise, but it was also to talk about modernity. During the 1920s, her defenders, who saw her at the vanguard of a new imperial reign—the Shōwa era—were optimistic. One, who placed her appearance at 1926, saw the Modern Girl evolving toward complete fulfillment. This journalist predicted that future historians writing the history of prewar men and women in Japan would call the year when the term *modan gaaru* appeared in magazines and newspapers "1 A.D." By the beginning of the Pacific War, however, boundaries reifying gender and culture (and denying class) were imposed: laws forbade women to dress in men's clothing, women's magazines were placed under tight controls, and supposed vestiges of Western decadence, including permanent waves, were outlawed. And although the Modern Girl reappeared after the war, freed of such restrictions, she was by then reduced to a witless mannequin.[51]

The Modern Girl, whose identity was originally split into the dual images of a working woman and a middle-class adolescent at play, expressed a new set of gestures with profound implications for social relationships. Some of the gestures were indeed grounded in daily life, as the work of Kon documented, but more often than not the Modern Girl represented conflicting fantasies about class, gender, and culture that were projected onto her. She was displaced by yet another embodiment of womanhood: the Japanese woman on the home front, a good wife and wise mother characterized by renewed ties of filiation to "tradition," state, and patriarchy. But the Modern Girl had made her mark. She appeared in the mass media through the 1930s as a signifier of the modern, even as the war on the continent escalated. Her figure will recur in the following segments, in such other sites of erotic grotesque nonsense, as the café. I see the café waitress, who was and is usually treated separately from the Modern Girl, as one manifestation of the Modern Girl, albeit one often far from militant.

2 The Café Waitress Sang the Blues

The Japanese café waitress was the working-class embodiment of the Modern Girl and as such she sang the blues. Let me elaborate. The Modern Girl was defined as promiscuous and autonomous for two reasons. First of all, women were now on the streets as workers and/or as women demanding rights and, secondly, male critics found a variety of new "modern" mores and projected their fears onto this Modern Girl. And just as the Modern Girl could and can be viewed in two ways—as a middle-class consumer or as a politicized working woman—the café waitress can be studied from two dimensions. While she was commodified as an erotic object, at the same time she articulated her own sensual desires and her protests against the constraints of her workplace. If freedom of movement was a hallmark of the Modern Girl, confinement defined the cultural milieu of the café, and neither customer nor café waitress transgressed gender or culture lines as did the Modern Girl.

I am not being literal when I say this café waitress sang the blues. Unlike her contemporaries, Bessie Smith, the Empress of the Blues, or Awaya Noriko, the Japanese "Queen of the *Blues*," she was not a singer. She may have sung an occasional tune, but unlike Awaya, whose hits, "*Parting Blues*" and "*Blues in the Rain*" were adored by Japanese troops on the continent at the same time that these very same songs were being forbidden on the home front, she was not known for her musical performance. Thus she shared neither raw musical style nor tone with the songs that emerged directly from African American history, nor did she, most of the time, exhibit an aggressive cultural politics. Rather, I use *blues* here metaphorically. I use it in the sense meant by Langston Hughes, who likened the blues to Negro life: sad but with an undercurrent of hope and determination. I also defer to James Baldwin, who used talk of the blues to discuss the African American survival of pain. The premise of my code-switching, of placing a cultural expression from within African American history into Japanese modern culture, is that the café waitresses were not passive servants of a male customer's objectifying actions, but like the black women blues singers discussed by Hazel Carby, Daphne Harrison, and, most recently, Angela Davis, they "attempted to manipulate and control their construction as sexual [I would say erotic] subjects."[1] In other words, I am using the concept the Blues to help formulate how the erotic subjectivity of this female, working-class member of Japanese modern culture was grounded in the social relationships of the culture of erotic grotesque nonsense. At the outset, we find the café waitress eroticized within one of the most commonly mentioned sites of Japanese modern culture, the café.

In many respects, the following social history of African Americans applies to their Japanese contemporaries in the cafés of modern Japan: "The mass migrations sent thousands of rural men and women into the strangeness of the city with its crowded housing, glittering nightlife, faster pace, and impersonal atmosphere. . . . Not just men but women and children often left their homes and kin to seek a better life. More of these women were single than married, many traveling to jobs promised in service to families—jobs that often did not materialize. . . . In the burgeoning working class, people began to exercise their newly gained freedom . . . and sought entertainment in the small bars and cafés that sprang up in the cities." But what interests me even more than this comparability is a similarity in affect and attitude that I place under the heading of "blues." This is to say that even as the Japanese café waitresses acknowledged that they were eroticized as impoverished sexual commodities, at the same time, they celebrated their own sexual desires.[2]

I do not want to downplay the historic specificity of the experiences of the Japanese or the American woman. However, like the American black woman blues singer of the post–World War I era, and like the black women in her audience (and like their Chinese contemporaries who sold their sexual services in Shanghai), Japanese café waitresses, often migrants to city life, were enmeshed in a series of relationships of domination. These relationships were at once economic, eroticized, and informed by at times contestatory agency challenging male power. Although I am aware of the danger of romanticizing resistance, I use the idea of the blues as a strategic means of highlighting the coexisting agency of the café waitress as both contained and resisting within a capitalist culture wherein she is both consumer-subject and commodified sex object, and of highlighting her subjectivity as possessed of sexualized, erotic impulses. The blues sung by blues singers (and avidly accepted by audiences) was a voicing or expression of sexual experience—experience that encompassed the range of interplay between male and female and between female and female. Similarly, the Japanese *jokyū's* words and actions voiced her experience of the erotics of male and female acting out of presumptions (and fantasies) of gendered domination. All this took place within the trajectory of the history of Japanese male "play" provided by Japanese women working to provide (or serve up) feminine pleasures.[3]

This segment talks about the café waitress in those two ways. She was eroticized by others, as working class (or colonized) sex worker within Japanese history and as expressing her own version of eroticism. What I wish to emphasize is that the *jokyū* participated in erotic relationships inside and outside of the café. When I refer to eroticism, within the context of the cafés in "modern" Japan, I refer to the desire for connectedness with an historically constituted other (male or female) associated with physical or psychic pleasure experienced differently by men and by women and mediated by the construction of gender. I also see expressions of desires for dominating the clearly gendered other or for being dominated by that other. Investigating the café waitress as an erotic being is one way of approaching the meanings attached to the *ero* of *ero guro nansensu*. By looking at the extent to which she may have conformed to expectations placed upon her and of how and when she may have resisted, we can also gain insights into the sexual politics of modern Japanese culture.

EROTICIZING THE MODERN JAPANESE CAFÉ WAITRESS

In a short story by Ozaki Midori published in the March 1929 issue of *Nyonin Geijutsu*, a solitary heroine seeks solace from her buddy, Kimi-chan, who works in a grungy coffeehouse. Kimi-chan lights a match for the despondent heroine and explains why it is not acceptable to be infatuated with Charlie Chaplin: "Nobody's going to be crazy about a guy who's not a loverman." Kimi-chan then adds her own illustration of the ideal loverman (*iro otoko*): "Even I stopped going to the flicks after Valentino died."[4]

The interaction between women, about idealized, eroticized males, places the waitress in relationship to her woman friend, to whom she offers the sorts of services dispensed by café waitresses to their customers—Kimi-chan lights her friend's cigarette, talks about contemporary culture, and offers solace. Although the scene does not take place in a café, it is very similar to the representations of the café waitress (the *jokyū*), whose image was almost as prevalent as that of the Modern Girl in the surveys, fiction, and the other documentary reportage of the 1920s and 1930s. By reading these materials, we can imagine the subjectivity and activity of the café waitress. This, in turn, raises a series of issues related to relationships between Japanese women and men during these decades, relationships informed by historically (and therefore culturally) specific constructions of modernity, class, gender, eroticism, and the merchandising of what was considered erotic. For example, not only does it take us into the social space of the interactions between waitresses and customers; it also hints at the meanings attached to the eroticized male (the *iro otoko*) by Japanese women. My main concern is to place the *modan* Japanese café waitress into the history of erotic grotesque nonsense as object and as consumer-subject.

Here *eroticizing* refers both to the process whereby the presence of the café waitress was made desirable to her male customers and to the recuperative task of discussing how these workers might have experienced their own erotic connections that were not business transactions while recognizing that ultimately real recuperation is not possible, for there is no easy archaeology of affective ties to be rescued from the earlier stages of Japanese history. I also see the dual dangers of either essentializing eroticism as frozen in time or place or of imposing aspects of Western conceptions of eroticism, sexuality, and the body onto Japanese experience.[5]

As I have argued, the Modern Girl was more important as an ideological construct than as an actual index of middle-class consumerism, as many have presumed. The mass culture of modern Japan presents the café waitress, in contrast, as a working-class woman selling erotic companionship at a moment in Japanese history when the erotic was overtly politicized. According to Tosaka Jun, such mores were threatening because they were new. They were politicized by the state precisely because relations between the sexes and representations of gender were being renegotiated in everyday life. But they were also politicized as a cover for repression of thought, as Tosaka pointed out in 1936. Tosaka made it clear that he thought the surveillance of cafés, revues, and dance halls absurd. He cited the prohibition against the gesture of wiggling the behind, calling the ruling a "masterpiece" in characteristically sardonic terms. At the same time, he pointed to a blatant contradiction: dance halls were the object of attack because they endangered the morals and mores of the people of the nation, but at the same time the pleasure quarters (where sex was sold) were given the protection of the state. Sheldon Garon's chronology of the crackdowns on what he calls "*café* culture" reveals both a continuity in state surveillance of cafés and an intensification of such repression in wartime, thereby conforming to

Tosaka's theory of displacement. In other words, the mass roundup of students in cafés in 1938, following the earlier morals campaign of 1928 through 1930, took place as the country was being mobilized for war. While the state's preoccupation with transgressive gestures, in alliance with Christian abolitionists and other private citizens, may have been a displacement or a diversion, it undoubtedly articulated official concerns about nation, gender, and sexuality, like the regulatory discourse on prostitution in China analyzed by Gail Hershatter. Here, however, I am concerned with the discussion about the *jokyū* solely as an expression of the negotiation of sexual politics. This is the representation of the *jokyū* that I found in the Japanese modern mass media. Like the Modern Girl, the café waitress could generate a disturbed tenor of discussion, whether in relation to frustrated customers, lonely housewives, or the down-and-out café waitresses themselves. However, unlike the Modern Girl, the café waitress did not cross the culture line; she was undeniably Japanese.[6]

The fact that the *jokyū* was marked as working class may account for the fact that while the term *café* was a transcoding from the French, the word "*jokyū*" was a Japanese word composed of Chinese characters, meaning "woman server." This term may have resulted from an attempt to render her less modern and thereby less threatening by distancing her from the Modern Girl within the modern surroundings of the café. Or the nature of her work, which was very much a continuity of earlier forms of sex work throughout Japanese history, may account for the absence of a code switch.[7]

In order to figure out how to frame the history of the Japanese café waitress it is also helpful to look outside of Japan. According to Joan Scott, in the United States, the study of the history of women has gone through four stages during the past couple of decades: (1) the study of woman's victimization; (2) the study of woman's agency (or of woman as subject); (3) a focus on the representation of women (which could be linked to either of the first two stages); and (4) the concern about the construction of such entities as "woman" and "the female body" and of cultural differences and lesbian relationships. This segment on the *jokyū* as one site of modern Japanese culture, engages in all four approaches. The still largely unwritten history of the process whereby the Japanese café waitress was eroticized by others and by herself must at the same time be a social history of Japan-specific working-class women's conditions of labor and a cultural and intellectual history of prewar forms of leisure and pleasure. Following this four-stage scheme, I study the *jokyū's* victimization, neither by retracing the political economy of Japanese capitalism during the modern years nor by recapitulating the conditions of rural and urban poverty that were, without question, the bottom line for understanding *jokyū* agency. Rather, I look at victimization (a form of self-victimization, it can be argued) by obsession within the subculture of the tenements that housed many café waitresses. I also look at agency in terms of the strategies employed by the *jokyū* to counter the power of the customer derived from his purchase of her company. Thirdly, the focus on representation is provided by the writings I term ethnographic, which were governed by the documentary impulse of the era. And finally, in terms of the fourth approach, in this segment, I focus on questions of cross-cultural comparability rather than on constructions of the female body. (It is in the following segment, on the consumption of movie imagery, that I discuss the constructed nature of the female body.)[8]

Let us place the café waitress on site. The workplace of the modern café waitress of the 1920s and 1930s had a prehistory. The first of these successors to the Taishō era "milk halls," wherein women served men, was Cafee Purantan (Printemps), established in 1911 and renowned for the graffiti on its walls, which reflected the artistic aspirations and occupations of its intellectually inclined customers. By 1930, in Osaka, there were eight hundred cafés and ten thousand waitresses. The cafés, which catered mainly to the salaried and to intellectuals, numbered 37,000 by 1933. According to statistics, three years later there were 112,000 *jokyū*, and as late as 1939 there were 90,200 even after a decade of crackdowns. (This continued popularity at a time of "spiritual mobilization" for war indicates that the draw of the neon lights of the cafés outweighed any fear of police action.)

The *jokyū* served all classes in varied forms of establishments. More than the food or even the drink, the café waitress, originally dressed primly in kimono and apron, lured the male customers into the cafés which were more bar than coffeehouse in atmosphere and menu. These working women served drink and food, poured the drinks, and joined in the drinking as they made conversation with their customers. The presence of the café waitress (and of her patrons) was sensationalized in such popular novels as *Jokyū* (The café waitress), by Hirotsu Kazuo and some *jokyū* were celebrities, comparable to screen and stage idols who sold their own form of spectacularized eroticism. In sum, the *jokyū* were immortalized in the print media in word and visual images, in movies (including the movie *The Café Waitress*, based on Hirotsu's novel), and in movie song lyrics.[9]

A history of the *jokyū* that looks at the process of how she was made to feel and to appear erotic within the café also calls for comparisons from within Japanese history. The *jokyū* was a type of sex worker who provided erotically charged services (usually for tips only). She was not a prostitute, because she did not engage in sexual intercourse. However, this distinction only begins to have explanatory value if we can associate her both di-achronically and synchronically with other categories of women who were paid to be erotic during the course of Japanese history. The labor of the café waitress has some precedent in the early modern work of the *meshimori onna* (literally translated as "food-bearing woman") of the Edo period. The job of this waitress was ostensibly to serve food and drink to the travelers at the designated way stations, but government proscriptions against various mores at these places of rest and recreation all but tell us that the serving woman did more than serve food. Not only were the *meshimori onna* called "prostitutes of the way stations," in addition the proscriptive language emphasized the need to distinguish the work of these serving women from the services of the courtesans in the pleasure quarters. Like the courtesans (and unlike the geisha), the *meshimori onna* had no training in the arts, and the various protocols made clear that the young women were compensating via self-decoration and availability in both the serving room and the bedchamber. One regulation stipulated that the *meshimori onna* was not to wear clothing that would lead to her being mistaken for a *yūjo* (courtesan), while others described in detail the subdued cotton clothing that was to have been her uniform (and clearly was not). Silver and tortoiseshell hair decorations, such as those worn in the pleasure quarters, were also forbidden, as were such practices of the quarters as the serving of ornate trays of food, the line-up of these sex workers for the customer's perusal, or the posting of their names. The regulation forbidding customers to spend more than two nights with a *meshimori onna* as much as tells us that these young woman did sell their bodies. The above regulations and implied conditions differentiate the indentured *meshimori onna*—whose servitude could last a decade if she survived to serve her term—from the *jokyū*, who was trapped in a different nexus of capitalist relationships that rendered her nominally free. But I would like to associate them diachronically by expanding on Sone Hiromi's idea of a "prostitution society."[10]

My point is that both *meshimori onna* and *jokyū* were sex workers who performed as entertainers, although they were not trained performers. The regulation forbidding the *meshimori onna* from dancing and playing the drum in the front room of an inn told her (and tells us) that she could do so in a backroom. The *jokyū* would also converse and sometimes sing. Just as Sone associates the sex work of the feudal era—the unlicensed prostitution, the woman of pleasure (or *yūjo*), along with the hidden unlicensed prostitute (the *inbaita*) and the *meshimori onna*—within a "prostitution society," I want to associate the *meshimora onna* selling eroticized services, with the *jokyū*. According to Sone, all the forms of women's work listed above, were prostitution: all these women sold their bodies through contractual agreement within this "prostitution society," which appeared along with a commercial, cash economy. Sone calls for a women's history that can take prostitution into account, specifying the social conditions enabling both its appearance and continuity. In response to Sone's call, we can say that in terms of appearance, the *jokyū* was an early twentieth century phenomenon who appeared full force half a century after the official disappearance of the *meshimori onna*, women serving food, drink, and sex. In terms of continuity, the *jokyū* was hired to serve up eroticized social intercourse, if not sexual intercourse (although there could be such a business transaction). The term *meshimori onna* may have in large part been a euphemism during the feudal era, but the eroticization of this task was one foundation upon which the conception of the *jokyū* relied.[11]

The *jokyū* was not a prostitute; she did not aim to sell her body for sexual intercourse in the marketplace of the consumer culture of urban Japan in the 1920s, although clearly this sometimes occurred. If we replace Sone's notion of the shared experience of prostitution as euphemistically broken down into different categories with the premise that the sale of Japanese woman's eroticized services has been broken up into categories (exemplified by the Yoshiwara hierarchy of women of pleasure) that have hidden the shared nature of eroticized practices, we can compare the *jokyū* to her non-Japanese counterparts, to her predecessors in the medieval and early modern period, and to other "women who served customers" (an object of study for Gonda Yasunosuke) during the 1920s and 1930s, including geisha, *shakufu* (sake-pourers), and both licensed and unlicensed prostitutes.[12]

As numerous theorists and historians have taught us, our discussion of erotic relationships must be delimited by the recognition that, in the words of Eve Sedgwick, *sexuality* or *sex* is "the array of acts, expectations, narratives, pleasures, identity formations, and knowledge in both women and men, that tends to cluster most densely around certain genital sensations but is not adequately defined by them." Nodding to Freud and Foucault, Sedgwick adds that "the distinctively sexual nature of human sexuality has to do precisely with its excess over or potential difference from the bare choreographies of procreation." The prurient question frequently posed by Westerners of the geisha, "Does she or doesn't she?" (that is, have intercourse with her customers) tells us more about the Western obsession with sex, discussed by Foucault, and presumptions of sexual difference, documented by Thomas Laqueur, than about the history of the *jokyū* as sex worker within a matrix of historically constituted set of interactions. The *jokyū* was seen as a worker selling erotic contact; but she was not usually identified as a prostitute, nor was her sex work equated with the labor of the geisha.[13]

Most prewar Japanese commentary on the café waitress, based on a knowledge of the training and practices of the geisha, implied that the café waitress did not have the *gei,* or skill in the performing arts, attained by the geisha and that she therefore was a very different sort of purveyor of services. But while texts from the café waitress' own time almost uniformly distinguish her from the geisha, largely because she needed no training to be eroticized, my argument is that she was already eroticized. Because of the construction of gender, of sexuality, and of eroticism in post-earthquake consumer culture, she shared in the same construction of gender and eroticism as the geisha. Clearly differences are crucial; women were placed into different categories of sex worker for good reasons. For example, the café waitress who found a job by reading a want ad in a window proceeded to make a living through her knowledge of baseball lore needed no extra training. As long as she knew about the annual competition between Waseda University and Keio University the job was hers. The skills required of her were determined by the desires of her clientele rather than by an established cultural canon. The café waitresses working at the Asahi Diner café in Osaka learned to sing labor songs along with labor organizers who were members of the progressive wing of the local branch of the Japan General Federation of Labor. (This shared activity with their customers led to the organization of the activist Jokyū Federation.) Such differences notwithstanding, there was a carryover of practices and presumptions about sex and gender among the women engaged in different forms of sex work. The word *sekkyakufu,* the Japanese term for sex worker, *sekkyakufu,* meant a woman who came into contact with customers. It linked to the six professions of prostitute, geisha, sakepourer, café waitress, waitress, and maid at an inn.[14]

The practices of the *sekkyakufu* purveying food and drink and then sitting with customers to visit, must be seen within the context of Japanese cultural history. The practice of a woman server offering food and drink and then socializing with customers was distinctively Japanese. (In contrast, in the French café—the ostensible model for the Japanese institution—food and drink were served by men, not women.) Japanese men on the town had been familiar with the eroticized act of the subservient female supplying their drinking needs within a consumer culture since the early modern era. The *jokyū*'s merchandising of her company comes out of the history of the erotic implications of the pouring of drink by women, for men. In premodern and post Restoration Japan, women and men knew that drinks were to be accompanied by the serving up of conversation and play (encompassing various forms of performance) by women for hire, who interacted intimately with male customers. During the modern years, there was diversification, as cafés vied for customers through such gimmicks as the match service *(macchi saabisu).* Customers who paid for this service lit a match and were allowed to "enjoy the pleasure of fleshly beauty" until the match went out.[15]

In 1930, the philosopher Kuki Shūzō pointed to a contemporary expression of female-male encounter that threatened the intrinsically Japanese codification of erotic play of the Edo era. For Kuki, this eroticism was characterized by numerous features, including a sense of resistance against the sexual other, along with a look defined by such attributes as a woman's bare feet or narrow face covered very lightly by makeup, and clothing in shades of deep blues and browns patterned in vertical stripes. All fell under the category of the Japan-specific term *iki.* Historians are quick to credit Kuki for the comprehensive nature of his study, yet they have also historicized *iki* as a word that shifted according to time, place, and class during the Tokugawa period. Nishiyama Matsunosuke, for example, places the term in the context of the rise of an urban merchant culture in mid-eighteenth century Edo that included the domestication of lower-level warriors as city dwellers rather than as samurai. He also traces the evolution of the term that came to imply a spirit of resistance, along with a refined eroticism. Nakao Tatsurō says that for the rich merchant *iki* connoted refinement, but for the urban worker it referred to a decadent, lustful, disorderly, aesthetic sensibility outside of the rules of propriety.[16]

What is important here is that while Kuki may not have taken a historicist approach, his concern for the proper eroticism and for its degeneration did show an historical break. In other words, while differences within the Edo period were not his concern, Kuki's treatise told his readers that the erotic relating of woman to man was shifting in modern culture. Kuki may not have granted legitimacy to the female figure he conjured up, but he offered a clear-cut picture of new gestures that was as evocative as his imagery relating to the Edo heroine: "the facial expression of *iki* is premised on a disengagement from the winking of one eye, the jutting forth of the mouth, and of such Western vulgarity as the performance of *jazz* with two feet." It is not far-fetched to imagine that he was condemning the new type of sex worker who moved among male customers, in syncopation to the rhythms of the jazz played in the cafés of the modern years. The reference to jazz is the giveaway that Kuki was not referring to other forms of *sekkyakufu.* While new gestures of eroticism were imposed on all *sekkyakufu* within what I will here term "the modern eroticism industry," we must keep in mind that there was a specificity to the eroticism commodified within the *jokyū*-customer relationship.[17]

The tension between the eroticization of the *jokyū* and that of her sisters in other occupations within the modern eroticism industry is best illustrated by the case of Abe Sada, the notorious heroine who was tried for cutting off and walking away with her lover's penis in 1936. The work history of this modern woman made famous in the West by Oshima Nagisa's movie *In the Realm of the Senses* (1976) reveals the range of jobs available to an uneducated woman willing to sell her body during the modern years: Abe Sada worked as a delinquent young girl *(furyō shōjo)* had moved from a position as low-class geisha *(geiko)* to labor as a prostitute *(shōfu)* by the time she was seventeen. She also worked as a high-class prostitute *(kōkyū inbaifu)*, a mistress *(mekake)*, and a café waitress *(jokyū)*. In all of these positions, Abe served male expectations regarding eroticized femininity, yet she lasted only two weeks in her incarnation as a café waitress in Kobe, before quitting. Why? In her court testimony, Sada dismissed her work as a *jokyū* as barely remunerative, but her account of her personal erotic needs upon becoming a mistress may reveal an equally pressing incentive to move on from that work. According to Sada, it was unbearable to sleep alone, even though she did stay in touch with a couple of her customers from her days as prostitute. Being away from men made her so jittery that she had gone to a doctor who had told her that there was nothing wrong that a good married life, and the study of books that cultivated the spirit, couldn't fix. An alternative way of phrasing Sada's need for physical contact is provided by Sada's biographers. They say that she saw through the theatrics of the romantic mood created in the café to recognize that what was taking place there was merely "managed romance," wherein the conversation and exchange of gazes between men and women were controlled. The conclusion of the biographers: Sada must have decided that if she was going to work in a situation where sex was transacted, it would be more "rational" to approach the interaction directly.[18]

While it is likely that Sada, the café waitress, next moved to prostitution (before becoming the servant in the house of her most passionate "loverman") for financial reasons, and that the sex work of the *jokyū* did not fulfill her need for physical intimacy with the other sex, her discomfort with the job of café waitress must also have had to do with the expertise of interaction required of the *jokyū*. Her biographers have called this interaction "managed romance." In other words, Sada had to rely on her own ability to marshal conceptions of the erotic and to place them in the context of exchanged conversation, including culturally coded teasing or flirtation, gazes, and other practices of female-male engagement. My guess is that Sada was not capable of such subtlety. A more metaphoric, blunt way of phrasing my conclusion is that Abe Sada was unable to "sing the blues," as evidenced by her inability to engage in anything but the most literal of actions when she affirmed her connectedness to her dead lover by taking his member with her upon leaving the scene of the crime—a crime which was an inadvert result of rough love play. If she had "sung the blues" she would have responded to her erotic desires and her pain in a form other than such acting out of eroticized violence. Sada would defend herself in legal testimony that made use of the term employed by the fictional waitress Kimi-chan, quoted at the opening of this segment: she proclaimed that she had taken the most natural course of action for any woman so passionately involved with a true "lover man." Abe Sada explained what she meant by the label "*iro otoko*" as she described him: "If asked what exactly about Ishida was good I couldn't answer, but as for the way he was, his attitude, and the way he felt about things, there is not one thing I can speak ill of him for, in any of those areas. I have never met such an *iro otoko*."[19]

Gender was eroticized for Abe Sada as for all other café waitresses and their customers before they entered the space of the café as were the presumptions about *iro otoko*. Men and women surely took presumptions and expectations (and disappointments) from the household to the café and back. To presume totally de-eroticized domestic relations at home or to separate the give-and-take of the café from dialogue within the households of café waitresses—who were often married—or of their customers, serves to conceal the cultural place of the café and to flatten out the complexity of human emotions structuring Japanese family relationships from the teens through the 1930s. Even the most cursory examination of women's magazines of the modern years, the magazines that were most popular among the *jokyū*, reveals that the relationships within families and between households and such public spaces as the café were not smooth either within the middle class or among tenement dwellers. (In contrast, in the mass press, the most aristocratic and imperial families were idealized as models for family life placed on a separate plane.) As early as 1916, the readers of *Fujin Kōron* were warned about the "*café* woman," in an article placing her in historical perspective: "For ages, sake had come with a woman who poured for the customer, but these young girls in white *aprons* were able to seduce their customers because they had been spiritually seduced by the vices of modern civilization." The *Fujin Kōron* firsthand accounts of a field trip by *katei fujin* (household women) to a series of cafés highlighted the tension between household and café. Twenty years later the preface of Yamada Waka's *My*

Views on Love (which was organized into the two categories of "love prob-lems" and "husband-wife problems") illustrated the persistence of conflict. Yamada presented a central issue that was foregrounded in many women's magazines of the era, if not in the café: the "making into one the everyday life *(seikatsu)* of two people."[20]

Among the methods of configuring and eroticizing gender in the café was the use of space in order to encourage intimacy and fantasy. Pho-tographs reveal the placement of the art deco sofas from the famous Ginza café Tiger. These were lit by stylized lamps in the shape of Japanese lanterns. The strategically placed shrubbery, and the division of the space by stand-ing panels, along with the high backs of the banquettes in the Star of Gold in Shinjuku give a sense not only of the cultural syncretism of the era but also of how customers were isolated and then organized and managed within groups of *jokyū*. Chinoiserie including the Chinese dress of café waitresses demonstrate the exoticization of the colonial experience. This orientalizing was also a Japanese variation on the imagery found in Japanese movie magazines of the era. The popular magazine *Eiga no Tomo* (Friends of the movies), for example, featured photographs of Hollywood female stars in captivating Oriental garb, including kimono with the requisite fan, and of the caricatured Chinese male. The Japanese waitresses in the Ginza Palace (Ginza Paresu) did play at being colonized "Salon Manchuria" on the second floor, an affectation that must have played into fantasies of colonial *seikatsu*, or everyday life. But while the power relationship between the café waitress and her customer may have passed as colonial, she could only pretend. Since in reality the *jokyū* did not come from a separate, colonial sphere she could not employ mimicry of the colonizer as a means of resis-tance. The foreign costuming was ancillary—a prop for the performance of femininity.

Customers at Ginza Palace more interested in another form of exoti-cization, the reworking of indigenous tradition, could patronize the Salon Momoyama, also on the second floor, where waitresses sat on brocade chairs and wore their kimono and their hair in appropriate medieval fashion, or they could drink and visit in a third area arranged on the same floor that had wicker and wood chairs, potted plants, and *jokyū* in kimono with their hair tied up in contemporary but modest buns. What brought several hundred young women together (the owners had advertised for three hundred *jokyū* at the time of the opening of the Ginza emporium) was their ability to act as desirable females.[21]

While masquerade may have prevailed over mimicry on Ginza, there was mimicry elsewhere in the café world. In addition to situating the colonial within the modern, the modern was also situated in the colonies, as evidenced, for example, in the mobilization of Chinese and Korean women in *modan*, Japanese-style bars, restaurants, and meeting places on the continent. This is one aspect of the pre-history of the horrors experienced by the so-called comfort women, the *"ianfu"* who were forced into sexual slavery by the Japanese military.[22]

The colonial came into the modern in the form of sex work. Korean women restaurant workers were first brought to Sapporo, Hokkaidō, in the 1920s to serve Korean laborers in Korean restaurants that were ghettoized behind a gated entrance. In 1935 and 1936 (just before the first "comfort stations" were officially first used extensively following the Nanjing massacre, known as the "Rape of Nanking"), there were six Korean restaurants for these workers. These were converted and expanded to over one hundred places serving Japanese customers who had expressed a taste for these women workers who spoke Korean to their Korean customers. Eventually there would be an attempt to eradicate the "Korean-ness" of these colonized night spots by changing such names as "Arirang" to more indigenous-sounding titles and by re-costuming Korean *jokyū* from Korean to Japanese dress. The Japanese women in Chinese dress could look exotically Oriental, but the Oriental Korean women could not. These changes were part of the cultural history of the relationship of colonial to modern culture within the *naichi*, the interior of Japan. The eroticism of the Korean woman may in fact have been more threatening than a mimicry that could enable the same Korean woman to pass as Japanese. Or this may have been an instance of a sex-blind assimilation policy that aimed to make Koreans Japanese through the mores of material culture.

In any case, such gender and ethnic relations in "modern" Japan as those found in the restaurants in Hokkaido were not easily separated into neat binaries of male/female or *naichi/gaichi* (interior/exterior). They were intertwined with conflicting formations of both class and race/ethnicity within the context of Japanese colonialism. For although the Korean woman might need to be deprived of Korean culture, her culture could also be held up as an example to Japanese readers. This can be seen in *A Guide to the New Korea*, part of a series on Korean geography and customs published in 1930 (the same year as Kuki Shūzō's disquisition on the erotic, the aesthetic, and the authentic). The guide featured photographs of the Japanese author in fedora and Korean garb, a young Korean girl in native garb, and a memorial to Koreans killed during the massacre after the Kantō earthquake of 1923 that included the murder of pregnant Korean women. It offers insights into how Japanese Orientalist writers negotiated the contradiction between

Korea as the oriental other and Korea as ostensibly one with Japan. Covering such topics as the superior beauty of the Korean schoolgirl, as compared to the Japanese schoolgirl, the body language of Korean women, and the practices of indigenous Korean courtesans. This served two purposes. First, it defined Koreans, including Korean women, as separate from the Japanese people *(minzoku);* and second, it called into question the modern mores of women in Japan.[23]

In addition to associating the *jokyū* with her Japanese predecessors of the Edo period, and with other contemporary sex workers in the colonies and the metropole, it is worthwhile placing her consciousness in cross-cultural perspective as a means of highlighting the Japan-specific aspects of her eroticization, especially because the ethnographers of the era were taking such notes. It is also worthwhile because European, American, and Chinese predecessors and contemporaries of the *jokyū* were also young women sex workers who made use of the commodification of the erotic in their efforts to please their customers under the guise of attraction and affection.

Comparisons can be made between the *jokyū* and the Victorian barmaid posited by Peter Bailey within the history of "open yet licit sexuality" (his definition of his term *parasexuality*), made possible by "capitalist cultural managers" of the nineteenth century. The British "cultural prototype," too, could earn more money than other working-class women by engaging in "sexualized social encounter" informed by the flow of banter and alcohol in the context of a "modern sexualized consumerism and of the blurring of class and gender categories due to the emergence of working women." (It should be noted, however, that a blurring of gender categories speaks more to the history of the Modern Girl than to the circumstances of the *jokyū* in her café.) The crucial difference between the history of the British woman worker and that of the *jokyū* is in the spatial construction of eroticized relations within the work space of the Victorian barmaid and the Japanese café waitress. As Bailey argues, whereas the *jokyū* sat with her customers, the barmaid stayed behind the bar. According to him, this physical distancing both eroticized and controlled the sexual relations between server and served. In his words, "It is the bar that constitutes the necessary material and symbolic distance that simultaneously heightens and contains the sexual attractiveness of the barmaid and qualifies her as a glamour figure."[24]

The *jokyū* was also a glamour figure, but her body was not distanced: it was intimately available, if not always available for the most intimate of sexual encounters. During the 1920s and 1930s, encounters between *jokyū* and customer at some cafés were increasingly sexualized. The desperation of competing café managers resulted in the institutionalization of such acts as "the underground" or "subway *service*," whereby the customer's hand could go "underground" through a slit strategically sewn into the *jokyū's* skirt, or the "match service" referred to above. The analysis of the social and cultural categories of nineteenth-century French courtesans, prostitutes, and barmaids provided by T. J. Clark in *The Painting of Modern Life: Paris in the Art of Manet and His Followers* is more suggestive for such Japanese history than Bailey's discussion of barmaid "glamour." [25]

According to Clark, the courtesan was the "necessary and concentrated form of Woman, of Desire, of Modernity." This "sphinx without a riddle . . . played at being an honest woman," but such artifice (here the Japanese word *gei* might be appropriate), including her claims to classlessness, was easily recognized as false. This very falsity made this category of woman "modern." Clark talks about relationships between prostitute and client as based on both class and gendered formulations of sexual desire: they often involved transgression of class divisions, and their context was a "set of sexual theatricals" wherein the client had to feel he had access to "some mystery," probably that "of Woman." Clark notes that the prostitute collaborated in the "game" of making herself desirable; she was trapped by this collaboration, but she also had critical distance from the relationship because she knew she was a member of the proletariat, a member selling "physical complaisance" who was dependent on market forces to determine what her labor power would yield. The notion of such sexual theatricals, and of the tension between collaboration and the consciousness of it within an economic relationship, can be applied to the experience of the Japanese café waitress negotiating charms for her tips, which were, as noted above, in most cases, her only income.

The Parisian barmaid, more than Clark's Parisian prostitute, or the French courtesan, most closely resembles the *jokyū*. This is because this woman sells drinks, oranges, and according to Clark, "most probably herself." For my comparative purpose, what is even more crucial is Clark's qualification: even if she is not for sale, some of her customers believe she is. In Clark's history, the barmaid "wears fashion as a disguise" to hide her class origin, and yet the "popular" face she wears is clearly not bourgeois. Clark argues that the detached expression and the fashion of the barmaid avoid class identity—and any identity, for that matter. Ultimately her self presentation represents her to the customer as an object for consumption, and the barmaid's work is to "maintain this illusion." In sum, Clark's focus is on the objectification of a woman sex worker within a capitalist nexus of commodities. What he terms a "collaboration" between an eroticized woman worker and her customer is also the basis of a contestatory *jokyū* agency including expressions of autonomy, if not total independence, and of challenge, although not absolute resistance, to a commodified relationship.[26]

The *jokyū* had something in common with young American women workers, too. Like the young workers in Kathy Peiss's influential book *Cheap Amusements: Working Women and Leisure in Turn-of-the-Century New York*, she belonged to a "working women's culture" within which she "carved out a sphere of pleasure." Peiss's notion of a "doubled vision" takes into account both working-class women's "autonomy and pleasure" and their "continuing oppression" in the history of their "embrace of style, fashion, romance, and mixed sex fun." Although it would be pushing the image of the *jokyū* to place her in even a limited sphere of fashion and mixed sex fun, because of the poverty of the Japanese café waitresses (and because many were supporting husbands), the concept of a "doubled subjectivity" does allow us to see the café waitress as an agent and not merely a victim within Japanese modern culture, even though her agency was exceedingly limited and her pleasure often confined to the realm of fantasy. Especially important is Peiss's documentation of how working women created "new manners and mores." Moreover, Peiss's discussion of the "woman adrift" has implications for discussing the *jokyū*'s autonomy from patriarchal ideas and structures. The most extreme case of the Japanese woman adrift (or traveling, like the American blues women), was the heroine in Hayashi Fumiko's *Hōrōki* (Tale of Wandering), discussed below, as a means of showing how *jokyū* subjectivity could speak to many of the issues raised by the study of European sex workers and American women workers.[27]

The French bourgeois social and cultural world discussed by Clark was different from the cultural order of the Japanese of the modern years, in which a new middle class may have dominated sites of leisure but was not an established arbiter of culture from within a private sphere as in the European case. And the *jokyū* created gender and sexual identity within the context of a working-class culture at the same time that she sold a commodified sexual identity within the class-based and class-coded leisure culture of the café. The term *café* denoted both the large establishments of Ginza and Dōtonbori in Osaka that attracted intellectuals, artists, and members of the new middle class, and smaller drinking establishments for those further down the social scale. In these cafes the café waitress both sold and experienced desire within relationships with customers, with café management, and with other *jokyū*, within the shadow of expanding state control and an expanding Japanese empire.

Writers and critics of this period make it clear that the men and women in the cafés took the empire for granted, just as they took for granted the fact that the *jokyū* represented a new form of erotic modern woman worker. Let us turn to how they documented her labors, keeping in mind that these documents may be used to deconstruct presumptions about the *jokyū* as available through representation. We can then reconstruct practices and relationships while realizing that we cannot reproduce them. What is important, no matter how difficult for the historian, is that the analysis of representation not be studied in isolation from the study of practices.[28]

DOCUMENTING THE CAFÉ WAITRESS

The novel *Jokyū*, by Hirotsu Kazuo, serialized in *Fujin Kōron* from August 1930 until March 1932, caused a scandal when the popular writer Kikuchi Kan recognized himself as one of the predatory patrons in the work. But the novel documents that it was not only patrons who strategized to have their way, for *jokyū* practices of selling their services were also made evident. Hirotsu documented the machinations of carefully organized groups of *jokyū* (ten *jokyū* divided into three groups of "red," "blue," and "purple" *kumi*), who drew men into their designated spaces within the café through careful gestures or motions (*mooshons*), and the ensuing flirtatious, high-pitched, coy banter of persuasion and flattery constituting the "handling of customers" (or "collaboration" in "sexual theatricals," to use Clark's idea). He also suggests a typology of *jokyū* that may have been in currency, making sure to point out the vamp type *(buampu gata)* and noting that *jokyū* specialized in certain topics of discussion (with some, one could talk about sports; with others, current literary trends). In addition, he suggests a typology of café managers, including a colonial type of woman who flaunted wealth gained in Latin America but at the same time exhibited a generosity of feeling not seen in women of the metropole. (Again, here is an instance of the colonial in Japanese modern culture taken as a given.) All of these women negotiated within a modern environment, a term Hirotsu used to refer to café furnishings and café customers in Western clothing.

While Hirotsu supposedly wrote about the experience of becoming an accomplished *jokyū*, more self-consciously documentary texts from the period give a much more complicated sense of *jokyū* voice and agency.[29] Early on, Kon Wajirō and Yoshida Kenkichi recognized that the café waitress was a worthy subject for their surveys, and they went on to publish two articles on the *jokyū* in the book *Modernology*. In the first article, the modernologists claimed that their sketches from 1926, comprising the clothing of the café waitresses of Ginza, would be worthy of inclusion if in the future "History of the Mores of the Professional Woman" were to be compiled. The sketches of a dozen or so figurines of somber young women in various combinations of kimono and apron, identified by the names of their employers, including some of the largest cafés on Ginza, like Café Lion and Café Tiger do indeed provide a vivid document of fashion distinctions between and among those in kimono and those in black dresses trimmed in white. The second piece, "Survey of the Café Waitress's *Apron*," was equally self-congratulatory. Recognizing the connection between the home and the café, the two ethnographers imagined how the object of their study, the *jokyū's* apron, might be placed under glass for study a century hence, if there were still an appreciation for a non-routinized household life and there thus were cafés and bars.[30]

Part of the value of this second study lies in its documentation of the needs and ingenuity of the café waitress, as illustrated by a sewn pocket behind a pocket that allowed for rapid insertion of her *tips*. But while the modernology studies documented such new mores, they provide little analysis. For example, the use of the term *professional woman* is undoubtedly a deliberate avoidance of class difference by critics who were concerned with the documentation of the slightest of class differences. (See, for example, Kon's surveys of women and men moving in public space and of the placement of their possessions in the domestic sphere.) Moreover, the significance of the tip is not explained. The inability of Kon and Yoshida to move beyond the term *professional woman (shokugyō fujin)* may be an illustration of T. J. Clark's argument that fashion is a disguise that avoids the display of class identity; yet it is hard to believe that neither of these two critics failed to associate the labor of the café waitress with that of other sex workers, who were never conceived of as "professional women." For a study that problematizes the category of "professional woman" while placing such new mores as the practice of tipping within the context of everyday life of Japanese modern culture, we can turn to the work of Ōbayashi Munetsugu published several years later.[31]

A NEW STUDY OF THE EVERYDAY LIFE OF THE CAFÉ WAITRESS

Ōbayashi Munetsugu's survey *A New Study of the Everyday Life of the Café Waitress* was conducted between April and June 1930 and published in 1931 by the Ōhara Institute for Social Research, the progressive research institute that also employed Gonda Yasunosuke.[32] Ōbayashi placed the "new profession" of *jokyū* within the context of woman's professional activities, making it clear that he did not classify the café waitress as a working-class woman or with chambermaids at inns or women ushers at the movies. Their jobs did not require training. Café waitresses, in contrast, were professional working women, even though their work did not require the same sorts of knowledge or training asked of women schoolteachers, doctors, "*typists*," nurses, or midwives (OM, 11–13).

Ōbayashi's survey first delineated the social spaces of this new form of *shokugyō fujin* (working woman): cafeterias, coffeehouses, bars, restaurants, and cabarets. The survey was based on 1,949 responses received from 515 such establishments. In his report, Ōbayashi included a copy of the survey, which positioned the Japanese café waitress within five categories of *seikatsu*: (1) place of work; (2) status relations; (3) related to changing jobs, management methods of owners of establishments, and thoughts on management and customers, based on previous jobs and on schooling; (4) income and expenses; and (5) particular attributes and disposition of *jokyū*, based on such information as hobbies and cultivation (a common term referring to attainment of culture or education) (OM, 1–5). Through such categories, the survey aimed to fix the *jokyū* within material, class relationships with family members, employers, and customers rather than to analyze the exact nature of her work. At the outset, when Ōbayashi distinguished the labor of the *jokyū* from both that of the professional, trained working woman and that of women laboring in factories and mines, he hinted at the eroticized dimension of the work, by observing that the labor of the *jokyū* was constituted by a social relationship: the *jokyū* was a *shokugyō fujin* because her work required her to relate to "various sorts of human beings," which in turn called for "quite a working of the mental faculties" and "actions of the emotions" (OM, 12–13).

The study posited the *jokyū* as a post-Taishō, nationwide phenomenon. The café waitresses were modern women with modern work. In a brief notation offering one of his few illustrations of the café environment, Ōbayashi commented on the ways in which this phenomenon was new. The large Osaka cafés employing over one hundred *jokyū*, he explained, stimulated the desire for pleasurable leisure through such modern trappings as the neon sign *(neon sain)*, the jazz band *(jazu bando)*, stage dancing *(steeji dansu)*, and decorations that changed with the seasons. (Ōbayashi used the word *kindaiteki* and not *modan* to denote the newness.) The unprecedented "modernity" of the café waitress's environment was expressed in the code-switching called for by the mention of neon, jazz bands, and stage dance that the description required: there were no Japanese equivalents for these terms. Ōbayashi further implied that other forms of labor "catering to the customer" were also not comparable (OM, 19, 22–23). The *jokyū* was thus a special category of working woman within a "modern" site of entertainment that was eroticized by means of a "commodification" of "atmosphere" that stimulated the sensations and emotions of customers (OM, 28).

The café waitresses reported that their brothers were predominantly unemployed or were students. Some worked in commerce, manufacturing (including construction work), or agriculture. And although Ōbayashi is not particularly concerned with presumptions of an urban/rural divide, the documentation of 165 brothers in agriculture speaks to the fact that numerous young women left the countryside to participate in Japanese modern urban culture. Older sisters were typically unemployed or also worked as *jokyū*. Thus the café waitress often worked to support siblings or, after divorce, her own offspring. Was she working-class? Working from such data as the information that more than 20 percent of fathers worked in commercial endeavors and that the majority of these sold goods, Ōbayashi said no. For Ōbayashi, "The café waitress was one form of small entrepreneur who used her ability and labor power as her only investment capital in participating in the industry of the café managers" (OM, 158).

Ōbayashi's denial of working-class identification or origin contradicts recorded instances of *jokyū* identification with the working class, such as the stated desire of one to marry a member of the proletariat. It also ignores the sorts of jobs held by the *jokyū* before they began working at the café. According to Ōbayashi's findings, most café waitresses had been maids, office workers, factory workers, and agricultural workers (OM, 71, 126). Ōbayashi also is critical of the tip system, which he revealed as defined by desperation on the part of the *jokyū* and her customer. According to Ōbayashi, the tip system was a working woman's problem because the *jokyū* had to stretch her income from tips, along with any money that she might have made on her days off, in order to cover such expenses as food, the public bath, the laundering of napkins and aprons, and toothpicks. Income that might have been made on days off is also used to pay for necessities. The system, which encouraged the customer to order food and drink at three times their price and to throw *tips* at the café waitress, resulted in artifice. Ōbayashi is not as confident as Clark in his analysis of *jokyū* deceit as the response to the commodification of the beauty of the young women. He cannot decide whether the *jokyū* responds to generosity by playing with her customer's affections, or whether she goes beyond this to offer her body, but he knows that her behavior has come to be defined by the term *eroticism*. The café waitress is trapped by a structural fact: the customers desired something other than what they were ostensibly paying for, and she would gain only by serving more than she was officially expected to serve. Ōbayashi puts this dilemma succinctly: the men did not want "the *service* of things"; instead they wanted to be served eroticism *(ero)* (OM, 186).

Thus the study gives some sense of the ways in which eroticism was defined by customers and management, the practices constituting the ambiguous but pervasive term *ero service*, and the ways in which these young women expressed their own desires for affective, sexual connection. Ōbayashi's findings reveal the desire for rigid gender differences in the cafés. The women offering *ero service* were to offer the ultimate in femininity to male clients whose sense of masculinity was to be stroked.

Ōbayashi openly admits to the significance of eroticism in the labor of the *jokyū*, who have been historically transformed from mechanical servers of food and drink within the capitalist system by "*café* capitalists." He points to the blooming "woman's beauty" of the *jokyū* between the ages of eighteen and twenty-one and to their heavy eroticism and fragrance (OM, 38–29). The eroticism is augmented by the atmosphere, the stimulation provided by the Western liquor, and the decor, including the *neon* and the *jazz*. Additional practices of eroticization are also recorded indirectly in police documentation. Ōbayashi cites 1,275 "corruption of morals" infractions over three days of police raids in July 1930. These ranged from the darkening of the customer seating area and the existence of secret rooms to customer nudity and prostitution. (OM, 30–31). Ōbayashi implies that such transgressions, along with other instances of violation of the October 1929 law legislating mores (which included a prohibition against nude dancing), were the fault of the café capitalists more than of the café waitresses.

Neither the survey data nor the ensuing report elaborated on regional, cultural, or class differences among women or between men and women in the cafes, although it differentiated between the workers who frequented the small cafés on the edge of town and the prosperous white-collar and student clients in the large cafés on the boulevard of Dōtonbori in Osaka. However, some sense of the waitresses' beliefs emerges in their answers to the question as to why they had become *jokyū*. Most listed financial reasons; some were "sick of the countryside"; and others gave such reasons as "I wanted to wear beautiful clothes" and "for revenge on a man" (OM, 80–82). It would appear that the image of the trangressive Modern Girl resonated with these women.

Unfortunately, the nature of the revenge is not described, but the acting out of relations of domination (and of manipulation) in the café, comparable to Clark's set of "sexual theatricals" and centered on drinking, is hinted at.

Jokyū opinions of their clients adopt a patronizing, critical distance: "Sake drinkers are fun"; "Gentlemen who do not drink are good"; "I give good *service*, make them satisfied, and treat them with care." In contrast to explicit discussion of the sexual theatricals by which they negotiated for tips, the women dismissed the men through such generalizations as "They all cheat on you," "It's like caring for an invalid," and "The youths of today have an air of delinquency about them."

These answers express a profound romantic disinterest, an impression that at first glance is strengthened by Ōbayashi's statement that most of the *jokyū* respondents did not understand his question about "experiences of having been seduced." Even from their limited statements, however, it is apparent that the young women did not necessarily equate *ero service* with either romance or sexual intercourse. In fact, according to Ōbayashi, numerous responses written on the back of the questionnaires expressed indignation at the popular image of the *jokyū* as a purveyor of sex (OM, 152). One response to the question about seduction that expresses the confidence of a *jokyū* in her ability to "play" with sentiments of love was: "I do the seducing." The café waitresses' presumptions about gendered differences were expressed in such statements as "Don't forget you're a woman." In the response to the query "List the good things about your work," one answer was, "I can find out all about men" (OM, 127).

One source of the café waitress's ideas about gender must have been her reading material. The survey revealed that waitresses read a broad range of women's magazines, which embodied different forms of femininity: the *fujo* of *Fujokai* (Woman's world), the *shufu* of *Shufu no Tomo* (Friend of the housewife), the more proper *fujin* of *Fujin Kurabu* (Woman's club), the *shōjo* of *Shōjo no Tomo* (Young girl's friend), and the *fujin* of *Fujin no Tomo* (Woman's friend). The survey also showed that these workers were reading women's magazines aimed at a middle-class, married readership. This is not surprising when the number of married and divorced waitresses (including single mothers) counted by the survey is taken into account. The married waitresses who were forced to play at being available single women while on the job apparently spent their free time reading about the ideal way to formulate family life.[33]

In spite of the variety of female personas made available by the women's magazines, the "favorite people" *(sukina jinbutsu)* listed by the *jokyū* in response to the survey were preponderantly male (though Murasaki Shikibu, the woman writer of the classical age, merited a mention). The responses most clearly offered a masculine ideal (not necessarily identical with the sexy *iro otoko*). The surveyors did not push the *jokyū* to elaborate why

Prime Minister Hamaguchi Osachi (who topped the list of favorites), General Nogi (the Meiji military hero lionized for his loyalty to the emperor), or the more "abstract personages" such as "a merchant" or a "manly" person should merit the women's affection.

The survey was sensitive to national difference, as when it referred to Japanese women born in America and Hawaii who worked as waitresses and to the existence of Russian and Chinese *jokyū*. Most attention was given to the Korean *jokyū*. When Ōbayashi mentioned the Korean café waitress in the first-class café who made more than two hundred yen per month (the average income was thirty yen), he was more interested in repeating what he had already said about the Korean *jokyū* in Japan. That is, that they were born and raised in Korea before coming to work in a café managed by a Korean for Korean customers. Twice the report stated that these *jokyū* were sufficiently bilingual to cater to Japanese customers, and that only their Korean dress identified them as non-Japanese. The Korean women were to be assimilated only so far (OM, 51–52).[34]

Just as Ōbayashi did not pursue the cultural politics of empire in his preoccupation with the Korean café waitress, he was content to quote, without critical commentary, the fantasy of one *jokyū* who articulated her goal in life as follows: "to engage in trade with Manchuria and Mongolia." Others sought petit-bourgeois careers such as inn-keeping with future (or current) husbands; 262 of the women wanted to be shopkeepers, in keeping with the occupations of male relatives. The comments "I'd like to go to a convent" and "I'd like a lover" indicate that it was not only the customers who were looking for some form of escape or love connection within the context of negotiations between customer and waitress in the café.

The café waitress may have sung the blues, openly admitting the need for love, but she also talked politics, albeit politics that accepted the colonial in the modern and vice versa. Expressions of class-based politics such as "I resent the *bourgeoisie*" and the hope for a café waitress labor union can be found in the report, along with the expression of hatred of "male oppression" and the desire for "equal rights for men and women" (OM, 126). Other "hopes for the future" were the aspiration to "married life with a manly man" or continued sex work in the water trade (a colloquial term for what I have called the eroticism industry).

It was not the politics of the café waitress, but the unprecedented nature of her art that contrasted with the *gei*, or art of the geisha, that made her modern to Ōbayashi. In Ōbayashi's eyes, the café waitress was modern because, unlike either the geisha or the prostitute, she was of the masses and open to the present. Hers was a "new social existence," illustrated by her ability to discuss topics of interest to her white-collar patrons—workers, wage-earners, and intellectuals, whose needs were met by the many café waitresses who had more than a middle-school education. Ōbayashi tried to come to terms with this new form of merchandising of the erotic, stating that the *jokyū* could not be seen only as an object of sexual desire. He granted the *jokyū* some leeway in allowing for her own experience of love while warning against the dangers of the "performing of love" based on falsehoods (OM, 149–153). The café waitress, whose company could be purchased for the price of a cup of coffee or two, who came with the modern music of the jazz band, the record player, the piano, and the radio, was as modern as her music, but it was clear from Ōbayashi's study that she also already had her own history. For example, she no longer wore the apron documented by Kon and Yoshida. The idea of the café was well ensconced in society, for it had been two decades since most of the Western restaurants in Tokyo had converted to cafés. These establishments had also displaced the milk halls where waitresses had served *milk, coffee,* and *cake.*

The café waitress was modern because she was of the post-earthquake present, but, working from Ōbayashi's material and not his explicit conclusions, it can also be said that she was modern because she was in motion, and that her being on the move is one way to think about her having sung the blues. This was not the frenetic movement of a Modern Girl, best pictured dancing the Charleston, but rather the movement from job to job of the itinerant woman. The reasons waitresses gave for switching jobs ranged from the blues-like explanations blaming "a situation with a man" or divorce, to the vague "the job didn't suit me." But whether they were pirated by *cooks* starting new cafés or merely answered the ubiquitous want ads posted outside cafés, these women had the opportunity to change jobs in a market that continued to expand along with the depression. Other forms of motion are described, including the travel of the *jokyū* from the countryside and the commute of these waitresses on the "*jokyū* trains." (Here is an example of the fluidity of rural-urban relation that I mentioned above within the context of imagining a social history that would capture the movement of people, ideas, and things.) What stands out is the autonomy captured in the statement of one respondent: "If they don't treat me right, I go elsewhere" (OM, 74–80, 88).

Others like the *jokyū* who imagined "the people of the nation all working together to abolish the national tax," and the *jokyū* who wanted the solidarity of a café waitress union, document that the favorite people noted above were not chosen merely for erotic attributes — the café waitress may have sung the blues but she also talked politics. There were also spiritual aspirations such as the voice, "I'd like to go to a convent." The expressions of class resentment such as the "I resent the bourgeoisie" cited above, articulations of sexual politics, such as the expression of hatred of "male oppression," and the desire for "equal rights for men and women" presented in Ōbayashi's survey may have come from such waitresses (OM, 127). In his conclusion, Ōbayashi placed the *jokyū* in the history of the liberation of women from family life under capitalism. He also positioned her within the process of changes in attitudes towards sexual discrimination, customs, and the legal system. He underscored his concern for contrasting the art of the geisha with the attainments of the café waitress through a class analysis that repeated some of his main points. The geisha (who served only bourgeois customers) was not capable of relating to the atmosphere of the "modern world of sports, modern literature, art, labor problems," and social issues in which the "mass-oriented, liberated" *jokyū* flourished. Such arts were definitely "*erotic service*" and not the "service of goods" as the well-bred young women responding to the earliest employment ad for café waitresses had discovered, much to their horror. Ōbayashi recounted how these *ojōsan* (an upper-class gendering of young womanhood), accompanied by their mothers, had responded to the call for "women boys" *(onna boi)* presuming that they would work for a trading company, only to find that they were being looked over for their "sexual draw" as women servers (OM, 163, 175, 245–247).

A CLOSE LOOK AT GINZA

In his vernacular ethnography *A Close Look at Ginza*, published in 1931, the art historian Andō Kōsei was much more specific than Ōbayashi about cultural practices that drew men to the *jokyū*. This was not the first examination of the cafés on Ginza: the second issue of the magazine *Ginza*, in its survey of Ginza architecture, had offered a brief lesson in British history along with its criticism that the décor of Café Kirin was derivative of the style following the Elizabethan age that stretched from the time of Charles I to Cromwell's era. This article had also offered its version of the modern lexicon of modern words that was to be found in numerous magazines during the modern years. This lexicon included such terms as *café, tippist* (a customer who left a ten-yen note for a three-yen dinner served by a café waitress). The definition of the English word *waitress* told what she was not— she was neither geisha nor telephone operator, as revealed by her clothing; she could not be an actress because she wore no gold wristwatch; and typists left for work early in the morning. Cafés were places where patrons indulged in sake and tasteless food, and sites of love and seduction. Ginza itself, according to this lexicon, had four meanings: it was a jumble of post-earthquake, makeshift shacks (barracks), night stalls selling food and drink, and concrete; it was a place where gentlemen in spats and torn socks, juvenile delinquent girls, children, and widows walked; it had streets where the dirt began to swim when it rained. And finally, given the tone of the first three definitions, what can be read as a tongue-in-check reference to Japanese expansionism: there was such an avenue in Tokyo, "the capital of the Japanese empire." (The mentions of the empire appeared matter-of-fact and accepting in the responses received by Ōbayashi from the café waitresses. Here, this citing of the imperial in the modern is jarring; it reads like a sardonic parroting of official references.)[35]

Another guide to the cafés of Ginza was produced by Kon and Yoshida, in addition to their surveys of café waitress garb. They produced a map identifying all the drink and food establishments on Ginza, including cafés. While this guide sold out in five days, leading to a second printing, neither this graphic nor the Ginza articles showed the café waitress in motion on the boulevard. (It should be noted that they did produce a study which calibrated the motion of the café waitress's feet.) It was Andō's work that placed her on Ginza, moving among customers, stores, and putting into practice her everyday survival strategies. Andō was specific regarding cultural practices that drew precise portraits of men attracted to the *jokyū*, as when he sketched the image of the café waitress wearing low clogs and walking by an interested customer who had stood in wait for her after hours. His ethnographic work also quoted the language created by the *jokyū*, who, as other sources confirm, could be identified in the Ginza by the small *furoshiki*, or knotted cloth bundle she carried with her to and from work.[36] The *jokyū* had their own version of *satokotoba*, the dialect spoken in the premodern Yoshiwara quarter. The café waitress actually engaged in a modern linguistic code-switching as she communicated with her coworkers. For example, within the café culture, "hot sandwich" *(hotto sandoicchi)* was shortened to *torisan* (short for "chicken sandwich") and then given the cachet of French terminology, as when a *jokyū* took the order for *"un torisan."* Andō, like Ōbayashi, placed the modernism of the café within the framework of capitalism, characterizing the café as "the dangerous stage on which capitalism is performed." Like Clark decades later, he was interested in the gestures constituting the relationship between *jokyū* and patron; and, like Peiss, he wanted to document the shaping of style within capitalism. As a result, he gives us some suggestions as to the relationship of style to gender and sexuality and the coexistence of differing styles of domination within the café.[37]

According to Andō, eroticism took on different styles in different cafés. He gave examples of styles, language, and body language that were considered erotic. At Lion the *jokyū* acted humbly toward her customers; other cafés, where the makeup was thicker and the kimonos more garish, and where the waitresses who wished to make the slightest of comments brushed their bodies against the customers, drew those in search of the erotic. (Andō did not elaborate as to the requirements for *hin no ii* [respectable], a term appearing to combine gender and notions of class, but he did oppose it to the vamp-style *jokyū*.) Such discussion of style, relating it to sexuality, taste, and, by implication, to class, compares with Peiss's notion of "putting on style," which she associates with dress as "a particularly potent way to display and play with notions of respectability, allure, independence, and status and to assert a distinctive identity and presence." Peiss's notion of prostitutes as cultural model, borrowed from the historian Ruth Rosen, also comes to mind as does Clark's association of appearance with the ostensible denial of class.[38]

Another dimension to Andō's guide to Ginza not found in Ōbayashi's survey is the relation of body type to gender and sexuality; there is physical typecasting. For example, the short stature of a *jokyū* is considered a "fleshly bad point," and the Takehisa Yumeji ideal of a slender woman is invoked as beautiful. In his revealing discussion of "Osaka Eroticism," Andō makes clear that style is a regional matter. In a joking reference, he combines class and intimations of sex: "the Osaka *jokyū* is a skilled worker in an *erotic* factory" and elaborates that Osaka eroticism is marked by its mass nature. In a vivid reference to connections among forms of commodified mass-oriented leisure, he remarks that all are welcome: to enter an Osaka café is like entering Cherokee (a department store), and on crossing the threshold, the Osaka customer yells out—with intimation of domestic spaces—a lusty "So-and-so, I'm here!" to his *jokyū* of choice. Tokyo culture is "conceptual" and "intellectual," in contrast to the *seikatsu* (everyday practice) of Osaka culture. Moreover, the Ginza *jokyū*, unlike the Modern Girl, is old-fashioned; but at the same time because of her intellectual nature she can converse with anyone.[39]

Andō's analysis of the *jokyū* as *courtesan* (spelled out phonetically) is reminiscent of Clark's analysis of class-based theatricals, but he is vague as to the national origin of the "courtesans from of old" to whom he compares these "free laborers." Although it is not clear whether Andō is transposing the history of European courtesan onto the ancestry of the *jokyū* or referring to her indigenous lineage, Andō's discussion of how she makes her income is clear. If Ōbayashi's *jokyū*—aside from the proud woman who claimed her rights as seducer—appears mostly passive (possibly because of the disembodied staccato nature of survey questions and answers), Andō's café waitress, like the women in the novel *Jokyū*, is manipulative as she "takes her love or bodies in silence." Andō describes a conspiracy among *jokyū* who label a customer "So-and-so's customer," thus granting one of the members of their group proprietary rights, a social practice also outlined in Hirotsu's novel. There is a code of behavior among the women, whose sense of community is forged at work and during off-hours at such places as the public bath (the Lion group habituates one, and the Tiger *jokyū* employees use another public bath in the Ginza neighborhood), where they use rough language to their heart's content (*rough* here meaning a code switch into the most informal of male vernacular) as they talk up a storm about the faults of customers, or badmouth the cooks.[40]

Andō discusses such aspects of the café waitress's everyday as the process by which she is trained, the methods whereby customers are assigned, maintained, or stolen, and off-duty activities. The informal survey confirms Ōbayashi's report that the *jokyū*'s routine of buying magazines and reveals that kimono dealers also entered the café. The tenor of interactions with clients after hours is evident in the section titled "Chasing after the Café Waitress," in which Andō describes such techniques *(tekunikku)* as a client's enlisting his ally, a coworker of the *jokyū* he is pursuing, and the various methods of "seeing her home," including the ruse of waiting near the café for her to walk by so that one can "just pass by" in a taxi, or telephoning her at the end of her shift to invite her to go to her favorite sweet bean restaurant or noodle shop where the hungry *jokyū* tended to congregate after work.

Andō also reveals that within these relations of power, the *jokyū* had their own techniques of responding to the above forms of "seduction." He recounts the story of the *jokyū* who wrote her address on the back of a ticket for one eager customer, who said he would visit her on her day off. In addition to giving her a big tip, he offered to bring her a treat of her choice, to which she replied (in terms that were marked as innocently feminine), "Well, you see, I do like cod roe." The gallant would-be seducer spent the following afternoon in a taxi, driving around in a neighborhood, pungent offering in hand, searching for an address that did not exist. Maybe the waitresses surveyed by Ōbayashi knew the meaning of seduction so well that they did not want to reveal the tricks of their trade! Hayashi Fumiko wanted to reveal all. That may be one of the reasons why her *Tale of Wan-*

dering was such a phenomenal best seller when it appeared in 1930.[41] In other words, the reader did not have to guess about the *jokyū's* experience of erotic desire, of erotic domination, or of confined but determined resistance to erotic and economic bonds.

TALE OF WANDERING

Hayashi Fumiko's autobiographical fiction, written in the form of a diary, is a documentary history that gives us the process of one woman's becoming a *jokyū*. It also offers a lyrical record of one woman's resistance during the Japanese modern years. When Hayashi referred to the work as a lengthy advice column, like women blues singers, she was "sharing experiences" and like her contemporaries in black America explaining to her eager audience (and possibly to women living, working, and loving in the back alleys of modern Japan) how the personal was social (HF, 307).[42]

It is neither surprising nor essentializing to conclude that more than any of the male writers I discuss, Hayashi Fumiko takes us into the culture of the café waitress. This was a subculture of the tenement houses, with its own rules for survival, of the café, and of the limited choices available to woman without skills. It was a subculture of the years before and after the earthquake of 1923.[43] Hayashi treats café relationships as defined by economic and gender domination. The account of a customer who absconded without paying is but the most immediate cause of her declaration, "It was after all nothing but a one-on-one battle between customer and *jokyū*. (I'm sick of it all when I think of the ruses of the *café*.)" When one *jokyū* likens the customers to Jews (exhibiting an anti-Semitism that emerges here and there throughout the media of Japanese modern culture), she is corrected by Hayashi, the narrator, who makes clear that all relationships in Japanese society are marked by greed. *Tale of Wandering* traces the process of becoming a *jokyū* within the capitalist system. When the heroine talks about having "fully become a *jokyū*," she is not merely referring to training for the acquisition of skills as implied by Ōbayashi or Andō; she refers to a process of eroticization that takes into account her own erotic desires as much as the needs of the men she serves (HF, 242).

The dated entries follow the *jokyū* from the time she first searches for work at cafés that are likely to have *"café* waitresses wanted" signs posted through time spent in training. Hayashi is informed of the price of the public bath, warned that she must not break things, and told that the boss lady, the master, the *jokyū*, and the cook sleep in one room. The narrator gives us life histories—her own and those of others. There is the story of Ohatsu-chan, for example, sold as a geisha to the colonies and brought back from Manchuria by a journalist. (Again, the empire is taken for granted.) The histories are as much about relationships between women as between men and women: Hayashi relates her "even more than sisterly" relationships with her intimates Ohatsu-chan and Kimi-chan, and describes a society of women sitting together figuring out how to construct a love letter or imagining upward mobility through the fantasy of "moving up to Ginza" or of rising through the *jokyū* ranks from the rough-and-tumble establishments in Asakusa to the costly cafés of Hibiya (HF, 85–86, 98, 100–101, 262).

Hayashi presents woman-to-woman interactions as intensely intimate, though not erotically charged, in such passages as the brief account of the heroine waking to find that she and Taiko-san have been holding each other while they slept. There is tenderness between women that Hayashi does not show taking place between women and men; she is happy under the quilts with a fellow waitress. Moreover, she talks about a relationship between two women with a fierce defiance: "The women who had the same fate laughed in a lonely manner, matching eye to eye in the same way. What the hell—Laugh! Laugh! Laugh! Just because two women merely laughed, does not mean we want anything from the heartless society around us." But elsewhere, she places herself within a social order that has compartmentalized women, giving them set opportunities and labels (HF, 279).

Hayashi does not deny her sexuality as the site of her oppression, for she recognizes that the eroticized woman has already been constructed as feminine. The heroine has been aware of the gendering of women in her society since the age of twelve, when she found it necessary to gender her desire for wealth in proclaiming her desire to become a "woman nouveau riche" *(onna narikin)*. She plays with fantasies of other embodiments of womanhood, imagining herself at various times as Kachusha, the leading stage heroine, and more prosaically as a "woman drunkard," a "woman thief," a "woman gambler," and "a mess of a woman" *(borokasu onna)*. When she gains work as a journalist, it is as a "newly rising lady reporter." Clearly, Hayashi is aware of popular conventions of womanliness and of how such glamour is being conveyed; her ideal of beauty is the actress Matsui Sumako "as seen in a photo" (HF, 106, 131, 132, 23, 284, 303). Hayashi's narrative links conceptions of femininity with the history of the café waitress when she claims that "in such a *café*, all you have to do is be a woman." But while she has her own idea about what makes her drinking partner, Toki-chan, a cute young girl and a woman with good parts to her, regardless of the fact that she is wild and has no sense of manners, she does not elaborate on what "being a woman" in the café context implies about male expectations (HF, 261, 266).[44]

Although Hayashi jumps into a "man-like ocean" at one juncture, she is more interested in following the shifts in her own erotic desires for men than in discussing the details of what makes them manly. She does not use the explicit language evident in her brief description of the "pertly pudgy youthfulness of the prostitute missing a finger, who seemed to have come up out of the working-class." She is far less specific about the men who love and leave her. Nonetheless she is seized by an erotic desire, as she reveals to her reader: "In the evening, when I was walking in the neighborhood of Shinjuku, for no reason, I was seized by the urge to cling to a man. Isn't there somebody around who can save me as I am now . . . I began to hiccup just like a child." Her sexual desire also appears in less seemingly infantile ways in her verse in such phrases as the graphic references in the poetry worked into Hayashi's story as:

> The young girls
> When it was night
> Casting up to the sky
> Their lips like fruit
>   (HF, 24, 27–28)

The heroine's desire is tempered by an ironic sensibility. When she pretends to fantasize that "maybe I'll just go home to my province and go be a bride," she knows that this will not satisfy her desires for erotic connection, or for the consumer items, that she craves including food and a shawl. The phrase "going to be a bride" implied fitting into a family and meeting the demands of an institutionalized kinship system. Hayashi is brutally honest about erotic domination that takes the form of violence made possible by obsession, as were her American blues-singing contemporaries. Because of an obsession with one man, she goes from café to café and because of men, in the second half of the book, after she has left the *jokyū* life, she is forced to back into the café life she has left. There she curses and mourns the departed man who abused her, and her poverty forces her to borrow money from a man who treats her as though he is coming home to a mistress (HF, 25–27, 263, 265, 282–283).

But Hayashi's *jokyū*, like the heroines speaking in the first person in the blues, also resists her fate in love, in part because, as the heroine says (echoing one response in Ōbayashi's survey), one loses one's illusions regarding men when one works at cafés. One example of a defiant response accompanying humiliation takes place after a customer wagers that she cannot drink ten bottles of King of Kings beer. All those nearby laugh, and the café proprietor is delighted when she takes on the bet: "I swear that I resent all and every one of the bastards. Ah, I am but a woman with no chastity. Shall I present you with one naked dance? All you fine personages . . . When I think of having to have a man provide for my board, I have to work one hundred times harder, don't I?" (HF, 103, 129).[45]

A more direct example of the *jokyū* challenge to domination by their customers is a trick: related by Hayashi in a wording that tells us both that this was but one of many "fads" and that the effect of such a challenge to the authority of the men who paid for their services was transitory. "Around that time, among the *jokyū* it was a fad to promise a number of customers that one would be with them on one's day off, then gather them in one place, and stand them up." Resistance is ultimately fruitless—the café culture will of course be impervious to their protests—but the *jokyū* must keep on resisting: "Of all of women's 'I've got to do something about this'—of all such things, there is not a worthwhile one. All one can do in front of such a fine, upstanding man is to open wide, and to be gobbling away at eating. Cracking a hard-boiled egg on the edge of the table, I eat with Oyu-san." The heroine's determination to register protest takes an alternative form of theatrics when she gets drunk, because she refuses to collude in erotic pretense. The café waitress is a woman without a man, like a friend whose apartment she visits: "When I opened the closet, I breathed in the sharp smell of a woman living alone" (HF, 138, 259–260, 265).

HOW THE JAPANESE CAFÉ WAITRESS SANG THE BLUES

The American woman blues singer's discourse from the post–World War I years into the 1930s belongs to a culture alien to Hayashi, but her voice is strong enough for me to want to use the metaphor in a way that does not deny the specificity of the Japanese *jokyū*'s experience, or of the African American experience, or of the African American woman's experience. The Japanese *jokyū*, like her African American contemporaries, was drawn to the big city, where she lived in the midst of small bars and cafés. The blues were inflected both by a culture-bound sexuality and by gender, as Hazel Carby and Daphne Harrison have shown, as was the language of the Japanese *jokyū*. I place the two side by side not to produce a universal history of women but to illuminate the concerns of the *jokyū* from the perspective of another idiom. Compare, for example, Hayashi's topics and the concerns of Bessie Smith (who was called a city type) and the other blues women whose heyday was the 1920s. The following were blues topics sung by women as catalogued by Harrison: "mistreatment, desertion, infidelity, revenge, sex, alienation, ambivalence about whether to go or stay or to defy sexual norms," and, as Harrison has noted "poverty was intertwined with the loss of love." Like the blues women, Hayashi expresses intense sexual desire for the very men who hurt her. Her struggle for autonomy within domination, expressed in such terms as "I swear the woman alone has it easy" and the intensity of her feeling when she desires to "act crazy to pieces," read like the expressions of resistance against male dominance in the blues. The politics of race were absent from Hayashi's narrative of oppression (except in the colonial context, which was denied or ignored), as were the politics of social protest well documented in the mass media, protests that are evident in all documented sites of Japanese modern culture that I discuss. But the following verse by Bessie Smith does describe the everyday existence of Hayashi Fumiko:

> It's an old story, every time it's a doggone man.
> It's an old story, every time it's a doggone man.
> But when that thing is on you, you just drift from hand to hand.[46]

Hayashi, like many women blues singers, felt herself to be "the only wretched one around." She also offered the *jokyū* version of the untrustworthiness of the very men she was tied to: "If you look at a man's state of excitement, it's kind of like that belonging to a politician. When they think it's all over, they're cool as can be." Such sentiment is a form of paraphrase of Bessie Smith's famous indictment of the man who has "a mouthful of give me and a hand full of much obliged."

Hayashi's *hōrō* (constant movement) is one main theme of women blues singers. These are the words of Alberta Hunter:

> I got a mind to ramble, but I don't know where to go.
> Yes, I got a mind to ramble, ooo, but I don't know where to go.
> If I'm lucky enough to leave here, I sho' ain't coming back no mo'!
> Folks, I ain't got a crying penny, my poor feet are on the ground.
> And if I ever want to be somebody, I sho' got to leave this town.[47]

These are the words of Hayashi Fumiko:

> Oh, I've also got no skills;
> and I also want myself a man,
> and I'm sentimental for my traveling.

Hayashi Fumiko gave voice to the eroticized, gendered experiences of the impoverished *jokyū*. Her words, and the numerous surveys, cartoons, and constructed fictions of the modern years illuminate the history of the *jokyū* in relationship to men, at her workplace in the café, and in the small, dimly lit tatami rooms of the cheap lodgings of modern Japan where women and men struggled toward and against each other, within structures of domination and resistance we have barely begun to know. But what can be known from this study of Hayashi Fumiko's "singing of the blues" and of the other documents about the *jokyū* examined in this segment, is that the gender ambivalence and androgyny of the era is not present; gender polarity is: men are male, and the women being pursued are always female. (It should be noted that when gender is ambiguous, as when the *jokyū* speak in a male voice, it is in the private sphere of the public bath.)

If we determine that *iro* was used to refer to women's desire for connectedness to men (as in Kimi-chan's desire for the *iro otoko*, Valentino); and *ero* for male pleasures of physical intimacy with women made available for domination (as in the *ero* services in the cafés that had degenerated into places of prostitution-brokering) one interpretation can be made regarding the negotiations between heterosexual males and females: *iro* was being renegotiated by women which may indeed account for the preoccupation with *ero* in the cafés and in the media of modern Japan. In the cafés, men and women were not confused about who was female or who was male, or how. But there was a pervasive dismissal of the erotic in the play of the café waitress and in the sensationalization of the erotic grotesque nonsense of the modern years. The complex legacy of this denial is graphically evident in the disembodied, violent representations of dominated women in contemporary Japanese mass culture half a century later, in a de-eroticized culture that has repressed any memory of the eroticized Japanese café waitress singing her blues, along with any sensation of the power of the empire within which she sang. The expanding empire was a presence alongside the celebration of eroticism in film culture as can be seen in the movie magazine *Friends of the Movies*, which is the focus of the following segment.[48]

3   Friends of the Movies

(From Ero to Empire)

The chatty movie magazine *Eiga no Tomo* (Friends of the movies), which first appeared in January 1931, offered a vision of modern, everyday gestures to its readers. In its monthly illustrated narratives of the private practices of stars and starlets, in its gossipy accounts of scenes on movie sets, and in its sensational ads for foreign and Japanese movies, the magazine firmly established moviemaking and moviegoing as embedded in *seikatsu*, with some meaningful shifts in emphasis over the decade. A close chronological reading of select material from the magazine from 1931 through 1941 reveals a transition from a focus on sensual pleasures grounded in sexualized gender difference, and on a discourse of national difference that also insisted on universalizing, to a transposition of *seikatsu* onto the Japanese occupation of China. This shift was accompanied by an increasing insistence on the distinctively Japanese nature of everyday experience. In other words, *ero* was displaced by reportage on empire. Throughout both phases, a series of photographic images required readers to code-switch, drawing conclusions about the relationship of culture to nation.

Gradually, *Eiga no Tomo* eased into an acceptance of the everyday experience of imperial expansion before it was overtly controlled by the state. Yet even as late as 1941, when the magazine was treating the film-going experience—based on a Nazi model—as a popular pleasure that could and should serve the national policy of building a new Asia, *Friends of the Movies* refused to let go of its Hollywood fantasies. This magazine functioned as a cultural mediator, giving the reader-spectator images and narratives about going to the movies. Like the magazine *Shufu no Tomo* (Friend of the housewife), *Eiga no Tomo* offered its readers community, presenting articles in a vernacular, easy-to-read language. It treats movie stars and readers (including café waitresses) as friends. The magazine does not give us an ethnography enabling a reconstruction of readers' responses, but it does tell us how writers wrote about the modern while giving us some understanding of how readers read about erotic grotesque nonsense and imagined the place of movies in Japanese modernity.[1]

ERO

In 1931 and 1932, *ero* was the keyword in *Eiga no Tomo*. In February 1931, the actress Uranami Sumako, in defensive response to the criticism that she had no qualifications to play vamp roles, promised that she would strive to show *iroke* and *ero*. Both Abe Sada's term of endearment, *iro otoko* (loverman), and the Japanese word *iroke* were variations on the pre-modern word *iro* which referred to eroticism. Yet the starlet also chose to use *ero*, the contemporary trendy abbreviation, as a means of promising that she would project sexiness. By using both words, she illustrated that in Japanese modern film culture there was a distinction between the erotic and the pornographic. In this case the foreign term *ero* appears to have signified the latter and *iroke* the former. But rather than inferring the definition of the second term, *ero*, the modern term with which we are concerned, it is much easier to read the explicit definitions, along with meanings implied in titles and in commentary, in the pages of *Eiga no Tomo* during its first two years of publication. An examination of how the film world defined *ero* may in fact be the easiest way to gain a grasp of how the *ero* of *ero guro nansensu* was understood during the early 1930s. This was a time when *Eiga no Tomo* and the more intellectually staid journal, *Eiga Hyōron* (Film criticism), were eager to offer their customers an understanding of this new word in its modern setting.[2]

The first installment of "Ero Encyclopedia," a series of articles in *Eiga no Tomo* beginning in April of 1931, illustrated how *ero* had flooded the culture in 1930 and 1931 by offering the following lexicon: "*Ero, ero revue, erononsense, erodance, ero100 percent, ero* actress, *ero* line of legs beauty, *ero* scenery, *ero* design, *ero* scene, *ero* café, *ero* café waitress, *ero* back alleys, *erogirl, ero* maiden, *ero* woman, *ero* old lady, *ero/guro*, and *eroeroero.*"[3] The author told the readers what "they already knew": that *ero* was shorthand for the English word EROTIC, just as *guro* stood for GROTESQUE, and that it derived from the Greek god of love, Eros. In the June 1931 issue, billed as the "Film World *Eroticism* Issue," the term no longer required much explication, although one article summed up *ero* as "a man seeing a woman and going lightheaded," and a woman seeing a man and going lightheaded, invoking a folkloric notion, it called *ero* "the catfish causing the earthquake."

Men, it went on to say, had a "man-smell" and women a "woman-smell" that could only be detected by the opposite sex. The meaning of *ero* was expanded in the other articles, and by the third installment of "*Ero* Encyclopedia," the magazine used code-switching mid-sentence to ponder how woman saw *It* in men, while detailing varieties of aphrodisiacs. The Hollywood marketing term *It*, denoting erotic appeal, was so embedded in Japanese modern culture that it required no definition. More esoteric terms did require explanation. In a special erotic section consisting of several articles, one article titled "The Secret *Ero* Language of Film People" elaborated on the erotic by sharing terms from the film world that had been adopted by the "*Modern Boy*" and the "*Vanguard Girl*." The neologism *location* referred to a faraway rendezvous, and a *set* was the rented site of this assignation. The erotic could also be perverse, as illustrated by the story in "Stars and *Erotomania*" of the man who bought 136 used handkerchiefs from a movie actress and had them washed before returning them to the actress's maid, his accomplice in these fetishistic transactions.[4]

In places, the "erotic" referred to woman's pleasure, as in the censored disquisition in Part 13 of "*Ero* Encyclopedia" on the "BOULE EROTIQUE" to be found in Japan, France, Germany, and Africa, and in the frustrated conclusion in the earlier segment on "Man's *It* as Seen by Woman." There, the author maintained that unless the women of the world explained their universal sighing for Valentino, woman's desire would be an eternal mystery for men.

Occasionally, *Eiga no Tomo* would also illuminate how modern sexualized gestures in foreign movies could be read in modern Japan, as in the article "Kiss *Notes*." The opening lines suggested that this gesture was being taken to heart by Japanese audiences: "The *kiss!* Do not think that this is a meaningless gesture of men and women placing lips together. I would want a modern *[kindai]* person to have read about the sources of the kiss in C. Wood's *The Art of Kissing* and *Studies in the Psychology of Sex* by Havelock Ellis in order to have more common sense regarding the kiss."[5] The author, Ogura Kōichirō, aimed to offer such education to his readers through a rendering of the variations of the term in French, German, Chinese, and in early Japanese history and by explicating the varying theories of the etymology of *kiss*. In addition to mentioning Anglo-Saxon, Bavarian, Spanish, Portuguese, Turkish, and Persian translations, he offered the variations of *osculation* and *smack* (both spelled out in English) along with German variants before moving on to the variations on the act itself. He told his readers that the *Kama Sutra* offered three forms of the act of male and female lips meeting, but there was also, he said, the familial kiss, the kiss in greeting, the kiss of respect, and the religious kiss. Finally, there was the given topic of the article, the kiss that appeared in the movies. It was this gesture that had most significance for contemporary Japan, although Japanese history offered a record of lips meeting. The author offered such examples as the folk adage that employed a euphemism rather than referring to the tongue directly, as in "the teahouse woman who looks like she will only engage in raw fish."[6]

Often *ero* referred to a graphic rendering of female body parts that did not stand for a woman in motion, but for a dissected and thereby immobilized woman as a body-in-parts. Only occasionally was a man's body taken apart in this way, as in "*Ero* Encyclopedia Part 3," an investigation of a woman's notion of *It* in a male. This was so obviously an inversion of the usual focus on women that its references to the male nape of the neck, the lines of a man's jaw, and the color of his lips appears almost parodic. More common was the sentiment expressed in the December 1931 "Memo of the *Revue* World of 1931," praising the success of the two Takarazuka musical revue stars whose stage presence is encapsulated by their hairstyles: "Tachibana Kaoru's ringlets falling over her forehead" and "Miura Tokiko's water-sprite *bob*." Regarding unnamed members of a dance troupe, the comedian Furukawa Roppa commented: "All, good legs. All, good kids." Elsewhere the author of "Studies in the Nude Beauty" paid lip service to the lure of the female silhouette (as illustrated by Betty Amann in *Asphalt*) and to the eroticism of female attire when he remarked on how common it was for a star to appear only in a chemise *(shimiizu)* in foreign films and bemoaned the absence of the Japanese woman's body in the movies. For him the image of the erotic naked female was encapsulated in "the exposure of Clara Bow's breasts, Mary Duncan's back, Olga Baclanova's thighs and buttocks—wonderfully profuse buttocks, breasts, backs, etc., etc."

This view was of course consistent with the identification of the Modern Girl by her Western garb but more centrally by her hair and her legs. It was also consistent with other, continued identifications of women's eroticism with woman dissected into parts in other expressions of visual culture. See for example, a 1938 photography primer that appeared several years after the first appearance of *Eiga no Tomo*. This book claimed that each individual woman should be found beautiful in differing, "nonartistic," and "ordinary" aspects, and then proceeded to take the woman apart. The primer then dictated that any likeness of a female body that was too fat or thin be rejected, before going on to mark the parts of a woman's body to be positioned as feminine through portraiture. Body parts were ordered in subheadings in the primer: the neck (not to be leaned backward, warned the author, lest the photographer detract from the subject's "womanly" gentle grace) was followed by the entire torso. The primer warned that apart from those women "who were altogether too thin," no body was to face front. Fat women in particular were to take care to drop their shoulders, as this would affect the feel of the "body as an entire body"; but rather than elaborate on the message to be conveyed by the entire body, the expert moved on to another part of the whole. The hands were not to stand out: they need not be altogether hidden, but were to be photographed in their "natural, womanly softness." A separate section was devoted to an elaboration of how the hands should be placed together to bring out a "well-bred eroticism." It was followed by directions as to seating that conformed to the modern obsession with the female buttocks. Body and clothing were combined in the final section, which covered such topics as the placement of folds of the kimono collar, exposure of the tips of the feet, legs, hair styled in the Japanese fashion, and a discussion of Western clothing.[7]

The male body was masculinized, molded, and enfolded in the same primer. The male ideal was based on a separate set of precepts, which were less dependent on body parts and more dependent on social forms than on physical formations. According to the text, man could be fat or thin; there was no restriction on body size. The expression of man's beauty was to be sturdiness on the outside and dignity within. Gendered, imagined masculine types were the military man, the politician, and the dancer. Like the female body, the choreographed male body was marked: face and neck (not to be "leaning too far forward in a feminine posture"), the upper torso, and legs. These were to be gendered and eroticized not by moving the body into positions but through the placement of objects. (Woman, in contrast, needed no props, because her body was the statement.) Such objects as the man's *"necktie"* and *"pocket handkerchief"* were identified with the upper torso (which was to be photographed after all pens and automatic pencils had been removed from the breast pocket). The hands were often best positioned by asking the man to hold a pen, and then by removing the pen from that posture. He could hold a cigarette, or place a book or magazine in his lap. The objects were to express his everyday life and hobbies. The photographer was to photograph all decorations and medals of civil and military officials with accuracy.[8]

The section on male formal dress, like the article on kissing in the contemporary Japanese arena, also revealed how modern culture was reformulating gesticulations. In a mixed message that found the Japanese people to be capable of affective gesture but forbade readers from expressing such gestures, this text confirmed and critiqued the new expressiveness of the era alluded to by the critics. According to this author's dictate, men posing in either Western or Japanese formal dress were to take care not to adopt a pose or expression drawing attention to themselves, for "unlike Western people, Japanese people were lacking in bodily expressiveness, and any expressions that stood out were considered low-class." This statement prohibiting any male expression of affect was illustrated by the advertisements appearing in *Chūō Kōron* during the modern years. From the late 1920s into the early 1930s in department-store advertising, Western clothing as uniform substituted for attention to physique. Man was featured in silhouette, sans any facial features (one sure way to prevent any expressiveness!) and in uniform both at work and at play. An authoritative, faceless figure often presented in a double-breasted suit was, in other words, also clad in suitable attire for the suitably middle-class male pursuits of skiing, hiking, and diving. There was also one formal variation on this hero: this was the use of caricature (cartoon-like drawing) in advertisements. In other words, one means of avoidance of reference to the male physique, in parts or as a whole in the flesh, was the use of caricature—another form, one can argue, of depriving the male of his physicality and his erotic identity. (By the late 1930s caricature took on another task in advertisements—simple line drawings could be used to express male anxiety about increased mobilization for war.)[9]

For a more direct definition of what *ero* meant in popular parlance, we can turn to the pages of the film journal *Eiga Hyōron*, which also provided some of the most comprehensive analyses linking *Ero* to *Guro* and to *Nansensu*. The editors of *Eiga Hyōron* were decidedly more highbrow and more left-wing than the staff of *Eiga no Tomo*. Nonetheless, in 1931, while offering such articles as "Studies in Russian Film," "Moholy-Nagy's Theory of Absolutfilm," "On the German Worker Film," and an account by the prolific critic Iijima Tadashi of the rise and fall of the *revue* movie in the United States and Japan, they also set aside space in the April 1931 issue for the "Erotic Film." Not only did this issue take up the meaning of *ero* in the world of the modern Japanese moviegoer, it also offered one of the few sustained discussions of erotic grotesque nonsense in a series of articles that confronted all three terms.[10]

The author of "Erotic Film," Yasuda Kiyoo, noted that "there is nothing so lonely as a life without *eros.*" He went on to distinguish between *ero* and the obscenity being sold with such desperation in the cafés of the moment. *Ero* could not be limited to the enjoyment of the *moga's* legs. Yasuda Kiyoo's explication of *guro* in relationship to *ero* made clear that the two were different points on a continuum of gestures: "The border between *ero* and *guro* is one sheet of paper. Depending on the performer, the same physical actions can become entirely different in feel." He claimed that contemporary Japanese actresses, regardless of their looks, failed utterly at *ero*, as was evident when they adopted the gestures and costuming of foreign actresses. This Yasuda blamed on directors, with the exception of Gosho Heinosuke, who had insight into the culture of the (premodern) pleasure quarters and had also captured the eroticism of contemporary hot-spring culture. Yasuda implied that Japanese directors were incapable of understanding that *ero* had a national aspect to it: "In Japan there is a Japan-specific *ero*."[11]

What is important for a rethinking of Japanese modern culture is not that Yasuda and others determined that Japanese actresses and actors failed at foreign gestures. What is significant is that such statements reveal the extent to which such new gestures were enacted and the ambivalence that critics exhibited as they tried to associate nation with gesture. For example, like the commentators examining the Modern Girl, Yasuda contrasted foreign with domestic eroticism through the portrayal of women's buttocks. He explained that in Japan, in contrast to the West, women considered a large buttocks vulgar. At the same time, since "woman lives for man," she had to draw men to her with her narrow physique, and did so through "an exceedingly *rhythmical* movement," contrasting with the Western woman's movement in *"high heels."* In an argument that implicitly denied a break between the premodern and a modernity, the author explained that this was a style of movement adopted during the Tokugawa era that could still be seen in the moves of the knowing geisha, but not in the obscene gestures of the waitresses in the bars and cafés who "blaspheme[d] the sanctity" of *ero*. The author did not attempt to explain how it was that Japanese women and men could engage in both the geisha culture, coded as Japanese, and café culture, coded as Western. He did acknowledge that *ero* took on different forms, depending on class and occupation. It was unattainable to those without imagination and to those who did not understand symbols. Here again, film directors illustrated the point: "The *ero* of G. W. Pabst's films was perverse, realistic, and rather than wearing the *veil* of *ero*, was the expression of sexuality itself." In contrast, Ernst Lubitsch had imagination, depth, and taste. Yasuda equated *ero* with Western technique. He was impressed with how Lubitsch could feign *ero*, only to pull back and not offer it to his audience.[12]

For Yasuda, the premodern Japanese geisha was the model for female eroticism, but the model of the modern (*kindaiteki*) erotic man was Maurice Chevalier, not a Japanese man. Yasuda implied that Chevalier met the test of authenticity, and dodged the question as to whether Japanese men could meet the standard. He concluded that Chevalier was an *ero otoko* whose eroticism was located in his lips: they drove the *moga* crazy. Clearly, Yasuda did not find only the indigenous erotic, but his gender bias was conventional. This bias conformed to the dictum cited in the Modern Girl segment that in societies undergoing rapid transformation, women stand for "the traditional" or the unchanging. At the same time, Yasuda acknowledged that the erotic was also in the eyes of the beholder: there were those who were unmoved by a woman's beautiful legs but who could not contain themselves when gazing upon a woman's lips. The story line of a film could also be erotic, but movies advertised as "100 *percent ero*," such as the *ero* revue movies, were nothing of the sort. Yasuda provided titles and parodies of the recent spate of *ero* film titles. Thereby "Please Love Me," "Oh, It's at That Moment," "Now, Don't Get Excited," and "I'm Feeling Strange These Days" were reconfigured as "But I'm Too Shy" *(Demo Hazukashii wa)*, "If There Were a Hole I'd Hide inside It" *(Ana ga Attara Hairitai)*, and "Oh, Is It This Sort of Thing?" *(Ara, Konna Mono Nano)*. In his conclusion, he placed erotic movies into recent Japanese history. Over the past two or three years, erotic movies had grown so popular that now, during the *"ero era,"* the censors were powerless to oppose theme. Yet one of the reasons for the ubiquity of the erotic film, Yasuda noted, was that it had been given the blessing of the government, which had seen this medium as a powerful counterforce to the left-wing "tendency movies" of the era; the *ero* film had served the function of opium.[13]

As if to illustrate Yasuda's own dictum that the space of one sheet of paper separated the erotic from the grotesque, the editors of *Eiga Hyōron* placed his article "Grotesque Film" immediately after his disquisition on the erotic. He listed such movies as *Phantom of the Opera* and *The Hunchback of Notre Dame* as embodiments of the grotesque, but not merely because they exhibited the strange and the weird. Rather, "the devilish, the vulgar, the coarse, the low-class had to be included along with an external strange weirdness." In Yasuda's definition, the blackest woman painted white was totally *guro*. It was not her blackness, but her attempt to escape her form, that rendered her grotesque. Persistence was another required ingredient. Yasuda's illustration of this point was that when one met a person with a strange face, this person appeared grotesque, as opposed to pathetic, if he persistently chased women. Before turning to an elaboration on the *grotesque* in film, he offered one more generalization: "That which leads to feelings of strong distaste, or creepiness as one turns away from a human being while at the same time wondering what it is, wanting at the same time to look, that is where the beauty of the *guro* is born."[14]

Yasuda set forth a three-part typology of the grotesque in film: the story could be *guro;* the actions of the actors could express the grotesque; or the costuming could be *guro.* In the first category Yasuda placed such films as *Dr. Jekyll and Mr. Hyde.* As for the grotesque in human actions, this was evident in Erich von Stroheim's *Greed,* when a man slowly chewed on a woman's finger in order to force her to hand over money: the "lewd tyranny" and the sexual perversion rendered this act grotesque. Actions appeared most grotesque, he elaborated, when related to sexual desire and its perversions. As an illustration from Japanese film, he related the scene in a samurai drama wherein the hero poured sake into his navel, without reminding his readers of any sexual desire exhibited by this act. As for *guro* in costuming, Yasuda observed, Lon Chaney was masterful in transmitting the feel of the grotesque through his makeup. In Yasuda's words, the grotesque being "exists cut off from other human beings, he moves on his own, alone." He implied that one example, beloved by the German people, who produced the grotesque Expressionist film, was pederasty. The Germans were not alone; this was practiced in a special category of Edo teahouses and was still in evidence in Hibiya Park. Yasuda's emphasis was not, however, that the grotesque was linked with the perversion of the sexual or of the erotic. Nor was his conclusion that Japanese grotesquerie could equal German grotesquerie. What was important to him was that a taste for true stories was no different from a quest for *guro.*[15]

For a discussion of nonsense, the readers of *Eiga Hyōron* needed only to turn to "Thoughts on *Nonsense* Films," which continued on the page where Yasuda's musings on the grotesque in film ended. The author of this essay linked the contemporary power of the term *nonsense* in Japan to the appearance of the nonsense (slapstick) film in America after the Great War. The nonsense film was not required to have meaning: it had only to produce laughter, something that "serious people who talked of *ideology* could not grasp." The genre of nonsense literature was duly noted, along with the element of reflexive satire in the period films that poked fun at the hero worship and mannerisms in that genre. The author defined the nonsense movie as "the film that asserts nothing." Although one could find examples of nonsense films in both the period drama and in such contemporary films as those made by Ozu Yasujirō, these films were never nonsense in and of themselves, but only in part. The author attributed the rejoicing of Japanese film companies, directors, audiences, and censors at nonsense films in part to national character. The Japanese had never been capable of totally understanding nonsense, and such an approach did not appeal to the European character either. Yankees *(yankii)* were the only people *(kokumin)* to fully understand nonsense; but the author predicted that the Japanese brand of nonsense film might retain its popularity in Japan for a while because of commercial viability. He added that the idea that nonsense meant "nothing" was accepted at face value, as a non-ideological truism, by most, without any recognition that apparently nonsensical behavior that might appear without import could very well carry a political punch. My premise goes further. I contend that the concept of nonsense and the notions of *ero* (except in the guise of the threatening Modern Girl), *guro,* and the composite *ero guro nansensu,* as they appeared in such popular media sites as *Eiga no Tomo,* have mistakenly been seen as apolitical. Moreover, by returning to the trajectory of the narrative provided by the articles in *Eiga no Tomo* during the 1930s, we can trace how a focus on the everyday both accompanied an obsession with *ero* and displaced it.[16]

ERO AT THE MOVIES

The intense interest in *ero* continued into the first half of the 1930s in the pages of *Eiga no Tomo.* In February 1933, part 7 of the series, "Thoughts on Ero Movies " looked back on the figure of Johnny Weissmuller as Tarzan clad only in loincloth in order to swoon over his *"love scene"* with Maureen O'Sullivan, whose attraction lay in her naked legs. Nine months later, installment 21 of *"Ero* Encyclopedia" titillated its readers with the section titled "Two Birds with One Stone." This article relayed the (ostensible) finding that in Europe, a man who snagged one lesbian would automatically, also, end up with the other. The article posed but did not divulge the answer to the question: Could Japanese women be likened to German women who engaged in same-sex love? In November 1934, *Eiga no Tomo* paired a roundtable discussion on men with a roundtable discussion on women. The women in the former group teased each other about same-sex love, spoke with a tone of intimacy about the inapproachability of German men, the allure of German actors, Conrad Veidt's style of smoking, Edward G. Robinson's forehead, and of "Gary" from the nose downward. (Aside from one indirect reference to a husband, no Japanese actors were mentioned.)

The men spoke of the draw of a woman with "man-like appeal" and wondered whether the presumed acting skills of the up-and-coming Shiga Akiko could be attributed to false eyelashes; they then turned to such topics as "Garbo" and to the question of Katherine Hepburn's sexual orientation. Any anxieties that the group of Japanese men in the roundtable discussion of November 1934 may have felt about Katherine Hepburn's sexual proclivities were resolved by their conclusion that she was neuter, thus rendering her female but sexless.[17] Both the group of women and the gathering of men raised the question of same-sex relationships. The erotic, it would appear, had become tied to questions of gender ambiguity that differed sharply from issues raised by Naomi's masquerade as sexy heterosexual female in male garb in Tanizaki's novel and from the sharply defined binary distinctions of male customer being served by female waitress in the eroticized space of the café.[18]

The participants in the *Eiga no Tomo* roundtable discussion did not pursue the question of same-sex relationships beyond titillating conjectures, but they were not alone in highlighting representation of gender ambiguity. This might be better conceived of as gender fluidity; free-floating gender markers recurred in the modern media into the first half of the 1930s. In January 1935 for example, an advertisement in the intellectually oriented, highbrow journal of opinion *Chūō Kōron* announced that *Utena Pomade* could be used by both men and women. It depicted a torso in profile. One subheading placed alongside a sketch of a torso in profile read, "For a new male beauty for 1935." The writing below the chin of this figure with slicked-back short hair was addressed to "the gentleman." And another segment of text, set along the bustline of the same torso—the bustline was curved and clad in kimono—was addressed "to the lady."

A second advertisement for Utena pomade appeared two months later. This time the ad was confident of its male subjectivity. It challenged readers in a highly assertive male diction to "look at my male beauty." But again there was a mixed message that could be called a code switch: the masculine text was contested by an image of a face and hand effeminate in features and gesture. The figure resembled one of the male impersonators *(otokoyaku)* of the all-female Takarazuka Revue, studied in depth by Jennifer Robertson. Robertson has discussed how "the femininity performed by the players of women's roles serves as a foil, highlighting by contrast the masculinity of the players of men's roles." She makes a compelling argument for the central place of the masculinized female both within Takarazuka and within the mass media that found such a figure so threatening. Robertson's point that "the markers distinguishing male from female, masculine from feminine, were losing their polarity" appears most relevant to the era. Nonetheless, this second Utena image belies that formulation, for the figure is male-identified, in contrast to the gender-bending women dressed as men in Takarazuka. Within the context of this ad, the figure in male garb seems more feminized man than masculinized female. While it is worth pointing to gender fluidity as an aspect of Japanese modern culture, in the pages of

Eiga no Tomo such ambiguity was rare. Aside from its occasional brief mentions of same-sex love, the magazine stayed safely within the Hollywood star system formula of "leading man attracts leading lady" and vice versa.

Rather than flirting with sexual ambiguity, and in contrast to the lasciviousness of the articles about *ero* in the pages of *Eiga no Tomo*, treatment of the erotic often took a material form that concentrated on everyday ritual. A pertinent question for the editorial staff, for example, might well have been whether the female figure gracing the cover of the "Film World *Eroticism* Issue" of June 1931 would be clad in Western or Japanese costume. In this case, the fresh-faced young woman in kimono and Japanese-styled hair won out over the Modern Girl, her hair bobbed and secured under an oversized cloche. (Such an image had been presented on the back cover *Eiga no Tomo* advertisement the previous month: a Modern Girl had advertised *Smile* eye medicine by provocatively caressing a tube of the product. The message of the picture conformed to Erving Goffman's "feminine touch": the girl's fingertips adhering to the surface of the product gave the effect of a "'just barely touching'—the kind that might be significant between two electrically charged bodies." With her other hand, she clutched the box to her bosom in similarly eroticized fashion.) Commentators such as Yasuda decried how Modern Girls showcased the Japanese inability to emote and the inferiority of the Japanese female body in comparison to the Hollywood model. Yet for that special issue, eroticism was signified by the demure figure in kimono.[19]

The everyday as erotic took other forms as well. Under a banner headline that promised "confessions" from women who had lived the daily life of the film star, the reader found an account of the downward spiral of one woman who had spurned the advances of a director and had thus plummeted, according to the title, "From Actress to Café Waitress." Another unfortunate woman had descended into the *seikatsu* of the nightclub revue. Articles offered the readers a view of their idols fallen on hard times. This came at a time, of course, when readers of all classes were experiencing the effects of the depression in Japan in terms of such hardships as salary reductions, unemployment, and starvation in the countryside, where many urban transplants sought haven. Even as articles about family suicides were appearing in the press, readers of *Eiga no Tomo* were treated to gossip about the star system. The June 1931 issue of *Eiga no Tomo* offered a photo layout of a Sunday with Kawasaki Hiroko, showing the young actress as mother's helper. The young actress was garbed in headscarf and apron over her kimono, she placed dishes into a wooden cupboard. She was also positioned with pen in hand answering her fan mail *(fuan meeru)*—a task said to take up most of her time at home. This, apparently, did not keep her from finding some time during her household life to play her *shamisen*, thereby expressing her taste for things Japanese. The magazine editors may have chosen Kawasaki, known both for her ladylike roles and her genteel off-screen manner, in order to code-switch or, in other words, to offset the photo offerings on the opposite page. There, the caption accompanying three photographs was placed under the heading "Who Is the Most *Erotic?*" The choices were Hamaguchi Fujiko, said to be exhibiting *ero* by means of her breasts; Irie Takako, whose breasts were hidden beneath her *"gorgeous chemise"*; and Nakamichi Fumiko, whose "more direct *eroticism*" was articulated in her shoulders. The editors offered one answer to the query: all three were too erotic. Yet while they might be "too *erotic*," they were given as prominent a place as the "ladylike" and domestically minded Kawasaki. The message was that all four women were in fact erotic and that there was no way to deny or negate their sensuality.[20]

Even after the Manchurian Incident of September 1931, the everyday could not be divorced from the erotic as was most evident in the special *Eroticism* issue of *Friends of the Movies* in July 1932. Officers of the Kwantung army had engineered this original incursion and by January of 1932, Pu Yi had been made regent of the puppet government of Manchukuo. But rather than celebrate Japanese victories, much less question the machinations covered by the euphemism *incident* or interrogate the investigation by the Lytton Commission of Japanese culpability, the *Eiga no Tomo* published an expose about sex. This article revealed the hitherto secret *it* aspects of various Hollywood and Japanese actresses, working downward from lips to nape of neck, to breasts, to underarm hair, and to buttocks. In yet another article that took apart the female form, and in national terms, the lips of Japanese women could not compare to those of foreign stars; Japanese actresses failed even at expressing eroticism at the neckline, which had been a Japanese expression of sensuality; not one Japanese star had a beautiful back; Japanese women did not show their breasts ("and if they did this would all be cut by the censors") and therefore were at their most provocative when wearing a chemise. The criticism hurled at Japanese actresses continued: the Japanese actresses struggled to shave underarm hair in summer; and as to buttock size, the large number of actresses abroad with large posteriors also set the standard against which the shape of Japanese women was studied and, it was implied, failed. An article about movie theaters and "sexual acts" described how eroticism moved off the film screen: it recounted how the on-screen gestures of male and female, heads placed together, each reaching out to grasp the torso and the buttocks of the other, were mirrored by the audience. According to the author, the story of boy A and girl B who were caught in their seats hugging and kissing under the bright lights, after Chevalier and Miriam Hopkins had jumped into bed and Lubitsch's movie had ended, was a well-known tale. To this possibly apocryphal story the author added a salacious account of goings-on in a rural movie theater in a special box not accessible to regular customers. Hearing a strange groaning, the theater manager had peered into the box to find a young lady and a modern youth engaged in "xxxxxxxxxx." (Only then had the author offered an evocative image of an unfastened kimono sash trailing as the active young couple was hauled to the local police station.)[21]

Hollywood stars were also given an everyday existence, comparable to the daily schedule of Japanese actresses monitored in the pages of *Eiga no Tomo,* but such articles did not mention eroticism. Rather, it was the gaze of the Hollywood star into the (ostensibly) intimate surroundings, off-camera, offering a view of the everyday, that must have been intended to draw in the reader, through pictures more than words (as was also the case of "Sunday with Kawasaki Hiroko.") Two months after the Manchurian Incident, the magazine featured "Household *Sketches*" from Hollywood in a photo layout inviting the reader to guess "What are the *stars* doing?" in a montage of overlapping pictures. The answers: Ramon Navarro (given his affiliation with MGM and seated at a table by a piano, cigarette in one hand and script in another) practiced his voice lessons; Paramount newcomer Sylvia Sidney enjoyed the crisp morning air in her garden; and on the opposite page Gary Cooper was spending his afternoon quietly reading. The Japanese reader saw that the new star Phillips Holmes was "relaxing with a pipe by his fireplace." (Note: the photo showed the actor in a stiff pose.) In a round photo inset placed above the pictures of these two male idols, the UFA actress Sari Maritza, "the very picture of health," appeared to be sitting astride a raised exercise bar. In "The Wife Seen from the Perspective of the Husband," subtitled "Dietrich, who is famous as a housewife in Germany," Marlene Dietrich's spouse revealed her skill at cooking German-style *pancakes.* An interview with Josef von Sternberg, ostensibly of a higher intellectual level, was not too different in tone from the above photo layouts, nor was it different from the account of a day in the life of Shirley Temple written for the *Eiga no Tomo* readers in November of 1935. But I am jumping ahead in the narrative of the trajectory of *Friends of the Movies.* Let us return to the time of the Manchurian "Incident."[22]

TOWARD EMPIRE

By May of 1932, the obsession with *ero* in *Eiga no Tomo* was projected onto battle in such articles as "War Literature and *Eroticism*" and "*Ero Scenes* in War Movies." The daily activities of movie stars retained their place, as evidenced in gossip featuring Clark Gable and in the prominently featured "Poor Thing! The Love of Chaplin," relating the history of Chaplin's two marriages in conjunction with his visit to Japan in May of 1932. But the everyday of war was starting to impinge on the film world: studios began to send personnel to film on location in Manchuria and to vie for acclaim as producers of the most popular of war movies. The editors of *Eiga no Tomo* devoted considerable space to war imagery, including a new line of airplanes flying across the top of the contents page. The invasion of Manchuria and the victory in Shanghai were duly documented in the section on war movies, in an article calling for exemplary naval battle movies in anticipation of the Pacific War, and in an account of the planning for a film of the bombing of Shanghai, which was to be the first Japanese war film specifically about war in the air.[23]

What is striking about this first coverage of the relationship of Japanese film spectatorship to Japanese wartime expansion is the tongue-in-cheek quality of the discourse, a tone carried over from the 1931 coverage of the erotic. I am not challenging the well-documented collaboration (and encouragement) of the press in state policy surrounding empire, which has been discussed by Louise Young and others. It is clear that the hegemonic message of the mass media was eager support for war, but, as in any such situation, there was room for countervailing positions. Whereas historians have discussed the shift in the press after the invasion of Manchuria offering both ideological and economistic arguments, articles in *Eiga no Tomo* illustrate a cultural continuity. In other words, while the major newspapers and the magazines supportive of state ideology, such as *Kōdan Kurabu* (Storytelling club) and *Ie no Hikari*, aggressively trumpeted the heroic successes and hardships of war, the transition into wartime did not mean the end of the irreverent humor and politics of the modern era. My point is that *Eiga no Tomo* existed alongside war fanfare. Japanese modern culture continued therein, but now there was a new form of montage with which to contend: war was juxtaposed against the celebration of Hollywood culture. My interpretation of the response of *Eiga no Tomo* is that it took war quite seriously while expressing critical sentiment through jest.[24]

There was a recognition in the pages of *Eiga no Tomo* that film heroes had to share media space with war heroes, as exemplified by the treatment of the case of the "Three Valorous Bombs." (These were three soldiers who were made into national icons after they were accidentally killed by their own weapons.) Because they had so captured the public's emotions (at the behest of the state), they were now being transformed by all major studios into film heroes as the fever for war movies emerged. At the same time, there was a strongly implied recognition that the audience was being manipulated. The author of *"Ero Scenes* in War Movies" did not reveal to his audiences that the self-destruction of the three young soldiers being drawn into a frenzied, state-sponsored multimedia hagiography was not an act of heroic suicide but of inadvertent death, falsely presented as an intentional act by the state-encouraged media. However, he did mock the inundation of the contemporary culture by military movies. The article listed seven variations on the same event: Kamata's part-talkie *The Manchurian March*, Shinkō Kinema's *The Three Valorous Bombs in the Flesh*, Kansai Film Distributor's *The Three Valorous Bombs*, Kawai's *Loyal Spirits: The Three Valorous Bombs*, Tōkatsu's *Unswerving Loyalty: The Three Valorous Bombs*, Nikkatsu's *Three Valorous Bombs*, and Akazawa Kinema's *The Military Gods of Shōwa: The Three Valorous Bombs*. Noting the proliferation of plays and popular songs dedicated to the martyrdom of the three soldiers, he then exulted, "It's *fascist.* It's *fascism!*" in no uncertain terms, with an irony not present in this entertainment following the Manchurian Incident.[25]

In another article that was much more than skeptical, Watanabe Atsumi, author of "War Films and the *Studios: Snapshots* and *Gossip*," explained how the term *Valorous Bomb* had become a slang term in the film world. He thereby revealed the ironic appropriation of state propaganda for private pleasure (or private politics), in memory of the three youths whose deaths had been coopted for capitalist pleasures, and for state propaganda purposes. In the film world "let's film this in a more valorous fashion" called for spirit, and if one complained that "these days my life's really a valorous bomb," this meant that times were tough. If "that guy's a valorous bomb for so-and-so," he had a crush on the girl. He noted that the term had spread to the streets of the city, where cafés displayed advertisements for "café waitress valorous *service*."

Watanabe's barbs were clearly aimed at the military. Switching to what he termed "non-*gossip*," he reported how the rage for war films had resulted in added support for the military, including the presence of troops with machine guns on the set of Nikkatsu's "Three Valorous Bombs." When these soldiers began to shoot their machine guns, the three heroes panicked and these actors refused to leave the set foxhole. It is difficult to read as entirely innocent the author's query as to why the military had to come to the set. A second stab at the military concluding the article on the studios talked of how a film crew had returned from Manchuria, bringing with them a Buddha taken from a temple as a memento. One response to this souvenir was "Why bother bringing back the head of a Buddha, how about the head of a Chinese beauty from Manchuria?"[26]

"Sensō Eiga no *Ero Shiin*" (Erotic scenes in war movies) made it clear that war was being manufactured in the studio. The most common constructs were of sets of Manchuria, those made to look like sets of Shanghai, and scenes of "Chinese and dark-eyed foreigners sitting around bonfires waiting to go on." According to my reading of the narrative provided by the articles in *Eiga no Tomo*, war was being spectacularized and thereby eroticized, and woman's relationship to eroticism was being redefined within this context. For example, woman as an erotic agent, as chronicled in the series "*Ero* Encyclopedia," was absent from the war coverage. In sharp contrast to earlier accounts of female desire, and in a revealing prelude to the "comfort woman" phenomenon that would be institutionalized by the end of the 1930s, Maruki Sunado, author of "War Literature and *Eroticism*," spoke with admiration of the tightly controlled military prostitution troops accompanying the European soldiers declaring that "for those going to war, it is only natural that morals regarding women be ignored." To underscore his point, in his overview of the satiation of male sexual desire as revealed in literature around the time of World War I he quoted a character from the German novel *Die Katrin wird Soldat* (1930). In the novel, the soldier declared, "For us women are the same as drinking and eating." The author also shared one story that had circulated on the battlefield to provide pleasure to soldiers during World War I. This was a tale that likened the female body to the battlefield: knees as hill, thighs as fields, hair as mountains, and breasts as rises. The wording was but another variation on the dissection of the female body found in so many of the *Eiga no Tomo* articles during the early 1930s.[27]

References to Japanese expansion found in *Eiga no Tomo* after the invasion of Manchuria were not all cynically critical. For example, the spectacular eroticization of empire through exoticism that relied on woman as object (as implied by the call for "the head of a Chinese beauty from Manchuria") was summed up in the illustrated plot summary for the movie *Shanghai* in the May 1932 issue. The synopsis referred to the city as the "wicked capital of the Orient," where women were openly sold off, and offered prospective moviegoers a vision of the Dance Hall International, wherein all sorts of races *(jinshu)*—those of color and those without—

danced madly amid freely flowing liquor, women and smoke. The desires of the people *(minshū)* of Japan had to be related to those of the races *(jinshu)* on the continent. Whether this phrasing meant that the Chinese were a race and the Japanese a people was not clear, though it was clear that the relationship of war to race and to eroticism was being worked through in the pages of *Eiga no Tomo*. But it was not a simple transition into war rhetoric, or from *ero* to empire.[28]

It is worth repeating that *Eiga no Tomo* refused to let go of Hollywood. Yet another special eroticism issue, appeared in July 1932, two months after the issue just discussed, that was devoted in large part to war coverage. Its table of contents made no reference to war. They read as though the Three Valorous Bombs had not been blown up and as if Shanghai were still intact. Nor did the headings in the table of contents refer to the invasion of Manchuria. It highlighted an everyday, local eroticism. The articles dissecting the female body in typical fashion did so in order to reveal women's own sexual desires, ignoring any reference to exoticized Chinese women as objects of Japanese military desire. Moreover, the ostensibly daily and ostensibly private life of movie stars was again foregrounded in the section on eroticism—*seikatsu* was still the priority. One article, for example, implied how in Japan, film culture had spread nationwide, when it empathized with actresses seeking to maintain anonymity, who could not plan assignations in private restaurants, in hotels, or on country roads usually set aside for such acts, without being discovered.[29]

The transition from *ero* to empire had still not been made three years later, as *Eiga no Tomo* refused to let go of its fascination with Hollywood, or of its presumption that the Japanese filmgoer was a member of a cosmopolitan, modern community. In the January 1935 issue of *Eiga no Tomo*, the article *"Dear* Mae West" quoted fan mail to "the boss" from such diverse fans as an American milkman, a Canadian farmer, a Frenchman suffering from tuberculosis, a student from Java, and a housewife (American?) bewailing a marriage gone bad. The woman writer of the article noted that fans were a special *jinshu*. In this context, however, the word did not refer to racialized difference. Fans were clearly a global phenomenon that could not be confined by national or regional boundaries or physical characteristics. Moreover, because in modern Japan, the term *boss (oyabun)* was associated with males who wielded power and often used for Japan-specific relationships of power and fealty, its use gave a masculinizing twist to this markedly female idol and at the same time brought Mae West home to a Japanese audience as a masculinized authority. In July 1935, Shirley Temple graced the cover of *Eiga no Tomo* and in addition she was one of the figures featured in the photo layout titled "Hollywood Special Photo *Snap-shots.*" The carefully numbered and captioned images in this montage also showed readers such familiar faces as Claudette Colbert (who reminded readers of her Academy Award), Clark Gable, Douglas Fairbanks, and Cecil B. DeMille. Four months later, "Twenty-four Hours for Temple" followed Shirley Temple off and on the set, describing her everyday life just as it had done for Japanese and Hollywood actors and actresses. If Mae West had been made indigenous, so had Shirley Temple, who had been given the diminutive name ending for a child. Temple-*chan* was at once the universal little girl and the little girl next door.[30]

The everyday life of the Hollywood film world was, of course, American—no reader could deny that Gary Cooper's summer vacation described in "The Brentwood Beach" took place in the United States. Even in the late 1930s, authors intimated that Hollywood culture, including the actual everyday lives of the stars and the everyday practices presented in their movies, had a universal relevance. According to Iida Shinbi, the author of the article "The Appeal of Marx Brothers Comedy," published in June 1936, the Marx Brothers made *"Yankee fantasy"* concrete through their *"nonsense, satire,* and disorder." The author found the *"essence"* of the brothers in Harpo and in Groucho—spelled out as *Gurūchō* so that it sounded like "Guroocho" in Japanese (thereby indicating but one of undoubtedly countless places where the Marx Brothers' wordplay must have been lost on the Japanese audience). Groucho's silliness, the author explained, in addition to his puns, irony, and disorder, coupled with the meaningless motions of the silent Harpo, who never uttered a word, exhibited a creativity unprecedented in the talkie era. The author took his readers through the Marx Brothers' oeuvre from *The Opera's for Dancing* (the Japanese rendition of *A Night at the Opera*) through *I Am a Duck* (*Duck Soup* was appropriated into the emerging Japanese cultural canon of film through the adoption of the wording of Natsume Soseki's classic *I Am a Cat*). The article identified the *"nonsense"* of the Marx Brothers as distinctively American. At the same time the humor was presented as speaking to a humanity (though ironically, a humanity willing to step on human emotions). The humor had "mass entertainment value" not "taken in by tradition." Tradition was rendered as history; it was presented as a hallmark of the Japanese notion of the *modern* (a term given credence in *Eiga no Tomo* into the second half of the 1930s). Iida was implying that the humor of the Marx Brothers was *modern* and therefore appealed to the masses, who lived in the present.[31]

The editors of *Eiga no Tomo*, albeit with some ambiguity, required their readers to place their own culture into a universal modern moment. This

tendency could of course be satirical. The October 1935 issue carried a satirical piece called "Woman's Heart—Man's Heart." This extended the early
1930s tradition of contrasting male to female erotic dispositions while recounting such "everyday" occasions as the leap, by a broken-hearted suitor,
from the top of a department store. The article called the present moment
"*modern*," defining the apartment building as a modern version of the *nagaya*, the one-story tenement row-house occupied by impoverished urban
workers and their families. In a slap at the sensationalism of the press, the
piece went on to accuse newspapers of "liking new things even more than
the Modern Girl." On the following pages, Japanese actresses modeled "the
sweaters of Autumn, and "*Autumn Vanity Fair*" offered a montage of text
and photographs of "*handbags*," a pair of gloves, a ring, and a bracelet. This
was of course modern merchandising and not Kon Wajirō's modernology,
but the comment that one of the handbags was appropriate for both Western and Japanese dress both illustrated Kon's attention to the appropriation
of things into contemporary culture and supported his refusal to separate
Japan from a non-Japanese modernity.[32]

Rather than give readers a clear-cut choice between the West and Japan,
Eiga no Tomo gave its readers a montage of images necessitating a constant
code-switching between and among people and possessions marked as Japanese and Euro American. For example, a two-page spread in the November 1935 issue featured an inset into an article titled "Miriam Hopkins's
Wardrobe." The inset featured "The *Top Half* of this Autumn," and the
three photos of the "*top half*" featured hats and the heads and necks of pale,
aquiline-featured mannequins. The pose of the Japanese models, (all actresses), hats at a rakish angle and hands on hips, mirrored almost exactly a
photo illustrating the article "*Hollywood Patter*: Clothes for Autumn
Walks" which appeared below "The *Top Half* of this Autumn." This article
also featured angular models. But there was a difference: the bodies of the
Japanese women were cut off just below the waist, whereas elongated figures of the Hollywood models were left intact. There is no way of knowing
whether the female Japanese consumer-reader of the article denied the difference by choosing to emphasize her ability to purchase modern goods not
marked by national origin. She may also have been led to view her own
body as inferior to the elongated Anglo-European female form. (Of course,
the female body was as exaggerated in the American advertisements of the
era, which depicted idealized female bodies physically unattainable by any-
body.) Ultimately the consumer-subject may have asked herself questions
similar to the queries put forth by the critics of the Modern Girl who attempted to ascertain whether she was Japanese or Western.[33]

If statements regarding identification with East and West were ambiguous in the pages of *Eiga no Tomo*, the Japanese modern emphasis on
gesture was emphatically asserted. The treatment of gesture as central to
the everyday was enshrined in its articles on Hollywood schedules and
domiciles, as was still evident in a November 1935 interview with King
Vidor, who told *Eiga no Tomo* readers the secret to becoming a film idol.
Focusing on the self-representation of the actress more than that of the
actor, Vidor called for the discovery of one's own voice, figure, rhythm,
pose, and individuality. But the stress on new forms of body movement
had probably already been better illustrated several months earlier, in a
February 1935 multipage photo primer "New Dance—An Introduction,"
that came complete with cartoon feet in position. Readers were encouraged to teach themselves the *"continental"* (danced by Fred Astaire and
Ginger Rogers and made famous by their kiss in the midst of the dancing).
They were also to gain mastery of the *"college rhythm"* by following the
smiling faces and dancing feet of the anonymous American couples performing the moves.[34]

The continental reappeared in March 1935, this time in the Japanese title
for the American film *The Gay Divorcée*. It was coupled in montage with the
opposite page. This page was an advertisement for the *"all-talkie"* period
film *Kunisada Chūji*. On this right side of the spread, Kunisada, the hero of
the historical drama, in topknot and simple, dark kimono, held his empty
sake cup in a masculine gesture. On the left-hand page, Fred Astaire and
Ginger Rogers danced above and below an inset of an adoring chorus. Although smaller in scale, Fred and Ginger were as prominent as Ōkouchi
Denjirō, the actor playing Kunisada, and the name of Yamanaka Sadao, the
renowned director of period pieces. Here was an occasion for the consumer-
reader-spectator to code switch, moving back and forth between the Hollywood ad and the signifiers of indigenous history. But to say that the audience had a choice only between West and East would be too simple. The
advertisement promoting *Kunisada Chūji* was written partly in the English
alphabet and partly in the Japanese syllabary reserved for foreign words.
Both the English and the Japanese words were rendered in stylized, "Oriental" strokes. (This was the phrase across the top informing the audience
that this was an *all-talkie* whose sound system was provided by Western
Electric.) The movie was thereby implicated in Hollywood codes of representation not only because of the style of lettering, reminiscent of all too
many Western versions of Eastern writing but also because of the mention
of the Western corporation. Even more important, readers knew that the director, Yamanaka, was largely responsible for the code-switching that al-

lowed characters in period films to speak in the contemporary vernacular, which is to say in a modern language.[35]

Sometimes articles in *Eiga no Tomo* relating Japan to the West were unambiguous. There was, for example, a politically charged article about the documentation of the news by film. Rather than applaud the use of the newsreel in coverage of Japanese exploits in Manchuria, "Speaking of *Newsreels*," published in April 1935, contended that Japan lacked a true newsreel. It compared the *Asahi Shinbun* newscaster at the Hibiya Theater unfavorably with his American counterparts, and expressed support for the news documentary made by a labor organization in the United States. (This film had captured a workers' demonstration in front of the White House that was pushed back by police forces.) It also quoted from the Paramount newsreel taken when Babe Ruth came to "our country." The article ended with the closing words of an American newscaster, translated by the author as "This is the biggest *news* in Japan." But the very last line of the article was in English: "This is the biggest news in Empire [*sic*]." Did the author compose his own English-language punchline? Was this meant ironically, like the treatment of empire in the magazine article about Ginza a decade earlier?

In October 1936, a similar article appeared equally dismissive of political authority and just as eager to identify with Western modernity. This article, "Ten *Modern* Commandments for Movie *Fans*," couched in the tone of the *ero* articles of the early 1930s, was even more tongue-in-cheek. It urged readers to keep up with the times by reading newspapers and magazines, including American movie magazines from "over there." Since such magazines were expensive, the reader of *Eiga no Tomo* was to take his (her?) English-Japanese dictionary to Maruzen. (This was advice contrary to the wisdom shared by Gonda Yasunosuke, who had told his followers to eschew this bookstore, which specialized in Western works, in favor of the authentically Japanese site of Asakusa.)[36] Among the commandments set forth in the article were the prohibition against viewing monster movies alone (without one's *avec*, or lover), and the warning to avoid becoming excited by newsreels. The extent to which the readership of *Eiga no Tomo* received the ambiguous message of either of the two articles referring to newsreels and or interpreted the first article as critical of the Japanese status quo is not clear. Nevertheless, it is clear that the advice that viewers should not become excited over newsreels would become a thing of the past. What is also clear is that any ambiguous representations of empire would disappear from the pages of *Eiga no Tomo* after the skirmish of Chinese and Japanese troops in July 1937 at the Marco Polo Bridge pushed the nation into a state of war.

Within months, as Japanese troops continued to move into China, the "National Spiritual Mobilization Movement" mobilized the domestic sphere. But while Japan might be at war, Hollywood would continue to occupy a prominent position in *Eiga no Tomo*. In March 1937, the magazine had featured a serialized "Tale of Walt Disney: The Creator of Mickey Mouse," the appeal of Ginger Rogers was investigated, and Charlie Chaplin "proceeded toward Russia." Nonetheless, in the words of the film critic Iwasaki Akira, the Japanese film world was "in crisis" because of rationalization. The term *hijōjidai* (emergency era) had been put into wide usage by 1933 in such propaganda as the "Emergency Era Proclamations" of the military and in the *talkie* film *Emergency Era Japan*, featuring War Minister General Araki Sadao. After the onset of war with China, it was now a repeated term in *Eiga no Tomo*, as in the article "Primer for the Emergency Era," which focused on restrictions on the importation of foreign films. At the same time, everyday life was being redefined as a Japanese rather than a modern experience. *Seikatsu* was also being termed "Oriental." For example the noted woman writer Kamichika Ichiko, in her essay "Why Women See Movies," put a twist on the gender differentiations of the "his take versus her take" articles of the early 1930s contrasting female and male *eros* at the movies. In her view, movies, especially those from the West, stimulated the woman spectator's senses, offering a multitude of suggestions for the *seikatsu* of the woman of the day—especially the everyday experience of the woman of the Orient.[37]

In the words of an article that appears in *Eiga no Tomo* in December 1937 looking back on the Japanese film world of that year, films were now being "forged" under the "wartime system" *(senji taisei)*. Ambiguity toward empire was giving way to debate over the relationship of the Japanese film world—including the Japanese spectator—to the West. The code-switching or freedom of the 1930s to move among languages, images, and films was no longer a given, and it was clear in the pages of *Eiga no Tomo* that state controls were tightening. Japan was armed for war, explained an article describing the situation at the Home Ministry censor's office. Any movie that had even one soldier in it was subject to the scrutiny of the military police, as in the case of *The Good Earth*. The North China Incident had "broken out" in July 1937—it would be renamed the "China Incident" in September—just as *The Good Earth* was being imported into Japan, and distributors had decided to voluntarily submit to a censor's review of this film. The film was suspect not because it dealt with war, but because it was about the unrest characteristic of the Chinese and the pillage that always accompanied such situations. The Japanese film world was on the defensive, it was clear.

But how should *seikatsu* and the relationship of the spectator to the movies be redefined during this new era? References to (a universal) eroticism, the parallel experiences of the daily life of American, European, and Japanese movie stars, and the merchandising of mass-produced Western-style apparel would not suffice to define the everyday. The everyday reality of war, and the Japanese interaction with the *seikatsu* of the Chinese during wartime, could not be ignored.[38]

Readers of the December 1937 issue of *Eiga no Tomo* were told by the famous director, Uchida Tomu, that "until now, aside from a few exceptions," there had been no *seikatsu* in Japanese film. He went on to say that the production of a new form of Japanese movie revealing the Japanese everyday was worth more than ten foreign films, and that the China Incident, instead of limiting the Japanese film world, had liberated it from feudal structures and now offered a rare opportunity for reflection. Uchida's narrative displaced the modern moment with feudal remnants but the implication was also that the Japanese spectator was coming out of an era of fantasy and worship of the West that was inappropriate to the national experience. This, however, did not stop the magazine's editors from featuring a two-page synopsis of the MGM feature *Parnell*, illustrated by a photo of Clark Gable and Myrna Loy with fingers and gazes interlocked. The hero's nationalism may have been the lead message in the plot summary, but when readers shifted their gaze, this picture told another story.[39]

To recapitulate, during the early 1930s, then, *seikatsu* in the pages of *Eiga no Tomo* meant the erotic life of the senses, along with the everyday gestures of Hollywood and Japanese movie stars. By the second half of the 1930s there was a shift from emphasis on *eros* to emphasis on empire, a shift that lacked the satirical edge of the articles that had followed the Manchurian Incident. By the late 1930s, *Eiga no Tomo* attempted to eroticize empire through an attempt to let go of Hollywood fantasies, through the redefinition of the priorities of Japanese spectators, and thirdly, through an engagement with the everyday on the Chinese continent.

A most striking example of the attempt to disengage from Hollywood was the characterization of the Marx Brothers in a February 1938 article about humor in the movies: "As for the Marx Brothers, that *humor* was fairly rare. It was not the raw stuff of *fantasy*. It was pure *grotesque*. Looking at it makes one's eyes spin. One's head hurts. One is made ill. One feels as though one is inspecting a mental hospital." This was a total volte-face (*tenkō*) from *Eiga no Tomo*'s earlier adoration of the Marx Brothers. The same article took a swipe at Hollywood (and the United States) with the critique that animated movies were aimed at the *"rough"* sensibilities of

American children. If the Europeans were to make animated movies aimed at adults, these would undoubtedly be more interesting, conjectured the critic, who clearly could not let go of the West entirely. Nor could *Eiga no Tomo*, as became evident in a debate conducted in a series of articles featuring literary and film critics in 1938 (the year that cafés were ordered to place the rising sun on their matchbooks) and 1939 (the year of the promulgation of the Film Law, which gave virtually complete control of the film industry to the state). This was when Gonda Yasunosuke became a member of the state Committee for the Reform of Theater, Film, and Music.[40]

This discussion among noted men of letters Niwa Fumio, Takeda Rintarō, and Takami Jun and the critic Kishi Matsuo is an example of how *Eiga no Tomo* gave its readers messages that often conformed more to the ideal of reform as a function of looking to the past for inspiration and affirmation than to the rejection of the products of the modern years. "Random Talk on Movies" began on a page opposite an advertisement for perfume. The advertisement featured a photo of a smiling woman pointing to a face partially covered by the contours of a softly sculpted Western-style face under a floating bottle of perfume, beneath a stark white inset whose text read: "Fragrant—the Beautiful Customs of the Women of the Home Front/The Dress of the Women of the Emergency Era." The home front referred to may have been Japan, and the woman of the era Japanese, but the photo was coded as an Anglo-European woman—it switched. Moreover, the men of letters used their so-called random talk to reminiscence about the golden (modern) era of filmmaking a decade earlier. Going to the movies might have become history by 1938, but they were not going to allow this history to be forgotten. In the roundtable, Takeda Rintarō took credit for having been the first to write film criticism, and Takami recalled (without any elaboration) the popularity of the left-wing "tendency" movies. Kishi Matsuo reminisced about how montage scenes had given him so much trouble, without overtly discussing possible links between form and the politics of culture: "That was when I really had a time with those *montages*. As soon as the sword fighting ended, suddenly those raging waves would dash up against those rocks. Now, when I think of it, there really were a lot of funny aspects." In a more serious tone, he observed, "That was a historic era for Japanese film. It was as if Japanese movies gained a certain social standing outside and inside the country."

A second article took up the theme of a historical shift that was not necessarily for the better. Yodogawa Nagaharu from the publicity department of Tōhō studios admitted that he was not that disappointed with Western films and that he awaited the day when he could see certain films that were not now available in Japan. He also noted that Japanese movies had improved recently, as had filmgoing practices. In the Kansai region, parents who had previously pulled their children out of movie theaters in the entertainment districts, for fear that their morals were being compromised were now going to the movies with their children in neighborhood theaters. Another change, however, was that the good cheer had gone out of contemporary Japanese movies. Instead, movies like *The Earth* (a 1939 film based on the 1910 novel by the same name documenting the details of the lives of impoverished tenant farmers) were popular, the author conjectured, because a movie had to fasten onto *seikatsu*. Everyday life was not the same: meaningful connections between spectator and movie were no longer available.[41]

The debate continued. The following month, in May 1938, Takeda Rintarō reappeared—now with authors Hayashi Fusao and Niwa Fumio—to defend his support of the Western movie and by implication, a modern way of life. This was part of his response to the interviewer's query regarding restrictions on the import of foreign films. Takeda wanted to allow the foreign movies into the country, whereas Hayashi said he felt "the most resentment toward foreign film" (possibly, he admitted, because Japanese movies were so bad). Both were willing to fantasize working as consultants to the Home Ministry, to cull the "good" from the "bad" foreign movies, for a substantial fee, but ultimately their views of the benefit of foreign films differed, as revealed in the following exchange:

TAKEDA: In any case, foreign films make a contribution.

HAYASHI: But not to Japanese culture. It's to Ginza.

TAKEDA: That's not true. I don't think there's any reason for Japan to arbitrarily become the countryside. Where does it say that it's necessary, by choice, for all of Japan to be rural? What I wish to say is that the sort of method that rejects foreign movies is not good for Japanese culture.

HAYASHI: That's *liberalism* of the *okonomiyaki* variety. It's first-class Takeda hodgepodge *liberalism*; it's *okonomiyaki liberalism*.

Takeda and Hayashi agreed that the Japanese moviegoer sought out movies once or twice a month as a diversion from exhaustion at the end of the day and that "high-class" movies would not sell to this audience. But their views of Japanese culture clashed. Takeda's position indicated that culture from abroad had permeated the Japanese everyday experience nationwide and that the alternative was an unnecessary provincializing. He was not interested in considering an urban rural divide or modern/non-modern dis-

tinction represented by the contrast between Ginza and the provinces. For
him the relationship of the province to a metropolitan culture was not one
between places within Japan, but one that saw Japanese culture as backwards
(or as "countryside") within a world order. Rather than see the syncretic,
Constructivist aspects of Takeda's position in the way illustrated by Kon's
modan images and essays, or in numerous other verbal, visual, and conceptual montages of the era, Hayashi accused Takeda of arbitrarily combining
markedly different ingredients into an *okonomiyaki,* just as the consumer
of this low-class delicacy chose which ingredients to place within a batter
and to be fried on a griddle.[42]

For Hayashi, the alternative to *okonomiyaki* liberalism was an approach
to culture that kept a clearly demarcated distance between Japan and the
West. Recognizing the lack of reciprocity between Japanese and foreign
filmgoers, he complained that the Japanese were whimpering about the ban
on foreign films because of their "traditional respect for foreign countries."
In contrast, Hayashi pointed out that foreigners had no interest in seeing
typical Japanese movies. They viewed Japan as an adjunct to China and had
been interested only in the strange world of the woodblock print. A year
later, Kawakita Nagamasa would second this sentiment by telling would-be
Japanese filmmakers that foreigners wanted to see only Japanese mores and
customs of the past. Among other pieces of advice were: He further advised
that while Mount Fuji and cherry blossoms were not required, filming
should take place within nature; male stars should not as appear to be passing as Western; and filmmakers should note that the gestures and speech of
the Japanese in everyday life were slower than those of the West. (This advice appeared to be offered in good faith, in contrast to the cynical words of
another critic, who voiced a common opinion when he suggested that the
Japanese film industry cater to foreign fantasies: "They want Mount Fuji
and geisha—so give them Mount Fuji and geisha.") Kawakita called for a
quicker *"tempo,"* ignoring the countless references to the lively tempo of
the 1920s and 1930s in the Japanese mass media and implying that the distance between Japan and the West could be bridged.[43]

When Kawakita demanded this increase in tempo from Japanese actors
and actresses, he compared Japanese movement to foreign movement. Was
he pointing to the fact that by February 1939, Japanese men and women
were not moving with the abandon of one decade earlier? In other words,
was he saying that the Japanese had never been modern or that their gestures were no longer modern? In either case, Kawakita did not totally distance himself from modern thought. Hitherto, articles in *Eiga no Tomo* had
not adopted the notion of "passing" as Western *(seiyōjin kabure);* and even

here Kawakita did not abandon the implication that there were no intrinsic differences between two racialized groups when he called for the Japanese actor to be possessed of a "Japanese-like mask." (Presumably that same actor could don a "Western mask.") He was adhering to a central presumption of the modern years; performance, and not essence, made the difference.[44]

In addition to Westerners, the Chinese were very much in evidence in *Eiga no Tomo*, but they did not count as foreigners. This was made very clear in the June 1938 issue, which raised the issue of Japanese attitudes toward China within movie culture. Film critic Iijima Tadashi bemoaned the fact that the Japanese masses felt superior to the Chinese people. One characteristic of the Japanese attentiveness to Western movies has been the Japanese audience's intense desire to absorb knowledge and to catch up with and surpass the West through what it learned at the movies. It was only natural, he concluded, that this audience had no interest in movies focused on the Chinese, such as one recent failure, *The Road to Peace in the Orient*. A roundtable discussion that included Iwasaki Akira took up the same issue, concluding that the movie had failed not (or not only) because of the prejudice against Chinese filmmakers but ultimately because the Japanese audience had no interest in China. They would have to be familiarized with "the thing that is China" and thereby come to feel an intimacy, just as the *talkies* had encouraged a familiarity with French film. Iwasaki—the only critic to go to prison for openly opposing the Film Law—disagreed: the problem, he said, was that the Japanese spectators did not want to go to the state-produced *kokusaku eiga* (government policy movies).[45]

This discussion revealed that the implied spectator desired by the state-sponsored producers of culture was only implied. Actual spectator-consumers had finally realized, in the words of one critic, that movies could be a healthy leisure activity for the home-front audience, who were willing to pay fifty sen for three hours' worth of entertainment. Such conflicting desires were confirmed in the pages of *Eiga no Tomo* by the continued presence of Hollywood stories and pictures. The cover of the July 1938 issue featured Ginger Rogers in a revealing halter top, and the stars caricatured in "Caricature Exhibition" were Louis Jouvet, Olivia de Havilland, Cary Grant, Dorothy Lamour, Gary Cooper, Annabella, and Errol Flynn. The following month, the reader could find the latest news about David Niven, Merle Oberon, and Lionel Barrymore in the feature "Hollywood Is All Agog," and in a feature reminiscent of the numerous *ero* features of the early 1930s, Takami Jun admitted to having desired such full-figured actresses as Clara Bow.[46]

Japanese modern culture was in love with Hollywood, but the *modern* had gone to war. "Hollywood Is All Agog" ended opposite the beginning of a scenario written by Ozaki Shirō titled "The Setting Sun on the Battlefield," which featured a "markedly modern youth" attired in *"golf pants"* and *"chrome* watch." The everyday had moved to China, and China was now being eroticized at the same time that the movie spectator was being nationalized. "War Movies and Women Fans in Great Britain," appeared in the September 1938 issue of *Eiga no Tomo*. Therein, author Okamoto Kanoko, wife of Okamoto Ippei, the caricaturist of everyday life, offered a soothing experience to her readers. Commiserating with the number of readers who after half a year of residing abroad were affected by nervous tension, she recounted how going to the movies had helped her frayed nerves when life in London had become unbearable, a condition in part induced by the fact that the Japanese body could not keep up with the speed of the British transport system. References to the difference between Japanese and foreign physiques were beginning to appear in *Eiga no Tomo*. The discussion of neckties in the November 1938 article "The Gentleman in Style" commented that the necktie had not suffered from recent restrictions on clothing, such as the new rule that the gentleman's hat return to its serious, standard size. The article recommended that given the difference between the Western and the Japanese male physique, the length and the width of the tie should be decreased. (Here we have prescription of fashion, in sharp contrast to Kon Wajirō's description.)[47]

Okamoto gave other culturally conditioned causes—including the distinction between Western food in Japan and British cooking—for her unhappiness in London. War movies had saved her. She had first been wary, afraid that they would not serve to lift her gloom, but she was delighted to find them exciting. What detracted from the cathartic experience as described by Okamoto was the behavior of the British women fans who would cling to her, shrieking, in the manner of Japanese women "responding to the spectacle of a ghost found in a ghost house on a festival day." However, there was a difference: very few Japanese women would respond so emotionally to an air raid, especially if it were merely in a movie. This difference reflected the vibrant personality of a prospering [Japanese] people. She had learned to sit herself between Japanese male friends, partly to insulate herself from the frenzy of the British women but also so that she could enjoy watching the responses of the Japanese men to the unexpected overtures from the British women spectators.[48]

Wartime pleasure could be exciting but in order for it to be eroticized, the Japanese experience had to be set apart from Chinese life. Just as the female body had been dissected in previous years, China was now being marked as a desirable site. An article on the documentary film *Shanghai* was discussed in terms of the sensations associated with the fall of Shanghai and Nanking. One article lauded the "subtle expression in the eyes of the Chinese as Japanese troops passed before a crowd" and attributed the new face of Shanghai—its "recovery"—to Japanese determination. In February 1939, Takami Jun reported going over to China to enjoy himself, only to find that the geisha in China had no sense of themselves as geisha. According to Takami's assessment, in Japan—"if you go to a *café* the café waitress is aware of herself as a café waitress, the geisha is as a geisha, and the man of letters is aware of himself as a man of letters." Takami continued, likening the approach of Chinese actors to the style of American actors: the Chinese were much more natural. His example was a Chinese actor as Modern Boy strolling in Shanghai: "There is a pre-*star* quality to it. The Chinese film may be infantile, but there is something carefree to it."[49]

The erotic pleasures made possible by filmgoing had now moved to Shanghai, as elaborated in the article "Report on Accompanying the Troops." The author, Niwa Fumio, reported triumphantly that he had been able to see *Peter the Great*, which was banned in Japan. He placed the theater in the French concession of Shanghai for the reporter, interviewing him, who was eager to hear about Shanghai movie culture. Niwa estimated that it would take the Chinese film industry at least four or five years to catch up with Japan, for the Chinese needed to overcome such obstacles as the audience's lack of willingness to believe that a papier-mâché tiger was real, and that one hand gesture could signify the opening and closing of a door. Niwa's domestication of the Chinese audience as childlike was coupled with the implication that the Chinese were docile, accepting of an expanding Japanese presence.[50]

Another document, this time by filmmakers, reinforced the image of the Chinese as childlike: leading director Kinugasa Teinosuke explained that the Chinese did not like to have their pictures taken, either because of superstition or for fear of ensuing problems, but that his all-knowing eye could detect which emotion was being expressed when the Chinese face was turned away from the camera. Kinugasa admitted that Chinese gestures could not always be captured or controlled, but other stories in *Eiga no Tomo* told of sentimental allegiances to Japan such as the loyalty of the Chinese people to Japanese troops. There was also, for example, the account of a sixteen-year-old Chinese youth who begged to return to Japan with a Japanese film crew. This kind of domestication had been lacking in the *Eiga no Tomo* articles about *ero*. And in addition, as noted above, China, like the female form, was being marked into different, geographic parts. The magazine told its reader-subjects that Nanking was now the way Shanghai had been when there had only been one movie theater, near Café Lion, which featured newsreels and naked Russian dancers. In Shanghai, the Japanese walking the streets need not be frightened, for it was the Japanese who remembered the eighteenth of September. Ostensibly, the Chinese had forgotten about the Japanese invasion of Manchuria.[51]

In order to mark China as an object for conquest, the Japanese nation (expressed in terms of character or spirit) has to be marked off or separated from China. Japan had to be projected as different, as in the March 1939 report from the front that noted that forty to fifty Chinese men had walked by unarmed film director Ushihara Kiyohiko, who was clad in his khaki uniform. If the situation had been reversed, Ushihara said, the Japanese would have cut open the onlooker's belly. Iijima also provided assistance in rendering the Japanese people different in *Eiga no Tomo*. In his article "The National Character of Film," he turned the universalist presumption of the modern years on its head arguing that both the talkie and the silent film had a distinctly national character. While it was usually said that the silent film was international, Iijima argued, the expressions and gestures taken to be universal in fact belonged to foreigners whose actions were translated into the spectator's native language. Iijima was worried that American movies that were divorced from current Japanese life ignored the emotions of the *seikatsu* of Japanese life. He called for movies "rooted in contemporary Japanese *seikatsu*." Two months later, his "What I Hope for in Japanese Movies," called for a realistic approach that acknowledged the speed with which Japanese everyday *seikatsu* was changing. In his call for the realization of the place of Japanese culture in the world, Iijima introduced a new term to *Eiga no Tomo* through the mid-1930s: *kokumin seikatsu* (the *seikatsu* of the nation's people) and noted that the recent "Incident" was grounded in the nation's people as a whole. As for the implications for going to the movies, moviegoers had to recognize that the realities of the planning and production of films were linked to a much larger force than individual wishes.[52]

Iijima and others might have wished to transmit the message that Japanese culture was different, but *Eiga no Tomo* still refused to let go of Hollywood during the remainder of the years preceding the Pacific War, even as Nazi cultural policy was referred to with growing admiration. The January 1939 issue sported Deanna Durbin. The table of contents page, highlighting the dialogue between Ishikawa Tatsuzō and Niwa Fumio resulting from their trip to China in large print, placed it next to a full-body photographic inset of an authoritative-looking Ginger Rogers, bag in hand and hand on waist. The November 1939 article lauding the attraction of the culture films *(bunka eiga)* was undoubtedly related to the requirement in the Film Law that every movie screening include at least 250 meters of these state-sanctioned, state-sponsored documentary films. The author shared the pleasures of an Italian *bunka eiga* on the invasion of Ethiopia, a moving German film about its air force, a British film on the making of a cathedral, a French series called "the three-minute science classroom *series*," and a Japanese culture film explaining the automatic telephone switching system.[53]

But while Japanese film culture mandated by the state was being played within world film culture, a "Special Report from Hollywood," titled *News Encyclopedia*, captured such news items as the decision to star Fred Astaire in *Girl Crazy* along with Eleanor Powell and Eddie Cantor. The Japanese Film Law might have been modeled after Nazi legislation and the culture film after the Nazi *Kulturfilm*, but anti-Nazi movies, including *Confessions of a Nazi Spy*, *Hitler*, and *Beast of Berlin* (listed both by their original English titles and in Japanese translation) were given space in the same issue. The January 1940 issue would pick up this topic to report on such anti-Nazi movies as *I Married Nazi* [sic] and on the banning of the popular ditty "Even Hitler had a Mother," from London's West End music halls.

The best example of the continued power of Hollywood fantasy over the everyday actions of the Japanese spectator appeared in a December 1939 article by the documentary photographer Kimura Ihei, titled "Fads and Witty Conversations." The author explained that he had originally aimed at a discussion of movie magazines but that the article had turned into a discussion of "the great gift" that the foreign movie had been to the young people of Japan.[54] Kimura's article illustrated the draw of modern culture. He had first noted a change in visual culture, in part due to the paper shortage. Moreover, cosmetic and medicine advertisements had begun to appear in movie magazines, in part because of the recognition that the large number of readers of movie magazines resulted from the "inability to separate movies from everyday life." Kimura did not underestimate the power of the photo illustrations of the stars. He provided an analogy from the mass media: women's magazines gave their readers practical information as to how to sew and cook, movie magazines also met concrete needs and desires. Men were thus able to make a style of clothing or hair their own, and women appropriated fashions in clothing, hair, and cosmetics. Kimura told the *Eiga no Tomo* readers that in his business of photographing people, he constantly came across cases of young people who had adopted styles in such a fashion, but even more common was the adoption of fashion from actual movies, rather than from the photos in the movie magazines. Moreover, these young people did not merely mimic the styles of the stars as they had in earlier years. Instead, they matched the styles (Kimura used the term *kata*) of America, France, and Germany to their own individuality.[55]

And not only had young Japanese spectators begun to dress in movie style, according to Kimura. These moviegoers had also begun to speak in talkie conversational style, adopting—through a form of code-switching—the pacing of speech and the spacing of laughter in the interstices between phrases found in the movies. Fifteen years after Kon's studies of Ginza styles, Japanese women and men were still creating new modes of self-expression, integrating aspects of Western culture into their own daily lives, and switching to new gestures. While it may be said that the state officially inaugurated an end to the celebration of the new with its celebration of cultural continuity marking the 2600th anniversary of the Japanese nation, photographs of stars discussed by Kimura were still omnipresent in *Eiga no Tomo* in 1940 and 1941.

In April 1940, Iijima Tadashi may have tried to persuade his readers that the bodies of the movie *stars* that film fans flocked to see were mere shadows—distinct from everyday life—and that they should focus on the spiritual qualities of moviemaking. And half a year later, a full-page ad for *Ohinata Mura* (Ohinata village), the movie based on the move to Manchuria of half the denizens of one impoverished village in Northern Japan, may have called for the "Building of Greater East Asia linking Japan-Manchuria-China." But opposite the photograph of two East Asian men, one clad in a Western suit, cigar in hand, the other leaning on his walking stick in the midst of a lush countryside, was a closeup of Myrna Loy, whose plunging neckline defied Iijima's exhortation to see "flesh" in spiritual terms. It is true that by 1941, *kensetsu*, or building (implying the building by the state of a new order, in contrast to the cultural constructions discussed by Kon or Kimura), was a keyword, and a glance at the January 1941 *Eiga no Tomo* reveals that *seikatsu* could no longer serve as a term for the everyday: it had been displaced by Iijima's term from 1939, *kokumin seikatsu*—"the everyday life of the nation's people."[56]

An article in the January 1941 issue, "Film and the Everyday Life of the Nation's People," announced that the new Film Law was making a new system and called for a revised understanding of movies by schools and households. Yet it also revealed that the nation's spectators had a will of their own, as it attempted to explain how "healthy pleasures" could be built. The writer, an official from the Ministry of Education, tried to tell his readers that the ban on morning movies (except on Sundays and holidays) had been implemented not only because of the war but also because it was necessary to create new forms of *kokumin seikatsu*. Yet he was forced to admit that movies were still about pleasure.

We can conclude that the people were inseparable from the nation but movies were still about pleasure and Hollywood fantasy was still the fantasy of the *Eiga no Tomo* readers. This was clear from the January 1941 issue of the magazine, therein the article "World Diary," a calendar of news events, including the fiftieth anniversary of the Imperial Rescript on Education, the closing down of dance halls on October 31, 1940, "Serve Asia Day" on the November 1, and the festivities surrounding the celebration of the 2600th anniversary of the nation, to be marked by the attendance of the emperor. On the opposite page a busty Deanna Durbin leaned into the title of her film, *First Love* (titled *The Silver Shoes* in Japanese), and two other Western actresses were pictured in heated conversation. One code switch went from Emperor of the Empire to Hollywood actress.[57]

In April 1941, *Destry Rides Again* was being advertised in *Eiga no Tomo*, but by spring of that year the pages were increasingly devoted to interviews with state officials. A hint that this shift was not made willingly was provided by one writer who shared with his readers his disbelief on hearing that the Imperial Theater was being used by the Cabinet Information Division. He had not believed this: he had gone there to see a movie and instead had seen the lettering for the new government office that would soon consolidate the information services of the Foreign, Army, Navy, and Home Ministries. The article recounted the journalist's interview with the new chief of the Cabinet Information Division, who during the course of the meeting praised a German-made movie on the invasion of Poland because people from the film world lost their lives during the filming. In other words, the bureaucrat explained, the filmmakers were being treated as military men.

In the eyes of the Japanese leadership, the movies had indeed gone to war, even as the pages of *Eiga no Tomo* continued to highlight modern gestures. A photo-essay in the July 1941 issue staged the dos and don'ts of movie theater behavior. In the montage of numbered photos, a man in suit and fedora and a woman in kimono sat together in varying poses. These ranged from the pose of the man leaning on the woman's shoulder and from inappropriate smoking or stretching to a pose of the two sitting upright (appropriate). There was, in other words, still a choice in gestures.[58]

While *Eiga no Tomo* clung to its photos from Hollywood, and gave its readers a choice in gestures, there was no denying that the movie magazine as a site for Japanese spectators to "go to the movies" was no longer a modern site by the end of 1941. The November 1941 reminiscence by a news photographer about how news reporting had increased after the Osada incident (referring to the Abe Sada case), along with his quick qualification that "of course we don't film anything like that now," was a clear reference to the end of *ero*. And the unprecedented racist sentiment expressed in an advertisement in November 1941 made clear that any fantasies blurring Japanese and Western identity, through identification with Hollywood and through the self-fashioning discussed by Kimura were to end. Facing this article, an ad for face cream featured a stylization of the word for "different" *(chigau)*, and the text read:

> If your country's different, your race is different
> If your race is different, your makeup is different
> As for long ago and now, the eras are different
> If the era is different, the make-up is different
> Throw different makeup clean away
> Be in good spirits[59]

4   The Household Becomes Modern Life

The photo-essay, "The Real Way to Eat Western Food," in the February 1923 issue of *Shufu no Tomo* (Friend of the housewife), led an unsmiling middle-aged woman in kimono through the stages of a meal that was to be fantasized by the housewife-consumer. This began with the placement of a napkin in her lap preparatory to sipping soup and ended with the use of a finger bowl. Such montage was a model for countless narratives in *Friend of the Housewife* that introduced new practices into Japanese culture during the modern years, although the word "Western" would disappear from these articles. Instead, *Shufu no Tomo* would discuss the modern both explicitly and indirectly. Like the other segments making up my montage, it spoke in terms of a post-earthquake break in history resulting in new expressions, an upbeat tempo, a questioning of gender categories, an intensification of erotic experience, and an association of all of the above with an everyday that extended beyond the borders of Japanese culture. In contrast to the state ideology positing a traditional woman within the family, this women's magazine sided with an idea of a modern woman within a modern home.[1]

This "friend" to modern Japanese housewives was launched in 1917, with the editorial intent of offering reading to the married woman who was struggling with the cost of living. The companion to the housewife was to become one of the most influential of the numerous women's magazines of the time. Its founder-editor, Ishikawa Takeyoshi, was proud of the criticism aimed at the magazine—that it read as if pickled in rice-bran soybean paste—because he accepted the implication that his magazine reached the common housewife. Because of its large circulation, *Shufu no Tomo* gives us one popular representation of the home of the *shufu* (housewife) and of the *katei* (household) which had for many displaced the patriarchal *ie* (family) of the *ryōsai kenbo* (good wife and wise mother). In this magazine, which often allowed the documentary impulse of the era to appear as satire in cartoon and textual reportage, we can begin to see how practices that were termed "fads" according to officials, were part of the "modern" experience celebrated in the Japanese press. This medium was one of many introducing new gestures and exhibiting an attitude towards the family-state that could affirm state ideology, indirectly challenge state dictates, or border on the disinterested.

Shufu no Tomo did not take on the order in any overt way; it was not a revolutionary magazine. After the earthquake, the magazine underscored that a new Tokyo of the present *(gendai)*, and thereby a renewed Japan, was being built as a part of "world culture moving forward daily." It was made clear that Japan moved forward with other modern cultures. Tokyo should, like the United States, establish movie theaters for educational purposes, and sites for cultivation of workers, like the Bryn Mawr Summer School where working women were given access to higher education. Suffering by individuals was exemplified by the case of the café owner who was reduced to selling curried rice to the masses in Asakusa (No mention was made of the fate of the six thousand murdered Koreans). Concern over social problems related to the colonial order in the Japanese metropole would not be voiced during the following two decades when circulation leaped from two hundred thousand (in the early 1920s) to one million (by 1934). The readership—composed of urban middle-class and petit-bourgeois wives and wives-to-be, rural housewives, and women workers— would be actively encouraged to support the Japanese war effort as has been well documented.[2]

But a reading of the journal today also reveals that by the 1920s, when the term *Western* had been displaced in the pages of *Shufu no Tomo* by exhortations to modernize made by bureaucrat and journalist alike, three types of articles stood out to challenge the official ideology pronounced by the state and taught in the schools. These were articles dedicated to choosing the ideal mate; those pointing to discord within the household; and pieces sending the modern Japanese woman out into the world (while at the same time encouraging her to bring the modern into her home). Like the Modern Girl's energetically articulated autonomy, like the antics in the café performed by Hayashi Fumiko's heroines, and like the fluid code-switching in the pictorial components of *Eiga no Tomo*, such a challenge was a form of resistance to the state ideology of family. Before examining each of the three topics it is worth looking back to the official version of the housewife's place in the family-state, relying on the extensive scholarship made available by Japanese scholars.[3]

THE FAMILY-STATE OF *SHUFU NO TOMO*

Basing his work on pre- and postwar scholarship, Itō Mikiharu provides a subtle analysis of how two combinatory premises held the prewar family-state *(kazoku-kokka)* ideology together: (1) the unity of loyalty to the state *(chū)* was conjoined with filial piety *(kō)* toward the head of household; and (2) the indivisibility of ancestors from descendants (or in other words, the identification of family with ancestry). The relevant task when studying the state of family life (in both its senses—the condition of the family and the national polity as it related to family life) as represented in *Shufu no Tomo*, is to untangle the extent to which *Shufu no Tomo* was about *kazoku*, or family (and what type of *kazoku*) and to what extent it spoke for the *kokka*, or state. Here, Kano Masanao's analysis of the appearance of the *shufu* (housewife) is apropos.[4]

According to Kano's narrative, by the late teens, as a result of the expansion of Japanese capitalism, a new middle-class man (the salaryman—another English term used by the Japanese) came into being in the big cities, thereby encouraging the dissolution of the *ie* or stem family of multiple generations living together in a household, under the rule of a patriarch, as envisioned by the Meiji ideologues.[5] A new division of labor, premised on a nuclear family, was put into place as the men commuted to their labors and their wives were placed inside the home. The wife of the salaryman was no longer tied to other (patrilineal) relatives in *ie* formation. Her identity and relationships centered on her household. The dismantling of the *ie* continued into the 1920s and 1930s, for three reasons. The first cause, according to Kano, was the Shōwa depression, leading to the sale of daughters into sexual servitude. Some fathers absconded, leading to the parent-child joint suicides by the women and children left behind. Second, the appeal of "red" or Marxist ideology from the late 1920s into the early 1930s threatened the family-state ideology of national essence. Fathers (the ostensible heads of the *ie*) were powerless before treasonous ideals brought into the *ie* by leftist thought. Kano's final reason is the most relevant here: the *ie* was forced to come apart because of public pronouncements of love expressed in both love marriages and "contract" marriages, along with the fad of modernism. Kano in part attributes this third factor to the marketing of romance in women's magazines. According to him, this emphasis on love was displaced as Japan became increasingly embroiled in war, and the focus on romance would be replaced by a concept of a sacralized "motherly love."[6]

State officials were clearly aware of the threats posed to the family-state ideology by such phenomena as women's unrest, juvenile delinquency, and the increase in family disputes. Surveys showed that the *ie* was in trouble and feminist activists demanded a reduction of the power of the household head, equal participation in education, remuneration for labor, and extra-familial institutions capable of fulfilling welfare functions. The Japanese feminist historian Miyake Yoshiko informs us that the family-state ideology was on the wane due to capitalist economic development, the development of the individual, and the notion of the family as part of the private sphere and not as a public institution.

Between July 1919 and December 1927, Diet members, legal scholars, and bureaucrats debated the meaning of *junpū bizoku* (pure morals and beautiful manners), but, no matter how steadfastly the hardline members of the Rinji Hōsei Shingikai (the commission established to revise the Meiji Civil Code, discussed in the Modern Girl segment) tried to define a traditionally Japanese *junpū bizoku* as the basis of the communal life of the family system, it was impossible to gain the full support of the more progressive members, who acknowledged that the Civil Code had to be adjusted to the social *jisei* (trends of the times). What was needed, argued some, was a reformed state-centered ideology that would emphasize the need for women's coming to consciousness of their identity as *kokumin* (members of the nation). To that end, the Shojokai (Unmarried Women's Organization) was transformed into a nationwide youth federation in 1927. At the same time a new federation of the Fujinkai (Women's Organizations) first established at the end of Meiji, was created. There was a double edge to this movement to inculcate an ideology of nationalism in the Japanese women members of these groups: women were told to reject the premodern notion of "respect men, despise women" but at the same time were encouraged to adhere to the precepts of "The Greater Learning for Women," another Tokugawa-era tract, which called for woman's unswerving obedience to her husband and in-laws. Ultimately, the members of the Rinji Hōsei Shingikai aimed to prevent discord in the household *(katei)*, saying that this was especially necessary given the "atmosphere recently in vogue."[7]

Articles in *Shufu no Tomo* illustrate that the state-appointed members of the commission to consider threats to the family had reason to be alarmed for all was not well for husband and wife from the 1920s into the 1930s. For example, in the official version of family life, the primary identity for the bride entering her husband's *ie* was not wife but daughter-in-law. In contrast, *Shufu no Tomo* gave its readers the message that being a *shufu* was about being half of a *fūfu* (married couple) in the modern world and noted that marriages were not always harmonious.

The friend of the housewife revealed the threat of discord in "Letters to the Editor on Household Law," and numerous articles on the married couple more than indicated that the patriarchal unit was not intact. In these accounts, women were active participants in determining the direction of family life, or were at least eager to turn to experts to have their options explained. Problems addressed to the attorney and professor of law writing for the magazine's legal advice column reveal the desire of women, writing as free agents, to map out household strategy. Letters covered such issues as successorship to head of household, rights of inheritance, and post-divorce proceedings. In the case of one letter regarding divorce, the writer's husband had been adopted into her household and had become the head of household. Now that a divorce had taken place, the former wife wanted to know which of them must leave the home, what would happen to the children, and what would become of the husband's assets. Although the answers to the queries regarding family law were clear-cut, *Shufu no Tomo* also addressed much more complex issues, including matters related to marital strife. And in both tone and content, the magazine countered the positions expressed in such sites as the moral textbooks written for young women. Concern about divorce was illustrated by the matter-of-fact legal advice in its Family Law Column, such as the December 1929 response to the husband who wrote in to explain that he and his wife concurred on the decision to divorce, and that his wife's parents were concerned that going to court would bring shame to the family. Couldn't he and his wife avoid going to court? He was reassured that this was indeed possible.[8]

In sum, in the pages of *Friend of the Housewife*, the housewife-consumer was faced with two alternatives if her husband's behavior did not correspond to her ideal. One option was to seek divorce. Alternatively, she could manipulate her husband in order to avoid the family strife that was documented again and again in *Shufu no Tomo* from its inception until the Pacific War.

WIVES AND HUSBANDS (THE *SHUFU* IN *FŪFU*)

The morals textbook for the upper-level education of girls in 1930, *The Revised Morals Teachings for Young Girls* concerned itself with the married couple and its relationship to the everyday life of family, household, and nation. (The only one of the terms evident in the morals text for boys—cited in Part One above—was *kokka*, state.) The text told the teenage girl that the married couple (the *fūfu*) was a constitutive part of the family (the *ie*). In the West, the *ie* was based on the married couple, and the death of the husband meant the end of the *ie*. The reader for girls underscored that in Japan, the family followed the way of the imperial household, thereby ensuring its continuity down through posterity. The caveat was that each member of the household was responsible for the continuity of the household, and the text made clear where the real power was to lie: as designated by the Civil Code, the head of the household was responsible for the family both within its confines and without. The primer told the girls to strive for mutual love and respect within monogamy; but agency in everyday life was not to be equally apportioned. The wife's place within this division of labor was to preserve and maintain rather than to discover or create. Moreover, *seikatsu*, a term associated in the mass press with moving and making, was associated only with the state, in the context of a discussion of *kokumin seikatsu*, or the everyday life of the people of the nation, and *kokkateki seikatsu*, the everyday life of the state. The advocacy of monogamy and the discussion of mutual love found in the textbook for girls were post-Meiji ideas, but this was hardly part of the modern discourse on the family (represented by the *fūfu* or married couple), in *Shufu no Tomo*.[9]

The *shufu* appearing in *Shufu no Tomo* was given her identity through the unit of the *fūfu*. She was seen to be one-half of this pairing, and to that end she was not hidden away in the newly constructed nouveau, middle-class *bunka jūtaku* (culture house). As I have argued, the Modern Girl existed largely as a phantasm of the anxiety-ridden critics who clung to a seemingly established order during a period of rapid transition. The *shufu* in *Shufu no Tomo*, in contrast, was legitimized in three ways that paraphrase the three themes I have just raised: finding a mate, discord, and the housewife in and of the modern world. First of all, once married, she became the domestic, rational force keeping the household on an even emotional keel. Secondly, she could have been a *shokugyō fujin* (working woman) of any class who worked outside the home. Finally, an appropriate *seikatsu* was maintained through a (usually) one-way dialogue with mores in (modern) Europe and the United States that were presented as rationalized models for household practice.

To read through the countless articles on the establishment of the *fūfu* in *Friend of the Housewife* is to see substantiated not only Kano's argument regarding the power of free love but also the sentiments of the state commission on the deterioration of harmonious relationships in the household. Articles did not overtly state that there was a new emphasis on love or freedom of choice in marriage. Instead, a series of pieces with matching titles indicated to the reader then, and to the historian now, that the magazine was challenging the patriarchal family-state ideology by offering a space to men and women (married and unmarried) in which they could reveal their desires. Women as well as men desired mates, and these desires, along with blunt criticisms, had to be channeled into an acceptable notion of the identity of the *fūfu* comprising housewife reader and her spouse.

Articles on desire—"hers" versus "his"—continued from the teens until the second half of the 1930s. An examination of the type of bride desired by a "young gentleman" in 1917 was countered by "My Ideal Husband" and "What Kind of Women Do Men Respect?" There were also paired articles asking women, "What Kind of Man Do You Want for a Husband?" and men, "What Kind of Woman Do You Want for a Wife?" By the early 1920s, the two halves of the *fūfu* were thus placed side by side in articles composed of the woman's voice and the feminine ideal sought by would-be husbands in a series of "She Said/He Said" proscriptions and suggestions. One young "gentleman," after watching the marriages of his friends fail—one as soon as a month after the wedding—set forth seven conditions to be met by his bride, the sixth of which was that she be *jōhin na haikara*. She should, in other words, be refined but of the moment with style—modern, in other words. The other prerequisites were conventional, as seen in his final wish showing that youths were not impervious to state ideology—his bride was to be optimistic because those who were brooding and hysterical could be neither good wives nor wise mothers.[10]

The defining features of the ideal male were established in *Shufu no Tomo* by the early 1920s, as evidenced in a section of the April 1918 issue devoted to "My Ideal Husband." A reader from Osaka wanted a "manly" man of fortitude, strong personality, and a cheery and vital disposition. Her ideal husband was capable of understanding others, including, most importantly, his wife. Another reader asked for a husband with religious convictions and a large heart who would be approximately five years older. Thinly veiled aspirations to a middle-class lifestyle were apparent: he could be a teacher, bureaucrat, or company employee. The author who wished for a husband who neither drank nor smoked, and proclaimed that the ideal size for the family was two people. The *fūfu* in other words, was being given its place as it strayed from the patriarchal *kazoku kokka* ideal of the multigenerational family.[11]

One woman, showing remarkable insight into both the lure of commodities in consumer culture, and an awareness of the complexities of desire as projected onto the opposite sex, likened the task of choosing a husband to deciding among beautiful wares at Mitsukoshi department store. The allusion to the department store was premised on her belief that as soon as a couple was married, their relationship, which had been defined by mutual respect and caring, turned sour. The advice columnist, feminist critic, and activist Yamada Waka (known for her stance advocating the protection of motherhood over woman's commitment to career), explained that women of differing nationalities applied equally faulty criteria when they chose a mate: American women went for money, German women loved soldiers, and French women were drawn to weak men. The task for the Japanese woman was to seek out the Japanese male who complied with etiquette, because etiquette was "the technology of human action." Yamada emphasized that the Japanese woman need not look beyond her national borders. She should seek out Japanese men who understood Japanese standards of etiquette; the mannerly man was the manly man.[12]

The articles in *Shufu no Tomo* posited an ambivalent division of labor. According to Yamada Waka, if there were only women and no men, the world would be full of hysterics, and if there were only men, it would be peopled by barbarians. Yamada apparently saw the role of the married couple as civilizing or domesticating disordered personalities. In contrast, some female voices called for a husband to play the pedagogical role of imparting knowledge. On the other hand, there was the articulate presence of the *shokugyō fujin*, such as the world athlete who warned against a social order wherein women were to be molded by men as though they were made of clay. The contradiction at the heart of *Shufu no Tomo*—the simultaneous celebration of a rational domesticity and the documentation of women's labors outside the household—could not have escaped its readers.[13]

In the words of *Shufu no Tomo*, the West provided models: there women had gained power and influence because they had been encouraged to work alongside their husbands, outside the household. But a change in editorial policy would ensue. As Japan broadened its presence on the continent, increasingly *Shufu no Tomo* would place the Japanese woman inside of and inseparable from her household. Now sounding very much like *The Revised Morals Teachings for Young Girls*, *Shufu no Tomo* also sent the message that the female half of the married couple was to be the comfort-giver within the household as haven. One author went so far as to declare that "for the modern person who has lost God, the household is, in one sense, a temple." (The textbook had also called the household sacred.)

The cartoonist Asō Yutaka, creator of *Lazy Daddy*, offered his audience in the pages of *Hōchi Shinbun* a commentary on the cultural change of the new era through his beloved comic strip. This starred the rotund figure in kimono and clogs who attempted to come to terms with the technologies of modernity, while exuding no sense of patriarchal authority. And although the cartoonist admitted to possessing a collection of over one hundred Western phonograph records, he nevertheless stipulated that his ideal wife should be prudent, modest, and schooled in "Japanese hobbies." She would ensure that their household was defined by Japanese practices. The cartoonist desired the patriarchal authority that his hero lacked.

While much of its imagery of the ideal wife appeared to conform to a culturally conservative ideal, the definitions of the ideal mother-in-law by the daughters-in-law quoted in *Shufu no Tomo* did not. For example, the multigenerational family system celebrated in state ideology was challenged by one daughter-in-law who complained that her mother-in-law was interfering with her child-rearing. She preferred to be alone and was neither ashamed of nor alone in insisting that life would be easier if different generations lived separately.[14]

Love, romance, and companionate marriage were idealized in the special "Love and Marriage" issue of July 1922 and in such articles as the January 1926 account of husbands of famous women. These legitimized both the notion of the working woman and the ideal of the household based on romance. In the 1926 photomontage, reminiscent of the accounts of the daily existence of Hollywood stars in *Eiga no Tomo*, readers found such affirmations as the account of how the understanding husband (a shipping captain and a pilot) of a noted artist contributed to their everyday life, and the love story of the Russian violinist Anna Ono and her husband (from the world of banking). There was also the message that the success of a popular actress appearing in the movie *Takahashi Oden* (about the notorious Meiji-era murderess) was related to the affectionate support of her husband. Ten years later, the magazine was still running features about famous pairings. Marriage was about neither *ie* nor *kazoku;* it centered on the *fūfu*, the married couple.[15]

THE *FŪFU* IN DISCORD/HOUSEHOLD IN DISCORD

The readers of *Shufu no Tomo* were duly notified that marriage could be fraught with problems. A series of short statements in "What Troubled Me Most in My Marriage" shared the experiences of wives of notables and working women renowned in their own right. The wife of Fujimori Seikichi (author of "What Made Her Do What She Did?") admitted to an upperclass upbringing that prevented her from checking prices. The wife of social reformer Kagawa Toyohiko wrote about the bedbugs and lice found in the slums where she and her husband had lived and worked.[16]

In the earliest days of the magazine, readers were given accounts of "good-for-nothing husbands." A decade later, readers were still being treated to the story of the wife who found a photo of a woman holding a child who resembled her husband. In August 1924, readers of "Sad Stories of Those Who Divorced" were told that divorce was a clear option "if there was a deep reason as to why a couple could not be happy." But the message was mixed. In one article, echoed by many other articles, readers were told to desist from divorce. Kagawa Toyohiko answered the letter from a woman who was considering divorce after determining that it was not her infertility but her husband's that had prevented them from having children. Kagawa suggested a change of setting, such as the trip to Taiwan he and his wife had taken, which had resulted in her pregnancy nine years into their marriage (the colonial as diversion). The wife whose husband had pawned her clothing in order to pay for his daily routine at the local café was told to be loving and patient. The mother of Hatoyama Ichirō, the minister of education, replied to the wife of the man who had set up a geisha as his mistress that "it would not be effectual for the wife to 'assert her rights.'" The angry wife who was told to treat her husband's mistress like a sister was also told by the expert that she should organize her marriage around her children and consider her husband's infidelity as a form of illness.[17]

Although the specialists brought in by *Shufu no Tomo* tended to want to keep the couple together at the expense of the pain of the housewife, the public show of marital discord in modern Japan could not be denied by legal experts. In November of 1936, attorneys and judges gathered to discuss the "fighting of couples brought before the court." The context was that the "couples problem" had so increased that in the previous year more than sixteen thousand cases had been heard in the Tokyo ward court. While one judge attributed this number to an increase in population, the discussion tended to go in another direction. Wasn't this due to woman's awakening? Until recently she had been willing to be beaten by her husband, but this was no longer so. The specialists agreed that something was not right— married couples and their relatives were actually battling in the hallways of civil court, in Japan, which prided itself on "a beautiful family system." Because of the family system, family members other than the married couple were inevitably brought into the fray, and one discussant-participant had even witnessed the lawsuit of a grandchild against grandmother. The fighting was new, "reflecting the times," but the men contended that it was not a modern phenomenon as might be expected. The "modern" divorce proceeding had emerged around 1915, when the nighttime pleasures of the married male had come up against woman's demand that her position be acknowledged. These cases, brought by "awakened" women, had recently been replaced by a new trend. Now, divorce on grounds of economic hardship was sought by women who wished to leave their husbands, to keep their children, and to demand child-support payments from the men they had left.[18]

Through the 1920s and into the 1930s a series of articles in *Shufu no Tomo* confirmed that marriage problems were on the agenda of women. No euphemism was used here: this was the couple's quarrel *(fūfu genka),* and the housewife-reader was given sets of machinations for working around what appeared to be inevitable strife between husband and wife. The articles were couched in a satirical tone and decorated with caricatures of everyday married life. These all-too-clear ink drawings illustrating dialogue (or lack thereof) between wife and husband appeared too often to be anything but meaningless nonsense. In 1917, "The Twenty Requests from Wife to Husband" and the "Ten Secrets of a Couple's Harmony" had appeared. The requests ranged from "Please do not oversleep in the morning" to "Please play with the children." The keys to harmony included the recognition that one's spouse was human, the admonition to "not get close when angry," and the need for similar hobbies. A decade later, instructions were much more detailed and more devious in "One Hundred Secret Ways to Prevent the Married Couple's Quarrel." The first premise of the article was that quarrels were inevitable, the solution was for the wife to contain herself, and the strategy was broken into numbered items: item 3 suggested "looking at her angry reflection in the mirror"; item 6 advocated, "When angry, remain silent." The savvy housewife was to realize that losing an argument could indeed be a victory and that to engage in fighting was to send her husband directly to the café. Two years later, the housewife was given "Forty-Eight Secret Means to a Couple's Harmony." The opening prescriptions disempowered the *shufu* by emphasizing that taking first place in school by no means ensured that she would meet the necessary ideal of the "sweet little wife" who placed her husband's interests above all else. Item 16 advised the wife to always respond to scolding with an abject apology. Item 22 denied her any kind of eroticism: she was not to take on the airs of a café waitress or a geisha. (This article likened the husband to a match and the wife to gasoline if she chose to let an argument ignite.) Item 31 summed up the strategy of the good housewife: when her husband was angry, he was to be treated "like a telephone pole," like something that was just there.[19]

Rather than being passively aggressive, the wife was to be passively responsive to all of her husband's expressed and non-articulated desires. The way to harmony required some manipulation through such strategic measures as light jokes (item 4) and practicing a smiling visage in front of the mirror (item 44). If she could observe the forty-seven rules, accepting the division of labor giving (financial) responsibility for the daytime to her husband and taking responsibility for the domestic pleasures of the evening, she would be able to experience the forty-eighth and last secret: the household of the couple would be the site of the constant forging of happiness.[20]

By May 1932, the battle rhetoric in *Shufu no Tomo* had so escalated that strife on the home front seemed as inevitable as the fighting on the continent. In "Ten Ways to Win a Couple's Quarrel," the housewife was told that war had to be won by strategizing "even if the opponent were her husband." The theme of battle was illustrated in a series of cartoons illustrating such strategies as "killing with laughter." If she refused to quarrel, the fight could not continue, just as sumo could not be conducted with only one sumo wrestler. This strategy was considered to be "even better than the explosives thrown by the Three Valorous Bombs." Only one weapon was inexcusable—the *shufu* could not damage her husband's honor.

The article made gestures toward respect for harmonious relations between wife and husband, if not between Japan and its enemies on the continent. It stated that although some warring between countries was inevitable, no couple's battle was inevitable. Nonetheless, the last cartoon in the series was the sketch accompanying the tenth way to win an argument: "If You Have Many Allies, You are Bound to Win." The housewife, garbed in belted Western dress, stood flanked by her mother-in-law and the maid, both of whom were in kimono. All three pointed rifles at the enemy; all three wore helmets inscribed with the word *Madam.* In contrast to the humor related to the Manchurian Incident in *Eiga no Tomo,* here humor seemed to lampoon marriage and not the actual war that gave rise to the imagery.[21]

WOMEN AT WORK

Even more challenging to the institution of the family (and of the *fūfu*) than divorce was women's desire to remain single. In one testimonial under the heading "Why I Don't Marry," a woman affiliated with the YWCA of Japan spoke glowingly of her rich personal and professional life in service to others. Another was equally forceful: she was single because she enjoyed the single life.

A journalist looked back to her childhood, when she had first concluded that there was no reason why women should not be independent. Although she preferred the company of men to the indecisiveness of women, she disagreed with those who voiced fears that the increase in professional women would lead to a decrease in marriages and would thus affect the population. This critic pointed out that not only did statistics show that the population was increasing; they also showed that the working woman was not necessarily an unmarried woman.[22]

The issue of profession versus marriage was debated in September of 1936 in "They Don't Want to Get Married: A Roundtable Discussion of Contemporary Young Women." These young women in their early twenties talked in terms of "continuing their own studies" (in painting, singing, and Japanese dance) instead of taking the option of sacrificing themselves to a husband's career. One twenty-six-year-old, who was studying Western dressmaking and art, had seen too many "marriage tragedies" to have any interest in marriage. Another had watched her classmates from art school marry fellow artists, only to find themselves supporting their husbands instead of continuing their own work. The words of a third were the most damning: "This is my personal opinion, but under the Japanese marriage system of the present, woman's position is disadvantageous." This sentiment was echoed by a twenty-four-year-old English teacher, who blamed the Japanese family system for burdening the housewife with too many chores. While the reporter offered some exceptions to the rule, noting that the poet Yosano Akiko and Imai Kuniko, the wife of a Diet member, had kept their careers, the participants remained skeptical as to the possibility of both maintaining a marriage and dedicating oneself to art.[23]

The Working Woman might or might not be married, but in the above discussion and in other forums the single *Shokugyō Fujin* was an object of great interest in *Shufu no Tomo* throughout the modern years. This focus on the working women out in the world and the assumption shared by interviewees that they would eventually join the ranks of housewives, created an intimate connection between housewife and woman worker. The housewife at home could be either a worker or a former worker. The connection of the woman outside the home to the housewife inside is a far cry from Gonda Yasunosuke's declaration that the bourgeois household was cut off from the *Strasse* and from the workers. These features were also a far cry from the article that had detailed "The Mission of Women outside the Household" in June 1917. That had been an overt call for *noblesse oblige*. Upper-class women were to accompany the "progress of civilization" by coming to the rescue of "lower-class society." The aid was to provide clothing, food, and housing. Material culture, in other words, was not to be chosen or put together from below, in the ways studied by Kon after the earthquake, but was to be granted from on high, through department-store-like establishments and bazaars that could distribute needed items.[24]

The discourse on the Modern Girl indirectly articulated the threat posed by the working woman to notions of "tradition," and the discourse on the café waitress offered a glimpse of a new form of sex work for working-class women. In contrast, the articles in *Shufu no Tomo* featuring the Working Woman presumed that she was an integral part of contemporary life and not to be isolated from the concerns of the household or the identity of the housewife. In May 1919, "The Experiences of Women Who Succeeded in Business" featured such working wives with economic needs as a rice-cake vendor. After the earthquake, more glamorous occupations were listed: one article told readers where they could train as typists, painters, doctors, and dentists. In addition, prison wardens were needed for the 1,712 women convicts unfortunate enough to be incarcerated. The need for beauticians trained to beautify the face, the article noted, was all the more important after the earthquake, a period during which Japanese women had never looked so ugly. Two years later, an unidentified "woman reporter" from *Shufu no Tomo* visited "Unusual and Different Women," such as the "old woman, known as the 'millionaire of the slum barracks,' who had worked as a nurse for forty years after being inspired by the story of Florence Nightingale." In one of *Shufu no Tomo*'s occasional references to the most destitute strata of contemporary society, the reporter noted that this woman chose to live among the hysterical voices of exhausted wives and the desperately drunken jeers of their husbands. The men could not find work, and, in this desperate setting, every once in a while "it rained blood." The process of defining the working woman reached Japanese readers in the colonies, as revealed in a first-person account by the sister of a bureaucrat in the engineering division of the Government General in Korea. She had determined to become a "working woman" and had figured out that the most lucrative position available to her as a working woman in Korea was that of schoolteacher. Here was the modern in the colonial.[25]

In June 1933, the magazine published "A Roundtable Discussion of All Model Factory Girls Speaking of their *Seikatsu*," featuring women factory workers who praised their meaningful work and dormitory life. Here the vernacular of the first-person voice, in addition to illustrations, offered intimacy, just as the *Eiga no Tomo* photo-essays had provided an easy familiarity. One factory girl (a worker at a candy factory) said that it wasn't the machinery but the spirit that counted; coverage was given to the extracurricular activities offered by the bosses; and an employee of a textile factory suggested that upper-class young people had gone wrong because of "thought problems" that were caused not by society's ills but by problems in the household. There was implied support for employers' paternalism and for acts of filial piety. For example, the article did not dispute working conditions or the capitalist system, as the above attack on left-wing thought indicates. In fact, these workers were still sending their salaries home to their parents as factory girls had done since the Meiji era of state-building. But there were some interesting modern touches, such as the statement by the cosmetics factory worker that "magazines are our best friend."[26]

The roundtable discussion among woman writer Yoshiya Nobuko and twelve department store employees in September 1935 considered the effect of department stores on family life in the major cities and provincial towns, along with the rising number of stores organized like department stores. It also recognized the tedious labor entailed in pleasing customers, in an article that was as much about the desires of consumer subjects as of the wants of the young women workers. In the words of Yoshiya, "Even if you kill your emotions with labor and service and work mechanically, since one is talking about a human being, it is inevitable that emotions will enter the picture." The discussion was punctuated by photographs that to some extent contradicted the text of the article: there was the employee dining hall, where "good friends make appointments to enjoy having lunch together," a photo of a "relaxation room set aside for women employees only," a picture of a *"morning concert"* at Matsuzakaya department store, and the photos of the young women studying calligraphy and flower arranging, and the singing of the company song at Shirokiya. The article did not deny social inequities. It reported that shoplifters and customers alike were allowed to return used merchandise after dressing their children in new outfits for the Seven-Five-Three festival, when girls of seven and three years in age and boys who were five were taken to pray at shrines. The working-class employees did not have this opportunity. But the gap between these working women and their customers was narrowed by the matter-of-fact admission of the young woman from the ready-to-wear Japanese-style clothing counter of Matsuzakaya in Ueno: "We are taught cooking, sewing, flower arranging, and sometimes tea ceremony in three-month semesters. We are able to prepare for the day when we will become housewives, while we work." The department store employee, like the factory girl, was outside of the household but was planning ultimately to be encompassed by it. Nowhere did it say that when she became a housewife that she would lose her connections to the outside world.[27]

The following month there was a roundtable discussion of "beautiful models." These women who posed for artists expressed pride that their profession afforded economic autonomy but were concerned that they were misunderstood by the public. The discussants endeavored to de-eroticize their profession, recalling their original embarrassment at posing nude. One proud participant made clear that models were the subjects of serious studies and works, whose bodies were transformed into works of art. But when it came to plans for the future, these women were no different from the department store employees and the factory workers. Some models such as the novelist Yokoyama Michiko and (blues singer) Awaya Noriko of Columbia Records, had gone on to fame. All agreed, but fame did not suffice. Although they would be prohibited from engaging in such household tasks as cooking rice because it would hurt their skin, like the department store employees, they looked forward to having households.[28]

While the models were not willing to discuss the relationship between their erotic lives and their occupation other than to disdain those who took the opportunity to stare at them salaciously, as late as January 1937 an article in *Shufu no Tomo* reported on a group of male critics gathered to lounge in easy chairs as they discussed such topics as marital fidelity and the duration of sexual attraction. (They thereby extended the preoccupation with eroticism into the end of the decade.) The gathering included Kiyosawa Retsu, who had written his "Studies of the Modern Girl" at the beginning of the modern era; Kataoka Teppei, who in 1926 had written "Woman's Legs"; and Kikuchi Kan, the popular novelist who had protested his inclusion in the novel about café waitresses. The men bemoaned the lack of opportunity for young men to meet young women socially, thus leading them to associate with café waitresses and geisha, and the inability of young Japanese women and men to express their natural desire for the opposite sex. They criticized women's schools for prohibiting men from attending school functions and debated the efficacy of arranged marriage before turning to a more graphic discussion of sexual behavior. When the discussion turned to marital fidelity, Kikuchi Kan quoted Bertrand Russell's opinion that it was unnatural for a couple to love each other forever inasmuch as it was like "asking someone to eat an apple a day." A man forced into such behavior was bound to resist, and it was impossible to keep him from falling in love with a beautiful young woman. He also noted, however, that a couple who had led a couple's existence for a long while created a "flesh-and-blood" link. Ultimately, this article was about a "couple's existence." Members of the group observed how in the United States couples separated for absurd reasons; that a solicitous, domesticated wife who had not lost her eroticism made the ideal partner; and that intellectual women were skeptical of such long-term relationships. The men placed the responsibility for the wife's sexual satisfaction with the husband, agreeing that frigidity was rare, that Western books explained that it was a question of timing, and that the trouble with Japanese husbands was that they finished much too quickly, leaving the women behind. On the other hand, the discussants had little sympathy for women who were not sufficiently vocal in resisting attacks on their chastity; it was "disreputable" to make an uproar that one had been attacked or seduced, after the fact.[29]

In October 1937, just months after the China Incident, Kikuchi Kan's "Discourse on Contemporary Marriage" eschewed any discussion of sex. In an essay that could easily have been approved by textbook censors for inclusion in *Girls' Morals of Today*, he eliminated any possible ambiguity about the relationship of the housewife to the working woman. Whereas a man could realize his talents without marrying, a woman could not. Only by combining the superior qualities of the man with the superior qualities of the woman could a unit of daily life be created: the married couple. Only within marriage could a woman bring to fruition her talents in household management, child-rearing, and especially, in expressing her love for her husband and children. No matter how bleak a marriage might be, it was better than remaining single for life.[30]

But Kikuchi had to come to terms with the state's need for the working woman. Not all discussions could afford to sound like the fantasies expounded by the bourgeois bride-to-be in "A Roundtable of Young Women of Osaka Talking of the Ideal Marriage" who was willing to compromise in marrying a merchant if her residence could be in the suburbs. After dismissing women doctors, women teachers, midwives, and nurses as irrelevant to his discussion, Kikuchi urged young women from "below the middle class" to become office workers, sales clerks, "*elevator girls*," and bus conductors. Not only was this pundit open to the notion of a working-class working woman, but he urged such readers to keep their jobs after marriage, if they were lucky enough to find a spouse, concluding that "being a working woman should be both a preparation for marriage and for the sake of married life."[31]

How are we to reconcile the coexistence of the concerns for the household—(1) the centrality of the quest for a mate, (2) the avoidance of housewife anger, and (3) the encouragement of a modern life for the modern women out in the world and home in the house—with the official state *ie* ideology? (It should be noted that the term *katei* was in use in the media by the turn of the century. See for example, *Katei Zasshi*, which translates as "Household Magazine"). Nishikawa Yūko argues that the *katei* (household) system and *ie* ideology were not diametrically opposed; she describes a system wherein the household and the family reinforced one another because the Civil Code encouraged second and third sons to create their own nuclear

families or *katei* in the cities or the colonies, leaving the eldest son to continue the line of the stem family. Systemically, this is true, and it is also true
that ultimately, as Nishikawa points out that the *katei* was used for the ends
of the state. The *shufu* was told that her husband was needed at the front.
The transition to this state of military readiness can be seen in such articles
as the May 1933 piece referring to the invasion of Manchuria that quizzed
the housewife about her preparation for the "State of Emergency." By May
1940 when "The Issues Relating to Women Working under the Incident"
implicitly supported the invasion of China, *Shufu no Tomo* had abandoned
any presumption that there was tension between working and maintaining
a household. Nonetheless, until the second half of the 1930s, a modern sense
of play and irony still countered the sensibility of the state ideology. This
was evident in the cartoons, interviews, and commentary relating to family
and male-female relationships in *Shufu no Tomo*.[32]

By following articles from the late 1930s through the war years, as
Wakakuwa Midori has done, in word and in image, we are soon made aware
that the modern moment had passed. The housewife was no longer half of
a couple; she was on the home front, and her husband was at war. The
shokugyō fujin had been displaced by the "working daughter," the "working wife," the "working mother," and the "working widow." The director of
the Tokyo Metropolitan Employment Agency looked back nostalgically to
the era when there had been "fads" in employment. In 1920, the few
women who had applied for work had all wanted to be office workers; the
next fad was employment in department stores (10,500 young girls had responded to a recruitment call based on the availability of one thousand jobs).
Now, "when factories are springing up like bamboo shoots after the rain,
women are wanting factory work." He asked the women to "take on the
burden of the workplace of Japan in the Emergency Era." But they were
not—like their European female predecessors at the end of World War I—
to presume that once the war was over, they should remain at their jobs.[33]

The model of a married woman was now nationalist, culturalist, and ma-
ternalist. The model housewife, in other words, was a model because she was
a Japanese mother. According to the reportage in *Shufu no Tomo*, when Yamada Waka visited Eleanor Roosevelt in the White House on December 7,
1937, she did not go to hear about American family values but rather to give
the president's wife access to the voices of Japanese women, since clearly
Mrs. Roosevelt had "already heard enough of the words of the women on
the Chinese side." After receiving a briefing at the Japanese Embassy that
included "A Documentary Movie of the China Incident" and "raw sushi,"
Yamada presented her case to Eleanor Roosevelt and to "American women

of the intellectual class" in terms of the suffering mothers in both China and Japan. Her concern, she insisted, transcended "the detailed problems of politics and economics." Aiming to counter the "terrible propaganda" by the women of China regarding "Japan's extreme barbarity," she told Roosevelt that "as mothers of the human race, we cannot bear that the blood of countless of our sons is flowing in the course of battle." Identifying herself as a member of the *Shufu no Tomo* staff and an activist in the Japanese "Movement to Protect Motherhood," Yamada protested that the "pure Japanese people, especially women," acknowledged that the Japanese were indebted to China. The "foundations of Japanese culture" had all come from China, two thousand years of friendly exchange with that country had been marked only by goodwill, and the current war "aimed firstly at the happiness of China, and then at the creation of the foundation of the establishment of world peace."[34]

Yamada's essentialist propaganda for the Japanese war effort was a graphic illustration of the end of the modern, as I have conceived it. There was no sense of historic break, or presentism, or eagerness to move between cultures; neither was there an awareness that the everyday was constantly being made anew, in part via new gestures. Nonetheless, it behooves us to remember that until the second half of the 1930s, a sense of play and irony coexisted with the belief that there was space for the housewife to move between the household and the outside world. In the pages of *Shufu no Tomo* during the years preceding the morphing of the Modern Girl into the mother on the home front, cartoons and interviews relating to the Modern Girl's family and to her male-female relationships challenged the culturalist asceticism of the era. To say that the Modern Girl had morphed into a Japanese mother is anachronistic, but it expresses the visual and contextual jump in *Shufu no Tomo* from modern to wartime imagery. Another example of this unexplained shift is the sudden appearance of garish, multicolored insets of mythical Japanese female figures in the pages of *Shufu no Tomo* where Hollywood starlets had once appeared. What I am concluding before further documenting the irony of the modern era that disappeared from historical memory, is that while the Modern Girl was given credit for new gestures, she was not allowed to mature gracefully in order to have a personal history. In this shift from one female icon to another, there were neither acknowledged historical breaks nor transitions. The Modern Girl did not age into womanhood. She merely disappeared and the wartime mother appeared. A wartime culture of new rituals was in fact being created; it was no longer acknowledged that the everyday was constantly being remade in innumerable movements and gestures. Instead of the whirling, unfixed, transnational figure of the Modern Girl moving within an unfixed, eroticized mass culture, Japanese housewife-subjects who picked up *Shufu no Tomo* were faced with the immaculate static mother without husband, who was married, as it were, to the nation.

But let us go back to the self-conscious alliance with the modern by looking at the discussion of the *seikatsu* of the Modern Girl and the other new gestures made available to the housewife-reader who just might crave *"toast"* rather than rice-bran soybean paste.

MODERN TIMES FOR THE HOUSEWIFE

The Modern took on different forms in *Shufu no Tomo* from the earthquake into the Pacific War. The Modern Girl, the most clearly recognizable and the most ubiquitous image of the modern, has her place alongside a modern imperial family, and such modern mores as moviegoing. Modernity could also be implied through the discussion of new forms of body language. By the late 1930s, however, such attention to new gestures was fading as a concern for the colonial and traditional and the increasing mobilization for war had displaced the interest in the new and the modern.

The Modern Girl was prominently displayed in the cartoon series *Mogako and Moborō* penned for *Shufu no Tomo* in 1928 by Tanaka Hisarō. In conformity with most representations of the Modern Girl, Mogako was given the main role. This Modern Girl was garbed in a flapper's dress revealing legs that were decidedly not slender. She accentuated her hips with a low-slung belt, called attention to her bust with lines of fringe, and was also decorated with a national symbol not usually identified with the Modern Girl. It is possible that this small Japanese flag fastened in her bobbed hair represented the position taken by some critics. In other words, perhaps it signaled that this Modern Girl was not to be confused with her American and European contemporaries. The flag figured prominently: at the beginning of each segment of Mogako's dialogue, where the cartoonist placed a smiling Mogako face with the flag tucked into a headband and perched at cocky angle. Mogako and her Modern Boy companion, who was fitted out in diamond-patterned jacket, cuffed baggy pants, cloth hat, pipe, and walking stick, appeared in three issues at the end of 1928.[35]

In September 1928, the episode "The Tale of the Vanishing Thin Clothing" had the heroine responding to an edict with private vigilante actions. From the outset, Mogako immediately takes charge by attacking a woman in a thin kimono, and explaining her actions in terms similar to the criticism mobilized against Modern Girls in the press.

> MOGAKO: Wearing such thin clothing is indecent, so you must stop it; you're shaming the women of Japan.
>
> WOMAN: What about your thin clothing?
>
> MOGAKO: Mine is mysterious, artful, original, cultured, maidenly, and expressive. Some things are just appropriate and some aren't, but yours are suggestive and degenerate.

Mogako then rips the kimono off the woman, yelling "Oh this is too much trouble—just go walk naked!" and hands her victim twenty yen in reparations, just as the shamed woman is boarding the subway. After victimizing various others in the name of the state, Mogako meets up with Moborō (whose dialogue is introduced by a narrow face defined by a flat Western cap, glasses, and a pipe). He persuades her to accompany him to the resort town of Atami, where there are both hot springs and ocean.[36]

The next episode, "The Tale of Atami Hot Springs," offers a twist on the popular image of the transgressive Modern Girl in bathing suit painted by both Yamakawa Kikue and Tanizaki Junichirō. Here Mogako confounds women bathers by wearing a bathing suit in the hot springs bath, where all go naked, and bewilders Moborō by baring her breasts to him from offshore while all around her are clad in bathing suits. (Her Japanese flag remains on her head.) Her lyrical defense against Moborō's accusation that her behavior is confused can be read as an ironic parody of the ideology of chastity and of the purity of maidenhood: "The translucent skin of a maiden under a translucent moon; the barrier of a bathing suit against the impure hot springs bathers; my behavior's not at all topsy-turvy."[37]

Mogako does not say that she is challenging the ideology of female propriety, but her extreme, alternative behavior must have given her readers pause. It is difficult to read either cartoon character seriously, but a third story does evoke a sense of sexually charged obsession and violent control. Here as elsewhere in the documents of Japanese modern times, the emphasis is on female sexuality. In this narrative, Moborō pleads with Mogako to bestow affection on him lest he be sentenced to live in the dark. When he places his hat over his face to invoke blindness, her response is to cut holes in the hat, transforming it into a mask that allows him to see out but renders him invisible. To call Mogako a sadist might be extreme, but she is clearly in control. She is self-centered and concerned only with sensual pleasures, and she is possessed of an extra touch of transgressive perversity.[38]

The 1927 article in cartoon format "A True Beauty," makes use of another Modern Girl to poke fun at the government regulation of culture. The introduction to this comic strip about the young woman who wishes to attract bourgeois men to dance to the *"jazz"* at her dance hall is framed by a drawing of a film strip and the reader is told the tale is an "educational movie" recommended by the Ministry of Education. Yet another detailed portrait of a Modern Girl in the same issue, "I Graduated from Girls' School, But . . . " puts a feminist spin on contemporary satires of the education system and the inability of the middle class to find employment by the end of the 1920s. The title provided a play on the buzz phrase of the era that was also voiced in Ozu Yasujirō's social commentary comedies, *I Graduated from College, But . . .* (1929), *I Flunked, But . . .* (1930), and his award-winning feature, *I Was Born, But . . .* (1932). The cartoon story is about a young woman with no marriage prospects who cannot sew, clean, or cook. She defends her inability to provide salted rice-bran paste for her father's breakfast by retorting that she has not even mastered this first lesson in the art of being a wife because she refuses to marry into a house where they criticize the pickled vegetables. Code-switching with ease, she also refuses to marry into a place that does not have *bread* and *oatmeal* and *coffee*. Her mother's lesson in cleaning is met with a disdainful "Japanese people are just really too fastidious; I really cannot stand it." The desires of this Modern Girl are to read, to dance so frantically to the strains of jazz that the family Buddha threatens to fall off the altar, and to sing popular songs while she has a chance, for she will not be allowed to sing after marrying. Ultimately, this modern girl is also defiant. In the segment titled "Learning," the mother tells her daughter that she has no need of schooling beyond girls' school, since her goal is to grab hold of a husband. The daughter repeats, "The era is different. The era is different."[39]

The humorous commentary on family life described above rejected the ideology of the harmonious family within the nation as family. Moreover, this attitude extended to the magazine's presentation of the imperial family. *Shufu no Tomo* offered its readers articles about the Imperial family that placed them within the nuclear family, within modern culture. The emperor and his family were ever-present in *Shufu no Tomo*, although the experience of living within a family was not defined, as in the state ideology, which celebrated a patrilineal *ie* that reached back over the generations into the mythic past. Instead, members of the Imperial family were presented in terms of a small-scale household. Monarchical power and disciplinary power may have come together under the Meiji emperor, as Takashi Fujitani had shown. But the images offered to the *Shufu no Tomo* reader were not about disciplining, nor about instilling a sense of nationhood, as traced by Carol Gluck. Instead, in words and photographs in *Shufu no Tomo*, the Imperial family was domesticated and commodified. By *domesticated* I mean that they were represented as members of a *katei* or household. As a result, they did not appear separate and apart from the readership. By *commodification* I mean that by the very nature of the montage within the magazine whereby articles about imperial personages were juxtaposed with numerous other articles and advertisements, they could be seen as one of many items being advertised within Japanese modern culture.[40]

In April 1930, readers were treated to a family album of the Shōwa emperor: this issue of *Shufu no Tomo* featured numerous pages of images showing the emperor, his empress, his siblings, his daughters, and other royal relatives engaged in such Imperial everyday royal doings as observing an army drill practice. The commodification process is evident in one two-page spread. A circular photograph of the emperor's nuclear family was placed across from the advertisement for Yamasa Soy Sauce, which urged the reader not to dismiss the cherry blossoms (and the emperor?) as outdated. The reader was also encouraged to recognize the taste of Yamasa as beloved in any era. It was "beloved, of high quality," it was "ever-improving," it was "progress." The same issue of *Shufu no Tomo* paired an ad for Higeta Soy Sauce—identified as the official choice of the Imperial household—with a photograph of a circle of imperial princesses and princes seated on rattan chairs and enjoying a mountain landscape. The "Gathering in Hakone" appeared no different from any gathering of upper- or maybe even middle-class modern men and women in this Japanese mountain resort. The men were adorned in suits and borselinos and the women favored the fashion sported by modern girls on *Ginza* and in the media. This was clearly an Imperial version of the *yuka* or leisure activity so eagerly theorized by such modern authorities as Gonda. The surroundings of this group enjoying a family outing may have been a bit more comfortable, but it was an experience as available to the modern middle class. This was the message given to readers who opened *Shufu no Tomo* to these two pages. The royal outing of this group was no different from the leisure activities engaged in by their family members.

There could of course still be overt reference to the family-state ideology in the magazine. A decade after the great Kantō earthquake, in the August issue of 1932, *Shufu no Tomo* readers were reminded of the benevolence of the empress dowager, who had chosen to eat plain fare and to wear domestically manufactured cosmetics in the days following the earthquake, as part of an effort to fund a home for "lepers." This discussion was placed in the context of the state ideology of family: the Japanese nation was an extension of the Imperial family, the emperor was its head, and the readers, as subjects, were subservient family members.[41]

Two years later, in May of 1934, the nuclear-family image was emphasized in an account of the first year in the life of the crown prince. The January 1935 issue was bordered by a drawing of fair-haired, winged cherubs and carried a full-page baby picture. In this issue the emphasis was on the noble motherhood of the empress, who, although by no means a *shufu,* or housewife, had set an example for readers by personally feeding the prince. Readers were to identify with the cuteness of the baby, not with their place in an ordering of Imperial family hierarchy. By implication, the emperor was the father of his private family, not the father of a family-state. Although the emperor was almost entirely absent from this family picture, readers were told how he entered the chamber of the crown prince in order to play with his heir. It is true that in January 1935, the ideologue Tokutomi Sohō offered a series of anecdotal stories illustrating the divinity of the emperor, his dedication to his people and to science, and his cosmopolitanism. But such articles were outnumbered by articles suggesting that the emperor, too, had a *seikatsu* and did not belong to a separate realm.[42]

While there were references to the new Japan of the Shōwa era in *Shufu no Tomo,* explicit references to *kindai* and *modan* made clear that the new moment was not only defined by transition in the imperial reign. Immediate material concerns close at hand were as meaningful (if not more so) to the housewife-readers as the achievements of those at the apex of their ostensibly nation-sized family. In March 1932, an advertisement heralded the modernity of a cosmetic product—it was *kindaiteki,* as was a bride featured in October of the following year. Western food was also modern, as were Mickey Mouse and the secret of buying inexpensive items at the department store.[43]

The imperial family was being modernized by implication but there were much more direct reference to other modern phenomena. The *Modern Manzai* (modern comedic dialogue) of Ōtsuji Shirō and Yokoyama Entatsu, one of the most popular duos of the time, associated modernity with trafficking in women. This was similar to the association of sex (and violence) with war in *Eiga no Tomo,* but with a lighter, less political touch. Their nonsensical dialogue of May 1936 was titled "A Show-Off Battle Comparing Tokyo Women to Osaka Women." The comics first exchanged ad hominem insults: Ōtsuji was likened to a monkey, and Yokoyama was alerted that his pose resembled Charlie Chaplin "turned inside out" and would cause indigestion. But the *fūfu* was still the topic for modern humor and the department store the emblematic site of the present (only months after the February 26 coup attempt on the government, which went unmentioned). In response to Ōtsuji's implication that Osaka women were tight-fisted, Yokoyama responded that Tokyo women were so cheap that they would pay off obligations by sharing bathhouse water with their neighbors. With sarcasm, Yokoyama admired the patience of the husbands of the Tokyo women who bought clothing on a whim when they determined that a clothing pattern did not agree with them, and then neglected to return the first, undesired purchase. At the department stores, these same husbands acted as "parcel-carriers" and babysitters.[44]

Two months later, in July 1936, Saijō Yaso, the lyricist of "Tokyo March" and numerous other popular songs, and the artist Miyamoto Saburō joined forces to caption a series of full-page tableaus of summer scenes, that were even more sardonic than Ōtsuji and Entatsu. In "*Album of Modern Tokyo Night Scenes*" the Ginza of Kon Wajirō (Saijō called it "*Café Corner*") was given its due, as was Gonda Yasunosuke's Asakusa ("*Cinema Corner*"). Saijō picked out people from the Asakusa crowd: the workers waiting for the discount bell at the movies, an old woman from the countryside visiting with her daughter, an apprentice geisha, and the inevitable *lumpen* or hobo asleep on a bench, his empty belly viewed with empathy by the overfed carp in the lake. The last of the ten tableaux told the story of a "*romance*" between a young woman and a Modern Boy who could only summon up the nerve to say, "I love you" (rendered as *ai rabu yuu*) when his roadster was going at "high *speed.*" When he was forbidden to speed, that was the end of their love. In sum, images and elements associated with the modern, such as the Modern Girl and Boy, speed, and selected sites in Tokyo were still in evidence a decade after Kon and his fellow modernologists studied everyday life, and half a decade after the invasion of Manchuria.[45] In July 1937, the month that saw the outbreak of the North China Incident, *Shufu no Tomo* made it clear that domestic tension between *fūfu* was still on the agenda, with "*Modern* Newlywed Photographic Verse." A series of verses accompanied by photographs told the story of a housewife forcing her husband to awaken on a Sunday so that she can clean house, while he worries about the lottery. The wife sits impassively by her husband's side as he tastes dinner, after which he comments that it is the smell of her makeup and not of the mushrooms that disturbs him. In the last photo, the modern couple wrangles over gender difference as they prepare for an outing: men's constant need to shave is disgusting, and women take too long in adjusting their *obi.*[46]

There had been more implicit references to modern transformation in the magazine—as when, in September 1932, Tokutomi Sohō decried two current fads in an article in *Shufu no Tomo:* according to Tokutomi, suicide and a Western-oriented philosophy of rights, based on the rejection of a three-thousand-year-old (imperial) spirit of loyalty and filial piety, had led to the degeneration of mores. Another article in April 1934 on cooking food that was popular in eateries frequented by the masses *(taishū shokudō)*, had shown that modern mores were being adopted by all classes. Moreover, in this article no distinctions were made among Chinese, Japanese, and Western food. *Ham* and eggs with *mayonnaise,* jellyfish with white vinegar, and *shūmai* rice (pork dumplings with a somewhat exoticized side dish of *raisu*) were not culturally different. They were associated because they could be made for little cost and minimal effort within the home. The article had blurred both class and colonial distinctions and any barrier between practices in public and household *seikatsu.* (The housewife-reader could choose to replicate the *"special lunches"* and the fixed-price dinners within her own household. It was implied that the reader might dine out inexpensively but that she had a choice as to when she would do so, just as she had the choice of what dishes to make for her family at the cost of ten or twenty sen per person, per dish.[47]

Not only did the pages of *Shufu no Tomo* offer the housewife-reader modern foods, it also allowed her to participate in the modern leisure activity of going to the movies. She was able to do this via the "Movie Tales" *(Eiga Monogatari)*. These were stories that were accompanied by stills, plot synopses, and a listing of such credits as screenwriter, director, leads, and production company. Modern food had not been marked as foreign and neither were the movies. For example, the 1927 American sensation *It,* a film central to the Japanese discourse of *ero,* was presented in the seven-part series "That" ("Are") in October 1927. The series in *Shufu no Tomo* opened with the following explication by the author of the original story, Elinor Glyn, and the Japanese wording was a fairly close translation of the words appearing on the screen at the opening of the American film: "That is a characteristic of certain people, and those people use that force of captivation to draw in all others. If you are a woman, you can have all men, and if you are a man, you can have all women if you possess *that.* In other words, *that* refers to an attraction of mind and of body."[48]

What followed in six framed boxes, each with a photograph from the film and a paragraph-long caption, was the story of Betty Lou, the character played by the "It Girl," Clara Bow. In the picture story, Betty Lou (after clearing up a misunderstanding regarding an illegitimate child) captures the heart of the boss's son, Cyrus, who runs Waltham's department store. The narrative of this tale was true to the original when it told the *Shufu no Tomo* readers that "he was captive to her That [It]" and that "his That [It] drew her to him." And it gave its readership some context at the end: *It* had been written by Glyn and had driven the youth of the United States wild when it had been serialized in *Cosmopolitan*. The *Shufu no Tomo* series taught the housewife-readers, that the words "that person's kind of got *It*" and "you've got *It*" were now in vogue. One inconsistency between the American film and the Japanese film-tale was the presumption in the Japanese version of jealousy among Betty's coworkers. This embellishment points up the fact that such narratives were not mere copies, but translations that were also active creations. The change was minor, but it was a code switch.[49]

The differences in script can be explained by the fact that the writers for *Friend of the Housewife* were working under some constraints. In other words, some plots sold, and working girls as Modern Girls with gumption, along with class inequity, poverty, and the triumph of the state of married coupledom over all, also emerged in the tales of other American films featured in *Shufu no Tomo*. In *The Sorrows of Satan*, translated into Japanese as *Satan no Nageki* (Satan's lament), directed by D. W. Griffith, the struggling writer (Tempest) leaves his equally impoverished love (Mavis) in pursuit of glory as a pulp-fiction writer. Tempest also seeks status by marrying Olga, a Russian princess, after Satan appears before him garbed in tuxedo and silk hat. Our hero soon becomes aware of his folly as his wedded state disintegrates into "marriage hell," and he begins to question the purpose of everyday married *(fūfu)* existence. In the end Tempest abandons all wealth and status to live happily ever after with Mavis. In *Ladies at Play*, titled in Japanese *Otoko o Miru Bekarazu* (Thou shalt not look at men), the heroine, Ann, receives word that she must marry within three days in order to receive an inheritance of six million dollars from a distant relative, who has also dictated that her two eccentric aunts must approve of the engagement. Ann and her little sister Betty—marked as Modern Girls not only by their willingness to manipulate men but also by a desire to cross-dress on occasion—decide to use Gilbert, a worker in charge of the mailroom in the hotel where the sisters are staying, in a scheme to elicit the approval of the aunts. Class resentment temporarily wins out when Gil refuses to play the role of Ann's fiancé, declaring, "Rich girls think they can buy anything." But in the end, all is well: Ann gets the money, Gil gets Ann, and Ann gives Betty her money—which she will not need in her new existence as the wife of a hotel worker.[50]

The reader who had no access to Hollywood movies because she was in the countryside, busy in the household or the workplace, or isolated at an

Imperial outpost could read the story from the text of the "Movie Tales." If she was not inclined to follow the fantasies so carefully in words, she could speed-read the tale by turning the pages to trace the narrative. Ideally, the photo on each page was to be read in conjunction with its text, but the message of these montages of word and image was fairly clear: these were picture stories—the photographs could take up twice as much space as the captions. In "That," the close-ups of Clara Bow, her lovers' spat (with Antonio Moreno), and the embrace marking their reconciliation said enough to fuel a fantasy. Such body language needed no translation. Similarly, the reader of the photo-essay "Comedy Routines from a New Household" might not be able to infer the punch lines from the photos, but the intimate, dialogic body language of the married pair leaning toward each other, gazing in the same direction, or separately but together engaged in the solitary act of reading within the same shared household space, sent a direct message that this story, while it might be billed as comedy like so many others in the magazine, was a serious celebration of the *fūfu*.[51]

The visual culture of *Shufu no Tomo* drew not only on body language but also on new forms of bodily practices. These were prescribed within the implicit discussion of appropriate modern behavior, and organized around code-switching, as in the case of the January 1930 "How to Cook Western Dishes for a New Year's Banquet." This article, which included such dishes as "pigeon fried in *butter*," "beef and vegetable *jelly*," "*sandwiches*" (which, in an article two years later, would no longer be identified as Western), "*royal pudding*," and "*hot lemon tea*," presumed that such fare had a rightful place in the national holidays, including New Year's, the holiday most identified as traditional. In other words, the implication was that these Western foods were being produced from within indigenous household and history. (To again refer to Todorov's formulation regarding intercultural relations and constructions, it was taken for granted that Western culture could be constitutive of modern, national Japanese culture, if not a traditional one.)[52]

The ink sketches of the seven banquet courses were not the only blueprints for new routines for the housewife's New Year. The following January, there was an article on appropriate comportment for guest and host during the New Year's round of visits. The written text did not always clearly conform to the uniform message offered by the photographs. The arrow above the exhortation that the housewife should introduce bright topics of conversation, such as memories of the past year and hopes for the coming year, pointed to a somber-faced young housewife seated primly with hands folded in lap, her kimono sleeves draped carefully over her *za-*

buton. She was seated next to a wooden brazier which was equally inert. The message in all nine images was the necessity for the careful alignment of the body—whether the housewife knelt on an Oriental carpet, served tea to a guest seated at a Western-style table, or bowed in New Year's greeting to the same guest in front of the same table.[53]

The ideals of health and beauty were added to the focus on disciplining body language, in an article on the correct way to sit. This prescriptive piece featured a series of images of a young woman, hair in a bun, rounded body in a bathing suit. The poses were: woman in bathing suit seated on a chair, seated on the floor, seated while writing; woman in bathing suit seated in proper floor sitting position; woman in bathing suit seated writing; woman doing calculations; and woman in bathing suit typing at the office. Two of the modern poses were sewing kimono material while seated on the floor and holding a tea cup demurely. (Here she was allowed to cheat, in a posture that allowed her to lean her weight on one thigh.) The woman also read at a low table, and sat on the floor with her hands on her thighs and her back arched. This article, illustrated by the proper bathing beauty was produced by such officials as a Ministry of Education official and the principal of a higher school that trained girls to be seamstresses. It offered the everyday activities deemed appropriate for a woman in September 1936 at the same time that it exposed body parts that had been subject to censorship during the heyday of *ero guro nansensu.*[54]

In December 1933, six differing uses of kitchen space were detailed in a photo-essay with diagrams more than worthy of Kon Wajirō's approval. The message was that the housewives of the "new family" were to move efficiently through kitchens like those of Madam Hatoyama Ichirō, the wife of the minister of education. In the photographs Madam Hatoyama and her daughter moved with no wasted effort, from chopping board to *"gas range"* to sink, and back and forth from knife holder, to broom holder, to dish pantry and cupboard. The rational face of a large, boldly numbered kitchen clock looked down in one of the pictures as though to remind the reader of an always present relationship between space and time. Another housewife, married to a well-known actor, offered her philosophy of "kitchen centrism" in a similarly outfitted kitchen. It was a hygienic room (complete with a large calendar marking each day) with a page to be discarded at the appropriate moment before the family could take advantage of the opportunity to spend the entire day in the clean, modern, rational space. The *shufu* was being encouraged to believe in simplification in *seikatsu,* or her daily life, as much as in efficiency.[55]

The woman in the bathing suit and the women in the kitchen fit into the history of the state's efforts to rationalize housework as discussed by Sheldon Garon. Here I place them into the history of Japanese modern culture experienced as *seikatsu* not imposed from above, but as a choice or series of choices originating from below. It cannot be denied that *Shufu no Tomo* did express a strong element of disciplining by rational state officials, and that there was also a marked increase in such discussion after 1937. The 1931 article featuring the bride in kimono greeting the New Year for the first time was similar to the 1936 article on "How to Sit." The body of the housewife was shown to be adjusted not only for the sake of ritual but also for the sake of efficiency, health, and appearance. But there were two very big differences: by 1937, the *shufu* as bride could easily connote a family larger and less flexible than a *katei*. Moreover, the choice of New Year's behavior, here marked as traditional, implied cultural continuity, not modernity.

Nonetheless, while the word *modern* was not always employed, and the above article about traditional New Year's behavior notwithstanding, it was clear that the editors and the readers of *Shufu no Tomo* (like the community of *Eiga no Tomo*) were not eager to let go of the modern during the 1930s. As evidence, Mickey Mouse appeared in May 1934, and a January 1936 article revealed the existence of secret dance halls. (All dance halls would be shut down for good on November 1, 1940.) In another example, a 1934 roundtable discussion on apartment-house living made no reference to a "family system" while recounting the experience of single and married women and men who had eschewed the "double life" of switching between Japanese and Western material practices. Apartment-house living was for those who had chosen a purely Westernized mode of life. For example, one could not choose to wear clogs in apartment houses; nor could kimono sandals be left outside the house, because they would be stolen. Participants in the roundtable agreed that what was significant was the choice by some to adopt what they thought of as strictly Western practices. Unlike other articles, this discussion did not displace the term "Western" with the concept of modernity; in this instance, it can be argued that the modern was not seen as universal.[56]

The article also revealed that daughters of the upper class were choosing the apartment-house *seikatsu* and that certain apartment houses could be used as marital references to attest to the character of the young, unmarried female. Apartment-house living was also redefining social relations by restricting the living space of the middle class. One participant implied how new configurations of privacy had to be created when he complained of the absence of a receiving area for guests who arrived early in the morning, before the host had risen. He also pointed to the American-style locks on the

Japanese Modern within Modernity

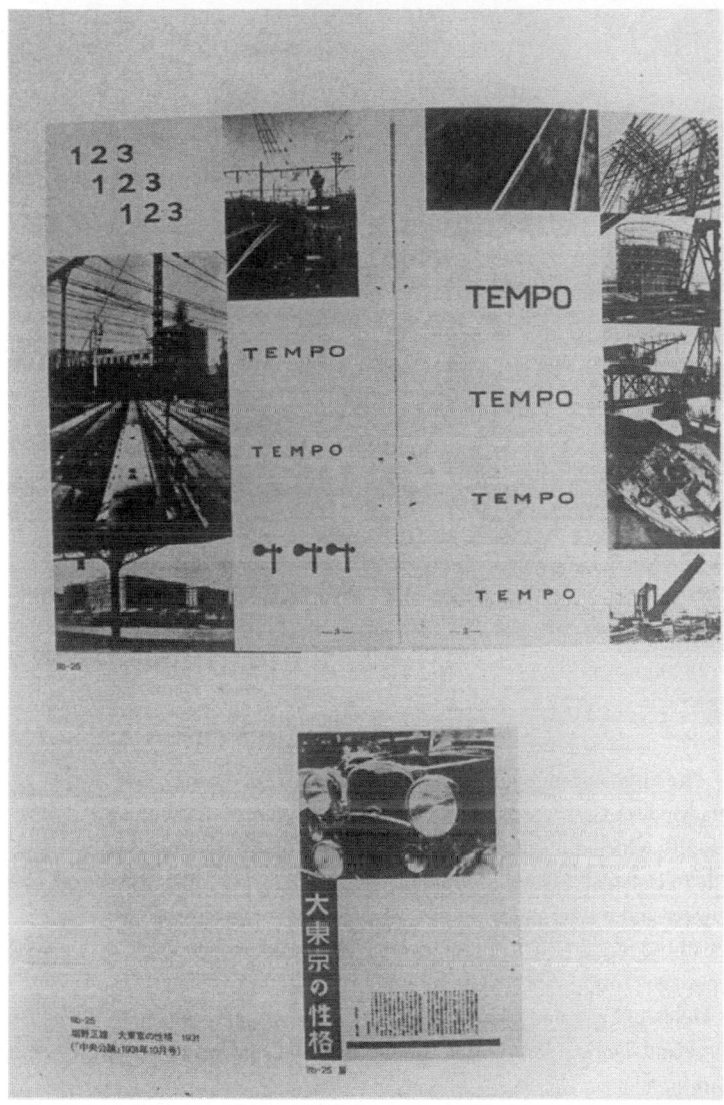

1. Photographs by Horino Masao from "Characteristics of Greater Tokyo," *Chūō Kōron*, October 1931. Courtesy of *Chūō Kōron*.

2. The English-language text under the title "The Day-Dream of a Modern Girl" reads, "Here is a fantastic picture of the modern girl, which our photographer, after an exhaustive effort, was able to construct. There seem to be dances, pictures, Cocktails, powder and rouge, and what not, all closely associated with the life of the modern girl and no more!" The sardonic Japanese-language caption refers to a camera fantasy, and the disinterest of Helen of Troy, and Cleopatra in the fleshy *moga*, who is to serve and dance. *Asahi Graph*, June 13, 1928. Courtesy of *Asahi Shinbunsha*.

3. The dreams of a salaryman are represented by such objects as
a restaurant menu, a box of the popular Golden Bat cigarettes, a
bottle of beer juxtaposed with the image of a café waitress, a
commuter train, and a pawnshop sign. According to the English-
language caption, this photomontage symbolizes the life of the
Japanese "salaried-man." The Japanese text interprets the montage as a commentary on the dizzying existence of the *sarari-
man*, who must measure the distance he walks and who is sur-
rounded by a complaining wife, management on cocaine, and the
threat of unemployment. The salaryman's commuter train is
placed in montage, along with the menu of a cheap establishment where he is allowed to unwind once a month. *Asahi
Graph,* June 20, 1928. Courtesy of *Asahi Shinbunsha.*

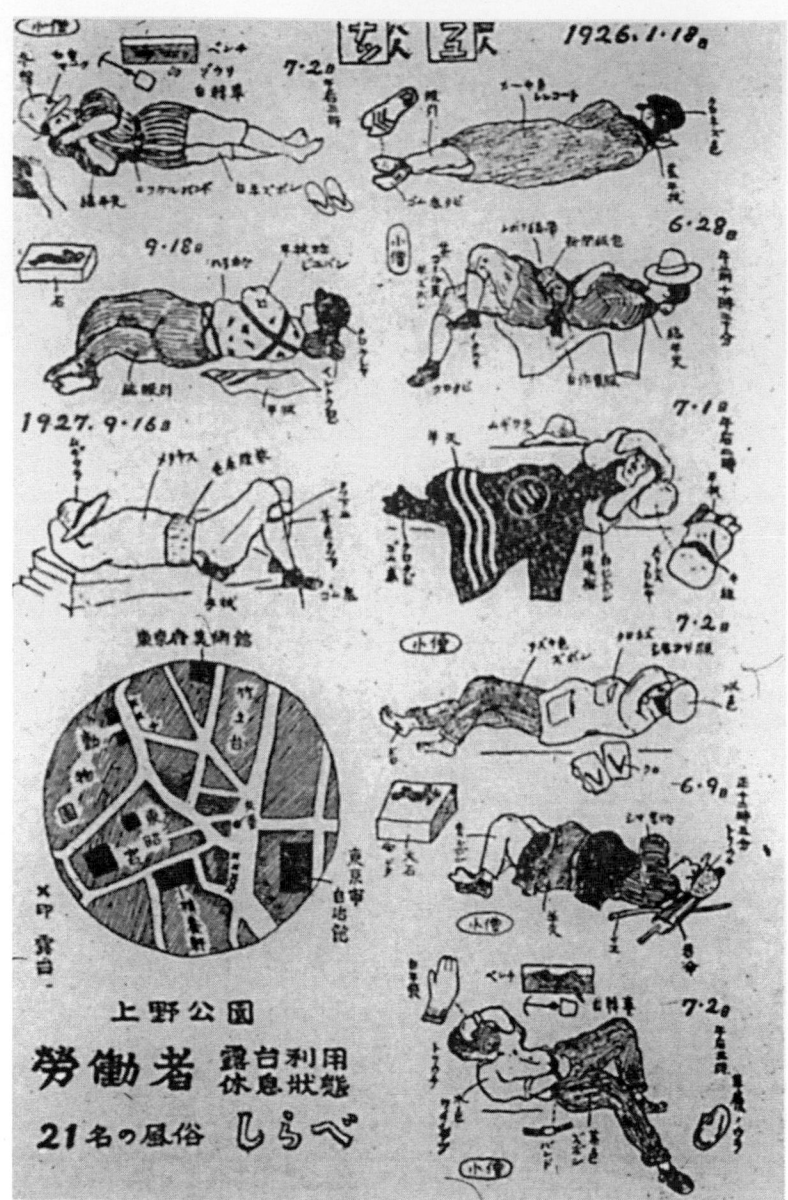

4. Arai Sen'o, "Survey of positions of laborers at rest in Ueno Park," January 18, 1926. From Kon Wajirō and Yoshida Kenkichi, *Moderunologio (Kōgengaku)*. This illustration by Arai pinpointed for each figure location within the park, date, time of day, and articles of apparel in addition to body language. Courtesy of Gakuyō Shobō.

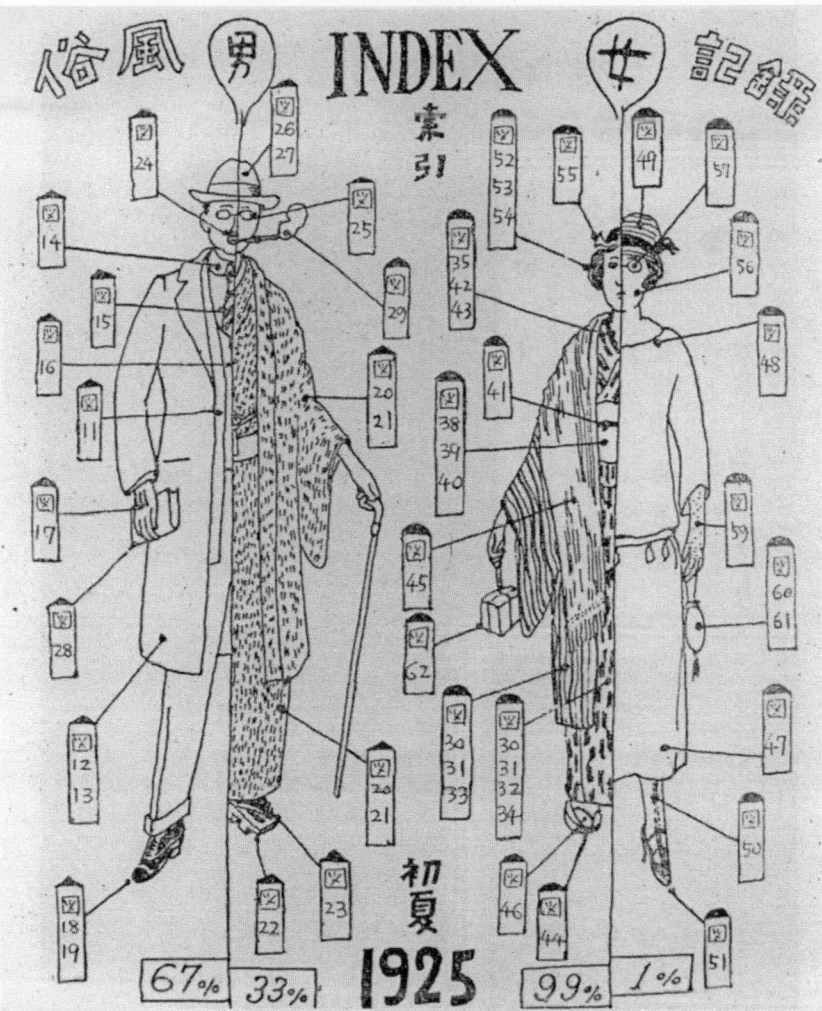

5. Drawing accompanying the article "Record of Tokyo Ginza Mores in the Early Summer of 1925," *Fujin Kōron* (Women's opinion), July 1925, republished in the anthology *Moderunologio* in 1930. This drawing illustrates the findings of Kon Wajirō's first modernology survey, conducted with Yoshida Kenkichi and assistants. The text explains that the numbers in the illustration refer to differences in the wearing of Japanese and Western clothing. The readers were asked to note that 67 percent of the men wore Western clothing, whereas 99 percent of the women were in Japanese dress. The data came from observing the dress of 1,180 people on Ginza at various times of day. From Kon and Yoshida, *Moderunologio*. Courtesy of Gakuyō Shobō.

6. Readers of the January 1931 issue of *Shūkan Asahi* were invited to join
in on the new, *modern* form of conversation for 1931, by sending in captions
to accompany the silent yet meaningful pose of the movie actress at the top
of the page. The model to follow was the interpretation of the gesture at bottom left as body language for 9:30.

7. "Clothing *Cocktails* of Students," *Asahi Graph*, April 9, 1930. Note the use of English and the caption below the title that reads, "Showing Japanese schoolboys and girls as they are usually seen in the streets. It is a curious sort of vanity that makes some of them proud of disfigurement." In contrast, the Japanese-language captions historicize styles from the Meiji and the Taishō eras. The rubber boots worn by the little *moga*s in the center of the montage are an example of one contemporary fashion. Courtesy of *Asahi Shinbunsha*.

The Modern Girl as Militant

8. Kageyama Kōyō, "Mogas' Beach Pajama Style," 1928. The photographer noted that at the same time as the skies were darkening over Asia, the emotions of the common people were taken over by sentimental songs. He added that around that time, vigorous *moga* dressed in beach pajamas and straw hats appeared on Ginza and were much discussed. Courtesy of Kageyama Tomohiro.

9. Advertisement for fountain pen. *Kaizō*, September, 1931.

10. The Lady Beauty Shop specialized in permanents. Courtesy of Fujimori Terunobu, Hatsuda Tōru, Fujioka royasu.

11. A Modern Girl in a café. The text reads: "I am completely drunk. So come on, please come unlock the door to my room." Courtesy of Shiseido.

12. Abe Sada after her arrest, May 20, 1936. Courtesy of Shōgakukan.

The Café Waitress Sang the Blues

13. The Salon Manchuria *(top)* shared the second floor of the Ginza Palace with Salon Momoyama *(bottom)*. In the Manchurian space, Japanese café waitresses dressed in Chinese fashion matched the decor, which aimed at a modernized Chinese look. The section dedicated to the Momoyama era catered to nostalgia for an earlier, decorative age. Courtesy of Fujimori Terunobu, Hatsuda Tōru, Fujioka Hiroyasu.

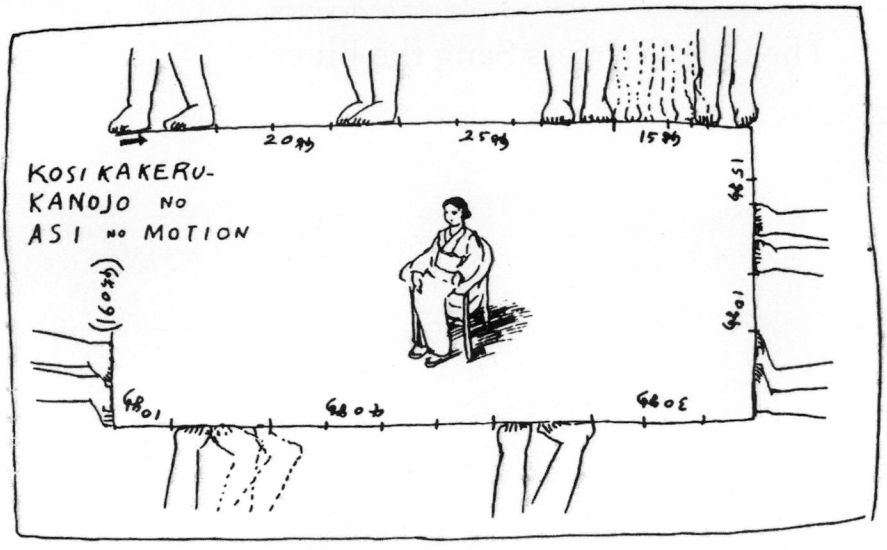

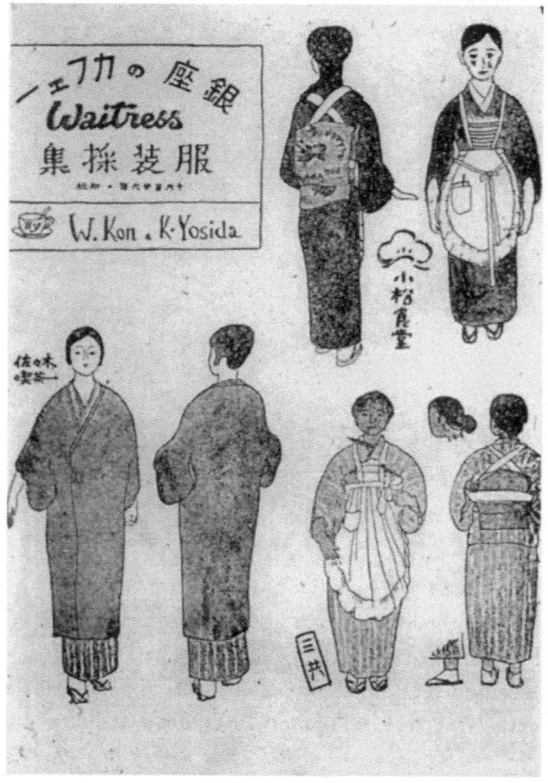

14. "Foot Motions of the Café Waitress," arranged by Kon Wajirō and published in Kon and Yoshida, *Moderunologio*. This sketch traced the movements of the feet of one café waitress in the space of 160 seconds. Courtesy of Gakuyō Shobō.

15. Part of a three-page spread documenting the clothing of café waitresses on Ginza. From Kon Wajirō and Yoshida Kenkichi, *Moderunologio*. Courtesy of Gakuyō Shobō.

16. The women's section at a movie theater. Kageyama Kōyō, 1931.

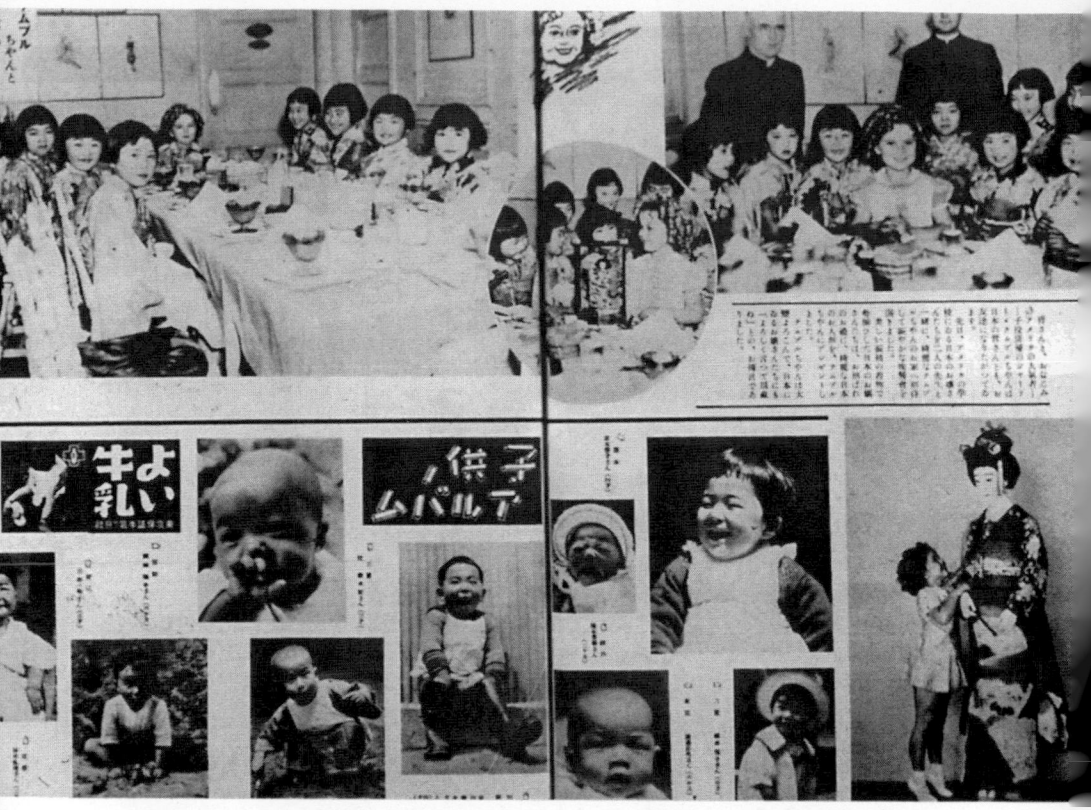

17. Shirley Temple *(Temple-chan)* has just received a Japanese doll from new friends in the United States. She sends regards to Japanese girls in Japan. Children's portraits and an advertisement for milk complete the montage. *Asahi Graph,* July 22, 1936. Courtesy of *Asahi Shinbunsha.*

18. Yamanaka Sadao's samurai hit *Kunisada Chūji* was promoted as a Western Electric–style "all-talkie." Across from this image of Japanese masculinity, the Continental (Gay Divorcé) promised 1935 style dance and song. In *Eiga no Tomo*, March 1935.

19. Cartoon of "Little Mickey" being congratulated on his seventh birthday, around the time of the attempted coup d'état in Japan. *Eiga no Tomo*, February 1936.

The Household Becomes Modern Life

20. "How to Make a Sandwich," April 1932. A housewife demonstrates each stage in the construction of such fancy sandwiches as the *asparagus sandwich*, the *rolled sandwich*, and the *hot cheese sandwich*. Nowhere is this fare referred to as Western; rather it is introduced teatime fare, to be served with black tea. Courtesy of *Shufu no Tomo*.

21. Appropriate posture for the housewife undertaking various tasks. *Shufu no Tomo*, September, 1936. Courtesy of *Shufu no Tomo*.

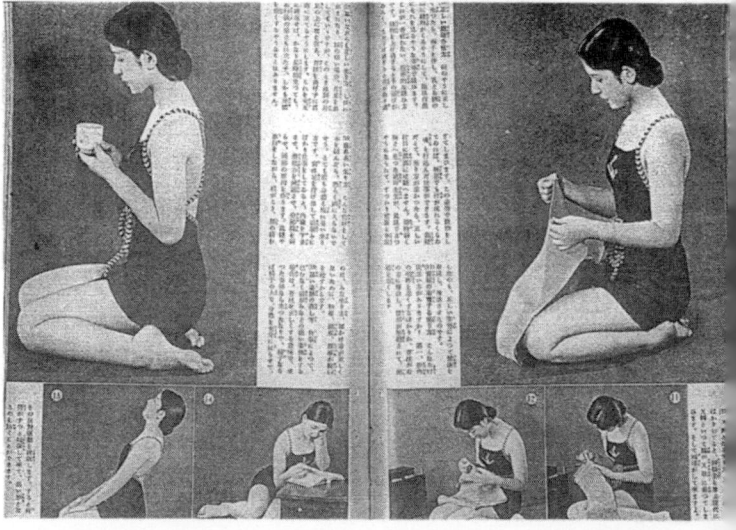

22. On the right-hand page of this spread from the April 1930 issue of *Shufu no Tomo*, Yamasa Soy Sauce was advertised as both timeless and a sign of progress. The reader, code-switching to the left, saw the imperial family presented in the most up-to-date fashion, as a modern nuclear family. Courtesy of *Shufu no Tomo*.

23. Here, in the serialized comic narrative *Mogako and Moborō*, Mogako flouts tradition by wearing her bathing suit in the hot springs bath and removing it while swimming in the ocean. On her head is a small Japanese flag. *Shufu no Tomo*, October 1928. Courtesy of *Shufu no Tomo*.

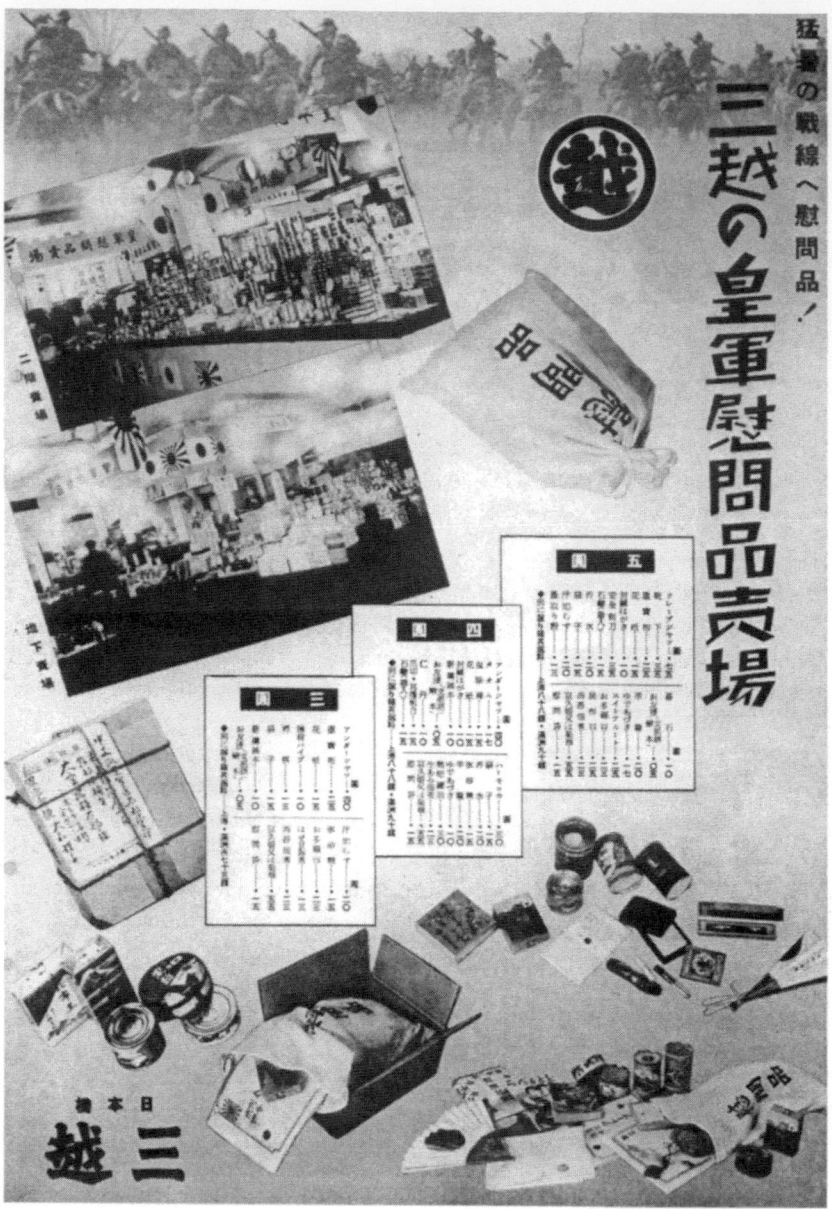

24. By July 13, 1938, Mitsukoshi Department Store had two counters selling a range of "comfort bags" priced between three and five yen. The bags contained such items as *undershirts*, tissue, harmonicas, and boiled sweet beans; the five-yen version also contained socks, perfume, and *sweet fruit*. *Asahi Graph*. Courtesy of *Asahi Shinbunsha*.

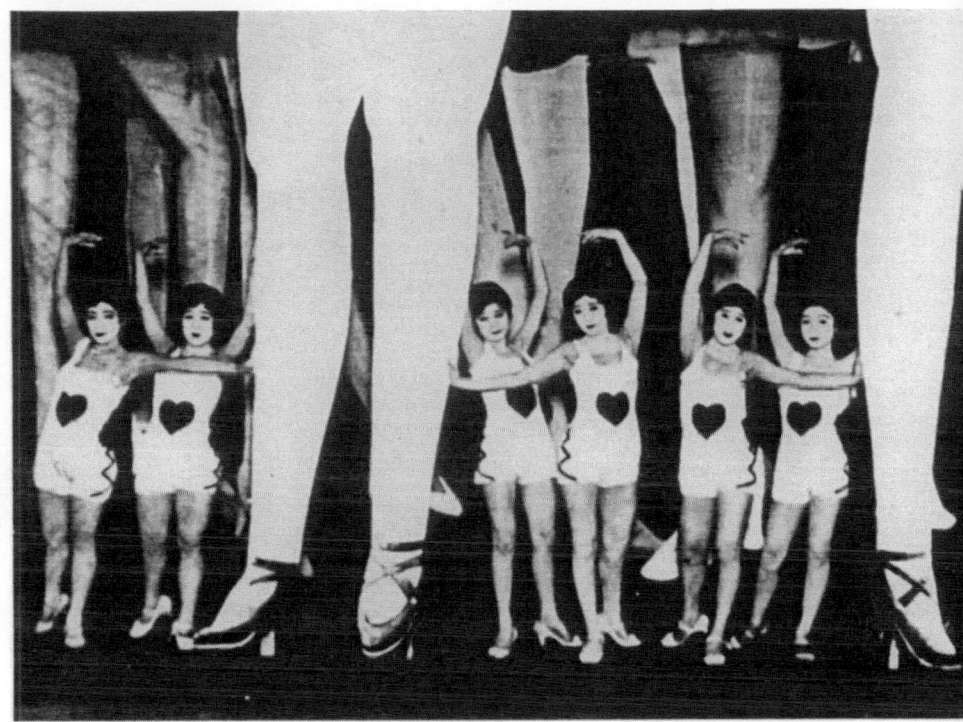

25. Long, exposed legs, marker of the Modern Girl, in a scene from the Casino Folies in 1929. T?
following year a law forbade the wiggling of the buttocks forward and backward or left to right.
Courtesy of Shōgakukan.

26. A grandfather with twin toddlers in front of the Taishōkan theater, which showed Western films, 1937. Courtesy of Kuwabara Kineo.

27. Shop boys on their day off in the sixth section of Asakusa, which housed the
movie theaters, 1937. Courtesy of Kuwabara Kineo.

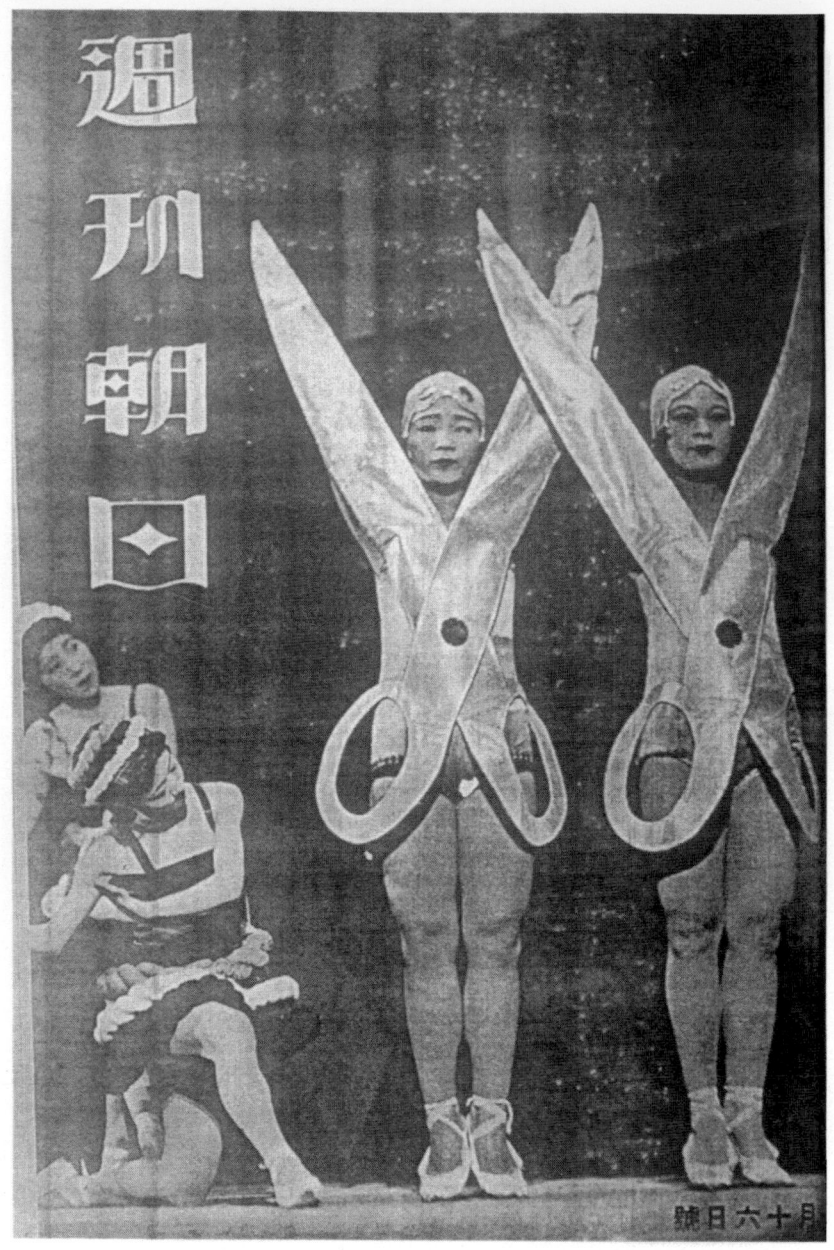

28. Erotic? Grotesque? Nonsense? All of the above? Cover of *Shūkan Asahi*, November 16, 1930. Courtesy of Asahi Shinbunsha.

Down-and-Out Grotesquerie

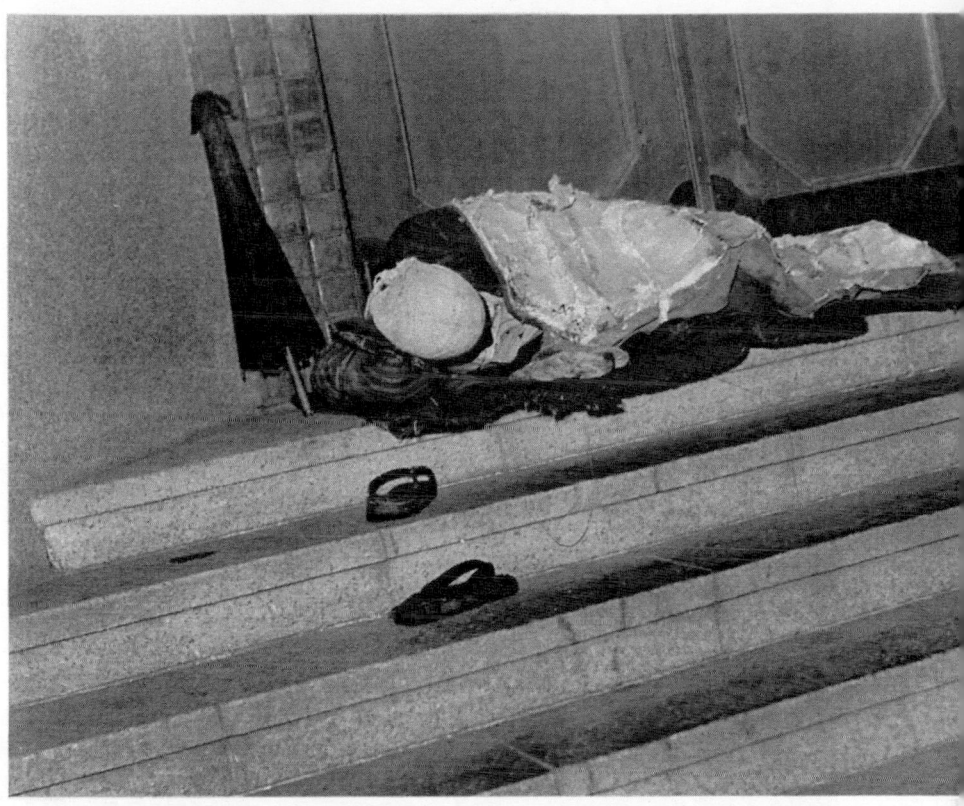

29. Ōkubo Koroku, from the "Tokyo" series, 1930–35. Courtesy of Ōnuki Minami.

30. Advertisement for Charlie Chaplin's *Modern Times*, *Eiga no Tomo*, August 1, 1937. The magazine announced that the "Genius Chaplin" had returned to the silver screen to pour heart and spirit into *Modern Times*.

31. Late Tokugawa traveling entertainers. Such performers were some of the down-and-out fig┄ whose existence spanned the early-modern and modern periods. From the F. Beato Collection. C┄ tesy of Yokohama Kaikō Shiryōkan.

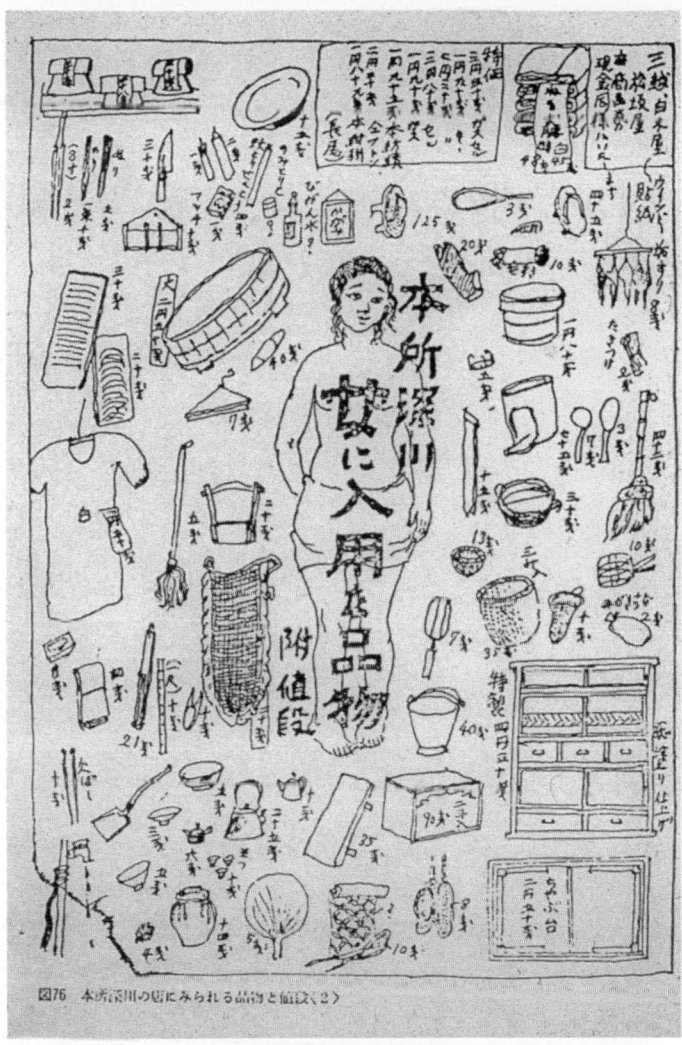

図76 本所深川の窟にみられる品物と値段〈2〉

32. Kon Wajirō, "Goods Needed by Women in Honjo-Fukugawa, with Prices." This drawing was paired with that of things "wanted by men" from the same survey of the Tokyo slum area Honjo-Fukagawa. Kon asked his readers to study these two illustrations, along with others in the essay, and consider what impressions were "etched in their minds" and "what kind of knowledge" they gained from this study. He added that it saddened him to share such findings at the end of a year characterized by bad economic times. From Kon and Yoshida, *Moderunologio.* Courtesy of Gakuyō Shobō.

33. Hashimoto Yaoji's ironic take on the "blessings of Spring" for hobos *(lumpen)* laboring in potato fields, after which they retire to *modern hotels. Shūkan Asahi,* April 26, 1931. Courtesy of Asahi Shinbunsha.

34. Program cover from the third show of the *Casino Folies*, August 11–20, 1929. The eight-part variety segment of the show included such acts as the "Spanish Dance," the "Oriental Dance with Swords," the "Happy Dance Kappore," and the "New York March." Courtesy of Hara Kentarō.

35. Scenes from the 1930 Casino Folies production of *Wondrous Adventures around the World*. The third actor from the left is the famed comedian Enoken. Courtesy of Hara Kentarō.

36. Ad for a film about Yaji and Kita, two popular heroes from the Edo period. *Kinema Junpō*, January 21, 1928. Courtesy of Hara Kentarō.

37. A *"Negro Dance"* with Enoken at left. Courtesy of Hara Kentarō.

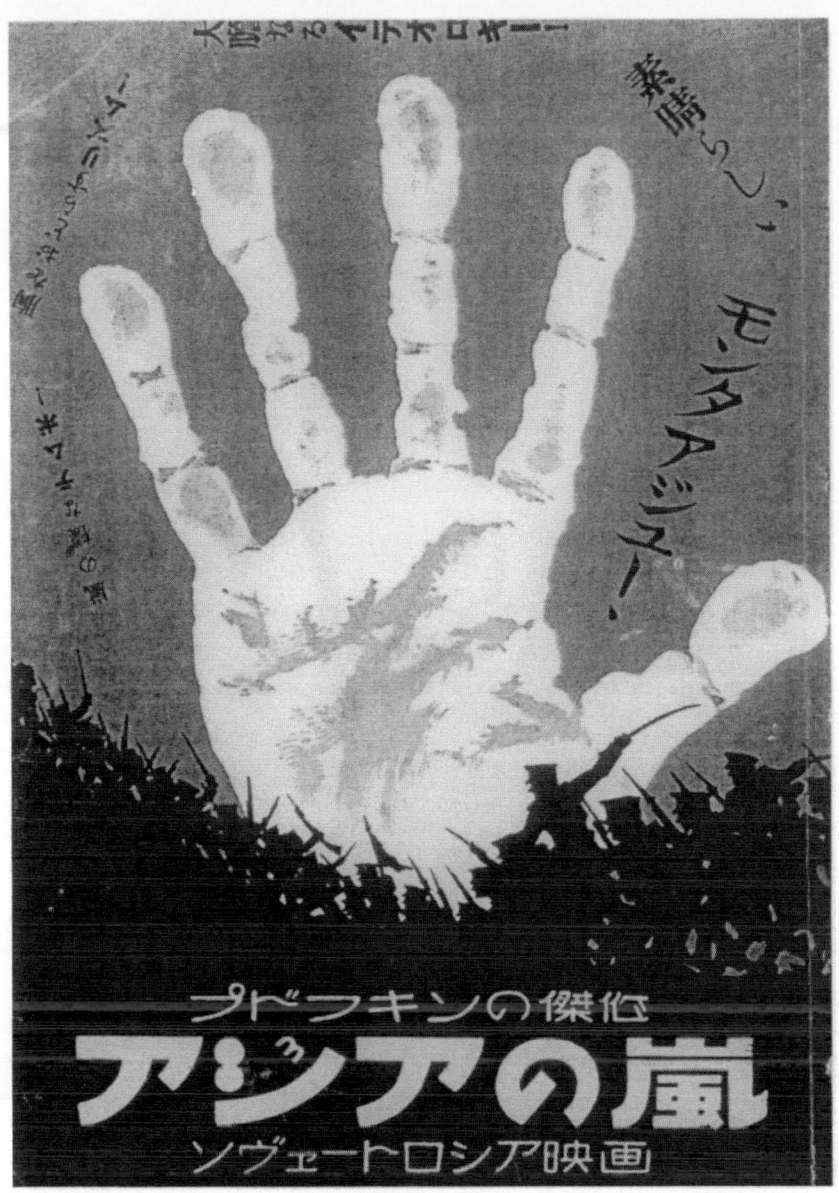

38. Ad for the Soviet film *Storm over Asia*. The word *montage* is followed by an exclamation mark. *Kinema Junpō*, October 1, 1930.

39. Nikkatsu ad for Yaji and Kita film, *Kinema Junpō*, January 11, 1928.

doors that had forced him to break and enter through a window of his own dwelling after he lost his keys. The roundtable members do not appear to be aware that the duplications and the consequences of this sameness that they recount in their anecdotes reveal how they are living the everyday of modernity, which is so often characterized by the principle of duplication. Instead, they merely recount how a group of young men, returning from an evening outing to the public bath entered not only the wrong entrance-way but also continued into the interiors of said apartment.[57]

Through the middle of the 1930s, the references to non-Japanese, modern living in *Shufu no Tomo* as in the case of the apartment-house dweller roundtable, served to equate the foreign either with American or European practices, as in the international roundtable on "Women's Views on Love and Marriage." The emerging admiration for Nazi Germany was revealed when the German participant contended that her countrywomen could not work after marriage because the country had to be kept strong: She was greeted by the moderator's response that "Hitler is a great man." The German contention that women should not marry outside of their own nation was greeted with as much respect. The following autumn, in November 1938, the wife of the German ambassador sent greetings to the women of Japan, accompanied by photos of Mussolini and Hitler. And just as there was a shift away from a valorization of the United States as implicitly most modern, there was a segue in the pages of *Shufu no Tomo* from a preoccupation with the modern to an emphasis on colonial life in Manchuria.[58]

The modern and the colonial were of course not mutually exclusive. When Ōtsuji Shirō (half of the comedy duo mentioned above) traveled to Manchuria in 1933, he conveyed in photographs, captions, and commentary how such notoriously modern institutions as movie theaters and fashion were a part of colonial existence. Two years later, during his interview in Paris with Josephine Baker, he focused more on racialized differences and similarities, as he identified with her treatment at the hands of whites. Four months after Ōtsuji's trip to Paris, *Shufu no Tomo* was praising the brides who had emigrated to Manchuria to be married, as pioneer members of a new form of *fūfu*. And by November 1937, readers of *Shufu no Tomo* were told to prepare themselves spiritually as Japanese. This was the same month that readers were privy to Yamada Waka's identification with the essence of the Japanese woman during Yamada's visit with Eleanor Roosevelt: the Japanese woman possessed a mother's heart. There is no way to deny that *Shufu no Tomo* was no longer presenting the *shufu* as half of a conjugal pair who could be housewife, mother, worker, or sometimes even unmarried professional. But no matter how much official ideology (as reflected in Yamada's rigidity) sought to deny history, change could not be undone. Humor did not disappear with the advent of war in China; nor did a nonsensical approach to Tokyo as a modern icon, as the following narrative tells us. In the July 1936 issue of *Shufu no Tomo*, "*Modern* Tokyo: An *Album* of Evening Scenes of Tokyo," entertained the housewife-reader. On November 3, 1938, Prime Minister Konoe announced the construction of a "New Order" in the Orient. In the November 1938 issue of *Shufu no Tomo*, the comedy team of Entatsu and Achako combined collaborative support for the government with nostalgia for the modern as they reported on their tour of Greater Tokyo. The grand tour covered not only the standard stops for all those in from the provinces to get a look at the big city, including Ueno Zoo and Ginza, but also included a people's bank and an employment agency. While delighting at the sight of a "typical Modern Boy" on Ginza, they argued as to whether women entering the employment market were acting in a masculine or a feminine manner as men kept proceeding onto the front. The last stop on their tour was the Asakusa Kannon. Asakusa, the site of this temple and of the adjacent park where the masses from the city and the provinces came together, was a place where the erotic, the grotesque, and the modern converged during the modern years; and Asakusa—I have added "Honky-Tonk" to evoke the raucous atmosphere of Asakusa—is the third part and the last of the five modern sites herein.[59]

PART III

Asakusa

Honky-Tonk Tempo

1   Asakusa Eroticism

When I say that Asakusa was honky-tonk, as when I say that the Japanese café waitress sang the blues, I am not being literal. I am referring to a similarity in atmosphere and to some extent, context. In the American South of the 1940s, *honky-tonk* referred to small tough bars that catered to white working-class customers who came for the prostitutes and for the syncopated rhythms of the "honk tonk" music. Thus the term honky-tonk could refer to the establishment, or to its music—which emphasized rhythm over melody. It could also be used as an adjective, to refer to the raucous, charged atmosphere encouraged by the beat of the honky-tonk music. (In some honky-tonks, patrons are said to have had sex while dancing—and with their clothes on—to the rhythms of the honky-tonk music.) Such imagery evokes the more desperate aspects (one could use the word *grotesque*) of modern life in Asakusa but I also use honky-tonk to help recall the energy, the tempo, and the sensuous pleasures to be had in this "park." Yet my comparison of honky-tonk culture with Asakusa happenings can only go so far, for a central element in the culture of Asakusa was the inseparability of worship from corporeal pleasures.

The modern play space of Asakusa, which housed Sensōji Temple, had indeed been the site of amusement and worship since the early modern era of Japanese history. By 1600, Sensōji had been designated the official place of prayer for the Shōgun and his family. By 1800 the ruling family had long since transferred its patronage elsewhere, but by then the temple and the area surrounding it were a thriving center of popular Buddhism. As Nam-Lin Hur has so compellingly argued, Sensōji culture was "a culture of prayer and play"; the two were inseparable. In other words, the worshippers who crowded into the temple grounds and immediately outside these borders were there as much for the sumo wrestling, the street fairs, and the shop girls in the teahouses and the toothpick stores, as for the opportunity to pray at the site of the legendary statue of the Boddhisattva of Mercy (the Asakusa Kannon). But by the time of the earthquake, the "live dolls" performing the tale of the forty-seven loyal retainers, the women acrobats, the elephants that refused to flinch when bonfires were lit under their bellies, and the Meiji peep shows had receded into history. The Meiji government had designated Asakusa as a park and the temple area had been divided into seven districts. By 1923 those going for prayer and play—they were now considered the masses—knew to go to the fourth and sixth districts for their pleasures. Such Meiji attractions as the Panorama House, which had drawn crowds to a simulated viewing of the Battle of Vicksburg in 1890, and the Asakusa operettas inspired by the West were things of the past. The oddities on display in the early modern period were called *misemono* (things being shown). Hur offers a compelling list of *misemono* including a self-boiling pot (1814), "scenic constructs depicting the secret lives of courtesans" (1820), "breathing dolls with foreign faces" (1855), and "models of an open womb showing the growth of a fetus" (1862). By 1923, the things being shown—the most popular of popular amusements—were the moving pictures in the sixth district of the park.[1]

By the second half of the 1920s, Asakusa was as erotic as it was modern. it was modern in Gonda's sense of the term, which corroborates my definition of Japanese modern culture as montage—implying active contiguities in time and in space. Gonda saw Asakusa as montage in motion, defined by class distinction and new mass-based entertainment along with class-based agency. I see Asakusa in the modern years as erotic in the following ways: it was erotic, and by this I mean that it celebrated the sensuality of both men and women, a sensuality encompassing an overwhelming number of sensations (a montage of senses, as it were), including taste, the thrill of motion, and a gaze defined not necessarily by domination but by exploration and imagination. In sum, the eroticism of Asakusa could be defined by sensation, food, motion, and vision.

No small number of writers, inspired by the "documentary impulse" of Japanese modern times and by the vibrancy of Asakusa, were motivated to guide their readers through the park. Three who stand out are Gonda Yasunosuke, the theorist of play whose documentation was also intended for the state; Soeda Azenbō, the composer/balladeer who created culture from within; and Kawabata Yasunari, whose documentary novel, *The Asakusa Crimson Gang*, juxtaposed social commentary with a careful, controlled nostalgia that relied on legend and an adamant emphasis that this year (1930) was not the past year. But it is the voice of the social scientist of culture, Gonda Yasunosuke, with whom we should begin, for his characterization of Asakusa clarifies how the notion of montage is appropriate for understanding the meaning of one very important neighborhood within a national, modern culture. Gonda's work sets the stage for investigating how Azenbō recognized that the past was history in a modern Asakusa obsessed with food at least as much as with sex, even as it provided a living for even the lowest of prostitutes and shared its patrons with the adjacent Yoshiwara, the pleasure quarters also on the northeastern edge of Tokyo. Gonda provides a historical grounding for Kawabata, who showed us Asakusa traditions—both new and old—within the modern moment, including the open acknowledgment of female desire, in modern colors. Ultimately, it was the movies that defined Asakusa modernity, as Gonda recognized. Thus, at the end of this segment, two film critics help to expand on our understanding of the erotic draw of the movies that is implied by Gonda's documentation of the film-going experience in the park. (I must note here that this segment deals only with the *ero*. I have chosen to place the *"guro,"* or grotesquerie, in Kawabata in the next segment, "Down-and-Out Grotesquerie."[2]

GONDA YASUNOSUKE'S ASAKUSA (AN OFFICIAL VIEW)

Gonda's first extended discussion of Asakusa, "Crossroads of Posters: The Popular Entertainment of 'Asakusa,'" written on the first day of March in 1920, sketched a day in the life of that urban place. Asakusa was in constant motion, and its constitutive parts could not be isolated, insisted Gonda, naming the key sites associated with Asakusa in the years leading up the earthquake. The *nakamise* (corridor of stalls) leading to the Kannon Temple, the movie theaters, the small eateries, and the well-known play sites (like the Twelve-Story Tower) all had meaning because they were in and of Asakusa. In the past, Asakusa had been the place of the Temple of the Kannon, but now, conversely, this temple was defined by its presence in Asakusa. People did not go to Asakusa to go to the movies, or to see inexpensive theater. They went to see *Asakusa* movies, and to enjoy *Asakusa* comedy. At the end of the day or the half day they took Asakusa treats home to eat, to try to extend Asakusa into their homes.[3]

In Gonda's view of Asakusa as a montage, it was a *"matomatta* [collected into place] world" with its own rules, view of humanity, karmic relationships, and history. Yet it was not, like the pleasure quarters of Yoshiwara, a separate world. Unlike Yoshiwara, which it had displaced, it was not a utopian space that leveled all social differences. Gonda defined Asakusa as "a place of Entertainment made by the people." And just as Asakusa was a montage of sharply defined places, the "people" *(minshū)* of Asakusa were made up of two clearly delineated classes: the *proletariat* and the *intelligentsia*. When, elsewhere, Gonda characterized Asakusa as *not* pulled together, and lacking a settled culture, thus seemingly contradicting his earlier notion, he was providing one illustration of the problem of relating the parts of a montage to its whole. In Gonda's writings, the second characterization, of a culture in pieces and in flux, won out. In his typology of Asakusa movie theaters (and their spectators), he noted that directly adjacent to the Fuji, where the voices of the working class resounded, members of the *haikara* (an outdated synonym for modern) student intellectual class thrilled to the foreign films of the Imperial. The Electric Palace catered both to the intellectual class and to wage-earners accompanied by their spouses, while elsewhere working-class parents and children were moved to tears. Such distinctions defined Asakusa.[4]

Gonda's concern with the historicity of Asakusa, its class distinctions, and the moviegoing experience were central to his writings on Asakusa. In "Centered on 'Asakusa,'" written on July 10, 1920, he took the part of the dilettante to examine "the wonderful social fact" of the enormous appeal of film by focusing on the "moving-picture fever" of Asakusa. Again, he associated specific classes of moviegoers with certain theaters. He recorded the jeering of laborers at the Fuji showcase for the swashbuckling idol Matsunosuke, and the dialogue yelled back and forth between film narrators and "girl and boy tykes" in the audience, while elsewhere women (and their husbands) wept to melodrama alongside vocational school students and a scattering of soldiers, who clattered their swords. There was also the rapt response of students and intellectuals who applauded when the names of their foreign idols appeared on screen. And there were finer distinctions: the Imperial claimed students from Tokyo Imperial University, while the Cinema Club catered to Keiō University students, and so on. The places that showed foreign films and played a smattering of Mozart and Beethoven for their audiences had "high-class" customers. Unlike other audiences, a couple of years earlier, they did not call out, "Hey Pearl White's gotten to be an old lady!" or "Kimball Young seems to have taken off some pounds!" to prove their knowledge of Hollywood.[5]

Gonda's concern for history showed in his narrative of changes in the qualifications of the "film buff." In the early days of moving pictures, aficionados had paid high prices for *"sensational"* stills, before turning to posters and other "everyday" items such as bookmarks, which were followed in turn by picture-postcard sets and small pictorial cards. This fad was succeeded by the mouthing of the terms *series, serial,* and *plot* and the memorization of both the names of foreign film companies and the original titles of films in their original language. Gonda also reported a code switch, in form if not language, mediated by the spectatorship of film: the cadences of various *benshi* (film narrators) had been adopted by junior high school students competing in speech contests. It had also become obligatory to learn the names of actors, beginning with the actresses: Mary Pickford, May Marsh, Norma Talmadge, Theda Barra, and "Gish." We can presume from Gonda's account that in 1920 junior high school students were inscribing these names in the margins of their textbooks. Gonda corroborates the fixation on parts of foreign starlets' bodies seen in *Chijin no Ai* (A Fool's Love) and in *Eiga no Tomo:* one heard discussions of "the way Marsh moved her eyes, of Talmadge's nose, of Pickford's shoulders." The worship of such male idols as Douglas Fairbanks had followed, said Gonda, along with the incantation of the names of directors and cinematographers and critiques of makeup, lighting, and camera angles.[6]

Of course Gonda was no dilettante. His highly numerical "Study of the Entertainment Center 'Asakusa,'" (March 1930), which he represented as unique in the realm of mass entertainment because of its incomparable *minshūsei* (quality of being tied to the people), was a detailed study of data collected from such government sources as the Asakusa ward office. It is not necessary here to recapitulate the contents of Gonda's "Study," which consisted of unexplicated, unannotated charts. What should be noted is the absence of any reference to the implication of the Japanese state in Asakusa as a residential and mercantile play space. Elsewhere, in "Centered on 'Asakusa'," his response to officialdom was a sardonic commentary on police control. The length of film footage censored by the police department, if placed end on end, would be one thousand times the height of Mount Fuji. If computed in terms of time (at the average world film speed of sixty *shaku* per minute), such a montage would last four months, twenty-six days, fourteen hours, and thirty-four minutes. Gonda also noted how the establishment of divisions of "Men's seats," "Women's seats," and "Family seats" had been mandated. No mention was made of his own appropriation of numbers (and categories) from the Metropolitan Police Office and Ward Office charts.[7]

The contradiction between an emphasis on mass, class agency and the need for state policy aimed at entertainment is evident when the reader compares Gonda's essays of the post-earthquake mid-1920s to his publications of the early 1930s. In 1924, as noted in part I, after the earthquake Gonda had been underimpressed by the government's control of leisure activity and, using one of his favorite metaphors, had concluded that entertainment could not be distributed as though it were unpolished rice. When he stated that the Metropolitan Police Board had ordered proprietors of pleasure quarters throughout Tokyo to engage in their business "'without the *shamisen*,'" his implication was that the entrepreneurs had taken the initiative and that the state was merely on the defensive as it attempted to contain the energized activity emerging from the urban rubble. By 1931 he was calling for a policy that could respond to the creation of people's entertainment from below. He was also formulating "social policy" aimed at the containment of such problems as the desire for titillation expressed by unsupervised, overeroticized film-going girls of the proletarian class. (These girls were eager to spend their time away from suffocating living spaces, and to spend their meager spare change on the stimulus provided by certain types of vulgar films.) A reading of Gonda's 1924 essay "Various Aspects of Entertainment at the Time of the Earthquake" reveals that even at the onset of the modern years, he was juggling his attraction to the notion of play created by the people with his recognition of the need for official policies that would respond to "the forms of entertainment that must come from an everyday consciousness shaken from its depths."[8]

Asakusa was definitely modern, according to Gonda's discussion if not his definition. In the essay "So-Called '*Modern* Everyday Life' and Entertainment," Gonda went to great pains to associate modern activity with the concerns of those not associated with labor (best represented by the Modern Girl and Modern Boy). Gonda's "modern" everyday is reminiscent of Ōya Sōichi's diatribe against the superficial: the modern mimics the foreign as an "arbitrary means of replicating power"; it is an *effeminate, neurasthenic dilettantism.* Admittedly, Gonda was referring to the street life of the boulevards (the *strasse*). Thus, the cafes, bars, restaurants, movie theaters, and dance halls mentioned are not those occupying the crowded streets and alleyways of Asakusa. But his ensuing discussion of the demise and revival of *yose* (a form of vaudeville) reveals that although Gonda may not have seen Asakusa as specifically *modan*, nevertheless, he saw it as a vibrant locus of contemporary agency and cultural transformation. Asakusa was where the masses created culture.[9]

For Gonda, technological advance did not necessarily denote cultural progress. A new form of live *yose* must, he said, combat the Edo tastes adopted by *yose* on the radio by incorporating a mosaic of the methods adopted on the Asakusa stage in the years following the earthquake including forms of comedy and the musical revue. The buttocks-wiggling modernism of the comedian Kingorō who shook to the *"jazz band,"* was almost there; but it was not *yose* made out of the "present sensibility of social *seikatsu" (gendai shakai seikatsu no jikkan)*—that is, from the everyday experience *(seikatsu taiken)* of the masses. Asakusa was where the masses were creating a new *yose*; it was not on the radio. Gonda told Kingorō it was not sufficient to swing his grand buttocks to the music of jazz: he had forgotten something big: the "everyday life of the Masses."[10]

Gonda did not use the word *modern* in anything but a pejorative sense; nor did he employ the word *montage*. However, his conceptualization of Asakusa, from the early 1920s until the early 1930s was marked by the mingling of classes and by forms of entertainment in which the past was being replaced by the actions of the masses. Those responsible for the transformation were sometimes referred to as the "masses" as in his prescription for a new *yose*; but he also referred to "the people," "workers," and *"intellectuals"* as the base for a new superstructure. This insistence on agency from below can clearly be linked to his appreciation for the rapid reemergence of Tokyo culture chronicled in his post-earthquake writing. As a play space defined by a religious marker, Asakusa was separate from other neighborhoods—as Gonda noted in his survey, some enterprises were unique to Asakusa. But as the most focused site of working-class culture, it was also representative of social and cultural change outside of its confines. In 1931, the year he conducted his detailed survey, the mass media was obsessed with the notion of *ero guro nansensu* as a characteristic of popular culture. But Gonda, who had been tracking play since the teens, did not talk about the erotic, he did not characterize the time spent by workers in Asakusa as in any way grotesque, nor did he refer to *nonsense*. In fact, he employed no hint of humor in any of his writings on leisure; this was serious business. One rare reference to *ero guro nansensu*, in 1931, dismissed it as a decadent, pornographic approach to the everyday.[11]

Keeping in mind what I see as Gonda's emphasis on Asakusa as a montage in motion, defined by class distinctions and new, mass-based entertainment along with class-based agency, I turn now to other chronicles of Asakusa from the "modern" years, chronicles that, along with Gonda's writings, contribute to my own definition of Asakusa as erotic, grotesque, nonsensical, and central to a Japanese modern, mass culture.

SOEDA AZENBŌ'S ASAKUSA (WORDS OF A BALLADEER)

The idea of Asakusa as play site central to the new moment is evident in *Asakusa Teiryūki* (Record of the undercurrents of Asakusa), by Soeda Azenbō, the anarchist songwriter, street performer and author of the topical song of 1924, "Earthquake Ballad." This work, which was organized in montage form opened with the segment "Fragments." Ever since Kawabata Yasunari appropriated "Fragments" when adapting Soeda's documentary account of Asakusa space and relationships to the seemingly documentary novel *The Asakusa Crimson Gang*, it has often been quoted in accounts of Asakusa.[12] Soeda began by offering an overtly erotic allusion to "naked human desires" before focusing on the movement of the masses within a constantly reformulated space. Like Gonda, Soeda was primarily concerned with the masses pursuing entertainment, in historical motion. Unlike Gonda, he allowed the modernist a place in Asakusa; more than Gonda, he wanted to represent distinctions within these masses. Here was an anarchist voice. Soeda expressed allegiance to neither state directives nor to the mandates of Marxist categories:

FRAGMENTS

In Asakusa, all sorts of things are thrown out in raw form.
All sorts of human desires are dancing naked.
Asakusa is the heart of Tokyo—
Asakusa is a marketplace of humans—
Asakusa is the Asakusa for all.
It's a safe zone where everybody can expose themselves to their guts.
The Asakusa where the masses keep walking hour by hour; the Asakusa
    of those masses, is a foundry where all old forms are melted down, to
    be transformed into new forms.
One day's dream. Fleeting adoration for the outdated.
Asakusa mood. Those without authority who grieve for the real Asakusa,
    ignoring new currents, withdraw.

You, proponent of cleanliness who aims to make Asakusa into a palace of
    lapis lazuli, pull back.
All things of Asakusa may be vulgar; they lack refinement.
But they boldly walk the walk of the masses, they move with vitality. . . .

The *Modernist* who inhales nourishment from the Western painting of
    the new era walks alongside believers of the Goddess of Mercy who
    buys favors from the Buddha with copper coins.
A huge stream of all sorts of classes, all sorts of peoples, all mixed up to-
    gether. A strange *rhythm* lying at the base of that stream. That's the
    flow of instincts.
Sounds and Brightness. Entangled, whirl, one grand symphony—There's
    the beauty of discord there.
Men, Women, flow into the rushing around of these colors and this sym-
    phony, and from within it they pick out the hope to live on tomorrow.
    (SA, 3–5)

Soeda's hero and agent of history is not Gonda's worker, whose time is defined by the factory clock. It is the beggar in "Asakusa from Morning until Middle of the Night," the chapter following *Fragments*. In this chapter, and throughout Soeda's mini-essays on Asakusa landmarks, language, and personalities, the desperate (but enterprising) beggar-vagrant is highlighted as living an active, enterprising everyday.

The term *ero* is not indexed in any of Soeda's carefully subtitled chapters, but if we adopt Audre Lorde's definition in "The Erotic as Power," we can begin to see how Asakusa modernity was erotic and how Soeda Azenbō's modern classic tells us it was so. For Lorde, the erotic is "an assertion of the life force of women; of that creative energy empowered, the knowledge and use of which we are now reclaiming in our language, our history, our dancing, our loving, our work, our lives." She does not deny the bodily dimension to eroticism, although, for her, the erotic power emerging from "sharing deeply a pursuit with another person need not be physical." She respects the body in rhythm and decries the Euro-American deformation of the erotic into the pornographic, for "pornography emphasizes sensation without feeling." Lorde, of course, was concerned with Euro-American, "women-identified" women as her subject and her audience at the end of the 1970s. Nonetheless, it is possible to adapt her definition. We can apply it to both the women and the men of Soeda Azenbō's Asakusa (bearing in mind that female and male experiences are always qualitatively different and that sensations are always culturally and historically defined).[13]

We are entering highly contested, complex territory when we attempt to differentiate the erotic from the pornographic, particularly when we are working with more than one language and one cultural order—which is to say history—of signs and passions. Yet I want to suggest that we view the Japanese modern era as characterized by Lorde's "electric charge," the creative energy that can exhibit itself in love, work, and other aspects of everyday life. A look at this eroticism in Asakusa should help us to rethink the significance of the preoccupation by the critics and scholars from the era with new mores and practices. Gonda and Kon Wajirō sought to investigate the creation of new customs, and Ōya Sōichi insisted that such concerns were but mimetic borrowings. The preoccupation with *seikatsu* (the everyday life of everyday practices) inside and outside Asakusa, along with the emphasis on the pleasures to be had by sensation, food, motion, and vision, was itself erotic.[14]

Of course Asakusa was pornographic. This term is as elusive as the word *erotic*, but it can be defined for Asakusa in 1930 through a montage of theoretical associations (as long as we recognize that conclusions from Euro-American history are being projected onto Japanese history). I have adopted the distinction between *erotica*, "based on mutual desire and affection," and *pornography*, premised "on male domination and exploitation of women." Moreover, "power" is central to the pornographic, which is never monolithic, and always relates to a "trafficking" in women. The definition of the pornographic element in moving pictures offered by Linda Williams is most apropos: this pornography is "a coincidence of sexual phantasy, genre and culture in an erotic organization of visibility" revolving around performance that "produces meanings 'pivoting on gender difference.'" The performances by women beggars and prostitutes in Asakusa at all levels of the public and private hierarchy of such sex work were indeed pornographic in this sense, "riding roughshod over the sexuality and sexual subjectivity of women" (to borrow Williams's phrasing again). But I see post-earthquake Asakusa as both pornographic and erotic: and here I make use of Williams's distinction between nineteenth- and twentieth-century Euro-American pornography to distinguish the "pornographic" from the "erotic" in Asakusa.[15]

According to Williams, during the nineteenth century the pornographic was defined by a "productivist mentality of work, rigid gender differences, and need for control." During the twentieth century, pornography shifted toward an emphasis on "a consumerist mentality of unending pleasures, shifting gender relations, and a desire for self-abandon." Women's desires were still considered different from those of men, but they were not outside the "economy of desire." The twentieth-century mentality was, according to Williams, more democratic in its treatment of women.[16] My position is that both phenomena were present in Asakusa during the modern years. Of course it was a pornographic space where women's services were sold, but it also included women as agents in its search for unending pleasures and shifting gender.[17]

In 1921 Gonda had written that those who came to Asakusa desired to "taste" of the intoxication of that world. His 1930 study of Asakusa documenting a panoply of over 275 establishments—many of which were aimed at consumers from outside—catalogued how food and drink could be consumed. Gonda's preoccupation with restaurants was a reflection of how central food was to the Asakusa sexual economy.[18]

Desperation notwithstanding, even during the heart of the depression, as Kon pointed out in 1929, the *motto* of the eating places in Asakusa was "cheap, fast, and good." In 1921, Gonda had pointed out how Asakusa defined its food—tempura in Asakusa was *Asakusa* tempura; one did not go to Asakusa to eat grilled eel, one ate "grilled eel *in Asakusa*." Soeda offered his readers an account of a man seeking the best tempura in Asakusa before taking the last train home to his village. His souvenir would be the memory of the food. The Asakusa segment of Kon Wajirō's *Guide to the Greater Tokyo* (1929) confirmed and qualified Gonda's typology of Asakusa food. Gonda had documented numbers, percentages, and locations of purveyors of the following foods: (1) a set menu of Japanese delicacies on a tray; (2) beef, chicken, and fish casseroles; (3) tempura, noodles, and sushi; (4) Western food (including food served at cafés and bars); (5) Chinese food; and (6) sweet bean, chestnut, and pounded rice cakes. The restaurants serving the tempura, noodles, and sushi were easily the most popular (seventy-one establishments, or 31.7 percent; followed by the fixed-menu restaurants and the "sweets *halls*"). At the height of the modern era, Kon offered his readers a choice of locale within Asakusa for each sort of fare, including the best places for beef, tempura, Chinese food, sushi, and noodles. Food was defined by its location in Asakusa, but Asakusa was also defined by its mass-oriented fare. The masses still had access to the erotic pleasures of eating, and the intellectuals continued to document this eroticism.[19]

Soeda Azenbō's chronicle of the down-and-out life of Asakusa documented prices from numerous cheap joints that were enjoying a "frightening" prosperity: ten sen bought Western food, fifteen sen bought a casserole, and sake could be had for fifteen sen. Eroticism, in the conventional form that I have herein identified as "pornographic," was also available for sale. Waitresses, including one who resembled Josephine Baker, flitted among the customers. In Soeda's account, Asakusa offered yet another form of eroticism: a consumerism that enabled women to stretch their senses. The cheap eateries had begun to welcome women with families, women with men, and women with women. This post-earthquake phenomenon ("one could not have dreamed of such a spectacle five or six years ago") was, according to Soeda, "a procession of women; a flooding." Here, undoubtedly, were the *Shufu no Tomo* readers eager to learn to cook the food aimed at the masses (SA, 84, 87–88, 90, 102).

If *Shufu no Tomo* can be partly characterized as encouraging the production of food, Asakusa discourse, without question, provided more than a counterpart celebrating the consumption of food. In this setting even the menus were titillating. Soeda offered a litany: one place was "neither God nor Kannon of Benevolence," but it had been the salvation of late-night customers, including taxi drivers, who were deprived of food stalls after midnight due to state regulations. The customers had been saved by "*rice* with bamboo shoots—10 sen, *ham-rice*—fifteen sen, *curry-rice*—10 sen. *Coffee*, tea, *soda*-water—each 5 sen" (SA, 92).

Soeda recorded the sensual crunch of the Asakusa specialty, "*high-collar*" mochi, white round dumplings grilled in sugar and soy sauce. "When you check it out and taste it, it's crispy—not much taste, but not unpalatable, more than anything it sticks hard to the belly." The treat was a recent innovation in Asakusa. It had been all the rage fifteen years earlier when the appellation of *high-collar*, connoting cosmopolitan and non-indigenous, had been attached to this most Japanese of foods. Soeda concluded it was a most Asakusa-like specialty, in name and in form (SA, 109–110). Soeda also led the reader to the quickest access to Asakusa eating: the "stand and eat" stalls serving "tea over rice with fishcakes, Chinese noodles, Western food, chicken on skewers, tempura, noodles with meat, beef over rice, fried beef, sushi, sweet beans, barbecued eel, authentic chicken on skewers, and tea over rice along with pickles." (These all sold "sake by the *glass, brandy, whiskey,* and grape wine.") In fact, the tempura served in tatami rooms (implying a higher-class establishment) was but a mere copy of the real thing offered at these stalls. Those in the know in Asakusa had long recognized "the happiness of Asakusa" that could be obtained from that tempura eaten on the run (SA, 104, 108).

Atmosphere contributed to the taste of Asakusa, as in Lily, one of a row of cafés:

> It's really a lively establishment. The waitresses are cheery, with no trace of vulgarity. Songs—songs—songs. Most melancholy is blown away. And this never means obscenity. The thirty-sen Ōzeki's [sake] the real thing. And the considerate, but not noisy waitresses who pour for one don't push the food. Don't take the customers for fools. That's why anybody can get pleasurably drunk.
>
> However. It's the *tempo* of Asakusa on the go. Even if one wants to stir up love in this busy *box*, there's no time. But the pointless fun is what's good about it. The food's not very good. The *cutlets* are shriveled up like deformed children. (SA, 99)

KAWABATA YASUNARI'S ASAKUSA (REPORTS FROM THE ALLEYWAYS)

Kawabata chose his guide wisely when he turned to Soeda as a reference for *The Asakusa Crimson Gang*. Soeda was clearly at home with the smells, words, and wishes of Asakusa, which for him was a modern site where traditions, including communal practices reinforcing a sense of community, were being created in the present and not being handed down by the past. It is most striking that Soeda did not refer to the dictates of *giri* (obligation) vs. the pull of *ninjō* (passion) even once in his account of Asakusa society, although these terms are almost always used to signify the traditional, communal culture of Asakusa and the rest of the so called "downtown" (*shitamachi*) area. Rather than concerning himself with unchanging mores, he wanted to discuss the code-switching that was going on in Asakusa, in the modern present and did so by quoting an Asakusa hustler who is trying to sell books:

> I listen to the old man who has insisted in proclaiming "Don't know anything about this English." He is giving directions to someone and what I hear is "Go to that area where that *bridge* is and when you turn at the corner of the *mailbox* that is beyond the *market*, there is a house with *glass doors*. There is a *bell*. That should be the house where the *modern girl* lives." It's all English, isn't it? This is how English has become Japanese, just as it is.
>
> This demonstrates how important it is to learn such words as *motion, erotic, anachronism, climax, combination, erotomania, communism, sex, ideology, nonsense*. (SA, 121)

Soeda's punchline in the words of the hawker are "It's the *speed* era! Everything is right to the point. It's *shortcut* [sic]." The audience will, in other words, get right to the point, and painlessly learn English. All they have to do is buy one book.

The foreign is indeed familiar in Kawabata Yasunari's documentary novel *The Asakusa Crimson Gang*, for it is the neighborhood of Asakusa that must be decoded for the narrator of the novel and for the reader. This novel might be better titled *The Asakusa of the Crimson Gang*. It is really about this one place at one specific time, and the spaces within Asakusa. *Asakusa Kurenaidan* appears to have been based as much on Kawabata's personal experience as on his study of diverse sources; it seems most appropriate to call it a work of documentary fiction. The characters placed into Asakusa by Kawabata follow the admonition of Soeda's hawker to respect the speed era; they move in and out of the story at dizzying speeds. Only Asakusa remains the constant in this pieced together montage of a novel, which Seiji Lippit has so aptly termed a "cartographic text." But the members of the *Crimson Gang*—aspiring child and teen-aged actors who take it upon themselves to guide the narrator through Asakusa's ways and alleyways are not unimportant.[20]

The cast of characters includes boat boy Tokikō (*fune no tokikō*) who joins the gang during his downtime as he waits for his father's barge to pick him up after school, Umekichi, who is introduced as a model delinquent of Asakusa (he will be discussed at more length in the grotesquerie segment below), and Oshin—legendary gang leader with an appetite for men (we can consider her kin to the gang). There is also a mad woman, Ochiyo, and then there is Lefty Hiko who falls for a "child of 14" who loves the Asakusa children's library. The girl's body was first sold one week ago, but she does not yet understand her situation. (KY 24, 26–27, 54–57). There is also a supporting cast of madams, pimps, beggars, salesgirls, police officers, and of course, those out for a day of fun in Asakusa.

At the center of what cannot really be called a story is Yumiko, the most multivalent of modern girls. She appears and reappears in various costumes as part of her plot to avenge her sister. Her sister is Ochiyo, the mad woman—seduced, driven mad, and abandoned during the chaos following the Great Earthquake of 1923. Yumiko retaliates by choreographing her own seduction of her sister's would-be suitor, Akagi. In the climax of this scenario Yumiko and her sister's seducer exchange mutually vindictive arsenic-laced kisses, leaving the reader to wonder about the intertwined fates of Yumiko and Akagi.

Kawabata was as explicit in his social commentary regarding the preoccupation of the media with what they termed erotic. In one of his documentary references, he cited the terms *eroticism* and *depression* that were appearing repeatedly in 1930. He also singled out the strange but now naturalized terms *children without food* and *family suicide*—at a time when the stakes continued to be raised in a journalism market incessantly seeking sensation. Kawabata noted a chorus line brimming over with *ero;* he remarked on the *ero* dances that had been censored; and he recorded the renaming of the Shōchikuza theater as Dance Ero, following the naming of the Nihonkan's Ero Ero Dance Troupe. This word appearing on signboards all over Asakusa had also led Kawabata to the dressing room of the Danislavski sisters, the "queens of *ero*" (KY, 167–168, 189). Kawabata, like Soeda and Gonda, also associated food with the erotic while acknowledging that food was the product of the active capitalist manufacture of desires. Soeda Azenbō, for example, sardonically quoted the advertisement for the sweet drink *calpis*—"the taste of first love" (SA, 56). One *Asakusa Kurenaidan* heroine explained: "Asakusa lets me eat because I'm beautiful" (KY, 25, 179–80).

Eating provided sensual pleasures but could also be an act of desperation for those in the depths of Asakusa society. Kawabata's Asakusa narrator-flâneur (in *The Asakusa Crimson Gang*) read the names of the alluring items on display at the Subway Restaurant, one of the post-earthquake landmarks. First the Japanese sweets, "fit to decorate a Girl's Day doll stand." Then *"fruit jellies, caramels, chewing gum, chocolate."* Kawabata also documented the contents of the display window of sample foods. This narrator and his teenage girl companion, one of the gang of young people, do not need the aid of a translator to decipher the imported words on the menu: by 1930, these were part of the everyday menu of Japanese subjects seeking to consume inexpensive pleasures. The Japanese term for rice was employed, but the *raisu* in the curried rice signified a foreign origin (if not an exoticism), as did the other borrowed signifiers juxtaposed in a montage of sensual sounds. The only foods to be fully signified by Chinese characters were rice *(gohan)*, black foreign tea *(kōcha)*, and fruit *(kudamono)*. All the other foods were signified by the katakana syllabary used for foreign terms. Yet the foreign was all familiar:

> *Rice, Bread, Coffee, tea*—5 sen
>
> *Lemon Tea, Soda Water*—7 sen
>
> *Ice Cream, Cake, Pineapple, Fruit*—10 sen
>
> *Fried Shrimp, Rice Curry, Child's Plate*—25 sen
>
> *Beef Steak, Cutlet, Croquette, Ham Salad, Cabbage Rolls, Beef Stew*—30 sen
>
> *Lunch*—35 sen (KY, 112)

The domestication was complete, in part because of the introduction of the foreign in such sites as the recipe for sandwiches in *Shufu no Tomo*. Kawabata embodied the desperation in Ken, the former *tsuge* (a free-agent beggar with no designated territory) in *Asakusa Kurenaidan*, who had once attempted to become a laborer. He had been forced back into "the park" by the economic hard times and now scooped the wheat bran meant for the carp out of Hyōtan Pond for his sustenance (KY, 11–12).

In large part it is not the discussion of food, but the stark images defined by splashes of color that lend Kawabata's noir tale its erotic tinge. Because of his idiosyncratic rendering of the visual impact of Asakusa, Kawabata employed the colors prevalent in the geometric imagery of Soviet Constructivism, which had been translated into Japanese graphics by the early 1930s. Red, green, and black were used in varying combinations to produce a sensual rendering of the narrator's interactions with the assemblage of teenagers who guided him through the landmarks of Asakusa and evaded him in its alleyways.

Red is the defining term in the gang name chosen by the Asakusa juvenile actors. It is the name of the boat featured predominantly in the story action, and the Red Obi Society is the name of an underground organization of politicized shopgirls. Red images stand out in the maze of events cutting back and forth in Asakusa, and between the intense present and the earthquake of 1923 that haunts Kawabata's heroines. First there is the red of the costume-like dress worn by the young girl playing the piano in the opening pages of the story. A little girl whistles a jazz-like tune to accompany her *"Charleston,"* in syncopation with one of the bouncing balls—the fad that year. She sports a red ribbon and deep red lipstick. A beggar sleeps, wrapped in a red blanket; red laundry is suspended from the brow of a boat; two red lines traverse the towels distributed after the 1923 earthquake in Asakusa. Clothing marks the bodies of the female leads, just as they punctuated the discourse on the Modern Girl, but Kawabata also applies red to the bodies of women—there are red traces of mosquito bites on the legs of the stockingless dancing girls in the musical revue, the *Casino Folies,* and their legs also turn bright red with the cold (KY, 17, 22, 30, 42, 52, 81).

It is not only women in red who decorate the streets of Asakusa. There are red flags advertising sales and performances, there is the red lighting of the neon signs, and there are the red palm-sized handbills. These are modern variations on the placards obtained at shrines and temples that the Asakusa Crimson Gang members use as "name cards, identification documents, and danger signals." They plaster them onto Asakusa's sacred and secular landmarks. At 5:30 in the morning, "the *asphalt* is dyed pink" and "the red strewn throughout the still sleeping streets floats up so brilliantly" (KY, 66, 150–151, 197–198). Photographers of the era such as Kimura Ihei have left us black-and-white photographs that captured the clutter of shapes and signs framing the crowds in Asakusa at the turn of the decade. In effect, Kawabata's use of red colors in these photographs for us.

Red predominates, but the small handbills distributed by the gang members come in both red and green—the narrator muses that the gang members have been inspired by traffic lights—and there are other juxtapositions of the red with green in Kawabata's novel: the little Charleston dancer is selling both red and green toy balls; a dirigible flashes its green and red lights over Asakusa; a beggar boy sells a toy that lets off red-green sparks (KY, 17, 73, 119, 150). There are also other color combinations: the white, bare legs of the girl playing the piano are freshly sensual against her red costume and the black of the piano; the Red Obi Society had been joined by the Black Obi Society; the red collar with white embroidery on "the dressed-up crazy lady" is "strangely sad" (KY, 15, 29, 153). The colors, including some purples and yellow, move through the story via Kawabata's preoccupation with costuming as sexual erotic disguise.

The theme of masquerade is first introduced when we read of the girl in red playing the black piano; her clothing is more costume than *semi evening* dress. Yumiko has a taste for disguising herself. When the narrator first meets up with Yumiko she is barefoot, with bobbed hair. She is the girl wearing the red dress, who plays the piano in the entranceway to a tenement house. Later, Yumiko disguises herself as a ticket seller at the merry-go-round and as a gentle young girl in a theater audience. And Yumiko is also the girl in braids in the audience at the Aquarium; she is on the lookout for Akagi, the man who violated her sister on the night of the earthquake. At the end of the story, the narrator meets Yumiko in the waiting area for the one-sen steamer. She is now masquerading as an oil seller from Ōshima and is still flirting.

Maeda Ai, in his characteristically erudite and sensitive reading of *The Asakusa Crimson Gang*, claims that Yumiko's disguise is a "metaphor for Asakusa, 'city of shadows'" and that her androgyny is the source of the ambiguity of her disguises.[21] But Yumiko's disguises can also be read as masquerades—of girl passing for boy and girl passing for girl, as in the Takarazuka theater. Yumiko is masquerade in motion, and, despite her avowals to the contrary, is very much in charge of her moves. She insists to Akagi that he "make her a woman," but that very insistence on submission is an instance of her power. Kawabata describes her as masculine. He even creates the male gang member Akikō, who turns out to be Yumiko in disguise. Yumiko's handwriting looks masculine; she also has the clean limbs of a boy (KY, 69, 97, 123). But Yumiko's masculinity is premised on her femaleness. This is the aggressiveness of the prototypical Modern Girl, who revels in her modern costuming. Yet her subjectivity is the idealized "normal" feminist consciousness set forth by Mary Russo in her idealization of the "female grotesque." Such feminism, says Russo, "would be heterogeneous, strange, polychromatic, ragged, conflictual, incomplete, in motion, and at risk." Yumiko actually proclaims that she is "half-man." But she is not male. She recounts with irony the self-determining prophecy of her response to her sister's descent into insanity after the earthquake: "I'm not a woman. Because of seeing my sister, ever since I was a child I've thought I would never become a woman. And really, men are weaklings—nobody wants to make me a woman" (KY, 39, 41).

Yumiko's grotesque masquerade as male, but even more so as female, fits the problematic elaborated and debated by feminists since Mary Ann Doane first revisited Joan Riviere's psychoanalytic treatment of the "masquerade" of femininity. In Doane's terms, masquerade "flaunts femininity." The femme fatale is threatening because she owns a critical distance between herself and "female iconography." Yumiko is such a seductress. She illustrates Doane's explication of the double standard that allows women to dress as men. Doane notes that "clothes make the man," enabling the woman to "at least pretend that she is other." The male, in contrast, is locked into sexual identity. Kawabata concurs: "Right nearby, there are any number of vagrant women passing, dressed in male guise. One can be done with that by laughing. However, a man powdered white in Japanese wig, disguised as a woman, stealthily disappears with a man along the darkness behind the Temple—this gives one the shivers, as though one has just seen a weird lizard" (KY, 66).[22]

Yumiko is fully aware that she projects the spectacle of a manipulative "femininity with a vengeance." She calls herself the *mannequin girl* of Asakusa, explaining that she wears fake braids (which inevitably arouse men) because they are least recognizable as inauthentic, enabling her to be like "a maiden in braids." She also carefully choreographs the seduction scene leading up to her attack on Akagi—by way of a poisonous kiss— through her clothing and the positioning of her body (KY, 47, 67, 69–101). She appears to be well aware that she performs femininity, a position celebrated by Sue-Ellen Case and clarified in Doane's second essay, but at the same time her anxiety suggests Doane's critique of Riviere's notion of masquerade "as a position which is potentially disturbing, uncomfortable, and inconsistent, as well as psychically painful" and "inappropriate for women" (KY, 225).[23]

The "impossibility of a stable female position" is illustrated throughout *The Asakusa Crimson Gang*. Like Tanizaki, the creator of Naomi, the heroine of *A Fool's Love* discussed in the Modern Girl segment above, Kawabata is aware of the gender fluidity of the Japanese modern moment and determined to maintain the separation of the two sexes in the face of this flux. Ultimately, he adheres to a gender binary. Unlike Tanizaki, however, he is not threatened by the incursion of foreign culture. For Kawabata, foreign culture is malleable; in Todorov's terms, it becomes constitutive of a new, modern Japanese culture. It is female masquerading as feminine, and not as Western, that poses the problem in Asakusa (and by extension, in Japan) in 1930. Men, in the end, do make women. Kawabata illustrates this with the "real woman" heroine Haruko, who is "made into a woman" when she affirms her female sexuality after she has been kidnapped, raped, trapped, and kept naked while captive (KY, 211, 216). Ultimately, neither Kawabata nor Yumiko challenges the binary essentialism of gender merchandised by the café waitress, but the visions of Yumiko's masquerades challenge and flaunt the erotic energy of Asakusa—an eroticism that makes room for women like Yumiko both as self-consciously female spectacles and as spectators. The participation of women in the modern space of Kawabata's Asakusa combines an erotics of both motion and vision. Women are commodified bodies, but they are also active consumer-spectators in the restaurants, the shooting arcades, the revue halls, and the movie theaters. The movie theaters were where erotic fantasies were most alive.

HOLLYWOOD AS FANTASY
(IWASAKI AKIRA AND THE PORK CUTLET PROBLEM)

As Gonda, Soeda, and others were quick to point out, movies were central to Asakusa culture. Asakusa was also central to Japanese film culture. Film company executives attended the weekly opening of each new movie in Asakusa to predict the nationwide popularity of the film by the length of the line outside the theater. Asakusa moviegoers were privy to the first *talkies* in 1929, and, even after the depression had almost totally curtailed commercial entertainment, the crowds continued to come to Asakusa. The typical moviegoer had to budget for one movie and a simple dish: a movie and a bowl of rice with tempura in 1930 each cost forty sen, at a time when day laborers were earning one yen and sixty-three sen per day on average (in contrast to a bank employee's starting daily wage of seventy yen).[24]

The eroticism of Gonda's "movie fever" was informed by motion and vision outside and inside the theaters of the "movie streets" *(eigagai)* of Asakusa. These settings themselves constituted a visual montage. Different syllabaries vied for prominence on the banners hanging in front of the theaters and suspended across the streets, and movie titles were juxtaposed with the huge billboards depicting samurai dramas and Hollywood heroines. These images, preserved in photographs of Asakusa, enable us to imagine the movement and energy there, but the question of spectatorship—of what going to the movies meant to the eager audiences of Asakusa and elsewhere in Japan—is much more elusive. The opinions of two leading film critics of the modern years expand our understanding of the Japanese modern "Hollywood Fantasy" that prevented *Eiga no Tomo* from letting go of Hollywood.[25]

In his stage-theory of film history, Iwasaki Akira stated that by the "American Era" (1914–1918), the capitalist large picture and the star system had advertised bourgeois consumer culture to Japanese petit-bourgeois and proletarian spectators, drawing them into an eroticism of a bourgeoisie on the decline. Here he made a point of distinguishing between healthy eroticism and the decayed eroticism associated with sexual fetishism. And just as there were two types of eroticism, the spectatorship of capitalist film within a consumer culture was also double-edged, as Miriam Hansen and others have noted. Hansen's analysis not only echoes Iwasaki's sense of the potential of film; it also contributes to my conviction that the modern spectatorship in Japan of the 1920s and 1930s challenged the insular official discourse of family loyalty and seamless historic continuity. According to Hansen, spectatorship can be seen as a strategy to stabilize the contradictions of consumerism. These contradictions included "the discrepancy between utopian images of abundance, exotic splendor, and sensuality deployed to create consumerist desire and the industrial-capitalist discipline necessary to produce the spending power." According to Iwasaki, film's modernity lies in its ability to reach a mass audience. Film is concerned with "what reaches out to the masses, what moves the masses, what organizes the masses, what has the power to give pleasure to the masses."[26]

Iwasaki's attitude toward the modern is very much part of the mass-media discourse of the era. Movies were the *"tempo"* of the present, and jazz provided a rhythm that passed on the emotions of the *"ultra modern."* Jazz was also relevant in present-day life, in its role of arousing action. Iwasaki also addressed the modern in his tribute to the montage. Because of its rhythms, he asserted, montage, which was structured by *"rhythm"* and *"tempo,"* led to fantasy and could be used to represent memory.[27]

In his essay *Eiga Ideorogii* (Film ideology), which first appeared in July 1930 in *Chūō Kōron*, Iwasaki offered a brief history of moviegoing in Japan. Ten years earlier, films had been considered "popular play," but at the same time "moving pictures" were seen as dangerous for elementary school students, who were forbidden to attend. Movies had become a profitable business, along with the production of such goods as perfume, packaged medicine, and steel. Film was now art, dissected by filmgoers who let their coffee grow cold over their talk of "the appeal of cinema, its *speed,* its *rhythm,* its modernity." In a discreet swipe at state ideology that passed the censors, Iwasaki noted that films had also become politicized: they could "lecture like the Imperial Rescript on Education." He made it clear that his sympathies lay with the cinema produced for the masses that was shown during "Proletarian Film Evenings" in such neighborhoods as Honjo and Fukagawa, the slum areas surveyed by Kon.[28]

Just as Iwasaki's "film ideology" was film history, his essay "history of film" was fiction. One of the "tales" within, *Kyarifoorunian Rapusodii* (Californian rhapsody), was clearly intended to be reminiscent of a Hollywood film scenario, complete with reference to "a kiss like a saxophone" and an opening scene set in the present at May 5, 1927, in the Beverly Hills boudoir and marble bath of an unclothed, languorous heroine. Its cast also included a capitalist with a monocle and a studio extra named Clara Brooks. Clara, the epitome of the Modern Girl, is a very thinly veiled composite of Hollywood starlets Clara Bow and Louise Brooks. She sports both a *"boyish bob"* and class consciousness. When Charlie Chaplin makes a brief appearance, by way of newspaper headlines referring to his divorce, the male idol, a cynical movie star, responds by noting, "A genius is worshipped by all of the women he does not marry and scorned by all he has married."[29]

The glamour of Hollywood is merged with Iwasaki's vision of class conflict in the final scenes, which are about a studio strike. Iwasaki closes in on an *"illumination,"* in boldface capitals twice the height of the rest of the print: HOLLYWOOD LAND. This spectacular vision is accompanied by Iwasaki's open-ended conclusion: voices can be heard in the darkness of Hollywood Land. Iwasaki does not tell his readers whether these are the sounds of directors controlling extras, or in fact the converse. The class struggle is up for grabs. In the meantime, Hollywood remains. Iwasaki would continue to celebrate and question its existence in his mixture of melodramatic imaginings and sharper attacks. His criticism was aimed at both Hollywood and Japanese film worlds.[30]

In the same essay by Iwasaki, a second vignette, *Amerika Higeki* (American tragedy), is set in El Paso, site of the Miss Texas beauty pageant, a "modern slave market." The pageant winner, Flobell Lee, spurred by her horoscope in *Motion Picture Magazine*, takes the Southern Pacific to Hollywood.[31] There she walks naked, drinking in the neon lights that advertise a litany of capitalist luxury items in a staccato of red and green capital letters. (The last four ad sound bites are typeset at drunken angles.)

ARROW COLLAR
DEVRYS MOVIECAMERA

HAPPY HIT
IT'S TOASTED
PEPSODENT!
HAVE A CHESTER

Flobell, along with a talking orangutan and an oversized Serbian, becomes a hit in Hollywood. However, she is ultimately and tragically abandoned for "the smell of the arms" of another. In sum, Iwasaki's Hollywood story highlights the fetishistic form of Hollywood eroticism in its image of the nude Miss Texas and of Hollywood dalliances.[32]

More direct political commentary is evident in Iwasaki's *Ai no Ansorojii* (Anthology of love), an imagined anecdote about a Greek classics scholar turned censor for the state of Pennsylvania. The censor crows that since he has been slumbering in the world of *Iphigenia* and *Electra,* he was able to show an almost 100 percent "rate of excitement" during a film screening, thereby beating out his opponents at this test of sensitivity to sex appeal. This is how he had triumphed to become a judge of moral conduct. The Japanese readers must have noticed that all of the morally coded words in this tale were adopted from the language of Japanese censors. When the jolly bureaucrat from Pennsylvania confessed that he feared for the *kokutai* (the term referring to the unique and sacrosanct Japanese national polity), this reverse code-switching was more than evident: an American had adopted an ideologically loaded Japanese idiom.[33]

Iwasaki framed his discussion of capitalism and the threat of state repression in joking terms, but he also had to come to terms with the danger of a "new Babel." Now that talkies had inundated the market, what was at stake was whether spectators could engage in a universal code-switching allowing for understanding and communication, or whether the silent film may in fact have been more international. In 1930 Iwasaki called the silent film *visual Esperanto.* In 1931 he attacked the "new Babel" that had already shaken the world of filmgoers in Tokyo, Berlin, and Paris. Five years later, in another Hollywood story, *Tookii no Nendaiki* (Chronicle of the talkies), he continued his assault: "the disorder of a new tower of Babel rose up. American films were no longer comprehensible to the peoples of Europe, China, Africa, and Latin America. . . . There was the need for a new messiah, just as the carpenter's son from Nazareth had stood between God and the child of man." Iwasaki concluded that a messiah had indeed appeared, not in the form of one white-skinned youth, but as men and women of red, black, and yellow skins. He did not refer directly to the writers of talkie captions, but instead referred to their "sacred rooms," decorated not with crosses but with gold lettering spelled out "Foreign Department." He chose to create a fictional group of new bureaucrats who produced language to be consumed within the world capitalist system. Included among the ranks of what he called a "racial exposition" were a short Japanese lawyer, a beautiful Irish maiden, a communist who had fled Italy, a Chinese who instigated anti-Japanese demonstrations in New York, and an Indian who was a disciple of Gandhi. (The disciple from the subcontinent lived in a fine hotel, ate *"beefsteak,"* and was a practitioner of the Kama Sutra.) The new Babel used numerous languages to give the same message. The translation was one-dimensional and unidirectional: the language of the American talkies was being translated for spectators in foreign cultures, but these spectators—captive to the power of American capitalism—could not communicate among themselves. "They cannot speak to each other at all, but they all do the same work, hitting the same *typewriter* keys. How do you say the slang, *'Oh Jimmy, you're a sheik. Look out, you're hooked onto my best shimmy!'* in Chinese? Or in Spanish, or Hindustani, or Japanese, or Persian?"

Not only was this Babel mutually unintelligible, it was monolithic. The entire world, he argued, heard only one culture and about only one economy: "*Talkies* carry not only American songs and *records*. They always carry with them American oil and steel and coal and automobiles and airplanes and battleships and foreign policy and imperialism on the wings of songs. To Cuba, to Costa Rica, to Guatemala, to China—throughout the world."[34] Iwasaki's attack on capitalist cultural imperialism extended beyond the world of films. When, in 1936, he published the opinion that Western music might be adapted to the Japanese context, but only to the extent that a *pork cutlet* was "*tonkatsu*" (the Japanese version of deep-fried cutlet), the staple of the reader of *Shufu no Tomo*. He appeared to use this transcultural, popularizing movement of modern culture as a degradation that was a disservice to the Western food and to its new incarnation in Japan.[35]

Iwasaki shared with his readers his own experience of this Babel when, in 1935, he apologized for his ignorance of Chinese lived experience: "To say that I am Japanese is not to say that I hold *kokusuiteki* views of love of native place. As a human being who practices a *seikatsu* and was educated as Japanese, and who has within him inevitably emotional and intellectual limits as a Japanese, I thus have 100 percent sensibility and understanding of Japanese film, but in terms of foreign films, especially in regard to Chinese films, that *percentage* is considerably lessened. In other words, I know little of the forms taken by Chinese *seikatsu* or of the shapes of its emotions, and I especially know not even one word of the language—it means I am that sort of human being."[36]

Although Iwasaki was critical of the Hollywood fantasy, his own Hollywood scenarios, in fact, included the coded and not-so-coded racism of American film culture: as early as 1927, *Kyarifoorunian Rapusodii* referred to "the laughter of a *negro* cook," and by 1936, in a discussion about the *stimuli* offered by film, he referred to the need to create racial, national *(jinshuteki, minzokuteki) appeal,* class *appeal* for the pure American *types,* and—for *niggers* and Chinese—references to invading oppressors. Iwasaki did not flinch at the slurs, which appear as natural as his description of Shanghai. He said that Shanghai had an American *chop suey*–like taste of the international, but he failed to consider that the Japanese presence was contributing to the flavor, when he recognized that exotic Shanghai was a Hollywood product. His conclusion: "One feels that in Shanghai, in reality, a lovely *Shanghai Lily* awaits on some street corner." In the end, Iwasaki, the critic of Hollywood, is a spectator taken in by the exoticism of Hollywood erotic fantasy.[37]

OZAKI MIDORI (LOVE FOR A CANE AND A HAT)

In contrast to Iwasaki's recreation of Hollywood erotics, Ozaki Midori flaunted her position as spectator, and moreover, as eroticized woman spectator. The object of her desire: Charlie Chaplin. In her film criticism, Ozaki Midori was able to communicate the emotional pull of the movies more than most Japanese critics writing about the modern. Although she refused to speak for other moviegoers, her representation of her own fantasy world gives a sense of how Japanese filmgoers allowed themselves to be erotically enveloped by images of movie stars and their gestures.

This cerebral and subtle writer respected fantasy while decrying false eroticism, contrasting the "tower of *erotic* starlets" cluttering film culture in 1930 with the fading memory of the rhythm of Josephine Baker's Charleston. Possibly unintentionally, this critic spoke for the female spectator when she recalled how even Josephine Baker had lost her sexual appeal. Baker's dancing had first made her nervous, then satiated her, and had finally led to boredom. Ozaki had grown sick of the rows of legs protruding from women's drawers. As bears noting more than once, Ozaki's erotic longing was directed at Charlie Chaplin and the physicality of his gestures. The eroticization of women in Japanese modern culture relied on the fetishization of parts of women's bodies, a process captured by the French writer Annie Ernaux: "The body under constant surveillance and restraint, abruptly shattered into a heap of pieces—eyes, skin, hair—that must be dealt with one by one to reach perfection." Ozaki saw this process in her recollection of Gloria Swanson's slowly unveiled legs. She knew that the male was eroticized differently; Charlie's gestures, along with his chosen costume, drew her to him. She quoted the character Charlie from the play *Chaplin:* "Charlie has said, 'We do not possess heads. We only possess hats. Hats make the person.'" Inverting Kon Wajirō's anticapitalist statement that "hats wear people," Ozaki imagined the hat as transformative and choreographed a fantasy wherein Charlie's hat landed on the heads of Buster Keaton, Harold Lloyd, and others.[38]

Like others writing about Japanese modern times, Ozaki is concerned with body language. In the "Random Writer," her alter ego is bewitched by the way Charlie's gestures meld his body with his fashion. She ponders what Chaplin's head must be thinking when it is hatless and concludes that it must be preoccupied with how to make that body come alive. Here is her rendering of Chaplin's choreographic cinematography: "Plots. Episodes. Techniques. Background. Costuming. Accessories. All are used by that body." In 1933, Ozaki would rework her random thoughts on Chaplin, as expressed in "Love for a Cane and a Hat" (subtitled "On Two Works by Chaplin") in an almost identical essay titled "Eccentric with Hat and Cane." Here she would add a close reading of her favorite scene from *The Gold Rush*, in which Chaplin's hands hold dancing human legs made out of potatoes speared by forks. Her description of a group of spectators delighting in *The Gold Rush* could very well describe an Asakusa movie hall:

> When Charlie, who'd been stood up by his lover, began to dance his potato dance, the workers, those in hunting hats, the old women and the young girls were drawn into an eddy of laughter. The grandson threw down his rice crackers to clap his hands, and even the bottles of lemon pop under the chairs raised their voices in rousing appreciation. My heart began to cry bitterly.

Ozaki's "random thoughts" also reveal other aspects of film culture. For example, each Wednesday she would scan the week's movie schedule to determine which stars would be appearing on screen. She would also study the programs, not only for memories of Chaplin but also for such information as glossaries of new, modern terms. She looks up (the Yiddish word) *kibitzers* but cannot find it in either her English or her German dictionaries. After conjecturing that this is too new a word, or that the dictionaries are too inexpensive, she is delighted to find the definition among the dozen or so offered in the program of the Musashinokan theater: "The sort *[jinshu]* who borrows your automobile and then telephones from the suburbs to announce that 'there is no more gas'—the sort who reads the outcome of detective novels at the very beginning—the sort who endlessly tells bad jokes, etc."[39]

Ozaki's filmgoing experiences are not recounted as "foreign" or "Japanese." (Note her use of the term *jinshu* above: there is no racializing here.) She is not unaware of some national characteristics as when, for example, she ridicules the conformity of Japanese intellectuals. Recently she has spied three Japanese youths, all carrying the same book, sitting in the same room, and all reading approximately the same page of this same book. Japanese people all believe, she declares, that one goes for a walk only with one's legs. She also acknowledges that Germans have national habits and that the voices of American actors, male and female, have a breadth and a depth not found in Japan. National differences are also gendered: German men are not American men. Nonetheless, distinctions in Ozaki's experience of filmgoing are based not on national identity but on venue. Among the movie theaters in Tokyo, she differentiates between the Musashinokan, which specialized in foreign films, in the entertainment district of Shinjuku, and the Hōraku cinema, which catered to a less elite clientele.[40]

Most important and most apparent in her discussions of Chaplin is Ozaki's presumption of an experience shared by Western and Japanese audiences. This view takes into account the "behavior of the urban girl" (Ozaki's version of the modern girl?)—an experience informed more by gender and by universal passions than by nationhood. The same presumption is the source of her sense of entitlement allowing her to critique all talkies for their slow tempo, and non-Japanese films for the shape of their costuming and for the miscasting of their heroes and heroines. Talkies disturb the silence that allows for clarity. Lillian Gish in *The Wind* is a far cry from those "emanating 'it'" who are currently in fashion, and at the same time is incapable of offering "more than the number of expressions that one can count on five fingers." *The Count of Monte Cristo* is boring. John Gilbert, who has the same laugh as the period-piece hero, Bandō Tsumasaburō, has redeemed himself in *Flesh and the Devil*.[41]

It would appear that Ozaki was pulled back home to the countryside by her family, and away from the Tokyo literary scene just as she was beginning to gain acclaim, for two reasons. Her health had been destroyed by medication taken for migraines and they disapproved of her living with a man ten years her junior. We do not know how she responded to the cultural shifts of the second half of the 1930s. The intellectual world was leaning toward support for the state, as revealed in the case of Iijima Tadashi. Here was a film critic who first talked in terms of the relationship of dreams to spectatorship, deferring to Freud and to the modernism of Clara Bow. Yet by 1939, in a move analogous to Gonda Yasunosuke's switch from *goraku* (play) to *kokumin goraku* (national play), Iijima had substituted the term *kokumin seikatsu* (national everyday life) for *seikatsu*.[42] The addition of the reference of the nation as integral to the everyday meant that the erotic was to be deemphasized, displaced by a regimentation of gestures and affect. And while the grotesque as commonly defined has an erotic (if perverse) element to it, the grotesquerie in this history of the erotic grotesque nonsense to be found in Asakusa was a grotesquerie of wants, rather than of desires. *Guro* was about the desperation of poverty.

2   Down-and-Out Grotesquerie

Asakusa grotesquerie must be defined by the tensions embodied in the co-existence of dire poverty with leisure, of resistance with surveillance, of un-precedented (capitalist and anticapitalist) attitudes with older forms of re-lationships, and of desperation with humor. Although it was a playground for those enriched by capitalism, it was also the home of Tokyo's most down-and-out.

The speaking orangutan and the giant Serbian imagined by Iwasaki Akira evoke two commonly noted aspects of the grotesque: the sideshow freak and the grossly oversized or deformed. We have now expanded the connotations of *ero* beyond manifestations and sensual consummations of physical desire, to include the sensual as experienced in gustatory pleasure and visual culture. What if we were also to rethink the grotesque beyond the common notions of unseemly, unwieldy, nonhuman, or the monstrous? What if we were to consider how just as Asakusa was about being out—out of one's work space, out of one's residential neighborhood, out in the streets surrounding the eating places and movie houses—it was at the same time about being down, at the bottom of the social order. It could be seen, in other words, as grotesque in the conventional sense, but it was also grotesque de-fined as down-and-out. Moreover, Asakusa grotesquerie included expres-sions of awareness and protest against this very marginalization. These were protests by those imagined as voiceless, far from able to give voice to a social critique. This is the meaning I am assigning to Asakusa grotes-querie.[1]

Let me elaborate by discussing meanings that others have attached to the term *grotesque*. Central to Mikhail Bakhtin's conception of the grotesque is a preoccupation with bodily needs of food, drink, digestion, and sex. Es-pecially important is the lower stratum of the body because digestion, defecation, copulation, conception, pregnancy, and birth are central to Bakhtin's concern for social life as a continual process of birth, death, and again birth; of becoming and growth—the eternal incomplete, unfinished nature of being. Bakhtin's grotesque is impossible without laughter. He contends that such humor, expressed in forms of parody, including exaggeration, hyperbole, and excess serves to defeat fear by transforming the terrifying into the grotesque. In Bakhtin's treatment of European folk festivity as revealed by Rabelais, popular play secularizes the sacred and challenges official power via negation. This world is peopled by extraordinary human beings—those with bodies of mixed parts (part human, part animal), giants, dwarfs, pygmies, and monsters. These individuals live, laugh, and die as part of an ongoing social whole as did the denizens of Asakusa.[2]

Others have adapted Bakhtin's version. Mary Russo has traced two approaches to the grotesque: the social dimension, as represented by Bakhtin, and the modern, psychological, interior dimension of individual experience as the word *grotesque* comes to be associated with the words *strange, remarkable, tragic, criminal*. By putting the psyche into the picture, Russo explores the long-standing and irreversible connection between the two concepts constituting the pervasive notion of the female grotesque.[3]

The scatological, sexual, parodic, antiauthoritarian, and feminized aspects of the grotesque were all present in the Japanese magazine *Gurotesuku*. So were racist and pornographic elements. During its brief life (from November 1928 through January 1930, with a final, "Revival Commemorative" issue appearing in April 1931), this self-consciously *modern* magazine added racism to associations given by Bakhtin and Russo. *Gurotesuku* treated such topics as "The World History of the Development of the Toilet," "Repulsive Chinese Eating Habits," "Meiji Peep Shows," "Georg Grosz," "The *Mobo* and the *Moga* of the Edo period," "Women Sumo Wrestlers," "The *Lesbian*," and "The Queen of *Negro* Dance, Josephine Baker." Its revival issue featured a roundtable discussion by survivors of everyday life in prison. My interest in Asakusa comes out of the down-and-out culture of its grotesquerie rather than the titillating topics set forth above. The two-part article "On Beggars" appearing in the renewal issue of *Grotesque* is most apposite to my concern with those who were marginalized in Asakusa and within Japan.[4]

Asakusa grotesquerie (I will from here on use *down-and-out* and *grotesque* interchangeably), including the celebration of food, the peep shows, and the valorization of group over individual in the park, must be framed within the intense poverty of the modern years and of the modern neighborhood of Asakusa where tourists "up from the country" prayed and bought trinkets at the Asakusa Kannon, factory workers on their days off went to the moving pictures, and where everyone, including the beggars, ate and drank a panoply of foods from East and West. Here the reworking by Peter Stallybrass and Allon White of Bakhtin's concern with the grotesque body helps us to place such texts as Soeda Azenbō's *Asakusa Teiryūki* into Japanese modern times. For Stallybrass and White, the "low"—"of the body, of literature, of society, of place"—is both reviled and desired. This is "the primary site of contradiction." Asakusa was such a "primary site of contradiction," as revealed by journalistic accounts of everyday life in Asakusa Park left to us by Soeda and others.[5]

When we follow the accounts of those who were infused with the documentary impulse in Asakusa during the modern years—the writings by journalists, the ruminations of novelists, and the notations of bureaucrats—how are we to separate fact from fiction? We cannot, and we need not. There is sufficient discussion of the culture of those struggling to stay alive in Asakusa as the depression deepened at the turn of the decade to enable us to use these sources as mutually illuminating. A picture-perfect representation of those on the bottom is unattainable, nor can the historian be sure that the voices were accurately recorded—even if the words are identical, meaningful affect and important gesture will be missing. The historian does not know for sure whether those at the bottom of the social hierarchy spoke what they saw as the truth, to power. In fact, more than one source makes it clear that those being surveyed were quite aware of the power relationship implied by such practices and that they evaded their interlocutors accordingly. Their interlocutors also recognized that they could not understand this society in its totality. As long as we place both survey categories and surveyors within a politicized moment that has been dismissed as the playful transitional time of a decadent erotic grotesque nonsense, a history of the Asakusa down-and-out can emerge. My history is premised on several precepts from Ted Porter's *Trust in Numbers*, including his characterization of social power: power must be exercised in a variety of ways to make measurements and tallies valid and his historicist and political conclusion (discussed in the context of the invention of crime rates and unemployment rates) that every category has the potential to become a new thing.[6]

According to contemporary commentators on Asakusa, its social formation was constituted by different groups, each with a strong identity made up of both unprecedented and continuing traditions. The parade of figures making up the social formation of Soeda Azenbō's Asakusa are (in order of appearance) the beggars, vagrants, hawkers, performers, rickshaw men, sad (and mad) women serving their fellow vagrants, juvenile delinquents, and

Koreans, Chinese, and Russian foreigners. Workers are not entirely absent, of course. One beggar, the survivor of a factory accident, plays the *shamisen* with the only finger remaining on his left hand (SA, 164, 176, 196).[7]

Five communities of what I have termed grotesquerie emerge from a synthetic reading of Soeda's documentation and other writings from the modern years—writings I consider to be both fact and fiction. These are the beggars, the vagrants *(lumpen)*, the hawkers, the juvenile delinquents, and the freaks (including foreigners). The notion of the grotesque as cut off from other human beings was mentioned above in the segment on going to the movies: this image of an isolated figure conforms to Yoshimi Shun'ya's notion, taken from Tsurumi Shunsuke, of "aloneness" in Asakusa. Yet the practices of the denizens of Asakusa appear to counter this characterization, for they reveal close relationships within and between down-and-out groupings.[8]

The attitudes and practices of these societies offer insight into Asakusa grotesquerie (defined as the product of the co-existence of need with abundance) at a time when all realized that a break with an earlier tradition had been made. They also suggest how Asakusa was not a hermetically closed free space, but a part of the montage of social relationships throughout the Japanese nation during the modern years. An examination of the cultural practices of each group within Asakusa reveals the tense relationship between agency and surveillance within one space, and the series of transformations in social relationships within Asakusa after the Meiji Restoration, the earthquake of 1923, and the onset of the depression in 1927.

BEGGAR CULTURE

Beggars are the first to appear in Soeda's chronicle of Asakusa. They float onto the scene at 5:00 A.M. to lift the lids off trash cans, querying, "Where'd you sleep last night—behind the moving pictures?" It is these men combing through garbage, and not Gonda's working-class heroes, who are important to Soeda: the "beggar philosopher" who talks of Newton, Einstein, and Carnegie, the widow of the Beggar Boss, and other sharply drawn personalities. These drifters gather *zuke*, slang for leftover food placed out back of the tiny restaurants. Asakusa beggars , in other words, consumed Asakusa eroticism in their own way. Not only did they take advantage of the abundance of foodstuffs, they also enjoyed movie culture, as they both monitored billboards and attended shows (SA, 6–7, 175–181).[9]

Ishizumi Harunosuke based his writings about beggars on more than ten years of living among them in what he termed "the play space of the *proletariat.*" In one work on Asakusa culture, he created a conception reminiscent of Bakhtin's discussion of the contradictions inhabiting the grotesque: he loved Asakusa because it was tomboyish, scatterbrained, vital, alcoholic, and openly, refreshingly unapologetically, stark naked, as though it had washed its backside in a big river—and, at the same time, had wallowed in Asakusa filth. Impurity and abhorrence were mixed together as though a human being's most unseemly belly had been pulled out. While claiming to present their daily lives exactly as they were, Ishizumi was less sanguine about his ability to present an accurate history of the beggars, who had first come to be associated as a social group in Asakusa during the Tokugawa period. He questioned the veracity of the story accounting for the ascension of Kuruma Zenshichi, the boss of these "nonpersons" in the ghettoized space of Asakusa. Three hundred years later, who was to say whether this was a lie that appeared to be the truth or the truth that appeared to be a lie? We may take the same cynical position regarding Ishizumi's description of Asakusa beggar mores, temperament, and methods, but his typology of the hierarchy of beggar positions and practices appears to be the product of a fieldwork that was sensitive to how the beggars represented themselves to each other by 1929.[10]

Ishizumi divided the more than one hundred beggars (men and women) into five categories. At the top of this social order, the *kenta* boss kept strict control over his jurisdiction, wherein almost sixty *kenta* commuted to five fixed, lucrative sites, such as spots en route to the front entrance to the Asakusa temple. There they could receive money from those praying. On the second rung, the *tsubu* had a freer but more precarious existence, for although they were not subject to the dictates of a boss, neither were they allocated a fixed site for begging. At the third level, both the *zuke*—the same word was used to refer to leftovers—and the *daigara*, like the figures who float to the fore of Soeda's book, subsisted on leftovers from Asakusa eateries. Beggars occupying the lowest rank were the *shiroi* (a rephrasing of the term *hiroi*, meaning those who pick up), who foraged for the foulest of refuse on which to subsist.[11]

Life could be good for the beggars at the top end of their social order. There was, for example, the mad old woman who ate only leftovers from sushi restaurants, and there were the bars in Asakusa that catered only to beggars. Kawabata described a gathering of drunken beggars grouped around a naked girl seated on a revolving tabletop in such a bar (KY, 45). Nonetheless, since the completion of the post-earthquake urban renewal, authorities were continually chasing beggars out of the park.[12]

Ishizumi makes clear that there has been a marked break in beggar culture with the Meiji Restoration. Begging had hitherto been either a sideline
to other work or vice versa. It was the social distinctions of the "civilizing"
of the Meiji era that had led beggars to adorn their bodies with dirt in unprecedented fashion, just as it was such "civilizing" that had led to the market in beggars' children—the more sickly the child's appearance, the higher
the price. During the Tokugawa period, beggars, because they belonged to
the *hinin* (nonperson) caste, had been forbidden to wear topknots. Thus,
when, under the Meiji Restoration, it was ordered that all do away with
their topknots to eliminate such marks of privilege, ironically, all appeared
to be "nonpersons." During this moment of transition, not only the samurai lost their emblems of prestige. The *"nonpersons,"* who were no longer
the only group to possess the right to work as beggars, lost community and
identity with the proclamation freeing them in the summer of 1871.[13]

Credit for the relatively orderly division of labor among beggars now
competing for limited resources in the confined space had to be given to the
kenpō, or constitutions regulating the *seikatsu* of the beggars from below.
The punishment for not following group rules was expulsion from the security of Asakusa Park. In a section entitled "Beggars in the Past and in the
Present," Ishizumi lamented how the struggle for survival had produced a
new type of cheating, utilitarian beggar who was a far cry from his early
Meiji predecessors. Meiji beggars had attempted to return large sums of
money and lost or stolen objects to those who had inadvertently been separated from their possessions, even though they knew they would be vio-
lating old pollution taboos by doing so. (Before the Meiji era, anything
touched by beggars was generally presumed to be defiled.) Ishizumi provided the following summation: the struggle for survival within material
civilization had produced beggars with the characteristics of modern men.[14]

When reading accounts of grotesquerie as documented by Ishizumi, it is
often difficult to distinguish between the beggar *(kojiki)* and the vagrant
(furōsha). For example, when discussing the Chinese and Korean candy sell-
ers as part-time vagrants, he acknowledges that while there is a difference
between the beggars and vagrants who spread out from Asakusa, the Chinese and Koreans living in slum conditions are no dirtier and no rowdier
than their Japanese counterparts. However, after his one-day survey of the
Asakusa temple grounds, the modernologist Arai Sen'o was able to conclude
that women and men beggars carried hats in order to carry their coins. Arai
called the top class of beggars who repeated their daily commutes to their
set workplaces, "professional" and shared his astonishment at watching a
beggar youth change out of his work clothes into a fresh kimono and new

clogs before leaving for the day. Vagrants, called *lumpen (rumpen)* by 1931, did not have access to such luxuries.[15]

VAGRANT CULTURE

The vagrant *(furōsha)* was the second social type to appear in Soeda Azenbō's day in the life of Asakusa. Playing off of Gorky's work, Soeda introduced the Asakusa vagrants as lying about, hunched over, standing, or leaning back as part of a continual "live performance of *The Depths*," in which the curtain never came down. The group included a forty-year-old confused woman and a young boy of thirteen or fourteen. In Soeda's report, members keep track of each other's whereabouts, sleep in close formation under the wisteria trellis in the Park, and share treasured food. Within a year, Kawabata Yasunari would echo this emphasis on community in his accounts of twenty vagrants sharing breakfast (KY, 24–25).[16]

According to Soeda, *vagrant* is a generic term covering those out of work, alcoholics, those who have not been able to return home after a bout of pleasure in Asakusa, embezzlers, fugitives, wives escaping discord in their households, street laborers, full-time vagrants, beggars, and the abandoned. For them, Asakusa Park is a haven made comfortable by the abundance of *zuke*, and, just as the beggars have their set places for business, the vagrants have their own established practices for making their form of livelihood. Soeda offers a montage of information: restaurants place leftovers on or next to garbage containers, and, in return, designated vagrants clean the area around the eatery. One vagrant divides a chunk of sugar and crumbs of cake among his silent cohort on a park bench. Another vagrant, contemptuous of the lifestyle offered by *Shufu no Tomo*, complains: "I'm sick of *cutlets*. In the first place, our standard of living's better than the middle class. No way those straight-and-narrow poor people living in the tenements could live like us." A third obsequiously feigns appreciation at soba scraps, tastes them, and discards them. After insisting to the suspicious proprietor (who threatens to leave no more food in the future) that he has indeed enjoyed the noodles, he walks away, muttering, "I might be a leftover gatherer, but no way could I eat anything like that" (SA, 153–158, 162).

Surveillance did not work among the Asakusa vagrant population who were making themselves at home. This illustrates Yoshimi's analysis that Asakusa was not only a destination for those escaping a specific place, but was also a sought after space to come home to. Soeda was quick to scoff at official use of surveys, noting that the Asakusa vagrant was suspicious of such bureaucratic practices.[17] He pointed out that the "vagrant hunt" by one police station found more than 600 vagrants in the park alone, whereas the official survey listed only 380 vagrants in the entire city. Vagrants could not stand questioning, he claimed, and as soon as they got a whiff of a survey— and they did have a keen sense of smell for such things—they moved to temporary hiding places. Those who were ensnared gave false information. Thus, both Soeda and Kawabata implied that neither the informants nor the numbers could be trusted: "You can't count vagrants on an abacus" (KY, 120; SA, 156). Most of the vagrants in Asakusa may indeed have been touched in the head—as Kawabata indicated, when he called Asakusa one large insane asylum—but they were not stupid (KY, 130). Maybe they sensed what Ted Porter has made clear in his discussion of the rise of the technology of cost accounting—bureaucrats with any real power did not need to take refuge in quantitative analysis. To do so was to constrain their own behavior as much as it constrained that of those being measured.[18]

The writings of Kusama Yasoo, much more than Soeda's reportage, are as much about both those who attempted to survey vagrants as they are about the vagrants themselves. Surveys, as a form of surveillance, were an integral form of Japanese modern culture as can be inferred from documents like the Ōbayashi's survey of café waitresses and the studies by Gonda. And Kusama was able to go beyond most social scientists to recognize the struggle for power between surveyor and surveyed. In his numerous documents we find the tension between surveillance and agency, along with the contradiction between leisure and want that defined Asakusa grotesquerie.

In 1927 Kusama issued an alarm: the number of vagrants, those who had fallen to the depths of society to stay there, groaning, as they wandered from place to place, had risen considerably. He noted the false definition that our nation *(waga kuni)* had placed on the vagrant: one without a fixed home. According to long-standing state and popular opinion, vagrants were those without address and fixed employment. This definition had long been employed in order to control vagrancy as a crime, but in fact, the number of vagrants wandering around Tokyo who were absolute proletarians was not low (these were workers with no financial reserves who had fallen into a state of unemployment or who had been compelled to stop work due to ill health in spite of their youth). Kusama was working with state statistics while at the same time cataloging and critiquing and participating in state surveillance practices. He was considered a master at his job by his colleagues in the Tokyo Municipal Bureaucracy. He was also greeted warmly as an insider when he approached groups of vagrants in the Asakusa temple yard. Kusama's intimacy with the improverished floating populace is attested to by a fellow bureaucrat who recalls being invited to accompany Kusama to Asakusa. Not only did the group of vagrants wave, but several sought out handshakes from the two city employees. Kusama's companion recalls that some showed advanced symptoms of what was then called leprosy. (Some were missing fingers; blood was evident on others.) Kusama's greeting in response was, "I've brought along a new guy. He's young, but take good care of him." Kusama had urged the young man to shake hands with these men. The above vagrants could easily have been Soeda's vagrants.[19]

Kusama's emphasis on the group nature of vagrant society in his 1927 study and in "The Poor as Seen on a Night in the Rainy Season," written in 1921, also resonates with Soeda's focus on *furōsha* community and antagonism toward authority. In the latter piece, the self-styled investigator's interview of two Imado Park inhabitants is interrupted by the entrance of three uniformed police officers. Kusama says he was curious to see how far the police would go in disciplining the vagrants; he had watched the three in uniform beam flashlights into a group of vagrants gathered on benches. When one young man had counterattacked, yelling at the police, "How dare you call me lazy?" those who had begun to disperse, gathered around in support. Kusama's conclusion: The currents of contemporary social thought had even floated over to these sort of *donzoko* (depths) and were making small waves.[20]

Kusama introduced a 1929 essay on vagrant practices of subsistence (as opposed to resistance) by pointing to the unkempt vagrants wearing clothing tattered like seaweed and moving through the shadows of the lively crowds at such sites as Asakusa Park (known as the fountainhead of pleasures) and Ginza at night, which was enlivened by Modern Boys and Modern Girls. Like Ishizumi, he explicated the beggar hierarchy, noting that the *takari* who warned the top-ranking *kenta* of approaching police was a form of *yōjinbō* (bodyguard) for these beggars who were allowed their allotted places. Kusama also set forth forms of labor adopted by vagrants, including legal and illegal trash collection. Vagrants could advertise moving pictures: some walked the streets of Asakusa with signs on their backs; others distributed handbills.

It is in the context of Kusama's discussion of a third form of subsistence (in addition to begging and various forms of menial labor), that a female grotesque emerges. The women vagrants *(onna furōsha)* lead their customers (male vagrants and sometimes laborers) into graveyards and empty houses. These prostitutes, who camp out with their unfortunate male contemporaries, are unseemly, Kusama implies, because most are over forty years of age. One is even close to sixty.[21]

Beginning in 1930 and most definitely by 1931, vagrants were called by another name in the writings of Kusama and the mass press. They were now *lumpen (rumpen)*—a tribute, no doubt, to the extent to which Marxist analysis had permeated Japanese social consciousness. The term may have also resulted from the fact that the worldwide depression had made vagrancy a universal as opposed to an indigenous problem. Kusama's "Tales of the *Lumpen*" took the latter approach. He traced the history of *furōsha*, beginning with the Tokugawa Shogunate's cordoning off of the unemployed and the ill in Asakusa. The Meiji state had made use of that site when it needed to hide vagrants and beggars from visiting European dignitaries in 1870. The beggars had been released, only to experience a second roundup, after which those unable to work had remained in confinement. Kusama made no distinction between vagrants and *lumpen*. Both groups shared the following five aspects: (1) lack of fixed domicile; (2) "inhuman" clothing; (3) neglect of personal hygiene; (4) absence of possessions; and (5) focus on life in the present, with no sense of the future. But Kusama did see a significant difference between the vagrants in Taishō and the contemporary homeless, who merited the new label of *lumpen*. Only 20 percent of the homeless at the end of the Taishō had ended up as vagrants because of their inability to find work. Most had been constitutionally unable to work because of infirmity, age, inability, household relationships, or disinclination. Now, five or six years later, there had been a complete reversal: 80 percent honestly desired to work.[22]

The persona of Charlie Chaplin, Asakusa film hero, fit all five of Kusama's criteria, and this may be one reason why he received such an intense welcome upon his arrival in Japan on May 14, 1932. Press coverage of Chaplin's trip helps us understand the popularity of Chaplin as expressed in Ozaki's fantasies, the workings of popular Hollywood fantasies regarding "Charlie" and others, and attitudes toward modern grotesquerie. Over a month before Chaplin's arrival, *Tokyo Asahi Shinbun* readers were forewarned in a message from Hong Kong, delivered by Chaplin's assistant, that he definitely did not want any kind of "festive commotion" as welcome. But Charlie was greeted with just that very sort of outpouring. By the time his ship docked, highbrow aficionados had been told that Chaplin occupied a unique position in the film world; he was likened to René Claire, maker of *À Nous la Libérté*. At the same time, he was proletarian. Chaplin's social concerns with the depression and the unemployment in the United States were quoted, and one article referred to his desire to visit a poor neighborhood like that seen in *City Lights* as part of his sight-seeing. The class theme was highlighted upon Chaplin's arrival, when the *Tokyo Nichinichi Shinbun* quoted his assertion "I am a friend of the poor" as a boldface headline.[23]

Not only movies prepared Chaplin's eager hosts and hostesses throughout Japan. *The Gold Rush* had been ranked first in *Kinema Junpō*'s "Best Ten" of 1927. And lucky Japanese consumer-subjects were privy to the "Chaplin Exhibition" spectacle, which had opened in Takashimaya department store in Tokyo, before moving on to Osaka and Kyoto. The consensus in the press appeared to be that while Chaplin was clearly not Japanese, he was kin. Anticipating his arrival in Kobe and then in Tokyo, police distributed two thousand platform tickets in an attempt to control the crowds. The next day a large advertisement for a special edition of Morinaga chocolate offered a special chocolate bar to fans of the "great artist." The wrapper was adorned with Charlie's face and the words "Welcome Charlie Chaplin" in both English and Japanese. In the same column, a Meiji milk caramel box featured a full-length, stylized figure of Chaplin painted by a Japanese artist, and bearing the following poem:

> Happiness Chaplin has arrived
> Lots of fun this caramel

On the same page, an advertisement for the June issue of the family magazine *Kingu* offered an article on the shining *bushidō* (warrior) spirit of the Japanese army. The May 15 issue of the *Tokyo Asahi* ran an ad similar to the Morinaga advertisement. This was a full page of photos of Chaplin with captions, along with ink sketches advertising everything from fountain pens to soy sauce and hair pomade. A *Kinema Junpō* jingle ran:

> Person of Cinema, Chaplin
> Person of the World, Chaplin
> Human Being, Chaplin.

Charlie belonged to Japan because he belonged to the world.[24]

The press followed the star's every step in Japan from the moment "Chaarii" was met by exuberant throngs. Articles catalogued every object of "Chappurin Kun's" consumption in Japan (*kun* being an affectionate diminutive), including two hard-boiled eggs in bed, tempura, and a new straw hat. The language of the press reveals a familiarity and affection for "Uncle Charlie" along with a desire to show him the real Japan—the real Japan being limited to kabuki, Mount Fuji (including the "Fujiyama" sketched by Chaplin), and, of course, tempura. Readers were told that Charlie was family. The coverage emphasized that his appeal crossed class boundaries in modern Japan. At the same time, they were told that Charlie had *"gypsy* blood" and that because he was *"Anglo Saxon"* he was horrified at the *"terrorism"* of the Inukai assassination.[25]

As stated in my introduction, the day after Chaplin's arrival in Japan (his stay was from May 14 to June 2), Prime Minister Inukai was assassinated by right-wing extremists. Other than the conjecture as to why Chaplin chose to return home far ahead of schedule, there was little discussion of how this socially aware Hollywood artist might have been interested in such expressions of political tension or in the profound urban and rural social change underlying such tension. Newspapers did offer carefully worded documentation of Chaplin's visit to the scene of the assassination and recorded that Chaplin took refuge in his hotel room for much of his stay, going out only in the evening to eat his daily tempura. One English language history mentions assassination threats on Chaplin by the same Kokuryūkai group that killed Inukai. Whether Chaplin's apparent depression was due to such threats or to boredom because of his isolation from any interesting or intimate dialogue is hard to say. Just before his ship sailed, he visited the prime minister's residence, where he lectured Inukai's son: "You had better keep a gun in your room."[26]

The coverage of Chaplin bespoke of of the Japanese intimacy with the heroes of Hollywood fantasy. In the February 1936 issue of *Eiga no Tomo*, for example, a cartoon illustration had Mickey-kun (receiving congratulations on his longevity by his good friends Chaplin, Garbo, Cantor, Brown, Keaton, Beery, Groocho [sic], Arliss, Laurel [sic], and Duranto [sic]. One aspect of the familiarizing (or should we say family-izing?)—in addition to the all-knowing tone taken by the movie magazine journalist—was the imagined placement of the Westerner into a Japanese cultural context. In other words, the pleasure of a Marx Brothers movie was likened to the enjoyment of a festival. Elsewhere the term *chambara*, applied to samurai dueling, was assigned to Hollywood antics. When the proverbial anger of woman was invoked, the author did not distinguish between Japanese or Euro-American women. And in an article titled "Hollywood New Gossip," gender categories served to familiarize Japanese readers with the common foibles of men and women: Martha Raye was displeased with Ray Milland and Louise Rainer was annoyed by Melvyn Douglas's tendency to forget his lines. The images of women were accompanied by the familiar Japanese folk saying "truly women are reckless and hot-tempered" *(mukōmizu no kanshakumochi).*[27]

Returning to the appeal of little Charlie, as Ozaki Midori noted, this was due in part to his body language. In an article in *Kinema Junpō*, dated May 11, 1932, Iijima Tadashi referred to Chaplin as genius in terms of the "mask" Chaplin made use of, and because of Chaplin's complexity of poetry and movement. A review of *Modern Times* six years later lauded him as the greatest mime among all movie stars. What is most important for our understanding of Chaplin's place in modern Japan is that the gestures that were so beloved by the Japanese audiences belonged to the persona of the *lumpen* hero.

The term *lumpen* was all over the Japanese media before Chaplin's trip to Japan, but he was most clearly identified with this down-and-out figure once promotion and discussion of *Modern Times* began. In March 1936, an article providing a summary of the plot referred to the hero as a *lumpen*, and the following year the character of "the gamine" was labeled a *furyō shōjo* (girl juvenile delinquent). When a journalist for *Eiga no Tomo*, writing from the Hollywood set of *Modern Times*, looked over a shared history of ten years with Charlie Chaplin, he mused on the appeal of a hero who moved one to a consciousness of *magokoro* (the true heart). He was expressing a connection felt by Japanese spectators when he referred to the little body of the little hero affectionately but not condescendingly. Chaplin was a modern figure, a Hollywood star. But he was also another modern figure—the *lumpen* whose imagined everyday life differed so much from the lives of the stars featured in *Eiga no Tomo*. He was identifiable to a Japanese audience facing modern times that were just as painful.[28]

One example of the press coverage of the *lumpen* as indigenous hero was the February 1931 "*Lumpen* Round-Table Discussion" published in *Bungei Shunjū*, the somewhat high-brow, somewhat intellectual popular magazine. (Kusama was one of the participants, although this was not the sort of policy-oriented, professional journal that usually carried his work). The feature was a fascinating representation of agency in the midst of state surveillance. It was also an ironic replication of the roundtable forums offered to intellectuals in higher-brow magazines and in the more mass-oriented *Eiga no Tomo* and *Shufu no Tomo*. Apparently, the publishing establishment had recognized that the homeless *lumpen* were as much a part of the social order as department store clerks or factory girls. And the *lumpen* (actually former *lumpen*) participants seated with Kusama and the director of a social welfare institution as much as stated that they both were and were not a part of that social order.[29]

One participant was a convert to social work. His sentiments illustrate the moralizing position described by Sheldon Garon in his analysis of state officials who advocated what Garon terms moral suasion: vagrants are incapable of unifying; anyone born in Japan must be guaranteed a daily life; each must work according to his ability. Most vagrants begin their downward spirals because of wine and women: almost all of those sleeping in Asakusa Park are sake drinkers. Another participant says capitalism alone is not to blame; workers must acknowledge responsibility.[30]

Other participants are critical of the state—cynical about an ideology of moralizing that talks of "Proper Guidance of Thought." One resents the *"police"* refusal to acknowledge any good deeds by *lumpen* and the police preoccupation with beating up and locking up vagrants. Even the participating director of an institution whose title translates as Tokyo Sacred Labor House states, "It's a mistake that those who are born in the Japanese state are not fed." Kusama's role in the conversation is to continually bring it back to Asakusa conditions and to elicit answers that reveal the desperation of the *lumpen*. Undoubtedly he knows the costs of flophouses, just as he knows that vagrants can get one sen for an empty beer bottle as well as he knows how vagrants search for leftover food in Asakusa (rather than shopping at the establishments in Tokyo which resell leftovers). He knows that a day without food has a name *(no chabu)* and that those who make do with water only are referred to as "goldfish *chabu.*" Nevertheless, he asks questions. Here, as elsewhere in his writings, Kusama does not moralize; he keeps returning to the question "What about leftovers?" in order, it would seem, to document the answer for the public record. It is as innocent-sounding as his query as to whether the prison-rooms for vagrants taken to Hokkaido are locked.[31]

If there had been any doubt that Kusama had his own grasp of the *lumpen* everyday at the time of the round table, this could not be said a year later, when his findings from an on-site survey of *lumpen seikatsu* appeared in the pages of the *Tokyo Asahi Shinbun*. The essay described his field method: he would yell out, "Hey, I've got *biscuits!*" and then the questions would begin. Among his informants in Asakusa was a *lumpen* wife. (Kusama noted that the October 1930 National Census had found forty *lumpen* couples, most of whom were beggars.) Significantly, Kusama identifies her as a woman *lumpen,* clearly as distinct a social category of the Asakusa *donzoko* as the woman vagrant. Kusama offered the woman's case—she had run away from home when young, to be with a lover. She had later attempted to flee from an older husband, who had sold her to an unlicensed brothel. Asakusa, with its plentiful food, was her final destination after years of wandering. Like other women, Kusama editorialized, she had chosen a mate whose qualities made him a good *lumpen*—in other words, he brought home the *zuke*. She, in turn, had sex with him and with other *lumpen* in the immediate vicinity. Some of the women *lumpen* catering to the male vagrants had become well-known names in Asakusa—celebrities such as Okiyo, the Red-Nosed Old Lady, and Oseki from the Tea-House.[32]

But were such informants to be believed? There appears to be some internal inconsistency in Kusama's fieldwork, but he knew that fact could not easily be separated from fiction and that those who were down and out used this truth to their advantage. The topic of the evasion of authority by vagrants brings us back to Soeda and to Kawabata, and to the heroines and heroes of Kawabata's *Asakusa Kurenaidan*, the girl and boy juvenile delinquents.

JUVENILE DELINQUENTS

Kawabata, who said he studied writings on deviance, may have read the following gendered definition that had pigeonholed one of two types of juvenile delinquents *(furyō)* by 1917: "These tough juvenile delinquents are masculine, wild and violent in speech and conduct, and take constant delight in acts of violence, assaults, and fights. Sometimes they carry dangerous weapons leading to bloodshed, but they have their own form of pride and a chivalrous side. They usually like judo, kendo, and sumo, and engage in theft, fraud, embezzlement, blackmail *(pakuri)*, and extortion of money *(takuri)*." *Pakuri* refers to the act of threatening students or girls and boys passing by and robbing them of money and valuables. In some cases, several delinquents band together to go in and out of coffee shops, cafes, and bars, challenging the students nearby to fight and taking their money. One acts as a so-called mediator-reconciliator to force the students to pay for food and drink.[33]

Asakusa denizen and playwright Satō Hachirō recalled that by the Shōwa era the "soft" juvenile delinquents had appeared in Asakusa, but Kawabata's Crimson Gang belonged to the hard category. Kawabata's Purple Gang, a group of fourteen-year-old schoolgirls who organized in order to exchange love letters with men, appears closer to the category of "soft" delinquents. In the novel, the Crimson Gang emerges as a series of sharply defined individuals. There is Yumiko, the multivalent piano player, merry-go-round ticket-taker, bewigged theater companion, and costumed hawker of oil discussed above in terms of masquerade and gender-bending. Another of the girls is Ochiyo, who appears to be a refined young woman with new grime on her body—giving her the smell of the dirt of the vagrant—who is continually drawn to the park. Kawabata cites Satō Hachirō's statement that it was currently trendy for gangs to have a beautiful girl at the helm (KY,

202). This is not without precedent, for there is the case of Oshin, the legendary heroine of all girl delinquents. Kawabata's narrator recites her achievements: she had organized an all-girl group by the time she was thirteen or fourteen, had twenty or thirty some followers, and by the time she was sixteen had been with 150 men (KY, 27). There are also delinquent boys. Umekichi is called a typical case and accordingly Kawabata gives the history of the youth who after having been imprisoned in the Kawagoe Youth Detention Center a couple of times, has been saved from "sinking to the depths" by the Crimson Gang. Kawabata employs the diction of a caseworker to relay this information and down-and-out grotesquerie in the form of sexual activity opens Kawabata's account of Umekichi. Kawabata then lists a staccato chronology:

1. Umekichi, age six. Toyed with by a woman over forty.

2. Age 13. Becomes friendly with a girl who is one year older while playing behind the stationery store in front of school; the daughter of an office worker. Invited to her house. Nobody home. The two cannot (the next word is censored). Goes back three or four times. Gossip spreads; the girl's family moves far away.

3. Age 14. Becomes acquainted with daughter of proprietor of sundries store when seated on the front bench of the bakery. The two go to Ueno Park and festivals and small eateries more than twenty times.

4. Age 15. Two young women sitting next to him in a movie theater in Asakusa Park. He sees one of them at another theater. Is taken to a house with two entrances of inlaid *glass*. (KY, 53)[34]

The time line continues. At age fifteen Umekichi had stolen money and seduced the seventeen- or eighteen-year-old daughter of a book lender at a play she was attending with her younger sister. The younger sister, seeing what the two were doing, pulled her older sister out of the theater. That same year Umekichi was to become the boy of a gang leader and would steal a total of 150 yen from the girl who lived in the house with the two entrances (KY, 55).

Kawabata is not merely interested in the crimes committed by Umekichi, or in the fact that another boy known as "Boy Kamakiri" (Kamakiri Kozō) knows the law so well that he knows he is protected until the age of fifteen, and that he therefore goes straight at that age. It is the family practices, or the lack thereof, that intrigue the author. Not only is Kamakiri Kozō unfamiliar with the practices in *Shufu no Tomo* such as the preparation of foods for the holidays or methods of greeting guests, he does not know the most fundamental of domestic tasks. When told to fold away his sleeping futon, he rolls this bedding together with the cushions for sitting. The notion of household and nuclear family in *Shufu no Tomo* may at times conflict with the state ideology, but boys like Umekichi and Kamakiri Kozō subscribe to neither ideology. Not only are they ignorant of the everyday practices of organizing a household, they have no sense of piety or ancestry as encoded in the morals textbooks. The boys have no sense of genealogy. When asked "What are your parents doing?" they reply, "I don't have any parents yet" (KY, 56–57).

Kawabata does not employ the term *grotesque* for his discussion of sexual improprieties; nor does he directly criticize the state. One reference to surveillance in Asakusa is discussion of the youth gang's appropriation of police property and method for their own end. The narrator reads a police signboard telling all to gather, which has been signed "The Crimson Gang." This of course is the official sign that also bears such official words as "The People's Signboard" and "Asakusa Branch of the Veteran's Association." The narrator recognizes the acumen of the gang members: no authority will notice writing placed so prominently adjacent to the police station. Elsewhere he notes that one young gang member cannot read the words for Home Ministry (KY, 53, 207). Kawabata provides no value judgment. However, his discussion of the plight of the youth gang members in the present (1930) reveals a concern for the grotesquerie of poverty brought about by the nationwide depression. He quotes again from Satō: "Even the juvenile delinquent youths can no longer eat" (KY, 202).

Kawabata observes that by 1930 the boundary between Asakusa and the rest of the city is blurred as the poor and laborers go to the vagrants to buy leftovers of leftovers. Forty or fifty thousand juvenile delinquents are under police surveillance, and they are former apprentices, shop workers, and so on. Kawabata defers to Tanizaki Junichirō to refine his argument: "But, if that is the case, what is the Japan of today? What is the Tokyo of the present? Aren't Japanese society of the present and the entirety of the city of Tokyo today one aged delinquent? In the midst of these aged delinquents, only Asakusa Park is a juvenile delinquent. Even though it's delinquent, this youth expresses love and respect, has vigor, has progress" (KY, 57).

Asakusa is different from the rest of Tokyo, but it shares in the depression with the rest of Japan. When the narrator says he has heard that the sounds of the Asakusa temple bells will be broadcast to the nation on New Year's Eve 1929, he fantasizes about gathering the Crimson Gang in front of the *microphone*, to have them yell "1930, *Banzai*." He explains: "We have this broadcast because Asakusa, as the heart of Tokyo, represents the New Year's Eve atmosphere of the *donzoko* year of the depression" (KY, 58).

Kawabata's work speaks of historic ruptures caused by the earthquake in 1923 and the depression in 1930, but it is to the work of Kusama that we must turn to understand the history of juvenile delinquency from the Restoration through the 1930s. There is of course some overlap: Kawabata, Satō, and Kusama all refer to the delinquent heroine Oshin. But as with the vagrant, Kusama's attempts to document the everyday of the delinquent offer us as much a sense of transitions in cultural practices engaged in by both teenage denizens of the park, as by those who attempted to control them.[35]

Kusama's 1936 study of the history of juvenile delinquency in Asakusa Park begins by assessing the significance of the Park for such youths during the Edo period. He takes this history through 1928, when he first observed numerous homeless youths in Asakusa Park, and into the early 1930s. The report notes a change in 1930: one gang leader, fleeing from police discipline, took his followers to Ginza; the gang had been destroyed. But by the summer of 1933, juvenile delinquents had returned to the park.

The practices and histories of Kusama's young men and women are reminiscent of those of Kawabata's tale. Kusama, like Kawabata, explains *pakuri* as the practice of forcefully taking money. His emphasis is on the vulnerability of young runaways to adult vagrants assisted by juvenile members of Asakusa down-and-out society. The victims are afterwards encouraged to join the gang. These youths then fall deeper and deeper into the ways of the gang as they steal from the temple offering box and scavenge for food. The crime of *gasebiri* calls for the collaboration of the "big brother" *lumpen*, one of his young subordinates, and a low-level prostitute. The unsuspecting victim is seduced into paying the prostitute in advance; suddenly her angry "lover" appears. The would-be customer loses this payment and sometimes all of the money he has on his person.[36]

Kusama's case histories of three girl delinquents sound very much like the histories of the Crimson Gang members, and also like the travails of the heroine of the left-wing movie "What Made Her Do What She Did?" that had packed in the Asakusa audiences. There is, for example, the case of the sixteen-year-old daughter of a carpenter, who had lost both parents by the age of four. Forced to quit school after two years of elementary education, by the age of twelve she had been sent to work as a factory girl in Osaka. She continued to flee from the advances of male workers until her uncle sent her to work as a babysitter at a merchant's house. After that, she had escaped from the *"hysteria"* of her mistress (one is reminded of the article in *Shufu no Tomo* regarding the cure for hysteria—this variation on neurasthenia appears to have been a common affliction of the housewife of the post-earthquake years) by stealing money from her master's household. Like many others, she ended up in Asakusa. After several days of enjoying the Asakusa pleasures of food and cinema, she ran out of money. Aimlessly wandering through the Park, she was pounced on by a *lumpen*. Now, Kusama observed, when this young girl was not working among older prostitutes, she was living on leftovers.[37]

Kusama's "true stories" about juvenile delinquents may be one reason why so-called experts called him unscientific. They may also reflect the fact that he had more power and respect in Asakusa than the more entrenched bureaucrats who needed the safety of numbers in statistical reports. A reading of his writings and of related documents makes it clear that he did command respect in Asakusa because of his sensitive interactions with the down-and-out who had nowhere else to go. His storytelling places the young women and men in the social and cultural history of their time and place. This history is informed by Kusama's determination as to what is and is not relevant. For example, he shares information that he has gleaned from his work at the Tokyo Youth Shelter.

Kusama's true stories illustrate how the Park provided a haven for the homeless adolescent without family. For example, he presents the case of Amakusa Kin, aged nineteen. Her medical examination has revealed venereal disease, and officials conclude that she contracted the disease while working as a low-level prostitute in the vicinity of Asakusa Park. Investigation reveals that soon after birth, Kin was abandoned near the Five-Tiered Pagoda but was taken into a loving farm household. Her true past was not revealed to her until the first day of school, when the discrepancy in her family name and that of her supposed family caused her great distress. It was then that Kin's downward spiral began. When she showed signs of delinquency, she was sent back to the orphanage, and by the age of eighteen, she was successful in her fourth attempt to escape from the institution. Despite Kusama's attempts at rehabilitation, by the time he is writing up this case, Kin has a pickpocket for a lover and is also training to pick pockets at the women's kimono counters of department stores in the city. There is also the tale of the young boy who loses both parents in the earthquake of 1923. He is adopted and trained by a kind man who teaches him to pick pockets. When he is arrested in Asakusa Park for attempting to pick the pocket of a man in Western dress, he is decked out in an outfit made of duck cloth, new socks, and red, high-top leather shoes. Kusama's eye for detail would have impressed Kon.[38]

Kawabata's character Oharu, whose fate has already been summarized above as the story of "the real woman" Haruko in my discussion of the Japanese modern desire for a fixed femininity, has also had a downward spiral into the depths. She left her job as a maid and came to Tokyo to pursue her dream of becoming a hairdresser, but, before she knew it, she found herself being sold from man to man. Kawabata traces this process: Oharu meets an old woman at the public bath who seems to befriend her. She has her back scrubbed, is treated to sweet beans, receives a theater ticket, and is invited to the woman's house. The public bath is in the Park; the old woman's house is not, but Oharu does not question this discrepancy. One day she agrees to deliver some packages to the old woman's house; the next morning she awakens to find herself naked. She finds her own nudity strange (here is the female grotesque, in Russo's sense of the woman freak) and then laughable. She stays trapped in the room for five days. Without her knowledge, Oharu has been sold to a house of prostitution run by the old woman. Within a month she is in turn deceiving a boy one year her junior: he is her follower, calling her "big sister," as she transforms him into a juvenile delinquent (KY, 208–12).

Kusama's response to juvenile delinquency was much more descriptive than prescriptive. In 1921 he responded to the "juvenile youth problem" by examining the statistics on crimes committed by boys and girls compiled by a police station in Asakusa the previous year. He was surprised to find that contrary to popular opinion, there were no arrests for sex crimes, and he commented on the large number of arrests of young children. Kusama divided delinquents into three groups: there were the hard-core delinquents, attracted to homosexuality, intimidation, and violence; the soft-core delinquents, who expressed their attraction to the opposite sex in groups; and the thieves. The soft-core group included both the *peragoro*, (*pera* being short for Asakusa operetta) who followed the actresses in Asakusa, and the *cafegoro*, whose prey were both delinquent girls and young women from good families who entered the park looking for recreation. Asakusa was the center for juvenile delinquent activity, and gangs (some with one hundred to one hundred fifty boys and girls) were growing in this area. Kusama blamed the widespread delinquency in the park on bad upbringing, leading to weakness of body and spirit. In 1927 he expressed concern for the increasing number of delinquent boys and girls, especially those who could not be rehabilitated and who escaped from shelters to return to the culture of Asakusa Park. By 1936 he was calling the protection of delinquent boys and girls a matter for the state and state officials, and warning of the danger that could be done by the delinquent child who, if neglected, would become a delinquent youth, a delinquent in the prime of life, and, finally, a delinquent old person.[39]

Kusama was concerned not only with relationships among the juvenile delinquents but also their relationships with their victims in the park and their fellow outlaws in Asakusa, such as the *tekiya* (hawkers), like the one accompanying Kin, the sixteen-year-old carpenter's daughter turned prostitute, and like the one employing Kawabata's "Little Boat Boy," a child member of the Asakusa Crimson Gang, as a shill (KY, 132).

THE HAWKERS

The hawkers are the second group to appear in Soeda Azenbō's tale of the underbelly of Asakusa. They set up their stands early in the morning and sell knitted goods, fountain pens, sandals, and other goods calculated to appeal to visitors from the provinces. Three hours later the police will appear to drive them away—or to catch them. These are shysters: one sells sixty-five-sen sandals for the price of one yen to a group of country bumpkins after leading them on a tour of the Asakusa sites (of which he has almost no knowledge). There are also street performers like the desperate young man who sings and plays the violin as a prelude to telling fortunes. Soeda rejects a new definition of the hawker based on the popular belief that the *yashi* (a word for hawker) is bad, and a cheat. One of the members of the Tokyo Municipal Assembly has said, "The hawker is an industrialist of small capital." No, Soeda says, "The hawker is a proletarian." Those without capital cannot have shops, cannot stock merchandise in bulk, and they require special sales techniques. Soeda says they are magicians, and illustrates this with the case of the *yashi* who carries a small *basket* and a *bucket* in which a *celluloid* duck is swimming and swirling. The secret? Those who pay ten sen will read the secret on a slip of paper. On the piece of paper it says "mudfish"; a fish swimming underneath the duck is causing the Magic motion (SA, 8–10, 111–15).

Another, more ethnographic approach to the hawker was provided by Wada Nobuyoshi, a reflexive writer who, like a gypsy, had traveled nationwide with hawkers (he uses the term *tekiya*, as opposed to Soeda's *yashi*, and states that he would be happy if the fruit of his observations could be used in sociological study). Wada's methodical (as opposed to Soeda's anecdotal) account includes the prerequisites for hawker status, along with the historical background of the occupation, a discussion of the hawkers' practices and code of conduct, an extensive typology of hawkers, and a lexicon of hawker argot. For our purposes, what is so significant is Wada's account of the hawker's own sense of the grotesquerie of social inequity.[40]

Wada gives his version of the relationship of the hawker to capital—

there is none and there need not be any: "First and foremost a hawker's only capital is the work done by his tongue. An extreme example would be the hawker who has not even one *mon* (penny), nor any merchandise, and of course no shop. If the hawker can find a place where there's already a cemetery and it's a place where children live, he will never know problems." Wada continues. As part of his elaboration, he asserts that if a hawker can find even a piece of paper, or a book, or an old newspaper to sell he has it made as long as he also has a relationship with a senior protector—and a knowledge of the hawker's secret language.[41]

Hawker culture is characterized by a code of conduct premised on a leader-follower relationship and an everyday centered on the premise of mutual aid. Rather than wield tight control over the hawker, the senior figure gives business advice. It is presumed that should either party seek aid, the other will, without question, provide it. (Wada calls this master-follower relationship a class relationship.) It may be well worth noting the order in which Wada catalogs aspects of hawker life. The very first item appears to point to household turmoil among the hawkers, for Wada devotes a long paragraph to what he calls "Woman Crimes and Dishonesty"; his main concern is wife-stealing. A wife-stealer can be killed for such an act with no moral outcry from his peers. Alternatively, the nation-wide network of hawkers in power will be notified, and as a result, the guilty lover's colleagues will no longer associate with him. Or, the more fortunate homewrecker will not be excommunicated from hawker community but will be recognized by the absence of his little finger, which has been cut off as a marker and a warning to his colleagues to follow the hawkers' code. The code also forbids hawkers to steal or to "sing," thereby revealing hawker secrets and also encourages the hawker to have a strong sense of *"pride,"* in part to counter public contempt for his way of life.[42]

Wada's hawker is highly aware of historical precedent, historical innovation, and the problem of historical documentation. He concludes that these merchants have been plying their trade for three or four hundred years beginning with the masterless samurai of the Warring States era. The range of wares has expanded from perfumes and medicines to over fifty attractions listed by Wada. This documentation is worthy of Kon Wajirō's annotations. The list includes old magazines, fireworks, balloons, old clothes, pipes, and neckties. The spectacle of performance is also offered: sideshows, fortune-telling, and the street performances of musicians and hypnotists who appear only at festival time. Venues now include steamships and wealthy mansions, where *tekiya* practice divination "in the manner of Rasputin." The big difference between past and present, Wada implies, is that the hawker now works alongside a capitalist political economy. He defends the shill (the cherry blossom, or *sakura*) as a legitimate innovation in advertising, pointing to the contemporary methods adopted by "sacred" capitalist gentlemen and their "sacred" commerce. Are not newspapers, magazines, signs, radio broadcasts also cherry blossoms? Like men in the "material culture" at large who take advantage of the gullibility of women, the hawker is adept at pricing. At first glance, this man of the "material culture" can calculate what each female customer is willing to pay.[43]

Wada documents the hawkers' own awareness of their position within a capitalist system. By the 1920s this brotherhood, sharing a code and set of relationships based on a social order predating the establishment of the modern state, had joined in the nationwide eruption of "thought activities" that challenged the state from the left. By January 26, 1924, a call for political organization that originated in Osaka, titled "Regarding the Establishment of a National Peddler Vanguard Federation," was being passed from hawker to hawker around the country. Just as he offers his readers a lexicon of hawker business language, Wada reports their political rhetoric by quoting from this document. The manifesto calls for "rational reform," and the authors identify the *tekiya* with the worker: hawkers may be like merchants, but they suffer all sorts of oppression and have little autonomy and the oppression they suffer is no different from that of the working class. Clearly the hawker organizers were employing the contemporary language of the Japanese left—the language of social protest employed by workers, women, and the outcast *burakumin*. For example: "We must awaken. In order to ensure our rights, and, as members of the working class, in order for us to build the peaceful and happy society that must come to be, we must, here and now, in a somewhat different sense, form the strongest of unions." The first leaflet issued by the Federation, the following month, reiterated that the *seikatsu* of the peddler was indistinguishable from the lot of the worker and condemned the "irrationality of class discrimination." At the same time it emphasized that the peddler, like the merchant, aimed for profit. It was inevitable that the hawker's prices would be higher than those of the merchant because the hawker had to bear the cost of transportation and lodging. The leaflet also set the peddlers apart because of their "spirit of mutual aid" and moral solidarity.[44]

Wada notes that tension between the "traditionalists" and those espousing the "new thought" must have ensued from the early organizing, and indeed the socialist and anarchist terminology does seem to conflict with the "Manifesto" issued by a cooperative of hawkers who identified themselves as agricultural deities watched over, in turn, by a guardian agricultural deity.

This statement said, "We revere the Imperial Line as Gods, take the traditional people's spirit as our life, and proclaim the faith of the essential familial love of the *kokutai*." This text illustrated notions of union and solidarity not premised on class solidarity. The family-state ideology in the manifesto was thus closer to the thought of the vagrants who in 1937 expressed appreciation to the soldiers in mutiny, taking up a collection for their assistance, because, they said, the soldiers were fighting on their behalf.[45]

We cannot tell how the hawkers inside and outside of Asakusa reconciled these conflicting sentiments, although some may have chosen to rely on the shared notion of *danketsu* (forged solidarity) as a guiding precept. What we can see is language articulated as an oppositional statement. Wada's form of ethnography paid special attention to dialogue, as is clear from his transcription of the stylized, highly honorific greeting of the hawker, and his Hawker Glossary. He points out that the hawker made use of linguistic reversal as one means of forging new, secret words. (One common example is the word *enkō*, which is the reversal and abbreviation of the syllables comprising *kōen*, the insider slang for Asakusa Park.) The hawker language was thus not unlike Cockney, because of its consciousness of class base, and because of its use of the back-slang terms that reversed syllables in order to make a political point. It was, of course, also Japan-specific—a product of the modern years with a Japanese linguistic and social history.[46]

Cockney words and the method of back-slanging can be traced back to the language of English beggars. In the Japanese case, the Japanese hawker argot was also shared; it was picked up by beggars, vagrants, and juvenile delinquents in Asakusa. However, whereas various accounts of Cockney vocabulary mention its emphasis on bodily parts and functions, Wada's glossary contains few terms for parts of the body other than the code words for the head, fingers, and face. Both Hawker and Cockney vocabularies contained numerous words for women; in the Japanese case the emphasis was on sex workers. (Again, the female grotesque reappears.) Most obvious in both lexicons was the extensive terminology for money. In the Japanese case, different denominations, for example, had different names.[47]

Whereas Cockney emphasizes the results of poverty—there is a term for exhaustion, for example, the Japanese hawker vernacular focuses on business practice. This was a craft brotherhood that took care to use its own terms—to code switch—for such words as "business," "travel fare," "wily deception," and "confession." The emphasis was on making money. The hawkers' preoccupation with state surveillance also features in Wada's list. There were hawker terms for guard on watch, detective, police, and chief of police station. Here, it does not seem a stretch of comparative scholarship to conclude that, as in the case of Cockney, the use of inversions expressed contempt. Almost all of the surveillance-related terms were inversions: *keibu* (police inspector) was turned into *bukei*. "Confidential" (*naisho*) became *shonai*, and so on. This was a form of opposition to state control; and the hawkers were by definition and by proclamation anticapitalist, as Wada's sources reveal. For example, the term for "socialist," composed of abbreviated and reversed syllables, was *gishu*. But even though the documents cited above contained left-wing sentiments, it would be unfair to the historic record to see the Japanese hawkers as active proponents of any sort of *yonaoshi*, or revolutionary rectification of the social order. Many hawkers may have had some notion of socialism, but much more relevant to their lifestyle was the category of people who were put on show in the peep shows and traveling acts. These were the *misemono* ("things to be shown"), known as *takamono* by hawkers. We thus come to the last group of grotesque inhabitants of Asakusa, the freaks. Within the Asakusa context, what Susan Stewart has referred to as "the freak of nature who is in fact a 'freak of culture'" is the foreigner.[48]

FOREIGNERS AS FREAKS

By *freak* I am not referring to what the first (and still foremost) Japanese scholar of the Edo sideshow termed "natural curiosities." In *Studies of Exhibitions*, Asakura Musei focused on a quest for origins and a description of unusual oddities. He found the first instances of the use of a disabled person as spectacle in a book from the Tokugawa era: a man missing both legs and an armless woman. According to his typology, the two other types of *misemono* were feats of prowess and such crafts as a giant, manmade elephant. A second, much more recent approach, adopted by the Heibonsha editors of a video compendium on traveling arts and sideshows, associates *misemono* sideshows, traveling entertainers, and street stalls as all run by *yashi (tekiya)* hawkers and all linked in the popular consciousness.

My sense from reading the Asakusa documents quoted herein is that the binary approach to physiological anomaly described by Susan Stewart did not exist in modern Asakusa. According to Stewart, "the physiological freak represents the problem of the boundary between self and other (Siamese twins), between male and female (the hermaphrodite), between the body and the world outside the body (the *monstre* par excess), and between the animal and the human (feral and wild men) player." According to Mary

Russo, freaks are, by definition, set apart, as beings to be viewed. This separation, she explains, is part of a modern discourse on "realness" that distinguishes between freaks as mediators between the natural and supernatural worlds and freaks as real, living, breathing monsters. The transition between a premodern and a modern epistemology was different in Japan, and it has been argued that *misemono* have only recently come to be seen as grotesque. My goal here, however, is not to pursue such a discursive transformation, but to note, by borrowing the phrasing of Susan Stewart, that in Asakusa during the modern years, the freak, doubly marked as object and other within the world of spectacle, was the foreign entertainer, the freak of nature who is in fact a "freak of culture." According to Russo, the freak in the freak show had a role that converged with the social roles of the racially marked and the underclasses. The foreigners working in Asakusa were indeed members of the racially marked underclass. To illustrate my point, I turn back to Kawabata Yasunari's *The Asakusa Crimson Gang*, taking the liberty of treating the fiction as fact.[49]

Among the sideshows described in the novel are attractions like the man with the mouth in his belly, wearing Harold Lloyd glasses and outfitted like a judo champion, who speaks with his mouth but eats through his belly. This sounds very typical of Asakura's attractions (KY, 35). But the narrator of *The Asakusa Crimson Gang* is much more interested in the *ijin* (or foreigners). There are foreigners and there are foreigners: there are the Chinese *(Shinajin)*, the Koreans *(Chōsenjin)*, and the white people. But unlike the indigenous *misemono* performers, they all fit the binary characterization of freak: within Asakusa, they define what is outside Japan. Moreover, like Russo's Western freaks, many are seen as sexually charged objects. For example, the narrator comes upon two young Chinese women dressed identically in yellow Chinese costume. Here, the grotesque as sexually and racially marked coincides with Kawabata's repeated use of the double in *The Asakusa Crimson Gang*. The use of the double is one of the characteristics of Freud's notion of the *unheimlich*. This *uncanny* refers to what is both familiar and frightening, and the doubles who people Asakusa in Kawabata's montage illustrate different aspects of Freud's definition. The identical twin boys, clad in navy pants and hats with green ribbons are, to borrow from Freud, "characters who are considered to be identical because they look alike," as are the Chinese girl entertainers. Yumiko as her brother Akikō comes closest to embodying the double as a thing of terror. The narrator is made uneasy as the cozy alleys of Asakusa are rendered unfamiliar by the mystery of Yumiko/Akikō's identity. Third, Freud's example of telepathy between doubles is well represented by the Asakusa Crimson Gang's shared knowledge; and, finally, the Freudian double's identification with another is exemplified by Yumiko's identification with her tragic sister. Through the different doublings, Asakusa as home is rendered unhomelike *(unheimlich)* and sinister; its inhabitants plot not merely to survive but also to avenge (KY, 14–15, 20, 106).[50]

Kawabata does not dwell on the modern approach, which focuses on interiority. In his presentation of the grotesque, Chinese children at play are marked as non-Japanese by their haircuts and as both human and animal by their "monkeylike" voices. A Korean woman is marked by her "Korean-like" way of carrying her baby along with her clothing (KY, 146). (Soeda had noted how Korean women stood out among the adults and children who went from bar to bar and who circulated among the western style restaurants, performing, telling fortunes, and selling such items as *"fried beans"* [SA, 198].) Kawabata also renders the South Seas exotic when in *The Asakusa Crimson Gang*, an Asakusa innocent covets a summer Kimono pattern known as "Evening in the South Seas" (KY 172–173). It is the white, female entertainers who are most clearly the objects of desire. Koreans are associated with the sale of candy as a front for more nefarious activities, and both Koreans and Chinese are seen as beggars and thieves. (This view is corroborated by the articles in the journal *Grotesque* on Chinese and Korean beggars.) Chinese thieves, moreover, are associated with murder.[51]

The post-earthquake *ijin* are white and mostly female. When a character in Kawabata's novel states that the Park has finally become international, because of the recent increase in foreigners, he is referring to the influx of delinquent girls from Europe, like the long-legged sixteen-year-old Russian refugee who blows a flirtatious kiss. She and her eighteen-year-old sister are dancers who stroll around Asakusa, whistling, stockingless, without underwear, in bright red, filmy costumes. They make fun of the desire of their Japanese observers by "acting as though it was absolutely the same whether their colored slaves did or did not see the skin of a white woman." There is also a young white prostitute passing as a revue dancer, a Finnish singer with her ten-year-old daughter, and a ten-year-old Russian girl who does a *Chaplin/Cossack* dance as a prelude to selling postcards (KY, 146–147).[52]

It is not new to say there was a double standard—that the Japanese discourse on Anglo-Europe was not the discourse imposed on their own empire. But it is too easy to conclude simply that Koreans and Chinese of

Asakusa were demeaned as colonized, whereas Europeans and Americans were seen as an eroticized species who served also as the object of intense sexual speculation. To complicate the issue of Asakusa attitudes toward whites, Chinese, and Koreans, we must turn to Asakusa humor and to the placing of the colonial within the modern in its jesting gestures.[53]

3   Modern Nonsense

In September 1931, the critic Iijima Tadashi defined the true nonsense film as "nearly meaningless." The director Itami Mansaku disagreed. Although he had been proclaimed the king of nonsense, he refused to see himself as a specialist in the nonsense film. Moreover, unlike others, he did not emphasize the influence of the slapstick of Mack Sennett, possibly because he was too well aware that "nothing" was not going on. In the words of Itami, in "Considerations on the New Period Film," the nonsense film could not be dismissed as "mere fun"; intellectual, artistic, social, and moral issues had to be taken into account. While it could not be denied that nonsense, a form of spirit, was smart, stylish, polished humor that took one aback, such characterizations were its surface manifestations. What really mattered was that nonsense tried to negate that which was treated with respect by society, just as the nonsense literature of the Tokugawa era mocked both Buddha and Confucius. It also lacked affirming characteristics: it was not about building, knowledge, health, or militancy, or waging battle. Itami concluded that nonsense had "not one thing positive about it." Even the spectator's sense of cheer disappeared as soon as one exited a movie theater. What, then, he wondered, was the appeal of this fad? His response to himself was that because it affirmed nothing, the nonsense film offended no one—not the censor, nor the shop clerk, nor the proprietor. The left could attend, reactionaries could go, men of letters went, and established religion could voice no objections. In this passage, the noted director and screenwriter came closest to hinting that in the politics of culture in this new era, nonsense as culture perforce took on new forms and new objects of disdain. He noted how he, the maker of nonsense movies, along with other filmmakers, was fettered by both capitalism and the censorship system; he was "like a bear pacing back and forth in its cage." Nonsense was "fine, dangerous thought" because of its refusal to offer respect to power. He concluded his essay by rephrasing this opinion within the context of the exigencies of the current historic moment. Nonsense's inability to speak positively also meant its inability to affirm lies. While he did not say so—after all nothing could be asserted—he may also have agreed with Iwasaki Akira's contention that comedy and satire were the only means of expressing antiwar sentiment under capitalism.[1]

Most others were less charitable to the nonsensical. The *Dictionary of Vanguard Terms* was disdainful. After telling its readers that *nonsense* referred to meaningless matters and that the fad for such foolishness had originated in America before spreading in Japan, it observed that nonsense, along with eroticism and *"high speed,"* was one of the three main constitutive elements of a class-based literature of modernism—part of a degenerate bourgeois consumer culture that had spread from the province of the "coupon cutters" of finance capital to a gullible petit bourgeoisie. For almost all who used the three-part term *ero guro nansensu*, the last term was clearly the least appealing.[2]

There were, however, commentators who were the exceptions, and one who stands out is Satō Hachirō. Satō—poet, playwright, ex–juvenile delinquent, and all-around Asakusa flâneur (we must of course substitute Satō's parks and alleyways for the shop windows and grand arcades of Baudelaire and Benjamin)—directs us to Asakusa as the site of nonsense. And whereas Itami is almost ironic, Satō is decidedly so.

THE IRONY OF PARODY

My notion of irony is premised on Hayden White's concept of its "transideological nature." In other words, irony can affirm, deny, or attempt to subvert. For the purposes of my discussion, Linda Hutcheon's treatment of the scholarship on irony and some of her own emphases are most helpful: according to Hutcheon, "the 'scene' of irony involves relations of power based in relations of communication." Irony is relational in several ways: "It happens in the space between the said and the unsaid" (Hutcheon notes that the emphasis is on what is not said.) Irony develops in a hierarchical setting containing the speaker of the nonsense, the audience, and the excluded— those who are the targets of the humor.[3]

Such communication relies on the preexistence of community and Satō Hachirō was adept at representing both community and hierarchies of power. Satō placed a section called "Asakusa *Nonsense*" in *Asakusa*, a book published in 1932. This series of vignettes was his tribute to eroticism, grotesquerie (including a jab at Kusama Yasoo), and nonsense in his own community. It was peopled by the down-and-out figures I have called grotesque—there are prostitutes, pimps, a hawker or two, and the requisite state authority, the police. The irony is mild, as tables are turned on shysters turned victims. Satō tells one story of the man who aims to take advantage of the *"spring woman"* who seduces men in movie theaters, only to have her drop her false teeth down his front. He also tells of a hawker whose "100 *percent nonsense* patter" does not prevent him from ending up drenched, in the pouring rain. The joke is on him, as it is on the others who ply their nefarious trades in Asakusa. But Satō's jokes are much more sharp-edged in his unctuous "Letter to the Superintendent-General of the Metropolitan Police," which appears in the final pages of *Asakusa*.[4]

The common association of irony with inversion of language or meaning is most applicable for a political reading of Satō's letter. In Satō's document, addressed to the Superintendent-General of the police, inversion masks the writer's anger. When combined with a literal rendering of the record, this inversion highlights repression while at the same time voicing opposition, if not resistance. Satō protests too much, with too many honorifics. He opens his letter to the "honorable" chief of police by warning him not to take his letter seriously. He is, after all, really a peddler of nonsense. Here is the irony: the Superintendent-General, who is the ostensible addressee of the letter, is excluded from Satō's intended audience. And the community of readers recognizes that Satō does in no way honor the police official, and that they should indeed heed the words in Satō's letter.

At the same time the readers must recognize that Satō's innocent-sounding sarcasm thinly masks the fact that not only is he pleased with the eradication of the well-organized right-wing gangs, as he says; he is actually displeased—although he expresses appreciation—with the recent success of a new policy regarding cafés. Indirectly but clearly, the letter informs Satō's readers that police officials have succeeded in shortening café hours. He pretends to commend the police for their *"teamwork"* in enforcing the change. The café customer, the writer states, had undoubtedly been used to returning home after the 2:00 A.M. close of business, comfortably sated with sake, if not with sex. Now erotic feelings that were repressed when the cafés were open until the later hour can be channeled into trysts between the rested customer and the equally alert café waitresses. Before, the women had been too exhausted to give in to overtures from their customers. Now the last trains out of the nightspots of Shinjuku and Yūrakuchō each evening were called "the *jokyū* express." The writer concludes by quoting the hortatory cry of police authorities, "Crack down on the *erotic*," suggesting that the longer hours be reinstituted. Quoting verbatim the order to "crack down" (issued in the least polite form of imperative) both reveals the language of the state, while revealing Satō's personal support for the eroticism of café culture. Satō himself admits to the ambiguous nature of irony when he confronts the Superintedent General for his department's treatment of one of Satō's so-called *It* ballads as "obscene." Readers could hardly have avoided seeing the irony in Satō's seemingly innocent suggestion that if his *It* song were to receive such serious treatment, then "*I Have No Bananas*" [*sic*] deserved the death penalty (SH, 265–284).[5]

In this fictive letter, as in other humorous works of the modern moment, the code-switching between imported terms *It* or *wife* and the Japanese language surrounding them employed by the writer (and shared by the reader) is a vernacular marker of cultural community and of irony based on shared knowledge. It is almost impossible to have access to conscious (much less unconscious) editorial intent in the cases of the image-based code-switching in *Eiga no Tomo* and *Shufu no Tomo*. But we do know that these mass magazines juxtaposed the indigenous with the foreign and the older with the modern, as discussed above. Working from discussions of code-switching by linguists, we can also conclude that Satō actively intended to code switch. Satō made use of a "socially agreed upon matrix of contextualization cues and conventions used by speakers to alert addressees, in the course of ongoing interaction, to the social and situational context of the conversation." He used a set of "repertoires" that he shared with his audience, and his audience was capable of understanding these cues that were based on the insertion of words and phrases in both Japanese and English. This negotiation of languages can take place for a variety of reasons. It is local and situational, and, like irony, it is transideological and unquestionably "bound up in the creation, exercise, maintenance or change of relations of powers."[6]

On the eve of the modern years, the word *wife* in Satō's disquisition on unhappy housewives undoubtedly reminded readers of the hit song mentioned in the beginning of this book. The narrator of the "*Croquettes* Song" had bemoaned the fact that he had taken a *waifu*, but all she ever served was croquettes. This tale was in fact based on a true story, but what made the tune a hit was the way in which this code switch could encompass, in shorthand, new conceptions of marriage and household within a new middle class that was importing new mores. The deep-fried food can be seen as emblematic of the sorts of Western foods, such as the sandwiches that were naturalized in the pages of *Shufu no Tomo*.

Satō's approach to language focused not on the direct syntax of code-switching, but, as noted above, on the use of a veiled sarcasm to make political points indirectly. When he voiced concern over the semantic mistake of the prison guard who called detainees who had not yet been sentenced "convicts," he was not really concerned with inaccuracies in the use of language, but with the absence of justice in the Japanese political system. And when he proclaimed admiration for the Japanese police system, it was assumed that the community of readers would understand his sarcasm—and would invert Satō's reading in a switch that would reveal the injustice. In other words, Satō was damning the police system, and he counted on his community of readers to decipher his code. When, in closing, he offered the police commissioner a parody of a recent election slogan, only the readers of this piece were to notice that in this case parody meant irony masking Satō's serious political commentary on state violence. The slogan quoted by Satō was "An Honest Vote—A Bright Japan." His deadpan parody: "An Honest Tokyo—A Bright Police Box" (SH, 277–279, 283).

THE *CASINO FOLIES* AFFIRMS THE FALSE

Through repetition, parody points to irony, as it did in the comedy of the Asakusa theater of the modern era. And the humor of the *Casino Folies* provides us with a rich sampling of such modern humor. Asakusa humor mocked how the present was related to the past in the cultural politics of that moment. Without saying so explicitly—for irony as we have noted, cannot be explicit—this humor also mocked the place of Western culture in the Japanese modern, along with the relationship of colony to the national polity.

Hutcheon defines parody as "repetition, but repetition that includes difference; it is imitation with critical ironic distance, whose irony can cut both ways." Asakusa parody was marked as much by incongruity as it was by inversion, and it played with geography as much as with history. In modern Asakusa the word for parody was "phony" *(inchiki)*.[7]

The standard narrative histories of the *Casino Folies* tell us that the revue company was established in Asakusa in the summer of 1929. It was located on the second floor of an aquarium in the fourth district and was named after the Folies Bergère and the Casino de Paris. This entertainment, modeled on European and American cabaret—in name and form—combined skits with song and dance numbers. The neologism *Kajino* (from the Casino de Paris) and the elongated *Fuorii* (from the Folies Bergère), we are told, were adopted in order to make the name more accessible to the Japanese audience.

After an initial poor showing, the *Casino Folies* were made famous by the publication of *The Asakusa Crimson Gang.* It also owed its claim to fame to the (apocryphal) report that the showgirls dropped their drawers on Fridays. (These of course were the legs that bored Ozaki Midori.) Reasons given for the failure of the first *Casino Folies* differ, but we know that it folded less than two months after its grand opening on July 10, 1929. And there was unanimity regarding the role that Kawabata's "documentation" of the revue in *The Asakusa Crimson Gang* played in its subsequent success. By December of 1929, the second *Casino Folies* was drawing intellectuals not to their usual Asakusa destination of the eroticized space of the Sixth District, with its movie theaters and places of food and drink, but to the Fourth District of Asakusa Park, which housed the aquarium building where the *Casino Folies* performed. Kawabata's documentary impulse had led him to set the stage. In the opening of the book, a little girl runs into view, exclaiming to her older sister, "They say the *Casino Folies* are going to appear at the Aquarium again!" Almost immediately, the author begins to refer to the bare-legged young showgirls (KY, 17, 42).[8]

There is no question that the *Casino Folies* were eroticized (and here I do mean linked to sensuality and sexuality) by Kawabata and by police regulations, but other perspectives suggest that just as in the cafés, eroticism usually moved in one direction. The "bloomer-dropping" rumor appears to have begun when the required wrapping around the torso of one dancer came unwound. Memoirs suggest that the dozen or so sixteen-year-old dancers who appeared on the small stage in this very intimate venue were deaf to erotic innuendos written into the script and choreography. While the come-hither, finger-crooking gesture may have been erotic to the male audience, to them it was merely a motion to be memorized; it was, in other words, one of many modern gestures. Apparently the young girls called their backstage admirers, including the writer-spectators Takeda Rintarō and Kawabata, "big brother."[9]

Soeda Azenbō's segment on the *Casino Folies,* in his documentary account of Asakusa, downplayed the erotic and played up the nonsense. What could this faded, dusty theater, equipped with uncomfortable, broken-down chairs and a rickety orchestra, possibly present to an audience, he asked. He answered by first offering a skit:

> The stage is supposed to be Ginza.
> A crowd of lonely people passing back and forth.
> A young man and young woman meet, nod, and hold hands.
> The crowd of people passing back and forth.
> The man and woman reappear, arms linked.

The woman glances at her watch.
"Oh my, it's been exactly an hour; I'll take the payment now
It's *yen*, you know."
The man,
"What you say, payment? Whatever are you?"
"Who am I? Why, I'm a *stick girl.*"
"Oh, Big Deal!!!!!!! I'm a *stick boy!!!!*" (SA, 48–49)

Soeda did not have to explain the terms *stick boy* and *girl.* They referred to people for hire who, for a fee would "stick" to the customer accompanying him (or, ostensibly, her) down the boulevard of Ginza. The words belonged to the new, "modern" lexicon that was understood on Ginza as well as in Asakusa. He did, however, have to elaborate on the brand of eroticism marketed by the *Casino Folies.* According to Soeda, the dancing is somewhat cold. The dancers have skinny, bare, yellow legs, and he wonders whether their totally flat breasts really need the legally required binding. He says he approves of the absence of eroticism in these children, but he is aware that the eroticization of the innocent young girls can be seen as part of the draw of the *inchiki.* When Soeda called the *jazz,* the song, and the dance "decidedly phony," he was merely echoing the self-mocking (but accurate) language of the intellectuals who produced the skits, songs, and dances that made up the revue (SA, 49–50). Satō Hachirō, for example, explained that the terrible acting of the *Casino Folies* was a plus for the very reason that the acting was so terrible. They could not even follow a script—which was all the better, because the Asakusa audience would not laugh at a script (SH, 19).

According to my reading of Asakusa "nonsense," when Satō and others termed themselves "phony" they were not looking down on the audience as members of a class that was incapable of appreciating a high or complex culture. They were, as one scholar has noted, playing to the "erotic, grotesque, and nonsensical" desires of their audience. If we are applying my revisionist conceptions of the erotic, the grotesque, and the nonsensical, "phony" folds into our understanding of parody. For these cultural producers, the phony, like parody, was a form of repetition. They appreciated the fact that through the new cultural form of the revue, which combined music, dance, and social satire, they could capture and criticize the tempo and social issues of the current moment. Enomoto Ken'ichi, the comedian (known as Enoken), drew crowds to a series of venues in Asakusa, beginning with the *Casino Folies,* and extending through the modern years. His narrative of the *Casino Folies* tells us that, like Kon Wajirō, Gonda Yasunosuke, and Kawabata Yasunari, the Asakusa icon associated the modern in Japan with a major social and cultural break:

There can be no doubt. After the unprecedented earthquake, the psychology of the audience became more modern *(kindaiteki)* and *speedy*. Those so-called good old days—that spirit of lazy, easy living—lasted only until the earthquake. After that, the rapidly changing social conditions continued to make a tremendous impression on the audience. A slow-moving *opera* could not ride the waves of those conditions. I wanted to try theater that would make the spectators gasp—a comedy with *speed*, classy, with musical accompaniment, and dancing. The audience would not be able to restrain itself from laughing at the comedy. This was new ground as yet untouched in our country.[10]

A dialogue between Satō Hachirō and Enoken illustrates the notion of "phony" and associates *inchiki* with parody achieved through linguistic and extralinguistic code-switching. According to Satō, Enoken had rushed into Satō's base of operations, the Miyako (café), saying that he wanted to put on a performance of *Chūshingura* (the classic story of the forty-seven samurai). Because the tale was as well known to these two as it was to their contemporaries, they could plot out their production via rapid references to key scenes and characters. The focus was on form and not on content: the two decided to do the play in "a really *phony* manner." For Enoken, here *inchiki* meant in Western dress, and Satō went along with the idea. They quickly concurred on a series of decisions that would result in the repetition of the *Chūshingura* tale, but *Chūshingura* with a new difference: in the opening scene warrior helmets would be replaced by *chapeaus;* instead of swords there would be slingshots; and *seppuku*—the highly ritualized and honored process of self-disembowelment—would be accomplished with the aid of modern technology—a safety razor would be the implement of choice. The leads would be outfitted in *knickerbockers* and *golf pants*, and one hero would wear overalls and sabots. A teahouse would become a hotel, the *tango* would be incorporated; and a *flute solo* would serve well instead of the standard *naniwabushi* (ballad recitation) (SH, 5–8).[11]

Such displacements provided an amusing series of incongruities, but this repetition went beyond such difference. Just as *Chūshingura* had served as a thinly veiled social commentary on the present during the Tokugawa era, Satō and Enoken now aimed to produce a sardonic satire on the times. Satire, unlike irony, takes a political stand—it aims to change the state of affairs. And without direct access to audience reaction we can fairly safely conclude that when during the course of the play one hero, who has just had his head neatly sliced off, placed a placard in front of his face reading "Unemployed," the ensuing laughter from the audience would express their recognition and derision of the grotesque state of the social order and the political economy of the modern years. The play was to end with the be-headed samurai leader parading through the snowy streets, accompanied by his loyal retainers. The creators of this parody agreed that this finale would be a "weird *demonstration*." They did not have to elaborate for the audience, for by 1930 the words *demo* and *demonstration* were widely used to describe the political protest that, along with the pleasures of the café, the movie theaters, the print media, and the stage, characterized the modern moment. Satō and Enoken knew that their audience would both recognize the allusions and appreciate the fact that censorship both necessitated such parody and lent it a critical edge (SH, 7–8).[12]

This is, in other words, not merely amusing extra-linguistic, apolitical code-switching between premodern, Japanese garb and codified gestures and contemporary clothing and activities. The parody is an instance of the ironic *acharaka* comedy of the modern years—comedy that commented on the strength of a capitalist class hierarchy, along with the power of modern mores that had originated outside of Japanese society. *Acharaka* comedy implied that both the class hierarchy and the mores were constructs, and that changes should and could be made.

The derivation of the word *acharaka* has its own irony, for, like the Cockney and language of the down-and-out in Asakusa, it makes use of wordplay. *Acharaka* is a vernacular abbreviation of the phrase *achira kara*, which means "from over there." And the words "over there" referred to over across the ocean, from Euro-America. (To repeat and redirect the famous modernist phrasing of Gertrude Stein, the Asian continent was never signified—there was "no there there.") My working assumption is that the humor in *acharaka* comedy was based on code-switching, gags (the neologism *gyagu* was used), and other gestures marked as *modan;* it presumed that whatever had been brought in from over there was now as much part of "here" as it was of "there." Non-Japanese mores were now part of Japanese history and geography. This did not result from a creolization, nor did it result in a hybrid culture of East meets West. What had resulted and was still in the making of modern Japan was a jagged montage that clearly revealed its points of conjunction. For audience and producers alike, this process of code-switching was just one instance of the creation of new cultural practices and capitalist social forms.

I do not want to exaggerate the polemical nature of *acharaka* comedy. It does not share the clear-cut class critique of the films, literature, theater, and art of the Proletarian Culture Movement of the same era. Its ironic code-switching and its parody alone would not have rendered it ideological, but these forms of what we can call nonsense appeared alongside representations of social relationships of power and inequity. It was this synthesis that made *acharaka* critically political.[13]

One of Theodor Adorno's commentaries from his montage *Minima Moralia* is most apposite here. Adorno recognized that irony "cancels itself out the moment it adds a word of interpretation." This means that as a historian of Japanese modern nonsense I am at a disadvantage three times over. The writers of *acharaka* would not have been explicit in their message: it would have ruined their punchlines; second, censorship precluded any direct attack on the existing order; and, it is not possible from the distance of over half a century to grasp the voiced or unvoiced opinions of the intellectuals, the performers, or their audiences. It is inaccurate to see *acharaka* comedy as merely a rephrasing of the East-West combinations of Meiji material culture, as epitomized by the attire of one of the characters in Futabatei Shimei's novel *Ukigumo*. The young man of the Meiji era aiming at a "civilized" look who has put together a uniform of fez and gold watch, differed from the consumers of Western clothing documented by Kon during the modern years. For by the modern years, *acharaka* humor, like a bowler hat combined with a caped coat and kimono, signaled a form of indigenous sophistication rather than a will to catch up with the West.[14]

The producers of the *Acharaka* Revue, such as the writers of "Salome Jazzes," staged in January 1929, wanted the audience to see juxtapositions as jarring—they were exposing montage. Even members of the audience not familiar with the story of Salome that was being parodied would catch the code switch within the neologism *jazuru*. They did not have to know the biblical story of the dancer who asked for the head of John the Baptist, or the Oscar Wilde play by that name, or the 1923 silent film version of Wilde's Salome to catch the humor in the code switch which combined the widely known term *jazz* with the Japanese language verb ending for the infinitive. The heroine and hero of the story journey to Paris, Tokyo, Hawaii, and finally New York, where they are arrested. Each city offers Salome and her hero, and the audience, a shift in cultural entertainment. They watch the can-can, the Japanese flower-viewing dance, *hula dancing* accompanied by Hawaiian music, and, preceding their arrest, *jazz song*, along with *jazz dance*, on Broadway. Such gags as the juxtaposition of plans for a lovers' suicide (worthy of Edo popular theater) with the use of a long-distance telephone to forestall the suicide paved the way for the antics of the *Casino Folies*, which would open half a year later. This theater was thus different from such entertainment as the "Mon Paris Revue" that had inaugurated the all-girl Takarazuka Revue two years earlier, and not only because the *Acharaka* Revue used male and female performers. Such performances as

"*Speedy* Yasubei" (Yasubei being a very out-of-date sounding man's name, contrasting with the modern ideal of speediness), "The Bride Contest" (a parody of the folk tale "The Crab Hunt," which was also performed), "Kabuki *Revue*," "Our Very Own Story of the Forty-seven Rōnin," and "Ballads of the Six Universities"—a clear reference to college baseball— could not rely on titles alone to draw or keep their audiences. Like "Salome Jazzes," they relied on the gags. The unrivaled king of such gesture, including various forms of gags on the Asakusa Revue stage in the 1920s and 1930s, was Enoken, a performer so beloved that the Asakusa audience delighted in referring to him with the parodic "*Eroken*" based on shorthand for his name. Enoken, they knew, was central to the culture of erotic, grotesque, nonsense.[15]

Enoken was in charge of the openly phony *Casino Folies* gags such as the large drawing of the automobile that was carried around the stage to produce a sense of movement and the waves that moved instead of the ship. He also produced parodies of Kabuki based on a process of code-switching whereby the plot remained the same, but gags and music were inserted. One of these routines showed a hero committing seppuku who would commence to disembowel himself at the appropriate moment while reciting the lyrics to popular tunes from abroad. Or he might plunge his sword into his belly to the rhythm of jazz. In "The Bride Hunt," the coastline instead of the waves moved; in "*Speedy* Yasubei," our hero ran in place while the hose and the telephone poles were rushed about. In another skit a sumo wrestler empowered himself by using a bicycle pump to inflate the rubber ball strapped to his chest. Other incongruities and code switches are available in the program notes of the *Casino Folies* programs, such as the one cited in *The Asakusa Crimson Gang*. The program note cited therein referred to such acts as an *Acrobatic Tango*, *Comic Songs*, and *Jazz Dance* Ginza. The role of the Modern Boy in "*Jazz Dance*, Ginza" was performed by young girls masquerading in sailor pants, their "*silk top hats*" cocked jauntily, walking sticks swinging at their sides. Their "Ballad of What's Up-to-Date on Ginza" was interrupted by another number. Again, these were girls dressed as boys, but they were performing a Japanese folk dance in the comic tradition—this "Fukagawa Kappore" paid tribute to the working-class neighborhood next to Asakusa that had been studied by Kon (KY, 40, 42, 43–44).[16]

The montage aspect of the *Casino Folies* was made concrete in the visual imagery of the program covers, such as the cover for the third performance, which placed a cartoon figure of a Modern Boy in porkpie hat, golf pants, and checkered vest, pipe in mouth, underneath and above photos of a body part—the female leg that was so ubiquitous in Japanese modern times. A suggestively dressed dancer went headless, and the lettering switched among English, Chinese characters denoting the Asakusa Aquarium, and the *katakana* syllabary reserved for imported words, along with a dollar sign by the Arabic numbers for thirty. What did the audience make of this construction? What did they make of the constructions of Enoken and the others performing the *Casino Folies*? How can we pin down the transideological ironic? While recognizing that we run the risk of having the irony cancel itself out in the face of interpretation, it is worth turning to two actual scripts from the era of *acharaka* comedy to investigate the politics of the parody. In examining these texts I am agreeing with Enoken, who took umbrage at the term *light theater* that was applied to the genre of *acharaka* that emerged from the *Casino Folies*. "What's so light about it?" he asked. These texts are not "light." In fact, these texts are worthy of our close attention because they give us the language of the modern moment.[17]

The title *Lumpen Sociology* combines two code switches: the audience moves from the vernacular term for vagrant, written in the *katakana* syllabary denoting a foreign derivation, to the official-sounding academic term for sociology, written in ideograms. The theme song of the play offers an ironic inversion: a hobo is disdainful of the self-satisfied specialist pontificating about sociology from within the salon; the real sociologist, the song implies, is the narrator of the song. In other words, this is sociology about the hobo, by the hobo. The true characterization of the *lumpen* repeats in the refrain: though he may be trash or rubbish, a *lumpen* is lighthearted. This down-and-out figure conflicts with Hayashi Fumiko's anxious *jokyū* persona and is much too blasé to correspond to the portrait emerging from Kusama's documentary evidence. The *lumpen* was there, however, not to confirm such findings, but through irony, and through irony as parody, to challenge the capitalist system that produces the vagrant. All this time, the Asakusa audience is being entertained. Not only does the object of sociology become the subject, in a second inversion, the class system and its propelling ideology are also inverted when the singer proclaims, "Whether or not I've got money, I'm a *lumpen*, a light-hearted one; that light-hearted one." The *lumpen* is to be emulated, if not envied.[18]

The setting is Tokyo, near Ginza; the time early January 1931. In six short acts, the white-collar worker suffers from the effects of the depression and the ensuing industrial rationalization. The drama snipes at the corporate culture of the modern years. Idle salarymen with no work to occupy them—although industrial strategy requires that they "appear busy"—bemoan that it is boring to make money. At the same time, they fantasize about get-rich-quick schemes, and their boss gives them an opportunity by asking them to conceive of a project that will make the best use of ten thousand *tsubo* in the suburbs of Tokyo.

The men belong to their times. They code switch, sprinkling their dialogue with such English phrases as *love letter* and *that's OK*. They are captive to the romance of film culture that is nurtured through the commodification of photographs of film idols and of women's clothing paid for by installment, and at the same time they are cynical about the possibility of a *happy ending*. One employee, Penkichi, thinks he has found the answer in leisure activity. His name is a play on *lumpen,* just as Buruta, the name of his boss, points to the bourgeois class position of the company president, and just as Runko, a female lead, is a feminized version of *lumpen*. Penkichi imagines an *ultra-modern, modern paradise*. The paradise will have a skating rink that converts into a hot spring at night. This heated tub will be used as a swimming pool in the summer. Youth will frolic by day, and flirt by night.[19]

Modern mores are mocked even more directly when Penkichi is taken in by a new, more militant form of *stick girl*. And like all other fads that are always in the process of being produced, reproduced, and replaced within the industrial formation parodied in *Lumpen Sociology*, the *stick girl* has been replaced by a newer, more militant model who explains her mission:

> Actually, I'm a *charming girl*—my job is to lure men. Since the existence of last year's *stick girl* was altogether too formalized, it couldn't be used for the '31 version of the hunt for the bizarre. This is what gives rise to us, the *charming girls*. First of all, when we find a man with earthly desires, we capture his emotions. Most men in this world instantly give in to the sexual enticement of a young woman. By doing this we've invested our capital. Just by a blink of the eyes we are able to do what we want with that sexual impulse peculiar to men. And then, just like a shadow, they follow us, matching our every move. Our union demands the fair price of two yen for the pleasures tasted during this half-hour. Do you now understand?[20]

Here indeed is a militant, unionized modern girl in control of the choreography of the situation, aware that the rules of even the recent past do not apply to the present. Another actress in this spoof, who captures the sense of rapid transformation and presentism of Japanese modern culture, declares she is "breathing the air of 1931." The conventional notion of *ero* is more applicable to *Lumpen Sociology* than is my revisionist emphasis on the pleasures of food and visual culture in Asakusa, although the play features kissing, café banter, and the sexual aggressiveness of women. Within the café, however, there is an ironic power shift when a vocal café waitress steps out of the *jokyū* role to castigate the company boss. She makes clear that "no matter how drunk he might get," he had better not forget that theirs is purely a business relationship, one based on her professional skills. She then encourages Penkichi to take on the boss, who is threatening to have him fired, in combat "man to man."

In the play the grotesquerie of economic desperation is presented as nonsense when the *guro* appears in the form of the ironically presented *lumpen*. But despite the cavalier refrain romanticizing the life of the light-hearted *lumpen*, when the Boss threatens Penkichi, the salaryman, with the life of "a stray dog on the prowl, looking for work" along with the rest of the unemployed, the terrified Penkichi begs for forgiveness. The *nansensu* is thus apparent in the parodies of class, sexual, and gender relationships and in the ironic shift between *lumpen* as hero and *lumpen* as failure. The "nonsense" lay in the ironic relationship between the said and the unsaid. At a time when work prospects were as bleak for students as they were for their white-collar predecessors and for workers, the Asakusa audience did not need to be told the unsaid—that the threat of unemployment was no joke. The weight given to the merry words of the song confirmed the profound anxiety of the clerk faced with unemployment. A similar irony was evident in the illustrated text opening the April 26, 1931, issue of the *Weekly Asahi*. The blurb, titled *"Lumpen* Blessed by Spring," claimed that the "winds of the depression" brought good cheer to the *lumpen*, who lodged in luxurious *hotels* equipped with *modern* conveniences. The line drawing illustrated men in the garb of workers bent over some kind of construction labor. In the background, a row of factory buildings, not hotels, sent smoke into the sky.[21]

The critique of capitalism in *Lumpen Sociology* takes place in conceivable settings—the office, the park, and the café. Thus the unspoken, ironic social commentary is driven by the spoken commentary of the script, along with the set, which may be considered a documentation of the modern. For a sustained illustration of the irony of incongruity as expressed in geographic dislocation, however, we must turn to the *Casino Folies* production *Storm over Asia*, written by the same author. Here the modern is transposed to Mongolia. It takes on intellectuals on the left, the film industry, and the highly vexed issue of Japanese identity as Asian identity, that the culture of modernity had not resolved. Japanese intellectuals with any interest in film would immediately have recognized *Storm over Asia* as the title of the Soviet epic about the transformation of a descendant of Genghis Khan from nomad to partisan during the civil war that followed the Russian Revolution. The movie, made by the theorist of montage Vsevolod Pudovkin in 1928, opened in Japan on October 31, 1931, and trumpeted its message to its audience in strong words and images that placed capitalist greed and conformity in montage with revolutionary fervor. In this film, Pudovkin practiced what he preached. He used montage to juxtapose good with evil: white capitalists with a multiracial rebel force fighting for Soviet victory. Bourgeois forces attempt to civilize the hero by dressing him up in a suit, but the masquerade is too painful. Refusing to be used as a puppet leader capitalizing on his lineage, he liberates himself.[22]

An amendment to the *Casino Folies* title signaled that *Tangled Lines, 'Storm over Asia'* would present some form of *acharaka* parody. In other words, the audience was warned that a cultural production from "over there"—in this case the Soviet Union—may have been intentionally scrambled. Through a stretch of analysis the historian can find parallels between the two *Storm over Asia*. The modern automobile occupies the same space as fierce natives on horseback in both works, the force of history places an advanced culture alongside a less advanced people, and the fast tempo of the folies production is matched by Pudovkin's use of montage juxtaposing (dignified) indigenous religion with crass, conformist capitalist actions. However, this is not what gives the *Casino Folies* version of *Storm over Asia* its ironic edge. From the outset of this *acharaka* play, in which the modern "over there" is Japan, code-switching implicates the colonial in and through the modern, by taking the modern to Manchuria.[23]

The *Casino Folies* version opens with a gag: the "Casino *Cinema* Film Crew" of a film to be titled *Storm over Asia* inadvertently departs for Manchuria without its pontificating director, who is left behind on the train platform, singing the praise of the Soviet *Storm over Asia*. The ironic treatment of the movie industry is clearly established through the linguistic code-switching practices of the crew members as they depart from Japan, mingling their "OK's" with their "*banzais*." The crew proceeds to the continent, where they meet up with the president of the Mongolia-Manchuria Railway Company and his daughter, an aspiring actress. This is a clear parody of the South Manchurian Railway Company, which controlled Japanese interests in Manchuria before the official establishment of colonial rule. The name of the "esteemed" president, Ōgane Arizō, is a play on the words for having a large amount of money. His daughter's name, Hadeko, can be read to mean showy or flashy (and thereby inappropriate to her class, as is her affinity for "*chewing gum*"). The region comprising Manchuria and Mongolia was referred to as "Manmō;" in this inverted code switch, the railway company is in the "Mōman" region.

The Mongolian hero, the bandit chief named "Storm over Asia," bears no resemblance to the ideologically motivated hero in the Soviet film of that name. Instead, this leader, like the boss in *Lumpen Sociology*, has been battered by the depression. It is no longer worth going out on the rampage because no one is willing to pay the ransom for hostages. He is contemplating forcing some of his legions to join the ranks of the unemployed by "engaging in that new-fangled fad called rationalization" (NS, 158–90).

Early in the play the notion of Japanese supremacy is parodied when a Japanese denizen of Manchuria, a judo expert, proclaims that he can play a *shishi* (an outmoded term for a noble-minded patriot on the eve of the establishment of the modern state) dedicated to saving the kingdom under heaven, but he will not play a bandit (which is to say a Manchurian). The *Casino Folies* scenario makes very clear that while emotional adherence to the significance of such racialized national difference might be deeply felt, it was not always easy to determine or maintain. The tangled deceit built up around national masquerade is illustrated when the Manchurian hero Storm over Asia, succeeds in kidnapping Hadeko by passing for a Japanese actor playing the *part* of Storm over Asia, and when her Japanese rescuer who in turn *passes* as Storm over Asia. When one of the film crew walks into a bar on the Manchurian plains, the proprietress asks the stranger, "Hey, you Japanese or Chinese?" The proud response: "I'm pure Japanese" (NS, 168, 193).

The Desert Bar, run by a former woman-bandit, O-Gin (who is the object of the bandit king's love-sick attentions) is one of the parodied sites of the modern. O-Gin, whose name is more appropriate for a geisha, stocks the Electric *brandy* that was so beloved by real-life Asakusa patrons of the Kamiya *Bar*. Her irony is based on her knowledge of the Asakusa audience and the rules of their theater. "This is a *revue*," she observes at one point. "If the play doesn't move quickly the audience will be bored." The gags in the story are also characteristic of the *acharaka* sensibility: the departure of the train from the station was undoubtedly performed in an overtly phony fashion, the bandits use a wireless to track the movement of the Japanese film crew, and with an incongruous flourish, our hero, the bandit, Storm over Asia, "departs for the front" to the sound of a *"saxophone"* (NS, 193, 162, 182).

What are the politics of this parody? The references to financial insecurity in this parody are clear, as are the references to class inequity. Gender, too, is targeted, but while both Hadeko and O-Gin (who admits that she possesses *It*) exhibit the characteristics of a Modern Girl, *Storm over Asia*, unlike most documents of the modern years, is more concerned with masculinity than with femininity. (Masculinity is equated with strength and sensitivity by both men and women.) What is left unsaid is that all the men deemed to be masculine in Manchuria are Japanese. This leads us to the question of the relationship of the politics of *acharaka* to the colonial in this play, written, produced, and published before the invasion of Manchuria (NS, 165–166, 169, 184, 203).

We can argue that Manchuria as a colonial place was parodied. When a film crew member promises to bring back as souvenir a Manchurian product—the head of a bandit—he is using the language of the day visitor to Asakusa. The references to Manchuria as a vast expanse, to the Japanese expatriates (such as the character of the judo expert from Japan who wishes only to play a patriot), and the reference to the "Manchuria Express" taking the crew overseas are undoubtedly not different from references of the late 1920s related to the fortunes to be made in this "exterior" space. But Manchuria is not only characterized as an exotic place for sightseeing; it is also placed in an incongruous relationship to the metropole.

In *Storm over Asia*, the interior is as implicated as the exterior in the *acharaka* sensibility: the director calls out to the (cardboard) "choo-choo train" leaving him behind. And, from the midst of the empty expanse of the Manchurian plain, the bandit turned café waitress realizes that fortune cannot be made on the continent. She then voices a euphemism worthy of a serious political analyst assessing the progress of the Japanese empire: "How's the *situation* in the interior?" And when the emasculated hero, Storm over Asia and his loyal followers ride in on bamboo horses, this is an example of a mocking *acharaka* humor. The hobbyhorses are comparable to such gags as the waves that moved while the ship stayed in place and the automobile that was carried around the stage.

Among the categories of irony listed by Hutcheon, are "playful," "belittling," "critically constructive," and "destructive." How are we to imagine the political stance of *Storm over Asia*? To answer this question we must work not from the position of our knowledge of the anarchist background of the *Casino Folies* writers and supporters, including Hayashi Fumiko, but from our analysis of the text of the encoded play that was to be decoded by the *Casino Folies* audience on the eve of the invasion of Manchuria. We also need to bear in mind that *Storm over Asia* entertained its Asakusa audiences almost a generation after the ceding of Manchuria to Japan in 1905 (NS, 160, 169, 172–174, 194–195).

The critical references to economic and social inequity appear unambiguous, as illustrated by the relationships of the head of the railway. But this play cannot be called a critique of colonialism because the economic relationship of colony to metropole is not examined: rather, both the "interior" (*naichi*—the Japanese colonial term for the colonial metropole) and the "exterior" (*gaichi*— referring to the Japan's holdings) appear to be subject to the same forces of rationalization. Moreover, the racist element in colonial consciousness might be present, but it is not transparently obvious because the emasculation of the Manchurian hero takes place alongside the belittlement of the Japanese men in Manchuria. Moreover, because the men who are proud of being "pure Japanese" are in no way heroic, their Japanese identity does not emerge as essentially superior.

Nonetheless, the Japanese men and women are technologically more advanced—they are more modern. (The only Manchurian women—presumably Manchurian, at least—appear in a harem-like dance sequence.) They have the cameras, the cars, the railroads. The *acharaka* here is about the incongruity of new and outmoded practices and objects. Ultimately, this is *acharaka* humor focusing on modern Japan as "hero" going over "there." And it is more about the ridiculous relationships of the new to the old within the capitalist "here" than about the relationship of a conquering here to a colonized Manchurian there. *Storm over Asia* may take place in a colonized space, but it deals with the place of the colonial in a culture that did not separate the colonial from the modern.

Storm over Asia was also prophetic. This is not the place to recapitulate the official Japanese colonization of Manchuria and the emergence of a colonial culture there—including the Manchurian Film Company Man'ei, run by Amakasu Masahiko—beginning in 1937. Here indeed was an inversion of justice. (Amakasu was responsible for the murder of the anarchists Osugi Sakae and Itō Noe, along with Ōsugi's six-year-old nephew, in the wake of earthquake, at the same time as the thousands of Koreans were being killed "for their own protection.") It is also worth noting how, even as the vitality of what we have termed the eroticism of the modern space of Asakusa dimmed after the invasion of Manchuria, a culture of the modern continued with the colonial as an undifferentiated part of that formation. The dimming of Asakusa eroticism and the increasingly loud drumbeat of empire must not be confused with the end of Japan's modern years. This was not a clear trajectory—the modern was not displaced by the colonial. The modern era continued even as the mass media was deployed to advertise the expansion of the Japanese empire into Manchuria and beyond. Yet modern energies dimmed during the 1930s, as illustrated by two documentary works of fiction set in Asakusa: Takeda Rintarō's *Asakusa Threepenny Opera* (*San Mon Opera*, 1932) and Takami Jun's *Under Whatever Star* (*Ikanaru Hoshi no Shita ni*, 1939).[24]

During the heyday of the *Casino Folies*, Takeda Rintarō had frequented the backstage, but his short story about the residents of an "*apartment building"* directly behind Asakusa Park was in no way *acharaka* parody. The pieces of the modern picture were there: the café waitress, the movie theater, the mass media, and the neon advertising of the "modern urban landscape," but Takeda did not celebrate the erotic as defined in our discussion of Asakusa eroticism. Neither did his down-and-out characters have the flair for poverty exhibited either by Brecht's characters or by the down-and-out figures populating Kusama Yasoo's reports. Surely Takeda was well aware that the play and the film version of *Threepenny Opera* had played in Tokyo, but his *Threepenny Opera* is mainly about the betrayal of erotic grotesque nonsense as has been discussed herein. There may be sex, but the erotic as defined in our discussion of Asakusa eroticism is not part of their lives. One member of the ensemble is a cook who works at a cheap bar in Asakusa and has never had a woman, although he is over thirty. The other residents include the pimps of the Yoshiwara pleasure quarters (with their bored wives). They are materially and sensually impoverished but have not created the politicized practices shared by the vagrants and hawkers whom I have termed grotesque. In Takeda's words, the down-and-out tenants "have had no training in communal living": they are to take turns cleaning, but the grime in the communal kitchen and bath area and the garbage make it appear "as though they are trying their best to make their shared space as filthy as possible." (This squalor is far from the humor, group leadership, and wily machinations in Brecht's *Threepenny Opera*.) When the apartment house occupants organize a rent strike, choosing as their spokesperson the smooth-talking film narrator, they all engage in mutual betrayal by secretly breaking a joint pact to refuse to pay the monthly rent.[25]

Takeda's documentary impulse is most visible as he illustrates the political organizing by movie narrators *(benshi)* who had been rendered unemployable by the advent of the *talkie* and had thereupon chosen to participate in what Andrew Gordon has called the "dispute culture" of the era. Takeda's report of sympathy strikes spreading, threatening a *"general strike"* affecting all of the movie houses in Asakusa, was published three months after a strike at the Asakusa Shōchiku Theater that had spread to those managed by Nikkatsu. Like the rent strike in the story, this unrest is also quelled, thanks to the active collusion of the film narrator, "the leader in white tabi" (along with the threat of right-wing violence and police "protective custody"). This nonparody with a parodic title has an ironic ending: a journalist tricks the "leader in white *tabi*" into feigning suicide so that this strike-leader can receive media acclaim for taking responsibility for the failure of the strike. However, there is no congratulatory article in the newspapers, and Takeda ends his story with the following moralizing: "The leader in white *tabi* with the winning ways, being awakened by nobody, will probably continue to sleep forever."[26]

Other than the title, there is no notion of *acharaka* in Takeda's story. There is however, another, very subtle (and not necessarily intended) parody that in part accounts for the absence of the nonsensical cultural commentary that pervaded the *Casino Folies*. In the course of rousing his fellow workers to strike action, the film narrator demands that his colleagues strengthen their resolve to engage in battle "in order to maintain our lifeline." Takeda used the state's keyword of 1931 *seimeisen* (lifeline). How are we to interpret his appropriation of the term underpinning Japanese expansionist ideology? (Manchuria was to provide the official continental lifeline in 1931, 1937, and 1941. Perhaps Takeda was arguing that the battle appeared to be lost as cultural forces began to move *out* onto an external *gaichi*.) Takeda saw that this new war culture was beginning to displace the modern, progressive focus on transformation through dispute culture and *acharaka* means. Yet, notwithstanding the new forces of repression, he and others refused to let go of the modern.[27]

In 1932 it was still possible for Takeda to see the moment as modern. By 1939, when Takami Jun began to serialize *Under Whatever Star*, this was no longer the case. In this work of fiction, the modern continued its move onto the continent, at the same time as the erotic, grotesque, nonsensical space of Asakusa culture was being actively transformed into war culture. The author gives his readers a big hint about his sense of historical transformation when one character explains to the narrator that those who have failed on the left are now called *tenkōsha* (those who have turned). Takami repeats the word often, usually in reference to Asakusa *yose* storytellers who have been forced into pairing up into *manzai* comedy duos to meet new popular demand; but the novella is also about the *tenkō* of Asakusa culture of the modern years. By the mid-1930s the term *tenkō* had found widespread use in the Japanese press. The term referred to the "turning away" of Communist Party members from their allegiance to the party and to the ideology of the family-state. Takami gives us a sustained analogy by offering a view of the energies of the neighborhood being dissipated. Although the author warns us that "they say that reality is stranger than fiction, but reality may be stranger than comedy *(manzai)*," his fiction and his comedy are so familiar it is easy to conclude that Takami's fiction documents the people and practices surrounding him. His writing shows that the term *modan* had not been forgotten at the end of the decade of the 1930s. Takami uses the word to refer to a drunken guest at a geisha party demanding of a dancer that

"Miss Modern" pour him a drink, and Takami refers to the modern architecture of the home of a priest.[28]

What makes Takami's setting most familiar, however, is the way he maps out Asakusa, citing familiar landmarks associated with the modern. The *Casino Folies,* for example, is so long gone that ghost stories circulate—stories that the tapping of the dancers' shoes can be heard late at night. The narrative revolves around the revue culture of 1939, featuring second-rate actors, aging dancers, those who serve them food and drink, and the voyeuristic intellectuals who come seeking cheap, strange thrills. When one character yells out to another, "Hey, has So-and-so been killed yet?" there is little doubt that Takami was privy to the everyday interactions among those who rehearsed in small spaces attached to the eateries. The eroticization of food is as ever-present herein as it was in Kawabata's novel. For example, the author lovingly includes a recipe for an inexpensive *"beef-steak"* dish, and his narrator-hero exhibits the documentary impulse worthy of Kon Wajirō when he begins to jot down all of the offerings at an *okonomiyaki* restaurant, in case he ever writes a novel set in such an eatery.[29]

Hollywood fantasy also continues at this late date. The young dancers have pinups of foreign male stars and of starlets in their dressing rooms, and Hollywood gesture has also reached them: the narrator conjectures that if he and his ex-wife's new husband had been born abroad, they would have hugged each other on meeting, just like in the foreign movies. Also the intense relationship of class to moviegoing culture is made evident when the narrator sees a movie for a second time. This is the story of a young girl from a poor neighborhood whose genius at sewing is picked up by the media and portrayed on stage before being documented on film. In one scene the girl's father, a tinsmith, comes home on New Year's Eve. He has not been able to receive money from the labor boss, and thus there is no money for the new year. The response of the father is to flail madly about the room. The first time the narrator saw the film, the response of the well-heeled audience in the Marunouchi Theater—who had never seen the tenement houses in Kōtō ward—was laughter. They had seen the gestures as slapstick—nonsense, as it were. The response in Asakusa the scene was met with silence and tears.[30]

In Takami's story, nonsense is personified by the hero in the figure of the *vaudevillian* who has chosen Chinese characters for his stage name. When transliterated, the name reads as *Bing Crosby (Biingu Kurozubii);* the reader (and the Asakusa audience in the story) need only code switch. In Takami's novel, Bing is a member of the guitar-wielding "Hilarious Four," but only his name betrays any humor. In the book an indigenous *modan* culture based on motions and objects from "out there" is no longer being invented, and the nonsensical irony and parody of *acharaka* are absent. Instead, the modern is being matter-of-factly transplanted onto the continent at the same time as it is being displaced at home by a series of practices affirming war and empire. Movement to the continent due to varied self-interests is taken for granted. The narrator's ex-wife, a former actress, goes to Shanghai to work in a bar; a dancer is to move to Manchuria with her father; writers' units are attached to the army in China; revue dancers are part of "solace groups" shipped over to China. Self-interest and national interest blur for the narrator as he ponders whether he should become one of these writers working for the state's efforts. In his mind the expansionist effort is clearly gendered: if he goes he will surely attain a new (masculinist) toughness. But although the China Incident has aroused in him the desire to go into the war zone so that he will be able to write novels to "exhilarate the spirit of his readers" he is ambivalent, for he also sees the trip as voyeuristic sightseeing.[31]

Takami's ambivalence emerges in several places. Employing a widely used state euphemism, a comedian who says he is busy undergoing *tenkō* to become a *manzai* performer asks the narrator to think of a stage name that will reflect positively on "the current situation." He wants a name like one he's just encountered: *Kunio Mamoru*, a pun for "Protect the Country" and a parody (or statement of support? or both?) of state sloganeering. And finally, the novel ends with the realism of the scene of a group of draftees being taken to the local shrine to pray. They are accompanied by members of the neighborhood association; all moved to the sounds of the "Patriotism March" (Aikoku Kōshinkyoku). Unlike his hero, Takami Jun did engage in *tenkō*. In 1941, a year after *Under Whatever Star* appeared in book form, he was drafted into the army as a member of its Information Corps, and by 1942 he had entered Rangoon with his army division. I am interested in his refusal to let go.[32]

Takami illustrates his refusal to let go of the modern when he refers to the nonsense of Asakusa entertainers in 1939. His story illustrates a documentary impulse—the performers of nonsense in Takami's work have a real-life counterpart in the Akireta Bōizu (I've Had It Boys). The four performers, Bōya Saburō, Kawada Haruhisa, Shibariei (a pun on the name of the French crooner Maurice Chevalier), and Masuda Kiiton (named after Buster Keaton), said to have been inspired by the Mills Brothers, made their debut in September 1937. What appealed to their Japanese audiences were their "changed songs" applying new lyrics to old tunes and their spoofs of current events. The nonsense in their *Dinah Rhapsody,* based on a silly code switch that resulted in the meaning "Dinah, Dinah, Whatever Is It?" *(daina daina nandaina?),* the impersonation of Popeye, the Hawaiian songs, and the staged fights among Walt Disney animal characters must have been both familiar and new to their delighted audiences. The nonsense of the I've Had It Boys was so popular that it went nationwide—it moved beyond Asakusa to reach the entire nation on the radio and on records. Their success was also evident in the number of copycat groups using "Boys" as part of their stage name. This nonsense lasted into the Pacific War, when the authorities began to treat the humor as protest. The performers were told that *akireta* (I've had it) was "undisciplined" and that *bōizu,* because it was English, would not do. As a result, the I've Had It Boys became the Newly Rising High Speed Squadron (Shinkō Kaisoku Butai). They had code-switched to the official lexicon, just as, by November 11, 1937, the Takarazuka All Girls Musical Theater was advertising its military revue under the title of the Nanjing Bombing Corps (Nanjing Bakugekitai). The advertisement for the revue, which showed women dressed as men in naval uniform, one as a mother on the home front, and one as a bomber pilot, screamed out, "Great Victory on the Shanghai Front! *Banzai! Banzai!*" and cautioned newspaper readers not to forget the valiant "Seahawk" that bombed Nanjing.[33]

LETTING GO OF THE MODERN—CHARLIE LEFT BEHIND

It is known that many comedians, artists, and writers traveled to the continent on "comfort missions." When they did so, entertainers such as Yanagiya Kingorō ("the performer swinging his big buttocks" who had been disdained by critic Iwasaki) and the *manzai* team of Entatsu and Achako had a dual task: they entertained the troops and, upon their return, reported to audiences at home. Because of this turn of events and so many others that must remain beyond the scope of my discussion of Japanese mass culture in the modern years, it would be intellectually dishonest and historically unwise to paint any sort of picture of sustained protest or massive resistance to Japanese expansion, or to unequivocally label the nonsense of performance a response to the tightening of state controls during the second half of the 1930s. Moreover, we still need (now more than ever) a serious study of just how it is that most of the so-called ethnographers of Japanese modern times whom I have deferred to herein, including Gonda, Kon, Hayashi, and Iwasaki, appear to have embraced state policy by the late

1930s. To engage in such a study of this *tenkō* of these intellectuals and their mass culture is beyond the scope of my attempt to produce a montage of Japanese modern, mass culture. I do hope that my segments have provided sufficient evidence to counter any argument that would contend that the Japanese modern culture was so superficial that it was easily abandoned.

I would like to suggest one interpretation. While many could not let go of the modern in Japan, by 1939, in some parts of Japanese modern culture, the emperor system, if not the nativist, statist, expansionist ideology, had clearly won out. The *Japan Culture Film Almanac* for 1939 makes it clear that the modern could not coexist with the official version of Japanese everyday experience. The brief blurbs in the *Almanac* gave full rein to expressions of ahistorical national definition. Sumo was placed as "beginning far off in the 'era of the gods,'" and the paragraph labeled "Talking about Baseball" told potential viewers that "Baseball has developed into a national sport and has even become Japanese-style baseball. . . . Today when there is a need for a training of the National Body *(kokutai)*, we must increasingly display the essential true value of baseball." All notions of the modern had lost their erotic, grotesque, and nonsensical connotations. The modern had been reduced to the Japanese term *kindaiteki,* with its connotations of efficiency, as in the battlefield postal service, in the "modern science" *(kindai kagaku)* of the (superior) Japanese sword, and in the reference in the almanac to the "modern culture" *(kindai bunka)* of Germany's cities. The only film to touch on American life was a documentary on Yellowstone National Park. The Euro-American (Ōbei) experience was now being featured in Japan by Nazi Germany, as in *Beautiful Germany,* a film on Nazi urban life produced by the German Railway Tourist Bureau. Another Nazi-produced documentary, *Marriage in Schwalm,* likened German rural marriage practice to Japanese marriage traditions (marriage being "the high point of rural *seikatsu"*). The German-produced documentary on the *The Great Processions of the German National People* was said to include footage of the 1936 Nuremberg rally, along with speeches by Hitler.[34]

In this almanac, non-Japanese Asians are treated with ambiguous care. The issue of colonization is skirted in the description of the movie *Ryūkyū Scenes and Manners* when the Ryūkyūans are treated as *kokumin* (a national people) with "a rich folk art." Ryūkyū culture is romanticized as local color (the term is actually used and pronounced *lookaru karaa*) but is treated in terms of nature and material culture as illustrated by the movie title *Ryūkyū Scenes and Manners.* The term *fūzoku* (mores), as keyword from the modern years employed by Kon and others, has been replaced by *fūbutsu,* encompassing both material culture and the landscape. Ryūkyūan distinctiveness is to be found not in sexuality but in "architecture, sculpture, music, dance, and crafts," as presented in a film claiming to explore a "spiritual *seikatsu*."[35]

A synopsis of *Thirty Years of the South Manchurian Railway,* produced by the Mantetsu Film Production Agency, represents this history of the company as a history of the pioneering efforts of the Japanese people *(Nihon minzoku)* and as a history of culture building on the continent. The present is the beginning of a new era that will eliminate ideological distinctions between China and Japan. (This was no *Storm over Asia.*) The blurb advertising *Scenes and Manners of Manchuria* did not tell its readers whether the movie made any distinction between Japanese daily life and Manchurian daily life a decade after the invasion of Manchuria.[36]

Thus the term *modern* no longer applied in Japan; and the notion of *seikatsu* had been relegated to the everyday life of others outside Japan, such as the "natives" *(dojin)* featured in the movie *Dark Congo* (renamed from the original 20th Century Fox title *Dark Rapture*), and the large-lipped comic strip characters in grass skirts who observed Chaplin's visit to "Africa" with admiration, in a 1933 publication of the family magazine *Kingu.* The almanac explained that the film featured the ancient, strange practices of the natives, including the love *seikatsu* of giant women over seven feet tall. The sensationalized text was illustrated by the close-up image of the face of a young boy who had been ritually scarred; his head held close to the camera. The movie was acclaimed not only for its treatment of animals in ways differing from earlier *"jungle* movies" but also for its treatment of the extremely "natural *seikatsu* of the native." The focus on their "sexual distinctiveness" leads one to wonder whether this "culture film" differed from earlier Hollywood films like *The Jungle,* that had been advertised so extensively in *Kinema Junpō* in June and July 1929.[37]

Whether or not the racism in the culture movie almanac indirectly recapitulated a Euro-American racial hierarchy is, for our purposes, not as important as Iijima Tadashi's concern that government programs such as the Ministry of Education's contest for the top ten favorite culture films, to be voted on "by the masses," were in fact not drawing in the masses. By 1943, he was explaining the exceedingly low numbers: "It is often said that cultural films were no fun." Iijima also lamented the power of the star system: the audience was drawn to the human being in the film, the human who had a *seikatsu* as well as a role. Filmgoers, he admitted, were possessed of a curiosity about worlds far different from their own, or even if not far different, about a *seikatsu* that was not theirs but which they could compare with their own. Iijima seemed to be saying the Japanese audiences needed to enjoy viewing identifiable movie stars or at least personable characters available in the realm of fantasy not available in culture movies. Movies were experienced as pleasurable, as *goraku* (play), because the viewer identified with them and felt that life could be enriched. (Such an idea conformed to the rhetoric of Japanese modern times because a non-Japanese *seikatsu* was not seen as qualitatively different from a Japanese *seikatsu*.) Iijima did not ask why, at this juncture when the Great East Asian War (Dai Tōa Senso) was supposedly galvanizing the people, they needed to imagine an ideal *seikatsu*.[38]

Iijima's concern over the popular disinterest in the culture film speaks to the power of Japanese modern culture. The case of Awaya Noriko, the blues singer mentioned herein, is one example of an artist constrained by the system who did not change her thought. She worked within the wartime system and was nominally subject to wartime restrictions, but she ignored the state's admonitions against the erotic. While other Japanese women also refused to give up their permanent waves and makeup to conform to the state's regendering of the modern women, Awaya Noriko took this refusal to the extreme. When she sang her *blues* for the troops (in concerts that were monitored), she chose to wear a military hat. But, as the government continued to proclaim "extravagance is the enemy" *(zeitaku wa teki da)*, she emphasized her feminine persona more strongly. In her memoirs Awaya recalls that military men became hysterical when the war did not go their way, acting as though women's fancy dress was the cause of their defeats. She found herself being attacked for wearing fingernail polish that was too red, *"high heels"* that were against the people of the nation, and an erotic black dress. Women dressed in the wartime uniform of *monpe*, the baggy cotton trousers ordinarily worn only by farm women, joined in the attack on Awaya, but her response was to draw her eyebrows longer and thinner and to darken her lipstick. And to one of the many women who were constantly forcing flyers upon her that denounced extravagance, she explained: "This is my preparation for war, this is not extravagance." Awaya's will to extend the modern years into the war years through a celebration of the erotic (and through a refusal to accept public behavior as defined by the authorities) was a form of resistance to the emperor system.[39]

A second instance of the distinction between adherence to the system and actual belief in the (emperor system) ideology involves Charlie Chaplin. (Chaplin remained a reference point long after all forms of American culture had been banned.) After Pearl Harbor, Iijima referred to Chaplin in an indictment of technology: "Human beings who make machines do not wish to be used by machines. But we cannot say that there are not instances wherein they are used by machines. For example, as evident in Chaplin's *Modern Times*, the tragicomedy of mechanized humans is often seen. And such a phenomenon is tied to the worship of machine civilization and gives rise to it." In the "Overcoming of Modernity" debate, while discussing machine civilization, the literary critic Kawakami Tetsutarō made his position quite clear: "It suffices if we have Chaplin and Quixote fighting against machines." The class identification of *lumpen* might have disappeared, but Charlie, along with modern technology, was still a welcome part of Japanese cultural consciousness. Even *acharaka* culture had not disappeared totally, for, according to the writer Takizawa Osamu, a Japanese movie made by Saitō Torajirō under strict Pacific War guidelines contained a scene of an automatic sushi-making device gone berserk. The little *lumpen*'s eating machine was in the collective memory.[40]

I admit I leave the reader with some ambiguity as to whether modern times ended at Pearl Harbor. Can we pick modern times up again after the Pacific War? My answer is that it would be too easy to draw a line of continuity, to pick up where I have left off. I admit that this would be somewhat closer to my own understanding of the history than to the common presumption in the West that Western mass culture, exemplified by the boogie-woogie, was exported to Japan beginning with the American occupation. However, this would also be wrong. The poverty of the post-war years would call forth a grotesquerie of vagrancy and homelessness, and eroticism would be evidenced in post-war filmgoing (albeit the sort Linda Williams would call pornographic), but the nonsense of *acharaka* could no longer be. The seemingly confident creations of *acharaka* had been premised on Japan's possession of an empire and an obsession with a Euro-American culture, including the European and American representations of people made to appear primitive—uncivilized. Now, the empire was gone and mass culture could no longer be freely brought from "over there." Now, an occupying force from "over there" was overseeing culture inside Japan. In other words, after the modern years there were new configurations of power both within culture and between cultures. But that is a story for another time.

Freeze Frames

(An Epilogue in Montage)

Tempo (1931)　A scene in the film *Madamu to Nyōbo* (Madam and the wife), directed by Gosho Heinosuke, highlights the truth that woman's eroticization during the 1920s and into the 1930s was emblematic of modernity. Our hero is overwhelmed by the freewheeling behavior of the women in the jazz ensemble gathered in the house next door to him in the suburbs. But it is the song played by the neighboring Mammy's Jazz Band—"The Era of *Speed*"—that punctuates an equally important aspect of the Japanese conceptualization of the modern by August of 1931, when the film was released. The hero is drawn in by speed, tempo, and rhythm. These are as seductive as the gestures of the female bodies during the jam session. But it is too easy to pit the "modern Madam" in charge of the gestures of the *"jazz ensemble"* against his "traditional" stay-at-home wife in kimono, who does not visit her neighbors. After all, she is excited by the prospect of an airplane ride at the end of the movie, just before the happy nuclear family goes off into the sunset. They stroll off to the strains of "My Blue Heaven" in a way prophetic of the denouement of Chaplin's *Modern Times*, wherein Chaplin and his gamine would depart in similar fashion.

Gestures (1932)　Cut to an isolated playing field in a very different kind of suburbs. These suburbs are different from the suburbs in *Madamu to Nyōbo*, which were defined by bourgeois propriety and decadence. The scene is from Ozu Yasujirō's *Umaretewa Mita keredo* (I was born but), a film from and about Japan released in June 1932. There, in the field, children compose their own set of modern practices based on mass culture materials: fantastic ninja movies and mass-produced illustrated boys' stories have inspired them to create their own hierarchy. The leader points two fingers in an imagined gesture of shooting his victim, who must lie down "dead" on his back. This boy is only allowed to arise from the dead after his tormentor makes the sign of the cross in redemption. When the assailant gestures, palm outward, for his victim to rise, the follower returns to a disciplined, standing pose, hands at his sides. This is a code-switching of Christian signs moving alongside visions of pre-modern Japanese heroes, thanks to the magic of gestures.

Umaretewa Mita keredo has been seen as a commentary on class inequity and conflict, and class tensions are set forth through the experience of two brothers, whose father has moved the family to the suburbs so that he can advance on the corporate ladder. The social commentary is evident as is an ambiguous message regarding the invasion of Manchuria. It is safe to say that the representation of mobilization for war is subtle—a sign in a school hallway celebrates the "Three Valorous Bombs." In addition, Ozu gives us gestures in a scene of schoolyard regimentation that may be read allegorically. At the end of the film, after the brothers have failed at a hunger strike aimed at their father's self-abasing careerism, the younger boy announces his plan to grow up to be a lieutenant general and not a general, because his brother will be the general. This is a far cry from a version of the script that did not see its way to Japanese spectators. In that version, the older boy is asked by troops on the move to buy some candy for them. He does so, only to find that they have moved on. He is thus drawn farther and farther from his home as he tries to catch up with them.

It is not the relationship with the military that is so fresh in *I Was Born, But. . . .* Rather, it is the modern gesturing—for example the younger boy creates a stance in a position worthy of a grimacing Kabuki actor frozen into a *(mie)* pose: Clogs in hand as a ready weapon, he prepares to meet his enemy. He must have learned the posture by going to the movies.

Code Switch (1936)   The movie *Utau Yaji Kita* [Singing Yaji and Kita] was a parody of the parody *Tōkaidō Hizakurige,* the picaresque classic of two Edo period ne'er-do-wells who travel the Tōkaidō highway at the turn of the nineteenth century. This movie displaced the often scatological humor of the original work by engaging in constant code-switching between the past and the modern and between Japan and the West—the comedy played with history. Some code switches in the film *Utau Yaji Kita* starring Enoken's rival, the large-bodied writer, comedian, and bon vivant Furukawa Roppa:

Dancing women in kimono at Nihonbashi at the onset of pilgrimage to Ise shrine suddenly and speedily transform themselves into Busby Berkeley–style kimonoed figures dancing in kaleidoscopic patterns.

Yaji (Roppa), his pilgrim's straw hat in hand—for he and Kita are traveling to Ise Shrine—says a fond, resonant "sayonara" to his wife, putting out his hand to shake it good-bye as he does so. She responds in kind, in the same kabuki intonations, and in English, bidding him *"goo-bai"* before all burst into song.

The soundtrack is a montage of popular songs of the era, including "Aishite Chōdaine," (Please love me), sometimes with no clear association between song and situation. These are *kaeuta*, the "changed songs" that had so intrigued Nakano Shigeharu when he came across the lyrics composed by young girl factory workers. We can think of changed songs—as we look back on such other examples as the *Dinah Rhapsody* by the I've Had It Boys (Akireta Bōizu)—as a form of code-switching. In *Utau Yaji Kita* our heroes, after asserting that they are fearless as sons of Edo, enter an enchanted forest, where it is believed that foxes morph into humans, to the strains of "My Blue Heaven." (Such combining should not be read as post-modern; it was highly modern within the mass culture of Japanese modern times.)

An impatient princess demands "words with *speed*" from a verbose samurai messenger who addresses her with too many honorifics. She then opens the contents of a present to find a message in English block letters—"I LOVE YOU"—before retreating to music that is both decidedly Japanese and decidedly premodern.

The heroes find themselves before a full revue stage, where dancers in kimono merge with chorus girls, and those in kimono dance a shimmy.

Kita sings the melancholy theme song from the contemporary hit *Samurai Nippon*, about a masterless samurai with a broken heart and no set allegiance. As he sings, a couple dances the tango beside him.

Yaji sings a dance-hall ditty about "Papa" and "Mama" that sounds very much like Chaplin's nonsense tune at the end of *Modern Times*.

Is this all merely nonsense as silliness? Yes and no. The heroes and their story have been ripped out of their narrative and thus out of their history and, at many junctures, out of their language and mores. This displacement is what elicits laughter. It also calls for the acknowledgment of change—change in tempo, language, and the intercultural as constitutive of the cultural. The displacement is what points to the constant contemporary production of the mass culture, and even of the changes in family relationships. The original Yaji and Kita, who delighted Japanese audiences from 1802 to

1822, could have been used as a basis for mere comedy, but they were employed for a very different modern parody, and for a finale which ended with the lyrics: "Fifty-three stops of the Tōkaidō, *oui, oui, oui*" *(Tōkaidō 53 tsugi, ui, ui, ui)*.

The film bombed not because mass audiences recoiled from modern references to the Edo duo. (Paramount films starring Wallace Beery and Raymond Hatton were being constantly advertised without any historicizing or qualifying parentheticals.) The original titles of these Hollywood productions: *Firemen Save My Child* (1927), *Now We're in the Air* (1927), and *Wife Savers* (1928); the Japanese language translations of the titles of these movies starring the Beery and Hatton duo: *Yaji and Kita Firemen, Yaji and Kita in the Air,* and *Yaji and Kita in Woman Trouble.*[1]

The code switches of the singing Yaji and Kita of 1936 were very different from the cultural synthesis advocated just one year later in the *Cardinal Principles of the National Entity of Japan,* distributed throughout the schools by the Ministry of Education in 1937. This history of Japanese advances (from "The Founding of the Nation" until the present state of imperial conquest) was attributed to the inherent difference between Japan and other nations, the basis of which was "the great spirit of the founding of the Empire." The text acknowledged the influx of Western influences since the Meiji era, denounced the unsettling influence of Western individualism, and called for "the creation of a vast new Japanese culture" that had characteristics peculiar to Japan and which would sublimate and assimilate foreign cultures. In other words, it continued, the natural sciences should be adopted, but the "views of life and of the world peculiar to the West, which were due to the racial, historical, and topographical characteristics of the Occident" were to be monitored. But views of the West were not always scrupulously monitored. If they had been, the film version of *Journey to the West* could not have survived.[2]

The Parody of Comedy (1940)　In 1923, the Chinese social commentator and philosopher Hu Shih called the legendary sixteenth-century Chinese novel *Journey to the West* "a book of . . . profound nonsense." He was referring to the tale of a monkey who, along with two other disciples possessing special powers, leads his master on a pilgrimage to obtain scriptures. This was a tale based loosely on the historical journey of Hsuan-tsang to India. Hu Shih did not deny the strong presence of Buddhism, Confucianism, or Taoist belief in the versions of *Journey to the West* available by the early twentieth century. His point was that the tale could not be a primer teaching religious practice.

In 1940, the Asakusa impresario and actor Enoken (as the monkey figure) took Hu Shih's point one step further: Enoken as Monkey led an ensemble of Japanese actors and actresses in a modern parody of the Chinese
parody. This was *Songokū*, named after the monkey hero. This comedy provided a vernacular expression of Kawamura Minato's eminently reversible
assertion that finding the barbarian (the *yaban*) without enabled Japanese
colonizers to self-consciously adopt the status of civilized.[3]

Kawamura concludes that the 1930 uprising in Taiwan confirmed the
deepest fears of the Japanese occupiers. (It can be added that Hollywood fantasies undoubtedly were major contributors to the formulation of these pro-
jections before 1930. For example, in 1929, ads for *The Jungle* in *Kinema
Junpō* played to the audience's desire for a view of the "primitive sex life of
the native" as part of the "unimaginable primitive everyday *seikatsu*." The
accompanying montage of stills and sketches emphasized the simple nature
of the pleasures and the weapons of the primitive people. There was also the
ad for *Taranga* (tribe wars), billed in English in the advertisement as "The
First Talking Picture of the South Seas." This was presented as the history
of the Taranga people—its *minzoku*. It was, moreover, a tale about primi-
tives *(dojin)*. At the same time that they were being taught racial categories,
Japanese audiences were urged to enjoy their distance from the uncivilized.
However, they were not supposed to distance themselves completely because of the ambivalent position of a racialized Japanese identity caught between Euro-America and Asia. The readers of *Kinema Junpō* were told to
look back at their own ancestry while watching *The Silent Enemy*, a movie
celebrating the struggle for survival of Native Americans. Japanese audiences were to learn that their forefathers had also killed in order to live; this
movie was not to be seen as a story of another alien *minzoku*. On the other
hand, the people of China were to be presented as unambiguously different.[4]

When *Songokū* appeared in 1940, this Japanese vision of a non-Japanese
Orient was being put into place by other films and film advertisements. The
dancing harem girls and the mysterious schemes of evil Orientals were familiar to the Japanese filmgoer who had studied such montages as the lush
Hollywood spread advertising *Secrets of the East: Scheherazade*. The Japanese film version of *Journey to the West* sported no naked women around
a pool, nor sailing ships, nor turbaned men, but the atmosphere of the film
did express the sentiment informing the ad for Scheherazade which referred
to an Oriental "land of secrets wrapped in purple dreams." This ad, along
with the advertisement for *The Mysterious Dr. Fu Manchu* that enthused
over the "Oriental taste" of the movie most definitely excluded Japan from

the world of mystery, as did *Songokū*. Fukuzawa Yukichi's call for an escape from Asia had indeed been achieved in this realm of mass culture.[5]

Songokū does illustrate the calculus of Kawamura's essay on the relationship between the discourse on barbarism and the Japanese experience of self-civilizing. In response to their encounters with conniving Orientals, the pilgrim heroes turn to modern technology: a *television* allowing X-ray vision into a room where one hero has been taken captive, a two-seater airplane which looks like a giant toy, but which does the trick of transporting our heroes, and an active machine gun. Hollywood fantasy does not take an exclusively Oriental form here in 1940. The heroes are also helped out by a can of spinach that emits the theme tune from *Popeye the Sailor Man* and by a rendition of "Heigh-Ho" by the Seven Dwarfs. In contrast, the Orientals, most of them female, are not merely passive harem dancers; they have evil designs on the heroes. One beauty attempts to eat a hero alive when he refuses her advances. She then code-switches into modern Asakusa parlance: "What should the flavor of the *sauce* be?" Not only does she have soy sauce, she runs through the list of *ketchup [kechappu]* and *mayonnaise [mayoneezu]*, mustard, and salt.

Thus, the primitive is also modern in this parody, in which the enemy is not merely alien in mysterious, backward ways but also inhabits a technologically advanced world. In one scene reminiscent of the management's control room in Charlie Chaplin's *Modern Times*, the Oriental inhabits a fortress of flashing buttons and robotic figures. And if the Oriental primitive can be modern, what is the meaning of this parody, which takes its inspiration from a Chinese legend at a time when Japan is at war with China? The repetition of parody and the irony of parody are present without doubt, but whether *Songokū* worked to challenge or to reinforce presumptions regarding the relationship of colony to polity remains unclear.

The celebration of transformation in the movie did have implications. If the monkey could turn into different figures and a magic rod into technological aids, could this not have encouraged audiences to envision alternative definitions of nation, just as the Modern Girl had challenged gender presumptions? Could it have led the audience to muse upon past and potential changes in the Japanese polity—to continue to recognize that neither culture nor nation was fixed? Most probably, the repetition of morphing was not taken as seriously by Japanese audiences as the transformations which they had watched in awe in 1914, when the hero Matsunosuke had turned himself into a giant toad, thanks to ninja sorcery.[6] What is clear, nonetheless, is the strong presence of the Hollywood repertoire in the Japanese imaginary, as late as 1940. The message of the parody was ambiguous: it could not as easily be said, as was said of *Casino Folies,* that its humor mocked the cultural politics of Japan's present. But this was not *inchiki;* this was for real, and although it might be dictated away, it would not so easily disappear from memory. What can be said is that the historicist parody in *Songokū* and its celebration of personal transformation, like the nonsense in *Singing Yaji and Kita* were a challenge to the sermonizing essentialism of the *Cardinal Principles of the National Entity of Japan [Kokutai no Hongi].*

ASAKUSA MEMORIES (THE 1970S AND 1980S)

One product of the Japanese economic growth of the 1970s was the *boom* in works about Asakusa and its environs, characterized as the "downtown" or *shitamachi* section of Tokyo. Another consequence was the "Loss of Experience" cited by Fujita Shōzō, who lamented in his indictment of the disappearance of the game of hide-and-seek from Japanese society when play space was displaced by automobiles. Experience, he said, was not "merely of the frontal lobe, or of the body, or only of the emotions"; children were being deprived of the negotiations between the combined mind and body and the material world. By losing the experience of hiding, both the children who were the devil ("it" in American parlance) and those who were pursued, were cut off from the experience of the loss of society, its recovery, and its reproduction. Instead of experiencing any critical distance or historical break, members of Japanese society were ushered through a system made up of "graduation," "job attainment," and "qualification examinations." Herein lay an unprecedented, new form of barbarism—Ernst Bloch's "rationalizing without reason" *(Rationalisierung ohne Ratio).* Fujita's opening salvo, an indictment of the fruits of high-speed economic growth, is reminiscent of Kon Wajirō's reference to heads serving hats. It is equally attentive to the modern commodity: "We are living in a terrible era." The essay went on to indict society devoid of craft. "All we have around us is given to us as an already manufactured item. The means to our everyday lives are given to us as finished equipment just like telephone boxes or gas ranges." Fujita went on to note that even food is "semi-manufactured" in order to give us the pleasure of playing house. The ready-made aspect of these new things and their givenness is diametrically opposed to the principle of montage, which for Fujita implies "mutual relationships of resistance among parts," "mediation," "reconciliation," and "metamorphoses." Readers are warned not to trust the presentist, trendy Japanese words for "now": *nau* and *ima*. To counter this temptation, he offers a "twentieth-century method of *montage*": one must attempt to piece together "the leap of one's imagination, the multiplicitous breadth of one's reason, along with reciprocity of experience." Then fragments from this assemblage must be put together to qualitatively resist the "reasonless rationalizing." Fujita makes clear that montage does not merely entail a putting together of pieces. Rather, through the process of reassociation, the fragments undergo a process of metamorphosis, and, as a result, a renewal of relationships.[7]

This sort of tension is missing from the odes to Asakusa published during the 1970s and 1980s. These works give little evidence of the culture of erotic grotesque nonsense documented by Kon, Gonda, Hayashi, Kawabata, and Kusama—the culture created by Hollywood, the *Casino Folies*, the hawkers of stolen goods, their customers, and beggar society. Instead, the culture of Asakusa becomes the culture of an old Japan, bound by the tradition of affective bonds. Even the claim by one author that Chaplin was "perfect for Asakusa" because most inhabitants had survived dire straits, which is accompanied by a discussion of the emergence of the homeless *lumpen* in Asakusa during the depression, is quizzical about Chaplin's appeal. The author concludes that Chaplin and *shitamachi ninjō* (the often-cited *shitamachi* human ties of close connection) shared unfathomable aspects of *ninjō*. What was implied was not only a uniquely Japanese affect that countered the cosmopolitan language of *Eiga no Tomo* but also a neighborhood-specific language, that like Kuki Shūzō's *iki*, made little room for historical transformation.[8] Here, a reminder regarding Soeda Azenbō's refusal to make use of the concept of ninjō in his documenting of modern Asakusa culture is in order.

There is no irony in such memoirs as the *Asahi Shinbun* compilation *Shitamachi* (1984). Nor is there a trace of Asakusa parody. The humor of *acharaka* theater has disappeared, along with any mention of the displaced foreigners who peopled *Asakusa Kurenaidan*. When war is mentioned, it is either without remorse or regret or with fond memories. Nonetheless, we can still seek out some of the history of modern Asakusa in postwar documentation. For example, the compilation based on a newspaper column, *Shitamachi*, a representative collage, not montage, of items (including the Electric brandy of the Asakusa Kamiya Bar, the Sumida River, the craftsman, and the Asakusa Kannon) concerns itself with disappearing traditions. Although the author does not make reference to any modern moment, his repeated reference to the earthquake as moment of change is significant. Readers are given anecdotal history reporting that the Japanese started eating soba in the Nara period and that tempura eaten over rice was suited to the sensibility of the *shomin* (common people) of the "downtown." A close reading of the book reveals the serious social history: the denial of class tensions or difference by the author is countered by the memory of hierarchy at the lowest, down-and-out strata. Beggars, we are told, had a class system; the beggar boss had both a main wife and a mistress; and those brought up in the *shitamachi* environment inevitably felt a sense of resistance toward power.[9]

One book with Asakusa as setting that does retain the sensibility of Asakusa humor is Kobayashi Nobuhiko's *Bokutachi no Sukina Sensō* (The war that we love, 1986), a novel consciously written, according to the author, as an exception to the postwar novels about Japanese defeat, victimization, and the heroics of fanaticism. Kobayashi Nobuhiko remembers the peak of Americanism in Asakusa in 1940, when audiences hungry for the American-style entertainment no longer available on screen turned to tap dancing as a "live *attraction*" preceding the showing of Japanese movies. In the opening pages of the satire about an Asakusa entertainer sent to the South Seas, the author talks about a *"sportsland"* with bumper cars, Minnie Mouse's face painted large on a fast-moving amusement ride, and "Mickey Alley," where Mickey dolls, Minnie dolls, and Popeye dolls are sold. The book provides nonsensical historical reportage in the Asakusa tradition of the modern years. When an Asakusa audience of 1940 roars at a performer masquerading as Groucho Marx, who parrots the state's aphorism that "extravagance is the enemy," the novel is, without question, resisting that ideology.

The more overtly documentary Asakusa memoir, *One Hundred Years in Asakusa*, also gives credence to the appeal of politicized nonsense. The author recalls that an impatient Asakusa audience of "industrial warriors"— workers and students drafted for the war effort—chose to wait over three hours for the arrival of the Asakusa comedian Shimikin (Shimizu Kin'ichi), the performer said to be the most hated by the censors, rather than seeking other Asakusa entertainment, "because the only movies to see were war movies." The beloved comedian, who fearlessly continued to challenge censors with his ad-libbing, had in fact been detained by the authorities, and the audience had no interest in consuming the fare made for them by state-sponsored artists working outside the confines of modern Asakusa culture.[10]

THE RETURN OF THE MODERN GIRL (THE 1990S)

In 1998 *Zola*, billed as the magazine for the (female) *"fashion egoist,"* devoted much of its first-anniversary issue to the "big feature" *Shōwa retro modan-*

shugi (Shōwa retro modernism), thereby concocting a postmodern term for modernism that added the Chinese characters *shugi* for "ism" to the katakana rendering of *modan*. It introduced the Modern Girls of the era of Kawabata's *Asakusa Kurenaidan* as "*bad girls*" who "wore makeup, rode in automobiles, and were crazed about *dancing.*" It also offered three biographical portraits of *moga* as path-breaking individuals: the writer Yoshiya Nobuko, who wore Western clothing when it was thought of as "non-Japanese" and came out as a *lesbian;* the movie actress Iriye Takako, who modeled her appearance on Greta Garbo and Marlene Dietrich as models for her own make-over; and the fashion designer Tanaka Chiyo, now known as the "designer for the imperial household." The emphasis on Modern Girl as fashion plate was reinforced by the feature "Portrait of the Ginza *Moga* of the 30s," which was based on the house magazine *Shiseido Gurafu*, published by the cosmetics company during the modern years. Although there were references to a special consciousness and sense of self, *Zola* did not represent the Modern Girl as militant, and the montage from *Shiseido Gurafu* was subtitled a *collage.*[11]

GIVING THE MODERN GIRL HER DUE

On December 22, 2000, the Japanese postal service issued a series of commemorative "Twentieth Century *Design* Stamps." In group four of the series, two cartoon figures from the modern years, Lazy Daddy and Shōchan, each merited his own stamp, and the Modern Girl was paired with the Modern Boy (contrary to most photographic representations of the era, which feature her alone or with other young women). What is even more striking about this stamp is that the *Modan Booi*—he is listed first, right next to the block letters (NIPPON)—strides purposefully forward, his expression framed by the fedora that is ubiquitous in photographs of men in kimono and suits taken during the modern years. In contrast, the *Modan Gaaru*'s face is totally obscured by her hat. This is not the Modern Girl of the modern years; this is not an image to be found from the documentary impulse of the era. She has been de-eroticized, depoliticized. It should be recalled that in the Mitsukoshi advertisements from that time, it is the male face that is rendered featureless.

THE END

If this book has revealed anything of the tensions, fissures, and energies released by mass culture that were coursing through the alleyways of early Shōwa Japan, my montage will have served its purpose. It is, after all, only one montage, only one series of juxtapositions, of angles, of perspectives. It is a series of moments and images that can be reordered in numerous ways to reorient us in our most necessary attempt to work through the narratives of the transition into and through wartime Japan. The *ero* made pornographic may have been grotesque at times, and the grotesquerie of the lives of those living in the depths of poverty may have at times appeared nonsensical, but the modern moment of Japan in the years of erotic grotesque nonsense was not in any way nonsense. The history of modern Japanese culture was suffused by meanings and tensions, created, consumed, and then not forgotten by the women, the men, and the children who went out to play in the city streets, and who were then sent to war, before they were told not to remember.

Abbreviations

EH	*Eiga Hyōron*
ET	*Eiga no Tomo*
GYS	Gonda Yasunosuke, *Gonda Yasunosuke Chosakushū*
HF	Hayashi Fumiko, *Hōrōki*
HRC	Hiratsuka Raichō, *Hiratsuka Raichō Chosakushū*
KJ	*Kinema Junpō*
KKMS	Kusama Yasoo, *Kindai Kaso Minshū Seikatsushi*
KNDS	Kusama Yasoo, *Kindai Nihon no Donzoko Shakai*
KSS	Minami Hiroshi, *Kindai Shomin Seikatsushi*
KTKS	Kusama Yasoo, *Kindai Toshi Kasō Shakai*
KWS	Kon Wajirō, *Kon Wajirō, Shū*
KY	Kawabata Yasunari, *Asakusa Kurenaidan*
NFMSS	Maruoka Hideko, *Nihon Fujin Mondai Shiryō Shūsei*
NMK	Minami Hiroshi, *Nihon Modanizumu no Kenkyū: Shisō, Seikatsu, Bunka*
NS	Nakazawa Seitarō, "Konsen 'Ajia no Arashi'"
OM	Ōbayashi Munetsugu, *Jokyū Seikatsu no Shinkenkyū*
SA	Soeda Azenbō, *Asakusa Teiryūki*
SB	Minami Hiroshi and Shakai Shinri Kenkyūjo, *Shōwa Bunka*
SH	Satō Hachirō, *Asakusa*
ST	*Shufu no Tomo*
TB	Minami Hiroshi and Shakai Shinri Kenkyūjo, *Taishō Bunka*
TNS	*Tokyo Nichinichi Shinbun*

Notes

Unless otherwise noted, the place of publication of Japanese-language works is Tokyo.

INTRODUCTION

1. Regarding Chaplin's arrival and the assassination, see Chiba Nobuo, *Chappurin wa Nihon wo Hashitta* (Seiabo, 1992), 37–100, and Charles Chaplin, *My Autobiography* (London: Penguin Books, 1992), 369–70.

2. Chaplin noted that he had visited Oscar Wilde's prison. Chiba, *Chappurin wa Nihon o Hashitta*, 118–21. Chaplin, *My Autobiography*, 371.

3. For a discussion of the history of "Tokyo March," see Miriam Silverberg, *Changing Song: The Marxist Manifestos of Nakano Shigeharu* (Princeton, NJ: Princeton University Press, 1990), 125–26. For "Tokyo March" lyrics, see Horino Hatsuko, ed., *Omoide no Merodii* (Seibidō Shuppan, 1992), 17. For its parody, see Chiba, "Seitō Botsuraku Kōshinkyoku," in *Chappurin wa Nihon wo Hashitta*, 100. I have not included a detailed political or economic history in order to avoid leaving the all too common impression that culture is a superstructural reflection of political and economic structure. I refer readers to Minami Hiroshi's "Shōwa Bunka no Haikei," an introductory essay that provides clear discussion of the depression of the late 1920s, foreign policy, and domestic political conflict. See Minami Hiroshi and Shakai Shinri Kenkyūjo, eds., *Shōwa Bunka* (hereafter *SB;* Keisō Shobō, 1992), 4–52. Katō Shūichi's treatment of the structural components of modern Japan into the 1930s is still one of the best explanations of why party government could not be representative. For a lucid presentation of the severe limitations on the power of the House of Representatives, along with the autonomy of the armed forces which had direct access to the emperor, see Katō Shūichi, "Taishō Democracy as the Pre-Stage for Japanese Militarism," in *Japan in Crisis: Essays on Taishō Democracy*, ed. Bernard S. Silberman and H. D. Harootunian (Princeton, NJ: Princeton University Press, 1974), 225–26, 229. Germaine Hoston, who also introduces her

analysis of Marxist thought with a "contextualizing" introductory chapter, relies on Katō for her discussion emphasizing the power of the bureaucracy over party leaders. She also discusses how, even after the passage of universal male suffrage in 1925, the populace remained alienated from party politics, in part because of the prohibitive cost of bonds. Germaine A. Hoston, *Marxism and the Crisis of Development in Prewar Japan* (Princeton, NJ: Princeton University Press, 1986), 14–15.

4. Sakakibara Shōji, *Shōwago: 60 Nen Sesōshi* (Asahi Shinbunsha, 1986), 8–80; Inagaki Yoshihiko and Yoshizawa Norio, *Shōwa Kotobashi 60 Nen* (Kōdansha, 1985), 74, 84. This approach is not unique of course; recently historians have also tended to rethink our bracketing of "Taishō Democracy." See especially Sheldon Garon, *Molding Japanese Minds: The State in Everyday Life* (Princeton, NJ: Princeton University Press, 1997) and Andrew Gordon, *Labor and Imperial Democracy in Prewar Japan* (Berkeley: University of California Press, 1991).

5. See Akazawa Shirō and Kitagawa Kenzō, eds., *Bunka to Fuashizumu* (Nihon Keizai Hyōronsha, 1993), 4; and Minami et al., *SB*.

6. Silverberg, *Changing Song*, 219–20, 227–28. Marilyn Ivy names the constitutive parts of modernity by relating the modern to the nation-state: "It indicates the problem of the nation-state and its correlation with a capitalist colonialism that ensured Japan would be pulled into a global geopolitical matrix from the mid-nineteenth century on. It indicates the changes effected in identities and subjectivities, through the emergence of individualism and new modes of interiority; in relationships to temporality, through the emergence of 'tradition' as the background against which progressive history could be situated; and in institutionalized procedures, through what Foucault has called individualization and totalization; bureaucratic relationships, Taylorized modes of production, novel forms of image representation, mass media, and scientific disciplines." I place Japanese modern times into this modernity. I would also add to this list the transformation of gender relations and forms of family; I also wish to differentiate Japanese modernity and the Japanese culture of the 1920s and 1930s from Western European modernity (and cultural modernism) by emphasizing the weakness of both bourgeois politics and culture. Marilyn Ivy, *Discourses of the Vanishing: Modernity/Phantasm/Japan* (Chicago: University of Chicago Press, 1995), 4–5.

7. To attempt to list all of the relevant books that have appeared in the past several years would be to risk excluding some new and important work. However, there are three works that are so close to the concerns of this book that they must be included. I refer the reader to Jordan Sand's path-breaking *House and Home in Modern Japan: Architecture, Domestic Space, and Bourgeois Culture, 1880–1930* (Cambridge, MA: Harvard University Asia Center; distributed by Harvard University Press, 2003). In the field of literary studies, Seiji Lippit has discussed topics and texts discussed herein in ways I could not begin to approach. See Seiji Lippit, *Topographies of Japanese Modernism* (New York: Columbia University Press, 2002). Barbara Sato's earlier work explained to me

why I kept finding references to this persona in the media of the modern years. She has now definitively placed the Modern Girl alongside the "new woman," where she belongs. See Barbara Sato, *The New Japanese Woman: Modernity, Media, and Women in Interwar Japan* (Durham, NC: Duke University Press, 2003).

JAPANESE MODERN WITHIN MODERNITY

1. William M. Tsutsui, *Manufacturing Ideology: Scientific Management in Twentieth-Century Japan* (Princeton, NJ: Princeton University Press, 1998) and Tatsuo Naruse, "Taylorism and Fordism in Japan," *International Journal of Political Economy* 2, no. 3 (Fall 1991): 32–48.

2. By "global" I am referring to the synchronous but decidedly different histories of peoples by the end of the nineteenth century, by which time capital and empire, generated by the nation-state, were firmly ensconced. See John Frow, "What Was Post-Modernism?" in *Past the Last Post: Theorizing Post-Colonialism and Post-Modernism*, ed. Ian Adam and Helen Tiffin (New York: Harvester Wheatsheaf, 1991), 139. For Frow, time is a component of modernization. He theorizes "a shift from the closed time of feudalism to the open-ended, dynamic, and godless time of capitalism" (specifically, the future-directed temporality of the return on capital and thus of capital accumulation); along with "the gridding of space and time into calculable units" (Frow, "What Was Post-Modernism?" 2). Minami Hiroshi has noted that presentist terms such as *modern, present,* and *vanguard* were used interchangeably in the media. See Minami Hiroshi, *Nihon Modanizumi no Kenkyū: Shisō, Seikatsu, Bunka* (Bureen Shuppan, 1982). My research suggests that the words *modan* and *sentan* (vanguard) appear most often. Jordan Sand's eye-opening work on domesticity during the era preceding the modern years historicizes new practices of the modern years that focused on *seikatsu*. See Jordan Sand, "At Home in the Meiji Period: Inventing Japanese Domesticity, " in *Mirror of Modernity: Invented Traditions of Modern Japan*, ed. Stephen Vlastos (Berkeley: University of California Press, 1998), 191–207, and *House and Home in Modern Japan*.

3. One illustration of the discourse on such progress was made by the photographer Ina Nobuo. Referring to a mass culture made possible by mass production and communication, Ina pointed to the *tie-up* between this art for the masses and mass production. According to Ina, "in present society, both under the capitalist system and the socialist system, mechanization *(kikaika)* and transformation by technology *(gijutsuka)* are the most conspicuous characteristics of their industry." See Ina Nobuo, "Shashin ni Kaere," *Kōga* 1, no. 1 (1932): 1–14. Hirabayashi Hatsunosuke's writing on technology is another example. See Barbara Hamill, "Nihon Modanizumu no Shisō: Hirabayashi Hatsunosuke o Chūshin to shite," in Minami, *NMK*, 89–114. Magazine illustrations are probably the best examples of representations of technical progress.

4. While the term *modanizumu* (modernism) was sometimes used alongside *modan* to refer to innovations in material culture and popular play, I will

not refer to "modernism" lest the discourse on the transformations of everyday modern culture be confused with the Japanese literary modernism that has usually been treated separately from the modern culture of pre–Pacific War Japan. As synchronic phenomena, they merit simultaneous treatment, but here I have chosen a more hermeneutic method of accepting the compartmentalizations of the era in order to come to terms with the consciousness of those years. The glossary of *modan* words appended to the October 1930 issue of *Fujin Kōron* by its editorial staff included both *modanizumu*, defined as "of the present" and translated as *kindaishugi* (implying an advocacy of the present state of affairs), and *modan*. The term *kindai* is used as a synonym for modern. ("*Modan* Ryūkōgo Jiten," *Fujin Kōron*, October 1930, 378).

For a sophisticated treatment of modernism as a category of literary history, see Lippit, *Topographies of Japanese Modernism*. For H. D. Harootunian, "modernism in Japan's interwar period was produced in a conjuncture that prompted the recognition of a vast field of economic and cultural unevenness that it sought to resolve, overcome, and even repress" (*Overcome by Modernity: History, Culture, and Community in Interwar Japan* [Princeton, NJ: Princeton University Press, 2000], xxi). For Harootunian, the uneven development resulting from capitalism is central to the way the past is experienced in everyday life (Harootunian, *History's Disquiet: Modernity, Cultural Practice, and the Question of Everyday Life* [New York: Columbia University Press, 2000], 21, 57). Arahata Kanson, "Kankōsha to shite no Omoide," in *Kindai Shisō Fukkokuban* (Chirokusha, [1913] 1960), 5, and "Dōtoku no Sōzō," *Kindai Shisō* 1, no. 5 (February 1913): 1.

5. Shimura Gentarō, "Kasekishitaru Gendai Seikatsu," *Seikatsu*, March 1, 1914, 23. "Kindai Toshi wo Setsudan shite: Kindai Seikatsu Zadankai," *Kindai Seikatsu*, April 1929, 64–82, and "Kindaijin no Kairaku Seikatsu," *Kindai Seikatsu*, June 1929, 29–43. Automobiles, moving pictures, and cafés were set forth as "symbolic of the fads of a new era" in the September 1918 issue of *Chūō Kōron*. See the contributions, including that of Tanizaki Jun'ichirō, comprising "Shinjidai Ryūkō no Shōchō to shite Mitaru 'Jidōsha'" and " 'Katsudō Shashin' to 'Kafee' no Inshō," in that issue.

6. Nii Itaru, Kataoka Teppei, Miyake Yasuko, et al., "Modaan Seikatsu Mandankai," *Shinchō*, January 1928, 123–47; Ōya Sōichi, "Modan Raifu Saiginmi," *Chūō Kōron*, February 1929, 177–82; and Inoue Kiichirō, "Modan Kairaku Seikatsu no Saiginmi," *Chūō Kōron*, January 1932, 127–31; Ōya Sōichi, "Modan Sō to Modan Sō," *Chūō Kōron*, February 1929, reprinted in *Ōya Sōichi Zenshū* (Sōyōsha, 1981), 2:5–8. Undoubtedly the impact of Ōya's essay was due in part to its inclusion in a book by the same name, published the following year. This volume included essays on such topics as the Modern Girl, the everyday existence of the salaryman, and the relationship between money and love. Richard Gid Powers and Katō Hidetoshi, *Handbook of Japanese Popular Culture* (New York: Greenwood Press, 1989), 311–12.

7. Matei Calinescu, *Five Faces of Modernity* (Durham, NC: Duke University Press, 1987), 41–46. For a discussion of the emergence of an economistic defini-

tion of the Japanese bourgeoisie following the original, more culturalist appropriation of the term *shinshi* by Kōtoku Shūsui and Sakai Toshihiko at the time of the translation of the *Communist Manifesto* in 1911, and for Nakano Shigeharu's critique of the cartoonlike nature of representation of class relationships, see Silverberg, *Changing Song*, 46, 152. According to Minami Hiroshi's calculation, the middle class of the Taishō era, living in the larger cities, with higher than middle-school education, and consisting primarily of mid- and lower-level bureaucrats, teachers, proprietors of small- and medium-sized businesses, and the new white-collar workers, made up a mere 7 percent of the populace. This new middle class bore some resemblance to the producers and consumers of the bourgeois culture described by Eric Hobsbawm in its artifice and social relations; however, not only was the Japanese group small, but it lacked the political autonomy that Hobsbawm ascribes to the bourgeoisie. See Hobsbawm, *The Age of Capital, 1848–1875* (London: Weidenfeld and Nicolson, 1975), 230–50. For more on European bourgeois culture, see *From the Fires of Revolution to the Great War*, ed. Michelle Perrot, vol. 4 of *A History of Private Life* (Cambridge, MA: Harvard University Press, 1990).

8. David Harvey, *The Condition of Postmodernity* (Cambridge: Blackwell, 1989), 10–38. The quote comes from p. 27. On Meiji ideology, see Carol Gluck, *Japan's Modern Myths: Ideology in the Late Meiji Period* (Princeton, NJ: Princeton University Press, 1985) and Takashi Fujitani, *Splendid Monarchy: Power and Pageantry in Modern Japan* (Berkeley: University of California Press, 1998). One aspect of American modernist ideology not found in Japan was the worship of the "therapeutic ethos" attached to the act of consuming. For this concept see T. J. Jackson Lears, "From Salvation to Self-Realization: Advertising and the Therapeutic Roots of the Consumer Culture, 1880–1930" in *The Culture of Consumption: Critical Essays in American History: 1880–1980*, ed. Richard Wightman Fox and T. J. Jackson Lears (New York: Pantheon, 1983), 1–38.

9. According to Minami, 18.1 percent of the populace lived in the cities in 1920; this figure rose to 21.7 percent five years later and to 24.1 percent by 1930. Minami et al., *SB*, 19.

10. Cf. Mariko Tamanoi's subtle contrasting of a "truly modern" woman with a "traditional" woman in a conservative agrarianist discourse on a "rural modernity" that recognized the inevitability of new practices in *Under the Shadow of Nationalism: Politics and Poetics of Rural Japanese Women* (Honolulu: University of Hawaii Press, 1998), 151–56. Minami notes how advertising for *Kingu* aimed at different classes, including reservists, bank employees, and village headmen. Minami et al., *SB*, 304.

11. For an English translation and extensive analysis of the Imperial Rescript on Education, see Gluck, *Japan's Modern Myths*, 120–27. When I refer to the absence of a notion of a universalist eternal, I am referring to the discourse on the *modan* in Japan, not to Frow's conception of modernity or modernization. Here Harvey's emphasis is on differentiations within the "historical geography of modernism" in his discussion of the modernism as an art of cities.

See Harvey, *The Condition of Postmodernity*, 10–13, 24–25. See also the "geography of modernism" in *Modernism: 1890–1930*, ed. Malcolm Bradbury and James McFarlane (New York: Penguin Books, 1976), 95–190, and Raymond Williams, *The Politics of Modernism* (London: Verso, 1989), 31–48.

Perry Anderson's discussion of modernism is similar, and the Japanese case can be said to meet two out of three of his criteria within a "cultural force field." Japan did have "the emergence of the key technologies of telephone, radio, automobile, etc.," as well as "the imaginative proximity of social revolution." Missing, however, was a "codification of a highly formalized *academicism* in the visual and other arts within regimes of state and society" dominated by aristocratic landowning classes. See Perry Anderson, "Modernity and Revolution," in *Marxism and the Interpretation of Culture*, ed. Cary Nelson and Lawrence Grossberg (Urbana: University of Illinois Press, 1988), 324–25. Minami's twenty-volume series, *Nihon Modanizumu no "Hikari" to "Kage": Kindai Shomin Seikatsushi* ("Light and darkness" in Japanese modernism: Texts on the everyday life of commoners) (San'ichi Shobō, 1984), is a compendium of primary sources that falls into Anderson's second category, pertaining to the study of mores. These volumes cover topics usually associated with *modanizumu* by scholars in Japan, such as "nightlife areas," "leisure activities," and "love, marriage, and the household." Japanese art historians and literary historians, by contrast, usually align *modernism* with the modernism identified with cultural or high modernism in the West, which pays attention to language or design.

12. Regarding "modernist" poetry, see Nakano Kaichi, *Modanizumu Shi no Jidai* (Hōbunkan, 1986). Sometimes the distinctions between *modan* and *modanizumu* have blurred. See for example, the listing of the dance hall and *"skiing"* as an expression of decadent modernism in Hayashi, "Modanizumu no Seiri: Seiritekina, Amari ni Seiritekina," *Chūō Kōron*, June 1934, 311–13. Also see Minami Hiroshi's discussion, in the introduction to an anthology, of a "Japanese *modernism*" that expressed itself in such varied media as art, women's behavior, and rationalism. Minami, *NMK*, vii–xiv.

13. I have chosen not to focus solely on the term *everyday life*, another possible translation for this word implying the significance of the quotidian, because of the existence of the phrase *nichijō seikatsu*, which translates much more directly as "everyday life." I also wanted to retain a vernacular flavor. Hereafter I use *seikatsu* along with the English terms *everyday life* and *daily life*.

By 1926, when Murayama wrote this essay, his Dadaist fervor (best seen in his journal *Mavo*, begun in 1924) had been displaced by his turn to Communist thought. According to his autobiography, when Murayama attended the founding meeting of the Japan Proletarian Arts Federation on December 6, 1925, he knew almost nothing about Socialism and "merely preferred *proletarian* art to *bourgeois* art." Murayama Tomoyoshi, *Engekiteki Jijoden 2: 1922–1927* (Tona Shuppansha, 1971), 317–19. The quote is from Murayama, *Kōseiha Kenkyū* (Chūō Bijutsusha, 1926), 37–38.

14. Five years later, Minami repeated his tribute to the importance of Hollywood, first made in *NMK*, when he pointed to two central aspects of the "modernist" Shōwa culture: the rapid development of the mass media and the overwhelming influence of American movies. (Minami et al., *SB*, 539.) My discussion of Japanese modern culture is also premised on these two points. Nagae Michitarō, *Eiga Hyōgen Keishiki* (Kyoto: Kyōiku Tosho Kabushikigaisha, 1942), 6–7. Murayama Tomoyoshi, *Engi Hyōronshu*, 7–9.

15. See G. C. Allen, *A Short Economic History of Modern Japan, 1867–1937* (London: George Allen & Unwin, 1946), 90–144. Satō Takeshi, "Modanizumu to Amerika ka," in Minami, *NMK*, 20–21. See also Minami Hiroshi and Shakai Shinri Kenkyūjo, eds., *Taishō Bunka* (hereafter *TB*; Keisō Shobō, 1965), 66–80; Minami et al., *SB*, 19.

16. Minami, ed., *NMK*, 153; Minami et al., *SB*, 68. Imai Seiichi, ed., *Shinsai ni Yuragu*, vol. 5 of *Nihon no Hyakunen* (Chikuma Shobō, 1962), 155–60. David Bordwell discusses Ozu's representation of the Japanese middle class and provides rich film synopses in *Ozu and the Poetics of Cinema* (Princeton, NJ: Princeton University Press, 1988), 33–35, 193–94.

17. Ishikawa Hiroyoshi, ed., *Goraku no Senzenshi* (Shoseki Kabushikigaisha, 1981), 50–56, 97–98, 104–9.

18. Minami et al., *TB*, 253–54, 361. For a discussion of how the "drama of consumption" was "concentrated in the Japanese department store," see Yoshimi Shun'ya, "Kindai Kūkan to shite no Hyakkaten," in *Toshi no Kūkan Toshi no Shintai*, ed. Yoshimi Shun'ya (Keisō Shobō, 1996), 137–64. On Takarazuka, see Jennifer Robertson, *Takarazuku: Sexual Politics and Popular Culture in Modern Japan* (Berkeley: University of California Press, 1998). On the entrepreneurial skills of Kobayashi Ichizō, who created two still-predominant features of contemporary Japanese mass culture—the railway terminal department store and the Takarazuka review—see Minami et al., *TB*, 143–44. On the emergence of credit, see Minami et al., *SB*, 68.

19. Newspaper statistics are from Sharon Nolte, *Liberalism in Modern Japan* (Berkeley: University of California Press, 1987), 19. Regarding *Lazy Daddy (Nonki na Tōsan)*, see Maeda Ai and Shimizu Isao, eds., *Taishō Kōki no Manga* (Chikuma Shobō, 1986), 70. On the commodification of the newspaper as big business, see 23–24.

20. On mass magazines, including the influence of a left-wing press, see Silverberg, *Changing Song*, 163. On the statistics of magazines registered under the Newspaper Law, see Gregory J. Kasza, *The State and the Mass Media in Japan, 1918–1945* (Berkeley: University of California Press, 1988), 28. For one history of the origins of the *enpon*, crediting the writer and labor organizer Fujimori Seikichi for asking the Kaizōsha publisher to offer inexpensive books to workers, see Minami et al., *SB*, 287–303. On advertising, see Minami et al., *TB*, 132–33.

21. For an early English language history of the Japanese film industry through World War II, see Joseph L. Anderson and Donald Richie, eds., *The Japanese Film: Art and Industry* (New York: Grove Press, 1959), 21–158. See also

Peter B. High, "The Dawn of Cinema in Japan," *Journal of Contemporary History* 1, no. 19 (January 1984): 23–57. Regarding "Tokyo March" as an example of the rationalization and repression of the culture of the mid-1920s, see Silverberg, *Changing Song,* 125–26. The theater where *Resurrection* was performed was the Teigeki, or Imperial Theater, famous from the most often repeated slogan from the earliest days of consumer culture in the 1910s: "Today It's Mitsukoshi; tomorrow, the Imperial Theatre" *(Kyō wa Mitsukoshi; ashita wa Teigeki).* Regarding *ryūkōka,* see Ichikawa Kōichi, "Ryūkōka ni Miru Modanizumu to Ero Guro Nansensu," in Minami, *NMK,* 257–84.

22. Minami et al., *SB,* 439–40, and *TB,* 162–63.

23. For a brief overview of the Taishō exposition, see Takemura Tamio, *Taishō Bunka* (Kōdansha, 1980), 40–43. The re-creation of the colonial holdings, the peace tower, the airplane, and the two-part structure of the spectacle into a bamboo pavilion and a pond's edge linked by a "Peace Bridge" are enumerated in Maeda and Shimizu, *Taishō Kōki no Manga,* 9. See also Edward Seidensticker, *High City, Low City: Tokyo from Edo to the Earthquake* (Tokyo: Tuttle Books, 1983), 257.

24. Kasza, *The State and the Mass Media,* 29–38, 89–90, 92. Minami, ed., *NMK,* 280–83.

25. Kasza, *The State and the Mass Media,* 55, 57, 61–70; Minami et al., *SB,* 169, 395–412.

26. Minami et al., *TB,* 162, 164, 166, 225. Takashi Fujitani, *Splendid Monarchy.*

27. Gluck, *Japan's Modern Myths,* 121, 267. For Minami's contrasting formulation of a shift from "subject" to "citizen," see Minami et al., *TB,* 150–54.

28. Kawabata Yasunari, *Asakusa Kurenaidan* (Tokyo: Senshinsha, 1930) [Facsimile ed. (Tokyo: Kindai bungakukan, 1980), 33] (hereafter cited as KY).

29. Maruyama Masao, "Patterns of Individuation and the Case of Japan: A Conceptual Scheme," in *Changing Japanese Attitudes toward Modernization,* ed. Marius B. Jansen (Princeton, NJ: Princeton University Press, 1965), 517–22. For a discussion of how the café waitress reformulated historical practices, see my essay "The Café Waitress Serving Modern Japan," in Vlastos, ed., *Mirror of Modernity,* 208–25.

30. While Foucault claimed that his repressive hypothesis referred to the West, its manifestation in Japan, in a form mediated by the West, bears examination. In other words, if the discourse on the erotic *(ero)* is taken literally, at face value, then this obsession with sex appears to be a variation on the Western "incitement" to speak about sex that accompanied a valorization that contradicted the presumption of the censorship of sex. While I am aware of this aspect of the culture of erotic grotesque nonsense, my emphasis differs, as should become clear. See Michel Foucault, *The History of Sexuality, Vol. 1: An Introduction,* trans. Robert Hurley (New York: Vintage Books, 1978), 22–23.

31. Andrew Gordon, in *Labor and Imperial Democracy,* notes the desires of the working class to partake of consumer culture. Takahashi Akira has been one of the few scholars to recognize the positive potential of a focus on the erotic.

In his essay "Urban Culture and Machine Civilization," he quotes from a 1931 essay that attributed an oppositional spirit to erotic grotesque publications and linked the erotic to the present destruction of the household, the bankruptcy of marriage, the socialization of women's work, and so on. The same essay also credited *nonsense* for destroying tradition, power, and all pretension. Takahashi refers to Yokomizo Seishi's "Tantei, Ryōki, Nansensu" in *Sōgō Jaanarizumu Kōza* 10 (1931), in Takahashi Akira, "Toshika to Kikai Bunmei," *Jiga to Kankyō*, vol. 6 of *Kindai Nihon Shisōshi Kōza* (Chikuma Shobō, 1960, 1982), 192.

32. For Eisenstein's definition of montage and for a discussion based on the premise that Eisenstein had no single "concept of montage," although he was consistently concerned with the *principle* of montage, see Jacques Aumont, *Montage Eisenstein* (Bloomington: Indiana University Press, 1987), viii–ix, 151–56, 171. On kabuki and "montage thinking," see Sergei Eisenstein, "The Unexpected," in *Film Form: Essays in Film Theory and The Film Sense*, ed. and trans. Jay Leyda (Cleveland: World Publishing Company, 1957), 18–27. For "The Cinematographic Principle and the Ideogram," see *Film Form*, 28–44. (The text I have quoted appears on p. 28.) In this essay, Eisenstein calls montage "conflict" and compares a "phalanx of montage pieces" to a "series of explosions of an internal combustion engine" that drive forward "the total film" ("The Cinematographic Principle," *Film Form*, 38). His concern appeared more narratological when he termed montage "the means of *unrolling* an idea with the help of single shots" (Eisenstein, "A Dialectic Approach to Film Form," in *Film Form*, 49). This was another way of talking about his concern for the embodiment and expression of a theme: see Eisenstein, "Synchronization of Senses," in *Film Form*, 69. The quote is from Eisenstein, "Word and Image," in *Film Form*, 35.

33. See Shimonaka Yasaburō, ed, *Dai Jiten* (Heibonsha, 1934). Claude Lévi-Strauss, *The Savage Mind* (Chicago: University of Chicago Press, 1966), 21, 33.

34. See Harvey, *The Condition of Postmodernity*, 21. Regarding Benjamin, see Susan Buck-Morss, *The Dialectics of Seeing: Walter Benjamin and the Arcades Project* (Cambridge, MA: MIT Press, 1991), 67. Maud Lavin explains Bloch's "anticipatory consciousness" as "the instances in life of desire for a better future, linking it to Bloch's notion of "nonsynchronism." See Maud Lavin, *Cut with the Kitchen Knife: The Weimar Photomontages of Hannah Höch* (New Haven, CT: Yale University Press, 1993), 29.

35. Hara Hiromu, "E—Shashin, Moji—Katsuji, soshite Typofoto, " *Kōga* 2, no. 3 (1933): 29–36, and Yamawaki Iwao, "Fuotomontaaju no Yorimichi," *Kōga* 2, no. 12 (1933): 32–33. According to Horino Masao, *Asahi Gurafu* was the first journal to adopt the form, followed in 1931 by *Chūo Kōron* and, in order, *Kaizō*, *Keizai Ōrai*, and others. He cited journals devoted to crime—*Hanzai Kagaku* and its spin-off, *Hanzai Kōron*—as journals especially committed to photomontage (Horino,"Gurafu Montaaju no Jissai," *Kōga* 1, no. 3 [1932]: 52–53). Ina Nobuo's reference to the "technology of photography" as both record and report follows his contextualization of the post–World War I speed up in *tempo* in a new capitalist, imperialist age reliant on machinery, heavy industry, and technology. Ina Nobuo, "Shashin ni Kaere, " *Kōga* 1, no. 1, (1932): 1–14.

36. See Matthew Teitelbaum, "Preface," in *Montage and Modern Life*, ed. Matthew Teitelbaum (Cambridge, MA: MIT Press, 1992), 7–8. Lavin, *Cut with the Kitchen Knife*, 9. See *Asahi Gurafu*, June 20, 1928, reprinted in *Asahi Gurafu ni Miru Shōwa no Sesō*, ed. Asahi Shinbunsha (Asahi Shinbunsha, 1975), 102–3.

37. See Tzvetan Todorov, *The Morals of History*, trans. Alyson Waters (Minneapolis: University of Minnesota Press, 1995), 77–78. See Penelope Gardner-Chloros, "Code-Switching in Community, Regional, and National Repertoires: The Myth of the Discreteness of Linguistic Systems," in *One Speaker, Two Languages: Cross-Disciplinary Perspectives on Code-Switching*, ed. Lesley Milroy and Pieter Muysken (Cambridge: Cambridge University Press, 1995), 68–77; and Peter Auer, "The Pragmatics of Code-Switching: A Sequential Approach," ibid., 117–30.

38. For more on Eisenstein's expectations of spectators, see Aumont, *Montage Eisenstein*, 167–69, 196. Aumont notes that Eisenstein was aware that "a montage of several fragments, let alone one single fragment, is never univocal" (169).

39. Monica Heller, "Code-Switching and the Politics of Language," in Milroy and Muysken, *One Speaker, Two Languages*, 158–61. To push the language metaphor a bit further, I work from the presupposition of John Gumperz, who says that "conversational code-switching can be defined as the juxtaposition within the same speech exchange of passages of speech belonging to different grammatical systems or subsystems" (John J. Gumperz, *Discourse Strategies* [Cambridge: Cambridge University Press, 1982], 59). Hayden White discusses code-switching in terms of a hierarchy of codes. Among the codes he finds in *The Education of Henry Adams*, for example, are those of history, science, philosophy, law, and art along with "social codes, cultural codes, etiquettes, protocols, and so forth." According to White, it is by means of codes that texts "emit messages." See Hayden White, "The Context in the Text: Method and Ideology in Intellectual History," in *The Content of the Form: Narrative Discourse and Historical Representation* (Baltimore: Johns Hopkins University Press, 1987), 193–212.

40. Tosaka Jun, "Ken'etsuka no Shisō to Fūzoku," in *Nihon Modanizumu: Ero Guro Nansensu*, vol. 188 of *Gendai no Esupuri*, ed. Minami Hiroshi (Shibundō, 1983), 44–47. Originally published in Tosaka Jun, *Sekai no Ikkan to shite no Nihon* (Hakuyōsha, 1937) but written in 1936.

41. Although Gordon includes some fascinating instances of parody and satire from within the labor movement, he makes clear that he has not included either family life or leisure in his study. Gordon, *Labor and Imperial Democracy*, 47–49, 158–59. Garon, *Molding Japanese Minds*, 11, 126–27. See the illustrated synopsis of the movie *Madamu to Nyōbo* in *Ie no Hikari*, September 1931, 67–71. For a celebration of *speed*, see Shibata Kiyohiko, "Kyōsō no Kisha Kisen," *Ie no Hikari*, October 1930, 71–74. For a discussion of spiritual mobilization, see "Seidō no Seikatsu Sasshin Undō," *Ie no Hikari*, September 1939, 121–26.

42. See Gluck, *Japan's Modern Myths*, 15–16, 237, 281–85, and Garon, *Molding Japanese Minds*, 6, 15.

43. Kuno Osamu and Kamishima Jirō, eds., *"Tennōsei" Ronshū* (San'ichi Shobō, 1976), esp. Kamishima's "Atogaki ni Kaete," 229–36; Kanō Mikiyo, *Josei to Tennōsei* (Shisō no Kagakusha, 1979); Garon, *Molding Japanese Minds*, 5; and Fujitani, *Splendid Monarchy*, 229–36.

44. Tomoeda Takahiko, *Chūgaku Shūshin*, vol. 5 (Tozanbō, 1922, 1928). Fukasaku Yasubumi, *Kaitei Gendai Joshi Shūshin*, vol. 4 (Okura Kōbundō, 1931), 5, 23, 29–30. Tessa Morris-Suzuki, *Re-Inventing Japan: Time, Space, Nation* (Armonk, NY: M. E. Sharpe, 1998), 97–98, 104,158–59.

45. Fujita Shōzō, "Shōwa Hachinen wo Chūshin to suru Tenkō no Jōkyō," in *Kyōdō Kenkyū Tenkō*, vol. 1, ed. Shisō no Kagakusha (Heibonsha, 1959), 35.

46. See Kano Mikiyo and Amano Yasukazu, *Han Tennōsei* (Shakai Hyōronsha, 1990), 133–36, and John Dower, "Sensational Rumors, Seditious Graffiti, and the Nightmares of the Thought Police," in *Japan in War and Peace: Selected Essays* (New York: New Press, 1993), 123–45.

47. For an illustration of the use of the idea of "borrowing," see Seidensticker's notion of a "double life" (Seidensticker, *Low City, High City*, 90). My term *documentary impulse* is more spontaneous and less literal than William Stott's term *documentary motive*. See Stott, *Documentary Expression and Thirties America* (London: Oxford University Press, 1973), 3–73. See also Tokunaga Sunao, *Taiyō no nai Machi* (Shinchō Bunko, 1953), originally published in *Senki* from June to November 1929.

48. Murayama included his own journal, *Mavo*, at the end of his list of the "New Arts Journals of the World" during its year of publication, thereby inserting the Japanese movement into an international Constructivist movement. The *Mavo*, with site of publication Tokyo, thus appeared alongside the addresses of *De Stijl*, published from Paris, *Blok* from Warsaw, and *Stavba* from Prague (*Mavo* June and July 1924, June and July 1925). Murayama's monograph *Studies of the Constructivists*, his essays on theater and art, his 1925 montage *Konsutorakushon* (Construction), and the stage set of the Japanese production of *From Morning to Midnight* attest to the influence of the Soviet avant-garde sculptors, architects, and set designers dedicated to exposing and celebrating the mechanization of life. See Murayama Tomoyoshi, *Genzai no Geijutsu to Mirai no Geijutsu* (Ōbundō, 1924); *Kōseiha Kenkyū* (Chūō Bijutsusha, 1926); *Nihon Puroretaria Engekiron* (Tenjinsha, 1930); and *Puroretaria Bijutsu no Tameni* (Atoriesha, 1930). The Japanese constructions of Murayama illustrate the Soviet Constructivist ideal that the "meaning of a work of art was contained not in the representational quality of the picture, but in the pictorial elements themselves, in their mutual relationships and interaction" and that construction should be dynamic, based on "motion-producing asymmetry." Barron, Stephanie, and Maurice Tuchman, eds., *The Avant Garde in Russia: 1910–1930* (Cambridge, MA: MIT Press, 1980), 29. David Elliott, *New Worlds: Art and Society 1900–1937* (New York: Rizzoli, 1986), 21, 110. Andreas Huyssen notes that Theodor Adorno's conception of the "culture industry" left no room for resis-

tance. In contrast, the Japanese ethnographers went where Huyssen conjectures Adorno might have gone. See Huyssen, *After the Great Divide: Modernism, Mass Culture, Postmodernism* (Bloomington: Indiana University Press, 1986), 19, 28. On the Marxist cast to Japanese intellectual life during the modern years, see Silverberg, *Changing Song*, 163–67, 224–29.

49. I thank Nimura Kazuo for introducing me to the work of Gonda Yasunosuke and would like to express gratitude to Henry Smith for introducing me to Kon Wajirō in "Tokyo as an Idea: An Exploration of Japanese Urban Thought until 1945," *Journal of Japanese Studies* 4, no. 1 (Winter 1978), 45–80.

50. Fujimori Terunobu, "Kon Wajirō to Barakku Sōshokusha: Shinsai Fukkōki no Kenchiku," *Karamu*, no. 88 (April 1983): 62–63.

51. On October 20, 1923, a new ordinance lifted bans on all articles relating to Koreans; but, at the same time, the press was urged to publish articles on Korean violence. The following day vigilante and official responsibility for the violence began to be underlined in the press, but the damage had been done, and the state had already begun a new campaign to associate the anarchist threat with the threat of Korean criminal acts. Miriam Silverberg, "The Massacre of Koreans after the Great Kantō Earthquake" (M.A. thesis, Georgetown University, 1979). Kon, *Chōsen Buraku Chōsaku Hōkoku Dai 1-satsu Minka* (Seoul: Chōsen Sōtokufu, 1924); Kon, "Kōgengaku to wa Nanika," in Kon and Yoshida, *Moderunologio (Kōgengaku)*, 353–55.

52. Kon, "Kōgengaku to wa Nanika," in Kon and Yoshida, *Moderunologio*, 357–58.

53. Kon, "Kōgengaku to wa Nanika," and "Tokyo Ginzagai Fūzoku Kiroku," in Kon and Yoshida, *Moderunologio*, 357–58 and 1–66.

54. Kon, "Inokashira Kōen Haru no Pikunikku," in Kon and Yoshida, *Moderunologio*, 144–46.

55. Kawazoe Noboru, *Kon Wajirō: Sono Genshōgaku* (Riburo Pooto, 1987), 221. Kon, "Kōgengaku Sōron," in *Kōgengaku Saishū*, 32. Kon, "Honjo Fukagawa Hinminkutsu Fukin Fūzoku Saishū," in Kon and Yoshida, *Moderunologio*, 69, 78–79. Kon, "Otaru-shi Fūzoku Chōsa," in Kon and Yoshida, *Kōgengaku Saishū*, 302.

56. Kon, "Depaato Fūzoku Shakaigaku," in Kon and Yoshida, *Moderunologio*, 206–16. Kon was the first social commentator to relate the department store to the manufacturing of desire. As early as 1909, the prescriptive text "Tokyo Learning" made such connections. See Silverberg, "Constructing a New Cultural History of Prewar Japan," in *Japan and the World*, ed. Masao Miyoshi and H. D. Harootunian (Durham, NC: Duke University Press, 1991).

57. Kon, "Shin Katei no Shinamono Chōsa," in Kon and Yoshida, *Moderunologio*, 155–73. Kon, "Kōgengaku Sōron," in Kon and Yoshida, *Kōgengaku Saishū*, 16–23.

58. Kon, "Inokashira Kōen Jisatsu Basho Bunpu Zu," in Kon and Yoshida, *Moderunologio*, 281–85. Michel de Certeau, *The Practice of Everyday Life*, trans. Steven Rendall (Berkeley: University of California Press, 1984), 98.

59. Gonda Yasunosuke, "Shakai Seikatsu ni okeru Goraku no Ichikōsatsu," reprinted as "Shakai Seikatsu to Minshū Goraku," in Gonda, *Gonda Yasunosuke Chosakushū* (hereafter abbreviated as *GYS*), 2:183–254 (Bunwa Shobō, 1974–1975; originally published in *Ōhara Shakai Mondai Kenkyūjo Zasshi*, 1924). See also Gonda Yasunosuke, *Minshū Gorakuron* (Ganshodō Shoten, 1931), reprinted in *GYS*, vol. 2. Gonda, *Minshū Goraku no Kichō* (Dōjinsha Shoten, 1922); and Gonda, *Gorakugyōsha no Mure* (Jitsugyō no Nihonsha, 1923), *GYS*.

60. Gonda, "Minshū no Goraku Seikatsu ni Arawaretaru Kokuminseijō," *GYS*, 4:35–37 (originally published in *Kaihō*, April 1921); Gonda, *Minshū Goraku no Kichō*, 371–74. Gonda, "Fukkō no Miyako o Nagamete," *GYS*, 4:130–46 (originally published in *Chūgai Shōgyō Shimpō*, January 11–18, 1924); and Gonda, "Shakai Seikatsu ni Okeru Goraku no Ichi Kōsatsu," *GYS*, 2:186–87, 239.

61. Gonda, "Shihonshugi Shakai to Ryūkō," *GYS*, 4:57–67 (originally published in *Kaihō*, July 1922).

62. Gonda, "Shakai Seikatsu ni okeru Goraku no Ichikōsatsu," *GYS*, 2:242–43.

63. Gonda, "Minshū no Goraku Seikatsu ni Arawaretaru Kokuminseijō," *GYS*, 4:35–37 (originally published in *Kaihō*, April 1921); Gonda, *Minshū Goraku no Kichō*, 371–74. Gonda, "Rōdōsha Gorakuron," *GYS*, 4:255–80 (originally published in *Ōhara Shakai Mondai Kenkyūjo Zasshi*, November 1933).

64. Gonda, "Minshū Goraku," *GYS*, 4:75 (originally published in *Chūgai Shōgyō Shimpō*, January 1923); Gonda, *Minshū Goraku no Kichō*, 400–401. Gonda, "Eiga Setsumei no Shinka to Setsumei Geijutsu no Tanjō," *GYS*, 4:119–29 (originally privately published by Oshima Hideo, August 1923).

65. Gonda, *Kokumin Goraku no Mondai*, *GYS*, 3:13–14 (originally published in 1941).

66. Gonda, *Kokumin Goraku no Mondai*, *GYS*, 3:13–14, 19. This volte-face in the mass media is illustrated by cultural messages in the cartoons produced by Okamoto Ippei, which were featured prominently in a variety of illustrated magazines during the "modern" era and during this moment of transition. Whereas his caricatures of everyday modern life, such as his treatment of the Modern Girl, are satirical, at the same time they can be seen as affirming. Tsuganesawa Toshihiro notes that Gonda was not in total accord with Nazi policy, but this is impossible to assess because Gonda's 1942 book on policy, used by Tsuganesawa to corroborate his point, is excluded from Gonda's collected works. Two additional articles from 1942 referring to Nazi policies are also excluded, although they are listed in the bibliography of his works. See Tsuganesawa Toshihiro, "Kaisetsu," in *GYS*, 3:442–43; Tamura Norio, "Kaisetsu," in *GYS*, 4:476; Tsurumi Shunsuke, "Minshū Goraku kara Kokumin Goraku e," *Shisō*, no. 624 (June 1976): 285. A book and two articles excluded from the collected works are: Gonda, *Nachisu Kōseidan* (Kurita Shoten, 1942); Gonda, "Kdf to sono Hoken Jigyō," *Onsen*, June 1942; and Gonda, "Kokumin Kōsei Undō no Nachisuteki Seikaku," *Doitsu*, July 1942. See *GYS*, 4:465–66.

THE MODERN GIRL AS MILITANT

1. See for example, Peter Duus, *The Rise of Modern Japan* (Boston: Houghton Mifflin, 1976), 187–88. See the segment devoted to the Modern Girl in "Nihon no Kokoro," ed. Takahashi Shōji, special issue of the magazine *Taiyō*, no. 54 (1986): 126–28 (the special issue is part of a series, *Modan Tōkyō Hyakkei*, edited by Unno Hiroshi); and the entry "Moga Mobo—Gaikoku Kabure no Danjo Moodo," in *Meiji Taishō Fūzokugoten*, ed. Tsuchida Mitsufumi (Kadokawa Shoten, 1979), 325–26. For an analysis of how the American flapper displaced the "social mother" of the preceding era, see Mary Ryan, *Womanhood in America: From Colonial Times to the Present* (New York: Franklin Watts, 1983), 220–23.

2. The movie, directed by Suzuki Jūkichi, drew unprecedented crowds when it opened in 1930. For a discussion of its appeal, see Tanaka Jun'ichirō, ed., *Musei kara Tookii e, Nihon Eiga Hattatsushi* 2 (Chūō Kōronsha, 1968), 178. *Nani ga Kanojo wo sō Sasetaka* first appeared in the January 1927 issue of *Kaizō* and was staged by the Tsukiji Theater in April of that year. I cite Fujimori Seikichi, *Nani ga Kanojō wo sō Sasetaka* (Kaizōsha, 1927), 1–160.

3. Kitazawa Shūichi's article is cited in Satō Takeshi, "Modanizumu to Amerikaka: 1920, Senkyūhyaku Nijūnen wo Chūshin to shite" in Minami, *NMK*, 41–42; Ueda Yasuo, "Josei Zasshi ga Mita Modanizumu," in Minami, *NMK*, 135–36; and Barbara Hamill, "*Josei*: Modanizumu to Kenri Ishiki," in Minami, *NMK*, 215–16. For a rich history of the appearance of the modern girl see Barbara Sato, *The New Japanese Woman*, 45–78.

4. Nii Itaru, "Modan Gaaru no Rinkaku," *Fujin Kōron*, April 1925, 24–31. Nii's colleague, Ōya Sōichi, attributed the piece to Nii, but Nii gave credit to Kitazawa; see Hamill, "Josei," 229.

5. Maeda Ai notes that the term *modan gaaru* won out over the label *shin jidai no onna* (woman of the new era). See Maeda, *Kindai Dokusha no Seiritsu* (Yūseido, 1972), 214–15. Ueda follows what he terms the discourse on the Modern Girl through articles published in *Josei* from 1924 through 1928. He cites the cartoon series penned by Tanaka Hisara as beginning in the September 1928 issue of *Shufu no Tomo*; see Ueda, "Josei Zasshi," *NMK*, 115–30, 127. For a commentary on the construction of the *moga* through the reinforcing "advertisements" of newspapers, magazines, and the movies, see Hoshino Tatsuo, "Modaan Shinbun Zasshi Eiga Mandan," *Kaizō*, June 1929, 42–45. See Minami, *SB*, 303–8. Regarding the extent of national distribution, see Ie no Hikari Kyōkai, ed., *Ie no Hikari Shijūnen* (Ie no Hikari Kyōkai, 1968), 126.

I elaborate on the place of the Modern Girl in my discussion of *Shufu no Tomo* as modern site in segment 4, The Household Becomes Modern Life, and in the conclusion.

6. Kataoka Teppei, "Onna no Kyaku" in *Ningen Seken*, vol. 1 of *Kindai Shomin Seikatsushi* (hereafter *KSS*), ed. Minami Hiroshi (San'ichi Shobō, 1985), 175–77 (originally published in October 1926).

7. Kiyosawa Kiyoshi, "Modaan Gaaru no Kenkyū," *Ningen Seken*, vol. 1 of

Minami, *KSS*, 143–58. Rosalind Coward, *Female Desires: How They Are Sought, Bought, and Packaged* (New York: Grove Press, 1985), 30. This volume offers insightful analysis associating fashion with the historical construction and representation of the female body. Kataoka Teppei, "Modan Gaaru no Kenkyū," in Minami, *KSS*, 1:163–64, 170, 172 (originally published on September 9, 1926). It was also included in Kataoka, *Modan Gaaru no Kenkyū* (Kinseidō, 1927). The term *ren'ai*, used to translate the Western term *love*, was, like the words for *philosophy (tetsugaku)* and *society (shakai)*, a Meiji invention. Two Chinese characters—*ren* (or, in the Japanese pronunciation, *koi*), alluding to feelings of deep affection between a man and a woman, and *ai*, meaning to be drawn to something and yearn for it or feel a tenderness toward it—were combined to create the new word, which could apply only to a yearning for a member of the opposite sex. See Tanaka Sumiko, ed., *Josei Kaihō no Shisō to Kōdō*, prewar vol. (Jiji Tsūshinsha, 1975), 166.

8. Kitamura Kaneko, "Kai Teisō," in Minami, *KSS*, 1:128–42, esp. 131–34 (originally published in 1927). Ueda, "Josei Zasshi," in Minami, *NMK*, 135; Kataoka, "Modan Gaaru no Kenkyū," 161, 168; Kitamura, "Kai Teisō," 133.

9. Kiyosawa cites in romanized letters a "Dr. Meyrick Booth," published in the "Hibert Journal." See Kiyosawa, "Modaan Gaaru no Kenkyū," in Minami, *KSS*, 1:152, 155–57. Nii, "Modan Gaaru no Rinkaku," 24.

10. Kishida Ryūsei, "Shinkō Saiku Ginza Dōri," in *Kishida Ryūsei Zenshū*, vol. 4 (Iwanami Shoten, 1979), 295–97. This essay was serialized in the evening edition of the *Tokyo Nichinichi Shinbun* from May 24 through June 10, 1927.

11. *Chijin no Ai* was serialized in the *Ōsaka Asahi Shinbun* from March through June 1924, and in *Josei* from November 1924 through July 1925; the version cited here is from *Tanizaki Jun'ichirō Zenshū* (Chūō Kōronsha, 1967), 10:1–302. For an English translation, see Tanizaki Jun'ichirō, *Naomi*, trans. Anthony H. Chambers (New York: Knopf, 1985).

12. Coward, *Female Desires*, 30. For a passage describing how the hero poses Naomi in various guises, and for the role reversal, see Tanizaki, *Chijin no Ai*, 45, 294. I am grateful to Lucy North for the concept of "mistress-slave relationship."

13. Tanizaki chose "Yankee girl," an unambiguously pejorative term that implied an unthinking copying of Western mores, over "Modern Girl." For a discussion of the term "Yankee girl," see Ueda, "Josei Zasshi," in Minami, *NMK*, 136–37. Tanizaki, *Chijin no Ai*, 126, 264. Tanizaki uses the Meiji term *haikara*, derived from the transliteration of "high collar," to mean fashionably Western, rather than *modan*, or "modern." Although it is common for scholars to assume that *haikara* was displaced by *modan*, the use of *haikara* continued until the end of the 1920s. The *bunka jūtaku*, or "culture house," was the term for the Westernized homes erected for the new middle class following World War I.

14. Kitamura, "Kai Teisō," in Minami, *KSS*, 1:131.

15. Ibid.

16. As E. Patricia Tsurumi has documented, women workers in the textile

industry constituted 71 percent of the private industry workforce by 1910, but this social reality was not reflected in official ideology. Kano Masanao suggests that not only have the two parts of the compound word *kokka* been separated into its constitutive *koku* or *kuni* (nation) and *ka* or *ie* (family) in order to posit an analogy between the two terms, but men have been placed within the nation and women within the family. See E. Patricia Tsurumi, "Female Textile Workers and the Failure of Early Trade Unionism in Japan," *History Workshop* 18 (Fall 1984): 5; and Kano, *Senzen "Ie" no Shisō* (Sōbunsha, 1983), 5. For the assessment that the Modern Girl was unfettered by tradition or fatalism and "more than anything respected herself," see the August 1924 issue of *Josei* (cited in Ueda, "Josei Zasshi," in Minami, *NMK*, 135). The introductory section to the Civil Code, which explained that Japanese law differed from Western civil codes because the familial nature of Japanese society displaced any notion of individuality, and the fourth book of the code, the *Book of Relatives*, placed women in a patriarchal web. For an example of the subjugation of woman within the family in the ethics textbooks, consider the elementary-school catechism about the loyal bride and mother-to-be who, with soft voice, engages in her needlework and cleaning; see Suematsu Kenchō, *Shōgaku Shūshin Kan*, parts 2 and 3 (Seikasha, 1892), cited in *Kazoku Mondai*, ed. Yuzawa Yasuhiko, vol. 5 of *Nihon Fujin Mondai Shiryō Shūsei* (hereafter *NFMSS*) (Domesu Shuppan, 1978), 369–70. See also Gluck, *Japan's Modern Myths*, 120–27. Hiratsuka Raichō, "Modan Gaaru ni Tsuite," in *Hiratsuka Raichō Chosakushū* (hereafter *HRC*), vol. 4 (Ōtsuki Shoten, 1983), 282–84 (originally published in *Dai Chōwa*, May 1927); and Hiratsuka, "Kaku Arubeki Modan Gaaru," in *HRC*, 290–97 (originally published in *Fujin Kōron*, June 1927).

17. Kitamura, "Kai Teisō," 135, 131. Kataoka, "Modan Gaaru no Kenkyū," 162–163.

18. Koike Tomihisa, "Marubiru Moga Sanpo Koosu," in Kon and Yoshida, *Moderunologio*, 131–37.

19. Rachel Bowlby, *Just Looking: Consumer Culture in Dreiser, Gissing, and Zola* (New York: Methuen, 1985), 18–34. Kiyosawa, "Modaan Gaaru no Kenkyū," in Minami, *KSS*, 1:157–58; Kataoka, "Modan Gaaru no Kenkyū," in Minami, *KSS*, 1:161–65. The notion is Kataoka's. See Kataoka, "Modan Gaaru no Kenkyū," in Minami, *KSS*, 1:164. The terms *sentan* and *zen'ei*, meaning *vanguard* and *radical*, were commonly applied to the Modern Girl. On this issue, see Minami, *NMK*, x.

20. Unlike other writers, who either marginalized the Modern Boy or ignored him altogether, Yamakawa placed no greater emphasis on the Modern Girl than on her male partner; see Yamakawa Kikue, "Modan Gaaru, Modan Booi," in *Yamakawa Kikueshū*, ed. Tanaka Sumiko and Yamakawa Shinsaku (Iwanami Shoten, 1981–1982), 4:268–71 (originally published in *Keizai Ōrai*, September 1927). Exhibiting a revolutionary optimism, Yamakawa also drew a second parallel: the interests of the decadent girls and boys were undoubtedly very similar to the diversions enjoyed by the Russian nobility and landowners

who were thrown off their land by the roughened hands of the ignorant muzhiks (ibid., 269–70).

21. Kiyosawa, "Modaan Gaaru no Kenkyū," in Minami, *KSS*, 1:153–57. Ōya Sōichi, "Hyaku Paasento Moga," *Ōya Sōichi Zenshū*, 2:10–17 (originally published in *Chūō Kōron*, August 1929). Hamill has concluded that the distinction between a (progressive) "real Modern Girl" and a "real" Modern Girl interested only in clothing and makeup was present in almost all accounts of the Modern Girl; see Hamill, "Josei," in Minami, *NMK*, 210.

22. Hiratsuka, "Kaku Arubeki Modan Gaaru," in Hiratsuka, *HRC*, 4:290–97.

23. Kataoka, "Modan Gaaru no Kenkyū," Minami, *KSS*, 1:173. The suffixes -*ko* and -*e* are feminine endings.

24. "Modan Seikatsu Mandankai," *Shinchō*, January 1928, 123–47.

25. The story of the woman who committed suicide after being called a Modern Girl may be apocryphal, but the strategic decision of these women not to adopt the label is in part explained by Hiratsuka Raichō's remembrance that no woman in short hair and Western clothes would call herself a "Modern Girl," just as the Seitōsha activists of her generation had actively resisted the label of "New Woman"; see Hiratsuka, "Modan Gaaru ni Tsuite," in Hiratsuka, *HRC*, 4:283. Ogata Akiko, *Nyonin Geijutsu no Sekai* (Domesu Shuppan, 1980), 38–39. Yamakawa Kikue, "Feminizumu no Kentō," in *Yamakawa Kikueshū*, 5:167–74 (originally published in *Nyonin Geijutsu* 1, no. 1 [July 1928]: 2–7).

26. Yagi Akiko, "Kotoba: Hyōgen," *Nyonin Geijutsu* 2, no. 1 (January 1929): 104–6. For Yamakawa Kikue's biting critique of the commodification of women, see Yamakawa, "Keihin tsuki Tokkahin to shite no Onna," *Yamakawa Kikueshū*, 5:2–8 (originally published in *Fujin Kōron*, January 1928).

27. A number of Kollontai's works were translated into Japanese between 1927 and 1936: *Red Love*, trans. Murao Jirō (Seikaisha, 1927); *A Grand Love*, trans. Nakajima Hideko (Sekaisha, 1930); *Great Love*, trans. Uchiyama Kenji (Sekaisha, 1930); *Working Women's Revolution*, trans. Ōtake Hakukichi (Naigaisha, 1930); *Motherhood and Society*, trans. Ozawa Keishi (Lo-gosu Shoin, 1931); and *Women and the Family System*, trans. Yamakawa Kikue (Seibunkaku, 1936).

28. "Tahōmen Ren'ai Zadankai," *Nyonin Geijutsu* 1, no. 3 (September 1928): 2–22.

29. "Zen Josei Shinshutsu Kōshinkyoku wo Tsunoru," *Nyonin Geijutsu* 2, no. 8 (August 1929): 2–3.

30. Yagi Akiko and Hayashi Fumiko, "Kyūshū Tabidayori," *Nyonin Geijutsu* 2, no. 9 (September 1929): 70–81. *Hōrōki* was serialized in nineteen installments between October 1928 and November 1930.

31. Nakamoto Takako, "Tōyō Mosu Daini Kōjō" (parts 1–4), *Nyonin Geijutsu*, July–December 1932. See Sata Ineko, "Kanbu Jokō no Namida," *Kaizō*, January 1931; "Shōkanbu," *Bungei Shunjū*, August 1931; "Kitō," *Chūō Kōron*, October 1931; and "Kyōsei Kikoku," *Chūō Kōron*, January 1931; all reprinted in *Sata Ineko Zenshū* (Kōdansha, 1977), 1:219–78. Sata has explained that the

women workers asked her for aid and that she had been outside the dormitory in Kameido during the strike (my interviews with Sata Ineko, in Tokyo, October 1982, and Karuizawa, August 1986).

32. Kiyosawa, "Modaan Gaaru no Kenkyū," in Minami, KSS, 1:158.

33. "Ryūchijō no Modan Gaaru," Nyonin Geijutsu 2, no. 12 (December 1929): 77–81.

34. See Watanabe Etsuji and Suzuki Yūko, eds., Tatakai ni Ikite: Senzen Fujin Rōdō Undō e no Shōgen (Domesu Shuppan, 1980), Undō ni kaketa onnatachi: senzen fujin undō e no shōgen, 194–214; and Rōdō Undōshi Kenkyūkai and Rōdōsha Kyōiku Kyōkai, eds., Nihon Rōdō Undō no Rekishi (San'ichi Shobō, 1960), 179–94.

35. In this sense the Japanese Modern Girl was not unlike the New Woman of Weimar Germany. In the words of Atina Grossman, "This New Woman was not merely a media myth or a demographer's paranoid fantasy, but a social reality that can be researched and documented. She existed in office and factory, bedroom and kitchen, just as surely as in café, cabaret, and film. I think it is important that we begin to look at the New Woman as producer and not only consumer, as an agent constructing a new identity which was then marketed in mass culture, even as mass culture helped to form that identity" ("Girlkultur or Thoroughly Rationalized Female: A New Woman in Weimar Germany," in Women in Culture and Politics: A Century of Change, ed. Judith Friedlander, Blanche Wiesen Cook, Alice Kessler-Harris, and Carroll Smith-Rosenberg [Bloomington: Indiana University Press, 1986], 64).

36. Ueda, "Josei Zasshi," in Minami, NMK, 120. The renovation and expansion of department stores between 1924 and 1930 also serve as an index of changes in consumer behavior. Hagiwara's reminiscence is from Hagiwara Yōko, Chichi: Hagiwara Sakutarō (1959), in Imai Seiichi, Shinsai ni Yuragu, vol. 6 of Nihon no Hyakunen (Chikuma Shobō, 1961–64), 165.

37. Minakami Takitarō, "Teito Fukkōsai Yokyō," Mita Bungaku, May 1930, reprinted in Imai, Shinsai ni Yuragu, 166–68.

38. Kon Wajirō, ed., Shinban Dai Tōkyō Annai (Chūō Kōronsha, 1929; Hihyōsha, 1986); and Kiyosawa Kiyoshi, Modan Gaaru (1926). Both cited in Imai, Shinsai ni Yuragu, 162.

39. The appearance of a number of surveys, by such pundits as Yamakawa Kikue and by government officials such as the unidentified gentleman who in 1931 ruefully admitted that Ibsen's Nora had been a prophet, aimed at scientifically analyzing this new social phenomenon and offered one index of the widespread concern over the definition of the working woman. See Yamakawa Kikue, "Gendai Shokugyō Fujinron," in Shichō (part 1), in Maruoka, vol. 8 of NFMSS, 334–44; Margit Nagy, "Middle-Class Working Women during the Interwar Years," in Recreating Japanese Women, 1600–1945, ed. Gail Bernstein (Berkeley: University of California Press, 1991), 199–216; and Maeda Ai, Kindai Dokusha no Seiritsu (Iwanami Shoten, 1993), 225–26. The term shokugyō fujin has come to be associated with a middle-class response to the creation of thousands of jobs in the expanded tertiary sector after the Russo-Japanese War and

accompanying the economic boom during World War I. See, for example, Margit Nagy, "'How Shall We Live?' Social Change, the Family Institution, and Feminism in Prewar Japan" (Ph.D. diss., University of Washington, 1981), 118–38; and Murakami Nobuhiko, *Taishōki no Shokugyō Fujin* (Domesu Shuppan, 1983). In many instances, however, the working woman was associated with the Modern Girl or the working-class woman. See Kataoka's contention that the term *Modern Girl* originated as a means of referring to the *shokugyō fujin* ("Modan Gaaru no Kenkyū," 164); and Ōbayashi Munetsugu's query, "Is the Café Waitress a Working Woman?" in "'Jokyū' Shakaishi," *Chūō Kōron*, April 1932, 151–62. Kon Wajirō, ed., *Shinban Dai Tōkyō Annai*, 281–81, 291–92.

40. Margit Nagy's essay documents the entry of married women into the workforce in the 1920s. For the monthly expenditures and income of the average salaryman, see Nagy, "Middle-Class Working Women during the Interwar Years" in Bernstein, ed., *Recreating Japanese Women*, 156–58. The consumption of the salaried worker must be placed in the context of the depressed food and housing prices that were part of the overall crisis of Japanese capitalism. When the world depression hit in 1929, the economy had not recovered from the shocks of the post–World War I depression, the 1923 earthquake, the run on banks during the panic of 1927, and the recession following the panic. By 1931, when Japan went off the gold standard, the country was in the midst of a severe depression.

41. Kano Masanao, *Senzen "Ie" no Shisō*, 112–15. The words are from the title of a critique by Oku Mumeo written in 1923, cited in *Kazoku Seido*, ed. Yuzawa Yasuhiko, vol. 5 of *NFMSS*, 28. Murakami goes in this direction when he notes the contradiction between the emphasis on love and romance in the Taishō era and the reality of the legal system that was challenged by women's new engagement in education and work; see Murakami Nobuhiko, *Taishō Joseishi* (Rironsha, 1982), 1–4. For excellent documentation of the debate on revision of the code and the discourse surrounding the debate, see Nagy, "'How Shall We Live?'" 198–219, 255. See also Maruoka, vol. 5 of *NFMSS*. For an article from 1924 on the destruction of the family which listed as three reasons for the collapse of the patriarchal system the end of the family as an economic unit, the power of the state, and the extension of individualism, see Kawada Shirō, "Kachōsei Kazoku Soshiki no Hōkai: Kazoku Seido Hōkai no Kiun," in *Kazoku seido*, ed. Yuzawa, vol. 5 of *NFMSS*, 438–53.

42. Sharon Nolte, "Women's Rights and Society's Needs: Japan's 1931 Suffrage Bill," *Comparative Studies in Society and History* 28, no. 1 (October 1986): 18–19. Although Murakami has argued that education and the increase in the number of working women, more than their organized protest movements, served to liberate women from the family system enshrined in the Civil Code, the role of a variety of political interest groups in changing the attitudes of women and men cannot be ignored; see Murakami, *Taishō Joseishi*, 2. For a use of the term *fūfu sōgi*, see Kitamura, "Kai Teisō," 137.

43. For an excellent chronology, see *Kindai Nihon Fujin Mondai Nenpyō*,

ed. Naruoka Hideko and Yamaguchi Miyoko, vol. 10 of *NFMSS*. Fujime Yuki provides an insightful history of the mobilization of café waitresses at a time when they were not taken seriously as workers by either most women's organizations or by most social commentators writing about them as sex workers. See Fujime Yuki, *Sei no Rekishigaku* (Fuji Shuppan, 1997), 288–94.

44. For detailed statistics, see Fujime, *Sei no Rekishigaku*.

45. Lois Banner notes that the flapper sent a mixed sexual message, and she makes the important connection between the flapper's play and the experience of the working woman: "The cultural focus on fashion and after-hours activities in the lives of these women glamorized the working world for women while trivializing it" (Banner, *American Beauty* [Chicago: University of Chicago Press, 1983], 279, 280). See Rayna Rapp and Ellen Ross, "The 1920s: Feminism, Consumerism, and Political Backlash in the United States," in Friedlander et al., *Women in Culture and Politics*, 52–61.

46. One metaphor for the contemporary woman's multifaceted image was that of a colorless proteus who has been liberated from the darkness of her household to take on the hues of her environment; see Kitamura, "Kai Teisō," 135–36. Three historians have looked beyond the stereotype of the Modern Girl to see a discourse constituted by contradiction. Satō Takeshi, who likens the Modern Girl to the flapper, traces a shift from the Modern Girl as emblem of women's new customs to the Modern Girl as juvenile delinquent ("Modanizumu to Amerikaka," in Minami, *NMK*, 26, 41–43). Ueda notes a multiplicity of definitions in his discussion of the relationship of women's magazines to a Japanese modernism ("Josei Zasshi," in Minami, *NMK*, 137). In a wide-ranging essay covering the working woman, women's education, advice columns, and women's magazines, Hamill, in her original work on the Modern Girl, like Ueda, talks in terms of a discourse. Adopting the term *modan gaaru ron*, she analyzes the coexistence of positive and critical assessments of the Modern Girl. She attributes the pejorative aspects of the discourse to the influence of Marxism on intellectuals who could see the "Modern Girl" only as an expression of faddish mores, and to sensationalism in the press. She sides with Hirabayashi Hatsunosuke to emphasize that the Modern Girl signified "the emergence of a new consciousness for women" breaking loose from traditional power relationships. See Hamill, "Josei," in Minami, *NMK*, 208–25. For Davis's "disorderly" women see Natalie Zemon Davis, "Women on Top," in *Society and Culture in Early Modern France: Eight Essays* (Stanford, CA: Stanford University Press, 1975), 143–45. Although Davis's claim that "a topos of sexual inversion placing woman on top in a hierarchy of power relationships was a resource for private and public life" (150) is far from definitive, and my discussion here has argued that the representation of the Modern Girl followed rather than encouraged political actions, the influence of the media on the actions of Japanese women during the interwar era deserves serious attention. In this respect the Japanese Modern Girl resembles her American sister, the flapper, for, as Paula Fass has shown, young women, even more than men, symbolized disorder and rebellion in the United States during the

1920s (*The Damned and the Beautiful* [New York: Oxford University Press, 1977], 6, 22).

47. Kitamura, "Kai Teisō," 137.

48. The concept of a "repository of the past" is provided by Sharon Sievers, who is working from a theoretical formulation by Hanna Papenak. Sharon Sievers, *Flowers in Salt: The Beginnings of Feminist Consciousness in Modern Japan* (Stanford, CA: Stanford University Press, 1983), 17.

49. Satō Takeshi, "Modanizumu to Amerikaka," in Minami *NMK*, 41–42. I do not agree with Satō's notion of a two-stage development of the term *Modern Girl*, in which she stood first for Western customs and later for criminal actions. The positive and pejorative connotations of her actions from the mid-1920s into the 1930s must be further explored. Ichikawa, "Ryūkōka ni Miru Modanizumu to Ero Guro Nansensu," 267.

50. Itō Shunsui, "Jidai Fūzoku Etoki," *Chūō Kōron*, April 1932.

51. Kitamura used the term *kansei* (completion) to connote fulfillment ("Kai Teisō," 139). Regarding the notion of periodization, see Kiyosawa, "Modaan Gaaru no Kenkyū," 158. See, for example, the exhibition catalog *Modern Boy Modern Girl: Modernity in Japanese Art, 1910–1935* (Kanagawa: Kenritsu Kindai Bijutsukan, 1998), 87, 89, 90, 94–95. Although it displays conventional photographs of women in flapper garb, it also includes satirical cartoon art that raises such issues as gender ambiguity, the politicization of young women (a "proletarian *moga*" is featured), and new attitudes toward the public display of the nude body.

THE CAFÉ WAITRESS SANG THE BLUES

1. Langston Hughes is quoted in Angela Davis, *Blues Legacies and Black Feminism: Gertrude "Ma" Rainey, Bessie Smith, and Billie Holiday* (New York: Pantheon Books, 1998), 145. See Hazel Carby, "It Jus Be's Dat . . . Way Sometime: The Sexual Politics of Women's Blues," in *Unequal Sisters: A Multicultural Reader in U.S. Women's History*, ed. Ellen Carol DuBois and Vicki L. Ruiz (New York: Routledge, 1990), 241, and Daphne Duval Harrison, *Black Pearls: Blues Queens of the 1920s* (New Brunswick, NJ: Rutgers University Press, 1988). For an overview of Awaya Noriko's career, see Awaya Noriko, *Wagu Hōrōki* (Nihon Tosho Sentaa, 1997)

2. Daphne Duval Harrison, *Black Pearls: Blues Queens of the 1920s* (New Brunswick: Rutgers University Press, 1988), 18–20.

3. Davis sees the blues as a working-class form set on an "African cultural continuum" informed by such elements as the poverty and racism of the 1920s, the transformation in sexual relationships after the end of slavery, slave culture, and West African religion (Davis, *Blues Legacies*, 33, 49, 67–69, 74). Elements such as community building could be found in *jokyū* culture also. For a wise warning against romanticizing putative acts of resistance that may in fact "ultimately legitimate dominant norms," see Gail Hershatter, *Dangerous Plea-*

sures: Prostitution and Modernity in Twentieth-Century Shanghai (Berkeley: University of California Press, 1997), 27–28.

4. Ozaki Midori, "Mokusei," in *Ozaki Midori Zenshū* (Sōjusha, 1980), 159 (originally published in *Nyonin Geijutsu*, March 1929). For my translation of this story, see Silverberg, "Osmanthus," *Manoa* 3, no. 2 (Fall 1991): 187–90.

5. I have chosen *eroticism* over *sexuality* because of the adoption in Japan of the term *ero*, although Foucault's conception of "sex" as an "imaginary" cluster is implied in the mass media of the era. He explains that the "the notion of 'sex' made it possible to group together in an artificial unity of anatomical elements, biological functions, conducts, sensations, and pleasures and it enabled one to make use of this fictitious unity as a causal principle" (Foucault, *The History of Sexuality,*154).

6. I am working from Gayle Rubin, who has said that there are "historical periods in which sexuality is more sharply contested and more overtly politicized. In such periods, the domain of erotic life, is in effect, renegotiated." Rubin, "Thinking Sex," in *Pleasure and Danger: Exploring Female Sexuality,* ed. Carol Vance (Boston: Routledge & Kegan Paul, 1984), 267. Tosaka Jun, "Ken'etsuka no Shisō to Fūzoku," 46, and, "Kenetsushita," 45–46. Regarding revue regulations, see also Seidensticker, *Tokyo Rising,* 77. For Garon's chronology, see Garon, *Molding Japanese Minds,* 107. For a rich, comprehensive discussion of the representation and regulation of prostitution in modern China, see Hershatter, *Dangerous Pleasures.*

7. Fujime Yuki is the only scholar I know of who has treated the sex work of the Japanese café waitress within a politicized labor history. See Fujime, *Sei no Rekishigaku,* 283–311.

8. On the stages in women's history, see Joan Scott, *Gender and the Politics of History* (New York: Columbia University Press, 1988), 15–50. Regarding "woman," see Denise Riley, *"Am I That Name?" Feminism and the Category of "Women" in History* (Minneapolis: University of Minnesota Press, 1988).

9. For statistics on café waitresses, see Minami, *SB,* 78, 169, 477–78, and Fujime, *Sei no Rekishigaku,* 288, 310. For a history of the café, see Andō Kōsei, *Ginza Saiken* (Chūō Kōronsha, 1977). Hirotsu Kazuo's novel *Jokyū* was serialized in *Fujin Kōron* between 1930 and 1932; it is reprinted in *Hirotsu Kazuo Zenshū* (Chūō Kōronsha, 1988), 5:7–242. Two films titled *Jokyū* were produced: the first, produced by Nikkatsu Uzumasa, appeared in 1930. The second, produced by Teikine and directed by Masune Junzō, appeared in 1931.

10. Igarashi Tomio, *Meshimori Onna* (Shinjinbutsu Ōraisha, 1981), 72–84, 140.

11. Igarashi, *Meshimori,* 181, and Igarashi, *Nihon Josei Bunkashi* (Agatsuma Shokan, 1984),133–48. Sone Hiromi, "Baitakū—kinsei no baishun," in Josei Shi Sūgū Kenkyūkai, ed., *Nihon josei shi seikatsu shi,* vol. 3: *Kinsei* (Tokyo Daigaku Shuppankai, 1991).

12. For a rich ethnographic treatment of the hierarchy and the complex practices and relationships of Yoshiwara, see Joseph Ernest de Becker, *The Nightless City: Or, The History of the Yoshiwara Yukwaku* (Yokohama: Z. P.

Maruya, 1899). To merely dismiss this as an Orientalist document is to ignore the wealth of material that makes historical change evident. On "classes of prostitutes" see, for example, de Becker, 44. Such sources must be linked to *shikidōron*, which Earl Jackson has translated as "theory of the ways of erotic love." The *Kinsei Shikidōron* cited by Jackson deserves further attention (Earl Jackson, Jr., "Kabuki Narratives of Male Homoerotic Desire in Saikaku and Mishima," *Theatre Journal*, December 1989, 459–77).

13. Eve Kosofsky Sedgwick, *Epistemology of the Closet* (Berkeley: University of California Press, 1990), 29. Foucault cites "the pleasure of analysis" made possible by the Western preoccupation with sex. Foucault, *The History of Sexuality*, 71. For a historical treatment of sexual difference in the West, see Thomas Laqueur, *Making Sex: Body and Gender from the Greeks to Freud* (Cambridge, MA: Harvard University Press, 1990). Mariko Tamanoi also makes this point when she criticizes Western studies of Japanese popular culture for following an Orientalist trajectory (she includes the study of geisha and bar hostesses in this category). See Tamanoi, "Women's Voices: Their Critique of the Anthropology of Japan," *Annual Review of Anthropology* 19 (1990): 17–37.

14. Fujime, *Sei no Rekishigaku*, 291, 310.

15. Awazu Kiyoshi, Ii Tarō, and Hosaka Kunio, *Shōwa Jūichinen no Onna: Abe Sada* (Tabata Shoten, 1976), 119. From the description of the authors it would appear that the pleasure was limited to looking.

16. Kuki Shūzō, *Iki no Kōzō* (Iwanami Shoten, 1979; originally published in the January and February 1930 issues of *Shisō*). For an in-depth discussion of the thought of Kuki, see Leslie Pincus, *Authenticating Culture in Imperial Japan* (Berkeley: University of California Press, 1996). Nishiyama Matsunosuke places *iki* within the history of the commodification of women in Yoshiwara, in *Kinsei Bunka no Kenkyū* (Yoshikawa Kōbunkan, 1983), 9:388–89. See also his *Edo no Seikatsu Bunka* (Yoshikawa Kōbunkan, 1983), 137, and *Edo Chōnin no Kenkyū* (Yoshikawa Kōbunkan, 1973), 64–65. For a good summary of Kuki's characterization of *iki* as characterized by flirtation, pride, and refinement that along with aspects of women's beauty, see Nishiyama, *Edo Kotoba Hyakuwa* (Yoshikawa Kōbunkan, 1980), 8–10, and Nishiyama, *Edokko* (Yoshikawa Kōbunkan, 1980), 146–50. For the approach of a historian who traces aspects of *iki* from Fukagawa and through Edo, see Nakao Tatsurō, *Sui, Tsū, Iki* (Miyai Shoten, 1984), 169–70.

17. Kuki, *Iki no Kozō*, 55.

18. For an explanation of high-class prostitution, see Awazu, Ii, and Hosaka, *Shōwa Jūichinen no Onna*, 121. According to the authors, these unlicensed prostitutes used the telephone and the *entaku* (taxi) as tools of their trade, and they tended to specialize: some catered only to student lodgings in Kanda, Waseda, and Hongō (Awazu, Ii, and Hosaka, *Shōwa Jūichinen no Onna*, 118–20, and Hon no Mori Henshūbu, ed., *Abe Sada: Jiken Chōsho Zenbun* [Kosumikku Intaanashonaru, 1997], 28–29).

19. Awazu, Ii, and Hosaka, *Shōwa Jūichinen no Onna*, 118–19. For *Abe Sada*'s testimony, see *Abe Sada*, 61.

20. See *Abe Sada*, 121.

21. Fujimori, Hatsuda, and Fujioka, *Ushinawareta Teito*, 77. For a series of richly detailed photos of café exteriors and interiors, that give a sense of the lush use of art deco see the section on cafés in Fujimori Terunobu, Hatsuda Tōru, Fujioka Hiroyasu, eds., *Ushinawareta Teito Tokyo: Taishō, Shōwa no Machi to Sumai* (Kashiwa Shobō, 1991), 76–95. Homi K. Bhabha, *The Location of Culture* (New York and London: Routledge, 1994), 85–89, 121, 167–68. It should be noted that the work discusses a "Mimic Man" but does not theorize the issues surrounding the possibility of the interactions of a "Mimic Woman." Undoubtedly the most successful case of (female) masquerade, an eroticized masquerade which passed as mimicry, was the ostensibly Chinese movie star Rikoran, who was in fact a Japanese actress. See Silverberg, "Forgetting Pearl Harbor, Remembering Charlie Chaplin, and the Case of the Disappearing Westerner," *positions*, vol. 1, no. 1 (Spring 1993), 24–30. For a fuller discussion of masquerade, see the section on Asakusa eroticism below.

22. For accounts of Japanese and Korean sex workers and a history of the rounding up of young women in Korea, by Koreans, see articles in the special issue of *positions* edited by Chungmoo Choi, *The Comfort Women: Colonialism, War, and Sex* (vol. 5, no. 1). I want to make very clear that I am not equating sex work with sexual slavery. However, it seems to me that a study of this colonial pre-history can add insight related to the ugly presumptions regarding sex, gender, violence, nation, and domination that made up the initiation and implementation of the *ianfu* policy. For a discussion relating the pre-history of sex work to the comfort women issue, see Song Youn-ok, "Japanese Colonial Rule and State-Managed Prostitution: Korea's Licensed Prostitutes," *positions* (Spring 1995), 171–217.

23. Regarding Korean women brought to Japan as sex workers in the drinking and restaurant trade, in relation to the history of the "comfort women" see Jūgun Ianfu Mondai wo Kangaeru Zainichi Dōhō, ed., *Watashitachi wa Wasurenai: Chōsenjin Jūgun Ianfu* (1991). See also Yoshimi Yoshiaki, *Comfort Women: Sexual Slavery in the Japanese Military during World War II*, trans. Suzanne O'Brien (New York: Columbia University Press, 2000). For a book-length account of the "*ianfu*" that preceded the recent ackowledgment by the Japanese government of guilt, see Kimu Irumyon, *Tennō no Guntai to Chōsenjin Ianfu* (San'ichi Shobō, 1976). The ethnographic guide is Moroo Genzō, *Shin Chōsen Fūdoki* (Banrikaku Shobō, 1930).

24. Peter Bailey, "Parasexuality and Glamour: the Victorian Barmaid as Cultural Prototype," *Gender and History*, vol. 2, no. 2 (Summer 1990), 148–72; quote is from p. 152.

25. The obvious issue at stake is the question of Japanese model(s). T. J. Clark, *The Painting of Modern Life: Paris in the Art of Manet and His Followers* (Princeton, NJ: Princeton University Press, 1984).

26. Clark, *The Painting of Modern Life*, 109–11, 245–46, 252–55. It is difficult to theorize resistance. My view of the inseparable nature of domination and resistance is informed by such sources as Timothy Mitchell's critique of

James Scott's *Weapons of the Weak*. Mitchell challenges such binary distinctions as selfhood versus the outside world, private belief versus public actions, and acquiescence versus private autonomy. Mitchell's critique of Scott's notion of the theatrical metaphors of "on stage behavior" and "full transcript" also contribute to the debate inasmuch as they serve to critique Scott's more recent *Domination and the Arts of Resistance: Hidden Transcripts* (New Haven, CT: Yale University Press, 1990). See Mitchell, "Everyday Metaphors of Power," *Theory and Society*, vol. 19, no. 5 (1990): 545–77. For a sophisticated analysis of the significance and limitations of Foucault's notion of resistance, see Robert Young, *White Mythologies: Writing History and the West* (New York: Routledge, 1990), especially Young's paraphrasing of Foucault: "Resistance does not operate outside power, nor is it necessarily produced oppositionally: it is imbricated within it, the irregular term that consistently disturbs it, rebounds upon it, and which on occasions can be manipulated so as to rupture it altogether" (87).

27. Kathy Peiss, *Cheap Amusements: Working Women and Leisure in Turn-of-the-Century New York, 1880–1920* (Philadelphia: Temple University Press, 1985), 3, 4, 6, 8, 72. Davis, *Blues Legacies*, 66–90.

28. See *Riddles of Identity in Modern Times*, vol. 5 of *A History of Private Life*, ed. Antoine Prost and Gerard Vincent, trans. Arthur Goldhammer (Cambridge, MA: Harvard University Press, 1991). A more comprehensive history of the *jokyū* must of course include the history of the state crackdowns on cafés and café workers and what I term the *tenkō* (political turning) of the *jokyū* as they were shifted into jobs perceived to be socially worthwhile and incorporated into the reformulated national polity in 1940. Here the work of Sheldon Garon, focusing on the attitudes toward prostitution by state officials and reformers during this era, is apropos. See Sheldon Garon, "The World's Oldest Debate?: Prostitution and the State in Imperial Japan, 1900–1945," *American Historical Review* 98, no. 3 (June, 1993): 710–33. This is the method utilized by Charles Bernheimer in *Figures of Ill Repute: Representing Prostitution in Nineteenth-Century France* (Durham, NC: Duke University Press, 1997).

29. Hirotsu, *Jokyū*, 234.

30. Kon and Yoshida, "Ginza no Kafee Jokyū-san Fukusō," in *Moderunologio*, 201–4; "Jokyū-san Epuron Jissoku," *Moderunologio*, 204–5.

31. Kon and Yoshida, "Jokyū-san Epuron Jissoku," 204–5.

32. Ōbayashi Munetsugu, *Jokyū Seikatsu no Shinkenkyū* (Ōhara Shakai Mondai Kenkyūjo, 1931 (hereafter cited in text as OM).

33. On the place of women's magazines, see Maeda Ai's pathbreaking *Kindai Dokusha no Seiritsu* and Kimura Ryōko, "Fujin Zasshi no Jōhō Kūkan to Josei Taishū Dokushazō no Seiritsu," *Shisō*, February 1992, 229–52.

34. The case of the Korean *ianfu* or "comfort woman" of course comes to mind, but the reference here is too early for an association with that most vulgar of euphemisms. For Japanese theories of assimilation within a comparative historical context, see Oguma Eiji, *Nihonjin no Kyōkai: Okinawa, Ainu, Taiwan, Chōsen Shokuminchi Shihai kara Fukki Undō made* (Shin'yōsha, 1998).

35. Yamamoto Setsurō, "Ginza: Kenchiku Inshōki," in *Ginza*, 2 (June 1925): 6–9. For the lexicon, see "Ginza Tsūgohen," *Ginza* 2 (June 1925): 20–25.

36. See the scene in Hirotsu's *Jokyū* in which the heroine is embarrassed by this, and the comment regarding the *jokyū* carrying a small basket containing cosmetics and a change of clothes in Maeda Hajima, *Shokugyō Fujin Monogatari* (Tōyō: Keizai Shuppanbu, 1921), 193.

37. Andō, *Ginza Saiken*, 16–17, 88. For discussion of "Kuruwa-kotoba," or Yoshiwara dialect, see de Becker, *Nightless City*, 136–40, and Ishii Ryōsuke, *Yoshiwara* (Chūō Kōronsha, 1967), 81–184. See Hirotsu, *Jokyū*, for examples of the café dialect spoken by the customers: Cat (Neko) was short for Café Kuroneko (Café Blackcat); *tora* was the slang for Café Tiger, (8).

38. Andō, *Ginza*, 79–83.

39. Regarding the links among forms of mass culture following the earthquake, see my article "Constructing a New Cultural History of Modern Japan," *Boundary 2*, 1991. On the difference between Osaka and Ginza cafés, and on the move to Ginza of Osaka-managed cafés staffed by *jokyū*-speaking Osaka dialect and behaving in "Osaka style" who were assigned one on one to customers, see Andō, *Ginza*, 115–20. Fujimori, Hatsuda, and Fujioka, *Ushinawareta Teito*, 77. For another comparison of Ginza and Osaka cultures, see Gonda Yasunosuke's essay "Ginbura to Dōbura: Santo Jōshu," in *GYS*, 4:68–71 (originally published by Chūgai Shogyō Shimpō, 1922).

40. Hirotsu also implies that not only did customers follow *jokyū* from café to café, but waitresses also moved to be with former coworkers who had found work elsewhere.

41. Hayashi Fumiko, *Hōrōki* (Shinchōsha, 1947; 1974); hereafter cited in text as HF. If *Hōrōki* were translated as the somewhat awkward "record of traveling," the documentary tenor of the work might be captured and my emphasis on the "documentary impulse" might be reinforced, but I have chosen to employ a more conventional, literary translation as one means of emphasizing the vernacular, familiar nature of the work to Hayashi's audience.

42. Angela Davis says that this sharing is a mode of community-building. Hayashi's community would have been limited to her readers. See, for example, Davis, *Blues Legacies*, 10, 91.

43. This culture may be compared to the subculture detailed in Ruth Rosen's *The Lost Sisterhood: Prostitution in America, 1900–1918* (Baltimore: Johns Hopkins University Press, 1982).

44. Kachūsha refers to the title of the earliest mass hit song in 1914, sung by Matsui Sumako, the earliest female stage star.

45. The reference to the naked dance is reminiscent of the powerful denouement of the short story "Draupadi" by Mahasweta Devi, translated by Gayatri Spivak in her *In Other Worlds: Essays in Cultural Politics* (New York: Methuen, 1987), 179–206.

46. Harrison, *Black Pearls*, 18–20, 39, 70, 75, 77. Carby, "It Jus Be's . . . Dat Way Sometime."

47. Harrison, *Black Pearls*, 77, 273.

48. Anne Allison's thought-provoking analysis in "Cartooning Erotics" suggests to me that relationships resented (and implied) by the Japanese "pornographic" *manga* are about a very different renegotiation of the erotic. See chapter 3 of Anne Allison, *Permitted and Prohibited Desire: Mothers, Comics, and Censorship in Japan* (Berkeley: University of California Press, 1996).

FRIENDS OF THE MOVIES

1. A serious study of reception should take into account film magazines. Yuri Tsivian's *Early Cinema in Russia and Its Cultural Reception*, trans. Alan Bodger, ed. Richard Taylor (London: Routledge, 1994) adopts an innovative approach that approaches film reception intertextually, taking into account such elements as art movements and technical irregularities. See Tom Gunning's foreword, xxi.

2. Regarding Uranami Sumako, see *Eiga no Tomo* (hereafter *ET*), February 1931, 139.

3. Tanaka Eizō, "Ero Hyakka Jiten (1)," *ET*, April 1931, 50–53. The quote comes from p. 51. See also the *fūzoku* category under *goraku* in Makino Mamoru, ed., *Fukkokuban Eiga Ken'etsu Jihō Kaisetsu* (Fuji Shuppan, 1985), 23.

4. Tanaka, "Ero Hyakka Jiten (1)," 52. The author gives a prehistory: as early as 1914, before the magazine was forced to cease publication, the word *érotique* had been used with more ease and intimacy in everyday discourse than even the newly coined popular term *building*. At that time, Japanese readers could buy a translation of the *Kama Sutra* for only five yen and a deluxe version for fifteen. The author had learned the name Havelock Ellis from the limited reading material available. Ono Kinjirō, "ERO Iroiro Goto," *ET*, June 1931, 68–69. Tanaka Eizō, "Ero Hyakka Jiten (3)," "Eigajin Ero Ingo—oyobi sono Yohō Kaisetsu," and Tōhukuji Sai, "Staa to Erotomeinia," *ET*, June 1931, 52–54, 64–67, 76–77.

5. Tanaka Eizō, "Ero Hyakka Jiten (13)," *ET*, April 1932, 50; Ogura Kōichirō, "Ero Eiga Kō 3: Seppun Nōto," *ET*, April 1932, 66.

6. Ogura, "Ero Eiga Kō 3," 67. According to censorship practices as recorded in the official Home Ministry bulletin, kissing fell under the category of lewdness *(in'yō)* and obscenity *(hiwai)*, which was a subcategory of the major category of mores *(fūzoku)*. See Makino, *Eiga Ken'etsu Jihō Kaisetsu*, 3, 37–38.

7. Tanaka, "Ero Hykka Jiten (3)," 52. "Eiga Joyū Rataibi Kenkyū," *ET*, June 1931, 64–65. Ezaki Kiyoshi, *Shajō Jinbutsu Satsuei Nyūmon* (Hikaridaisha, 1938), 185–215.

8. Ezaki, 173–75, 181–83.

9. Ezaki, 182. For a more extensive discussion of the attributes and place of prewar Japanese advertisements that notes a shift from *fūzoku* (mores) to *fūkei* (landscape), see Miriam Silverberg, "Advertising Every Body," in *Choreographing History*, ed. Susan Leigh Foster (Bloomington: Indiana University Press, 1995), 129–48.

10. Kikumoto Takeo, "Doitsu Rōdōsha Eiga ni Tsuite," *Eiga Hyōron* (hereafter *EH*), April 1931, 36–41; Shimizu Hikaru, "Mohori Nagii no Zettai Eiga Ron," *EH*, April 1931, 52–59; Azuma Ryōji, "Roshia Eiga Enkyū," *EH*, January 1931, 26–31. Yasuda Kiyoo, "Eroteikku Eiga," *EH*, September 1931, 35–41.

11. Yasuda, "Eroteikku Eiga," 35–36. Yasuda's contempt for a mimicry of Hollywood style is somewhat similar to the gist of Deguchi's article, titled "What Brought About the White Person Complex?" Quoting from such sources as Tanizaki's *Chijin no Ai*, the author focuses on a racially based inferiority complex leading to a desire by the Japanese masses to emulate the looks of Hollywood stars. Although I do not dispute Yasuda's documentation of the mimicry—indeed, any cursory glance at *Eiga no Tomo* reveals a kinship between film idols ensconced in Hollywood and in Japan—I cannot so readily endorse his claim that material culture was borrowed because there was a concern that Japanese filmgoers could never transform their bodies to make them white. What seems important is not the sense of inferiority so much as the sense of possibility and fluidity of a mass of spectators who determined that they could take on the look of their idols. See Deguchi Takehito, "Nani ga Hakujin Konpurekkusu wo Umidashitaka," in *Nihon Eiga no Modanizumu 1920–1930*, ed. Iwamoto Kenji (Riburopooto, 1991), 104–23. The photographs accompanying this essay are especially compelling.

12. Yasuda, "Eroteikku Eiga," 36–37. Yasuda lists Lubitsch along with [von] Sternberg and Chaplin as the three giants of the film world.

13. Yasuda, "Eroteikku Eiga," 38–41.

14. Yasuda, "Gurotesuku Eiga," *EH*, September 1931, 42–43.

15. Yasuda, "Gurotesuku Eiga," 44–45. For another discussion likening gesture to the grotesque, see Yamamoto Roppa, "1930 nen to Kabuki Eiga," *ET*, February 1931, 56–58.

16. Miki Tsunehiko, "Nansensu Eiga Kō," *EH*, September 1931, 46–47. The literary figures were Satō Hachirō and members of the Shinkankakuha, the group often referred to as modernist writers. Regarding the period film, Miki cited Itami Mansaku, "Shinjidai Eiga ni Kansuru Kōsatsu," *Eiga Kagaku Kenkyū*, vol. 8 (April 1931).

17. Ogura Kōichirō, "Ero Eiga Kō (7)," *ET*, February 1933, 72–73. Tanaka Eizō, "Ero Hyakka Jiten (21)," *ET*, November 1933, 58–59. Roundtable discussion with Takada Seiko, Takehisa Chieko, Kitamura Shizue, and Minami Yoshio, "Otoko o Kataru Zadankai," and another roundtable discussion with director Gosho Heinosuke, Iwata Sentarō, Itō Tatsuo, et al., "Hiroin o Kataru Zadankai," *ET*, November 1934, 56–59, 140–43.

18. Jennifer Robertson, *Takarazuka*, 56, 59, 70–73. For an excellent overview of the discourse on sexual deviance during the prewar years, see also Donald Roden, "Taishō Culture and the Problem of Gender Ambivalence," in *Culture and Identity: Japanese Intellectuals during the Interwar Years*, ed. J. Thomas Rimer (Princeton: Princeton University Press, 1990), 37–55. I tend to agree with Robertson that the concern with the unsettled nature of gender and sexual

identity was aimed mostly at women and rarely at men. However, new research into the discourse on masculinity from the late 1930s onward may yield new subtexts from the modern years. I translate *chūsei* as "neuter." See Robertson's discussion of the use of the term (which she translates as "neutral," or in between woman and man) as a means of avoiding considerations of eroticism (49).

19. Cover page, *ET*, June 1931, and back cover, *ET*, May 1931. Erving Goffman, *Gender Advertisements* (New York: Harper Torchbooks, 1979), 29. Goffman gives credit for observations on the role of fingers to a Michi Ishida, who appears to be Japanese.

20. Haruyama Kimiko, "Joyū kara Jokyū e," and Sawayama Akemi, "Rebyū Seikatsu e," *ET*, April 1931, 68–70. "Kawasaki Hiroko no Nichiyōbi" and "Dare ga Ichiban Erochikku deshō?" *ET*, June 1931, no page numbers. The photos of the three actresses in "Dare ga Ichiban Erochikku deshō?" were almost as revealing as the come-ons in words.

21. Ijūin Yoshi, "Seiyokukan o Chūshin toshite Mita Eiga Joyū Nikutai Kō," *ET*, July 1932, 51–53. The timing of this article conforms to Louise Young's narrative identifying the two moments when "war fever" was dominant: The first "media boom" took place from the time of the Manchurian Incident in September 1931 until the summer of 1932, when the press turned its attention to the Japanese Derby, the Los Angeles Olympics, and a series of love suicides. The second followed the release of the Lytton Commission report in the winter of 1933. See Young, *Japan's Total Empire*.

22. Hosokawa Harumi, "Otto no Mita Tsuma," *ET*, November 1931, 97; "Katei Sukecchi," *ET*, November 1931, 86–87; Katsumi Kōtarō, "Yosefu fon Stanbagu," *ET*, March 1932, 50–53; Azuma Yōko, "Temupuru no Nijūyojikan," *ET*, November 1935, 136–37. Clearly these presentations are based on imported advertising. For example, the Dietrich offering was one of many fan magazine articles in the West that emphasized "her off-screen role as devoted *hausfrau* and mother." Although Judith Mayne has argued that this was because "the androgynous sexual figure projected on screen required some form of counterpoint," I believe that placing Dietrich, along with leading Japanese women intellectuals and performers, firmly in the household was one way of celebrating the practices of modern times and of creating intimacy by bringing the foreign onto home terrain. Judith Mayne, *Cinema and Spectatorship* (New York: Routledge, 1993), 65.

23. Maruki Sado, "Sensō Bungaku to Erochishizumu," and Ogura Kōichirō, "Sensō Eiga no Ero Shiin," *ET*, May 1932, 48–51, 62–63; Ōguro Toyoshi, "Aware! Chappurin no Koi," *ET*, May 1932, 120–23; "Goshippu," *ET*, May 1932, 102; Ogasawara Meihō, "Kaiyō o Mamoru Fujō: Kaisen Eiga o Miru Hito no Tameni," and Ina Seiichi, "Kūbaku no Seiei: Aru Satsuei no Oboegaki," *ET*, May 1932, 52–55.

24. During a roundtable discussion among leading intellectuals in 1955, Kuno Osamu recalled that the newspapers originally critical of the state had changed their position when the war intensified. Fujita Shōzō countered that in-

tellectuals had foreseen the war and had rushed in to speculate (see Kuno Osamu, "Nihon Shisōshi to Tenkō," in *Kyōdō Kenkyū: Tenkō,* ed. Shisō no Kagaku Kenkyūkai [Heibonsha, 1959–1962; rpt. 1973], 363). More recently, Ikei Masaru has documented the "escalation" of competition among newspapers eager to capitalize on the "event" of the invasion (Ikei Masaru, "Senkyūhyaku Nendai no Masu Media," in *Saikō Taiheiyō Sensō Zen'ya: Nihon no Senkyūyaku Sanjū Nendai Ron toshite,* ed. Miwa Kimitada [Sōseiki, 1981], 143–91). Louise Young states that journalists believed in the cause and also tends to emphasize the economic incentives of "war fever" (Young, 54–114). The continuity in the tone of *Eiga no Tomo* is consistent with Young's discussion of critical journalism that escaped the censors but less consistent with her contention that "Taishō culture" was replaced by war fever (85–87).

25. Ijūin Yoshi, "Bakudan Sanyūshi Oboegaki," and Ogura Kōichiro, "Sensō Eiga no Ero Shiin," *ET,* May 1932, 70–71, 62–63. Regarding the propaganda aspect of the Three Valorous Bombs affair, see Young, 77–78, and John Dower, *War without Mercy: Race and Power in the Pacific War* (New York: Pantheon, 1986).

26. Watanabe Atsumi, "Sensō Eiga to Sutajio: Snappu Shotto to Goshippu to," *ET,* May 1932, 67–69. The ironic appropriation contrasts with Louise Young's catalog of products endorsing the hagiography, including the "Three Human Bullets Sake" and a dish called the "Three Human Bombs special," made of radish strips representing the explosives (78). Movie theaters reported a two- to threefold increase in attendance for the "valorous bomb" movies. Ikei, "Senkyūhyaku Nendai," 175.

27. Ogura Kōichi, "Sensō Eiga no Ero Shiin," *ET,* May 1932, 62; Maruki Sado, "Sensō Bungaku to Erochishizumu," *ET,* May 1932, 48. The quote from the soldier is from the German novel by Adrienne Thomas, *Die Katrin wird Soldat* (1930).

28. "Shanghai," *ET,* May 1932, 148. I note the contrasting use of *jinshu* regarding those on the continent and *minshu* for native Japanese in order to contribute to a much-needed study of the lexicon related to race, nation, and peoples during the imperial era. Here, denizens of the continent (including Anglo-Europeans, it would appear) seem to be the only people who are racialized. Kurashima Yasuzō, "Eiga Joyū Seiseikatsu Bunryushō," *ET,* Tokushū Erochishizumu (Special eroticism feature), July 1932, 45–46.

29. My reading of *Eiga no Tomo* shows a continuity from 1930 into the second half of the 1930s and beyond. This is one example of a critical stance toward state expansion on the Asian continent that was also disinterested in emphasizing the difference between Japanese *seikatsu* and the Anglo-European everyday as evidenced through representations of films and film stars.

30. Minami Yoshiko, "Dia Mee Uesto," *ET,* January 1935, 104–5. It is worth comparing this re-gendering of Mae West to the masculinization of the Takarazuka *otokoyaku* and to the domestication of Dietrich in the fan magazines. The term *oyabun* may have been appropriated because there was no other way to grant a female the power clearly wielded by this female figure.

Mae West's manipulation of female wiles through ribald humor may have also allowed for the gender crossover. "Hariuddo Tokushu Snappu," *ET,* July 1935, 26–29. Azuma Yōko, "Tempuru no Nijūyojikan," *ET,* November 1935, 136–37.

31. Yodogawa Nagaharu, "Burentouddo no Kaigan," *ET,* September 1936, 120; Iida Shinbi, "Marukusu Kigeki no Miryoku," *ET,* June 1936, 44–45.

32. Matsushita Fujio, "Onnagokoro—Otokogokoro," and "Shine Fasshon Rando," *ET,* October 1935, 92–93, 94–97.

33. "Miriamu no Wōdorōbu," Okada Tomiko, "Konshun no Toppu Haafu wa?" "Aki no Kokoroyoi Kanshokuni," and "Hariuddo Pataa: Aki no Sanpofuku," *ET* (November 1935), 164–65. On the visual culture of American advertising, see Roland Marchand, *Advertising the American Dream: Making Way for Modernity, 1920–1940* (Berkeley: University of California Press, 1985), 209–33.

34. Kingu Vuidaa (trans. Yodogawa Nagaharu), "Kosei Daiichi," *ET,* November 1935, 150–51; "Shinbuyō Goshōkai," *ET,* February 1935, 70–79.

35. The ads for *The Continental* and *Kunisada Chūji, ET,* March 1935, no page number. Yamamoto Kikuo has discussed how Yamanaka Sadao injected contemporary realism into his pieces, in stark contrast to the romanticism of other period pieces. *Kunisada Chūji* in part borrowed from *Grand Hotel.* See Yamamoto Kikuo, *Nihon Eiga ni okeru Gaikoku Eiga no Eikyō* (Waseda Daigaku Shuppanbu, 1983): 515, 521–25.

36. Shimizu Shunji, "Nyūsu Riiru o Kataru," *ET,* April 1935, 56–57; Kitamura Komatsu, et al., "Eiga Fuan Modan Jukkai," *ET,* October 1936, 94–96.

37. Seno Atsushi, "Uoruto Dyizunii Monogatari," Okada Shinkichi, "Roshia ni Katamuku Chappurin," and Nanbu Keinosuke et al., "Jinjaa Rojaasu no Miryoku Tankyū," *ET,* March 1937, 58–61, 66–69, 74–78; Ad with Shirley Temple, *ET,* December 1937, 115; Shigeno Tatsuhiko, "Shōwa Jūninendo Nihon Eiga Kaisōki," *ET,* December 1937, 78. Iwasaki Akira, "Nihon Eiga no Kiki," April 1937, 50–51; "Tokushū: Eiga no Tomo, Hijōji Dokuhon," October 1937, 130–35; Kamichika Ichiko, "Josei wa Naze Eiga o Miruka," November 1937, 60–61.

38. Shigeno Tatsuhiko, "Shōwa Jūninendo Nihon Eiga Kaisōki," *ET,* December 1937, 78–80.

39. A roundtable discussion with Uchida Tomu et al., "'Kagirinaki Zenshin' Gappyō," *ET,* December 1937, 113–15; "Aikokusha Paaneru," *ET,* December 1937, 94–95.

40. Shishi Bunroku, "Eiga ni Arawareta Yūmoa," *ET,* February 1938, 56–57. The Film Law went into effect on September 27, 1939. For the text of the law, see Sakuramoto Tomio, *Dai Tōa Sensō to Nihon Eiga; Tachimi no Senchū Eigaron* (Aoki Shoten, 1993): 7–15. For an analysis of control over the industry, see Gregory Kasza, *The State and the Mass Media,* 232–48. The philosopher Watsuji Tetsurō was also on this committee to reform film.

41. Kishi Matsuo, Takeda Rintarō, Takami Jun, Niwa Fumio, Sasami Tsuneo, and Ōguro Toyoshi, "Eiga Hōdan," *ET,* April 1938, 113–15; ad for perfume,

"Kokusan Kappii Kōsui," ET, April 1938, 12; Yodogawa Nagaharu, "Eiga Hogo-chō," ET, March 1938, 120–21.

42. Takeda Rintarō, Hayashi Fusao, and Niwa Fumio, "Eiga Tateyoko," ET, May 1938, 56–62; the quoted exchange is from p. 61.

43. Takeda, Hayashi, and Niwa, "Eiga Tateyoko," 62; Kawakita Nagamasa, "Nihon Eiga no Kaigai Shinshutsu ni Tsuite," ET, February 1939, 62–65.

44. Kawakita, "Nihon Eiga no Kaigai Shinshutsu ni Tsuite," 64.

45. Iijima Tadashi, "Eiga to Taishū," ET, June 1938, 50–51. A roundtable discussion with Iwasaki Akira, Hazumi Tsuneo, et al., "Nihon Eiga o Kataru," ET, June 1938, 62. Regarding Iwasaki's opposition to the Film Law, see Kasza, The State and the Mass Media, 241.

46. Cover page and "Karikachua Tenrankai," ET, July 1938, 133; "Horiuddo wa Ōsawagi," ET, August 1938, 128–30; Takami Jun, "Joyū ni Tsuite," ET, August 1938, 70–71.

47. Ozaki Shirō, "Senjō no Rakujitsu," ET, August 1938, 131–40; Okamoto Kanoko, "Sensō Eiga to Eikoku no Josei Fuan," ET, September 1938, 52–53; "Shinshi no Oshare," ET, November 1938, 154–55.

48. Okamoto, "Sensō Eiga to Eikoku no Josei Fuan," 53.

49. Asano Akira, in a roundtable discussion with Satō Haruo et al., "'Shan-hai' Gappyō," ET, March 1937, 114; Takami Jun, in a discussion with Abe Tomoji, "Taidan: Eiga Hōdan," ET, February 1938, 77.

50. Ishikawa Tatsuzō and Niwa Fumio, "Jūgun Hōkoku," ET, January 1939, 83–87.

51. Ushihara Kiyohiko and Kinugasa Teinosuke, "Taidan: Chūshi, Nanshi Jūgun Hōkoku," ET, March 1939, 66–71.

52. Ushihara, "Taidan: Chūshi, Nanshi Jūgun Hōkoku," 70; Iijima Tadashi, "Eiga no Kokuminsei," ET, September 1938, 50–51; Iijima Tadashi, "Nihon Eiga ni Nozomu Mono," ET, November 1938, 86–89.

53. Itagaki Takaho, "Chikagoro Mita Bunka Eiga," ET, November 1939, 138–39. Also see Kasza, The State and the Mass Media, 129.

54. "Hariuddo Tokuhō: Nyūsu Ensaikuropejia," ET, November 1939, 82–83; "Han Nachi Eiga Ōkō," ET, January 1940, 152–53; Kimura Ihei, "Ryūkō to Wa-jutsu," ET, December 1939, 69–70.

55. Kimura, "Ryūkō to Wajutsu," 70.

56. Iijima Tadashi, "Eiga no Nikutai," ET, April 1940, 62–63. Ad for Ohinata Mura, ET, October 1940, 15.

57. Oda Nariaki, "Kokumin Seikatsu to Eiga," ET, January 1941, 46–47; "Sekai no Nikki," ET, January 1941, 85.

58. Itō Nobumi, "Eiga o yori ijō Jūyō seyo," ET, January 1941, 8–9; "Eiga Kanshō ni Kokoroe Okubeshi," ET, July 1941. The news photographer had reason to be nervous. Between 1937 and 1940, the highest number of instances of censorship by far were in the "sex-related" category under the "manners and morals" section. See the Home Ministry charts reproduced from Home Ministry material in Kasza, The State and the Mass Media, 238–39.

59. "Nyūsu Kyameraman 'Jūgun Hōkoku' Zadankai," *ET*, November 1941, 65–69. Ad for Reon Sengan Kuriimu, *ET*, November 1941, 64

THE HOUSEHOLD BECOMES MODERN LIFE

1. Okamoto Shigeo, "Seiyō Ryōri no Honshiki no Tabekata," *Shufu no Tomo* (hereafter *ST*), February 1923, 225–29.

2. Tanaka Hisara, "Saigo no Robō Sukecchi," *ST*, October 1923, 195–203. Uehara Shizuko et al., "Saiken no Tokyo ni taisuru Fujin no Yōkyū," *ST*, November 1923, 22–33.

3. A stem family was a multiple-generation family living in the same household, in which the relationship between family members extends vertically—for example, a household consisting of a married couple, their children and the husband's elderly parents. In the event an elderly man lived with his son and daughter-in-law, the man usually remained in his position as head of the family until his death.

4. Ogawa Shigejirō, "Furyō Shōjo no Kanka wa Ika ni Subekika?" *ST*, February 1918, 16–20. "Watakushi no Risō no Otto," *ST*, April 1918, 81–93. Katō Setsudō, "Danshi wa Ikanaru Fujin wo Sonkeisuruka," *ST*, December 1918. Yamada Waka et al., "Otto toshite dōiu Otoko wo Nozomu ka? Tsuma toshite dōiu Onna wo Nozumuka?" *ST*, January 1922, 27–41. "Gobunsō no Yutaka naru Suminomiyadenka no Gokinjō," *ST*, March 1922. "Renai to Kekkon Gō," special issue of *ST*, July 1922. "Cafe no Shōjo" (illustration of painting), *ST*, February 1923; "Seikatsu no Yōfūka wo Ika ni Miruka," *ST*, January 1923, 61–71.

5. Itō Mikiharu. *Kazoku Kokkakan*. (Mineruva Shobō, 1982), 2–4. Kano Masanao, *Fujin, Josei, Onna* (Iwanami Shoten, 1989), especially 102–4. It should also be kept in mind, however, that a household-based division of labor, based on Western bourgeois notions of monogamy and shared family time activity had been in place since the turn of the century. The magazine *Katei Zasshi* had first appeared in 1892, and the term *shufu* first gained currency at that time. See Ueno Chizuko, "Kaisetsu," *Fūzoku Sei*, vol. 23 of *Nihon Kindai Shisō Taikei*, ed. Ogi Shinzō, Kumakura Isao, Ueno Chizuko (Iwanami Shoten, 1990), 505–18. No laws or policy changes emerged from the debate. Margit Nagy, "'How Shall We Live?'" Katō Akemi, "'Minpō Kaisei Yōkō' to Josei," in *Onnatachi no Kindai*, ed. Kindai Joseishi Kenkyūkai (Kashiwa Shobō, 1978), 228–54. My argument closely follows Katō's analysis of state intervention as regards education, the *shojokai*, and the *fujinkai*. See Katō, 249–53.

6. Kano, *Fujin, Josei, Onna*. Manipulation could work both ways. Isono Seiichi and Isono Fujiko, *Kazoku Seido* (Iwanami Shoten, 1958), 100–104. Okamoto Ippei et al., "Otto, Saikun, Koibito Sōjūhō," *ST*, August 1927, 86–91.

7. For excellent documentation of the debate regarding revision of the code and the discourse surrounding the debate, see Nagy, "'How Shall We Love?'" 198–219, 255. See also *Nihon Fujin Mondai Shiryō Shūsei*, vol. 5: Yuzawa, ed., *Kazoku Mondai*. For an article from 1924 on the destruction of the family which

listed the end of the family as an economic unit, the power of the state, and the extension of individualism as three reasons for the collapse of the patriarchal system, see Kawada Shirō, "Kachōsei Kazoku Soshiki no Hōkai Kazoku Seido Hōkai no Kun," ibid., 438–53.

8. "Katei Hōritsu Sōdan," ST, December 1929, 345.

9. Fukasaku Yasubumi Kaitei Gendai Joshi Shūshin (Okura Kobundō, 1931), 41–43, 47–48, 60, 64–65.

10. "Wakai Shinshi no Nozomu Risō no Hanayome," ST, May 1917, 71–74.

11. Mitsukoshi, "Shōrai Yūbō no Seisen Naraba," in "Watashi no Risō no Otto," ST, April 1918, 83–85. "Watashi no Risō no Otto," ST, April 1918, 81–93.

12. Yamada Waka, "Hontō no Imi no Otokorashiki Otoko wo," in "Otto toshite dōiu Onna wo Nozomuka," ST, January 1922, 27–30. For Yamada's ideal, "Otto toshite Douiu Otoko wo Nozomuka? Tsuma toshite Douiu Onna wo Nozomuka," ST, January 15, 1922, 27–30. The requirement of a "large heart" rated as the fifth of thirteen requirements in "Watashi no Risō," ST, April 1918, 90. This quality was referred to as "a grand personality" in Uehara Sawayo, "Onna wo Ikashite Yukuhodo no Danshi wo," ST, January 1923, 35.

13. Yamada Waka, "Hontō no Imi no Otokorashiki Otoko wo," 27–29.

14. Asō Yutaka, "Nanigotonimo Tsutsushimi no Fukai Fujin wo Nozomu," in "Watashi wa Donna Fujin, Danshi to Kekkon wo Nozomuka?" ST, April 1926, 23. "Yome yori Shūtome e no Yokkyū, Shūtome yori Yome e no Yokkyū," ST, May 1922, 20–24.

15. "Gendai Chimei Fujin no Otto Shirabe," ST, January 1926, 135–43. See an article regarding famous people, including a sumo wrestler and a woman in androgynous hairstyle, "Fūfu Enman Tetsugaku," ST, April 1936. Those accounts were a far cry from the anxiety-ridden letters written by brides-to-be who were plagued by such issues as the fear of venereal disease and the need to prove one's virginity. "Kekkonmae ni Shitteokitai Koto no Sōdankai," ST, May 1932, 314–21.

16. "Kekkon shite Ichiban Komatta Koto wa Nanika," ST, April 1926, 16–21.

17. Nitobe Inazō, "Otto no Ikujinashi wo Nageku Tsuma e," ST, March 1917, 10–13; "Rikon Shita Hitobito no Kanashiki Monogatari," ST, August 1924 32–39; "Fūfu Seikatsu no Himitsu Tankenki," ST, March 1927, 45–46; Kagawa Toyohiko, "Konaki ga Yueni Rikonsen to Suru Tsuma no Nayami," ST, September 1932, 206; Hatoyama Haruko, "Rikon Shiyouka Dou Shiyouka Mayou Fujin no Minoue Sōdan, " ST, September 1932, 213–18; "Rikon shita Hitobito no Kanashiki Monogatari," ST, August 1926, 32.

18. "Hōtei ni Mochidasareta Fūfu no Arasoi," ST, November 1936, 112–21. The views regarding divorce are substantiated by scholarly findings. Taimie Bryant notes that Japan had the highest divorce rate in the world between 1882 and 1916. She cites the findings of Japanese scholars that divorce and remarriage were highest among agricultural families who were in need of farm labor. The divorce rate continually decreased after the turn of the century. See "Mediation of Divorce Disputes in the Japanese Family Court System: With Emphasis on the Tokyo Family Court" (Ph.D. diss., University of California, Los Angeles,

1984). Takashi Fujitani has determined that between 1881 and 1897 one of three marriages ended in divorce, in Tokyo, half of all marriages were dissolved (*Splendid Monarchy*, 187–88).

19. "Tsuma kara Otto e no Chūmon Nijukkajō," *ST*, April 1917, 82–85; "Fūfu Waga no Jū Hiketsu," *ST*, June 1917, 30–33; "Fūfu Genka Yobō Hiketsu Hyakkajō," *ST*, June 1929, 46–51; "Fūfu Wagō no Hijutsu Yonjūhatte," *ST*, August 1931, 114–28.

20. "Fūfu Wagō no Hijutsu Yonjūhatte," *ST*, August 1931, 114–28.

21. "Fūfu Genka no Hisshōhō Jukkajō," *ST*, May 1932, 126–33.

22. "Watashi wa naniyue ni Kekkon shinaika," *ST*, February 1922, 46–49.

23. "Oyome ni Ikitagaranu? Gendai Musumesan Bakari no Zadankai," *ST*, September 1936, 100–109.

24. "Kateigai ni okeru Fujin no Atarashiki Ninmu," *ST*, June 1917, 2–10.

25. "Samazama na Konnan to Tatakatte Shokugyō ni Seikō shita Fujin no Keiken," *ST*, May 1919, 27–44; "Gendai no Fujin Shokugyō to Shūshoku Annai," *ST*, April 1924, 220–22; "Mezurashii Fujin, Kawatta Fujin no Hōmonki," *ST*, February 1926, 82–87. See also "Jokyū to natte Hataraku Wakaki Kyōdai," *ST*, September 1924, 6–9; "Binbō to Arasoinagara Kugaku shite Seikō shita Fujin," *ST*, January 1927, 45–46.

26. "Mohan Jokōsan no Jokō Seikatsu wo Kataru Zadankai," *ST*, June 1933, 140–53. The statement regarding magazines as friends is consistent with Kimura Ryōko's point that the editorial policy of *Shufu no Tomo* was to reach all who had completed elementary school, a category that would include working-class women. It also confirms her discussion of the highly personalized relationship between the *Shufu no Tomo* reader and her magazine. Kimura Ryōko, "Fujin Zasshi no Jōhō Kūkan to Josei Taishū Dokusha no Seiritsu," *Shisō*, February 1992, 236, 244.

27. "Godai Depaato Daihyō Joten'in Zadankai," *ST*, September 1935, 198–212.

28. "Utsukushii Moderu Onna no Zadankai," *ST*, October 1935, 142–58.

29. "Otoko no Tachiba kara Renai to Kekkon wo Kataru Zadankai." *ST*, January 1937, 102–13.

30. Kikuchi Kan, "Gendai Kekkonron," *ST*, October 1937, 122–28.

31. "Osaka no Musume san ga Kekkon no Risō wo Kataru Zadankai," *ST*, March 1938, 92–99.

32. Nishikawa Yūko, "The Changing Form of Dwellings and the Establishment of the *Katei* (Home) in Modern Japan," *U.S.-Japan Women's Journal*, English Supplement, no. 8 (1995): 23, 24, 27, 33, 34. Nishikawa, *Shakuya to Mochiie no Bungakushi: "Watashi" no Utsuwa no Monogatari* (Sanseidō, 1998), 5. "Hijōji ni Shosuru Katei no Junbiwa?" *ST*, May 1933, 75.

33. Wakakuwa Midori, *Sensō ga Tsukuru Joseizō* (Chikuma Shobō, 1995), 145–49. "Jihenka ni Hataraku Fujin no Mondai," *ST*, May 1940, 82–91.

34. Yamada Waka, "Beikoku Daitōryō Fujin to Kaiken suru ki: Rōzuberuto Fujin ni Nippon no Hahagokoro wo Toku," *ST*, February 1938, 84–89.

35. Tanaka Hisara, "Mogako to Moborō," *ST*, September 1928, 94–97; October 1928, 128–31; December 1928, 188–91.

36. Tanaka, "Mogako to Moborō," *ST*, September 1928, 94.

37. Tanaka, "Mogako to Moborō," *ST*, October 1928, 128–29.

38. "Mogako to Moborō," *ST*, October 1928, 131. For the episode "The Tale of Atami Hot Springs," part 2, in which Mogako cuts holes in the hat, see *ST*, December 1928, 188.

39. Nakajima Rokurō, "Manga Fuirumu, Makoto no Bijin," *ST*, January 1927, 86–89.

40. The presence of an orthodoxy does not necessarily mean that the orthodoxy is adhered to. See Gluck, *Japan's Modern Myths*. For Fujitani's revisionist application of Foucault to Meiji Japan, see *Splendid Monarchy*, 144–45. His discussion of the "production of an image of the imperial family as a nuclear family" supports my interpretation of the representation of imperial family members as members of *katei* (*Splendid Monarchy*, 239). Gluck's entire book is about such myth-making. See her epilogue regarding the enduring sense of belonging to a *kokumin*.

41. Pictures of the Shōwa emperor, *ST*, April 1930. The captions read "Tennō Kōgō Ryōheika to Terunomiya Denka" and "Hakone no Otsudoi: Chichibu, Takamatsu no Miya Ryōdenka Narabini Asaka no Miya Dōhi Ryōdenka to Ōji Ōjo Denka." *ST*, April 1930. Such an interpretation is not a stretch of the imagination if one considers Makise Kikue's account of how her mother and older brother had snickered at the Taishō emperor and how her mother had told him "Everybody speaks ill of the Emperor when they're in the shadows. They have no problem in crumpling up newspaper pages with his photograph and taking them into the toilet." Makise Kikue, "Jibunshi no Naka no Tennōsei," in *Josei to Tennōsei*, ed. Kanō Mikiyo (Shisō no Kagakusha, 1979), 139. Nevertheless, some people clearly believed that the emperor was either a god or different from other human beings. For the results of a survey on this issue, see Kamishima Jirō, "Atogaki ni Kaete," in *"Tennōsei" Ronshū*, ed. Kamishima Jirō and Kuno Osamu (San'ichi Shobō, 1974, 1976), 453–54. I have used the term *leper* to represent Japanese attitudes toward Hansen's disease during the prewar era, when the state was increasingly isolating sufferers from society. The empress dowager prominently advertised this process in a positive fashion. Tokutomi Ichirō, "Kōtaigō no Gojintoku," *ST*, August 1932, 126–30.

42. "Hatsu no Sekku o Mukaesasetamau Kōtaishi Denka Goyōiku no Onmoyō," *ST*, May 1934, 74–79; Tokutomi Ichirō, et al., "Seijō Heika no Goseitoku ni Kangekishita Hitobito no Kinwashū," *ST*, January 1935, 68–75. The full-page photo of the crown prince appears in *ST*, January 1935. Tokutomi Ichirō, "Gakumon ni Hijō ni Gonesshinna Tennō Heika," *ST*, January 1935, 74–95.

43. Advertisement for *kindaiteki* cosmetics, *ST*, March 1932. "Katei de Dekiru Kindaiteki no Hanayome no Okeshō to Kitsuke Gahō," *ST*, October 1933, 67–82.

44. "Tokyo Onna to Osaka Onna no Jiman Gassen," *ST*, May 1936, 470–76.

45. "Modan Tokyo Yakei Arubamu," *ST*, July 1936, 55–69.

46. "Modan Shinkon Shashin Senryū," *ST*, July 1937, 307–12; Tanaka Kinuyo and Uehara Ken, "Shinkatei Manzai," *ST*, September 1936 26–33.

47. Tokutomi Ichirō, "Watashi no Mita Gendai Sesō no Samazama," *ST,* September 1932, 114–17. "Taishū Shokudō no Hyōban Ryōri no Tsukurikata," *ST,* April 1934, 543–54.

48. "Eiga Monogatari: *Are,*" *ST,* August 1927, 65. The opening frame of the original movie *It* (Paramount, 1927) reads " 'It' is that quality possessed by some which draws all others with its magnetic force. With 'It' you win all men if you are a woman—and all women if you are a man. 'It' can be a quality of the mind as well as a physical attraction."

49. "Eiga Monogatari: *Are,*" 79.

50. "Eiga Monogatari: *Satan no Nageki,*" *ST,* June 1927, 63–85; "Eiga Monogatari: *Otoko Mirubekarazu,*" *ST,* August 1927, 63–83.

51. Tanaka Kinuyo and Uehara Ken, "Shinkatei Manzai," *ST,* September 1936, 31.

52. "Ichininmae Ichien de Dekiru Shinnen Enkai no Seiyō Ryōri no Tsukurikata," *ST,* January 1930, 356–62; "Sandouicchi no Tsukurikata," *ST,* April 1932, 84–88.

53. "Onenshi Mawari no Kyaku to Shujin," *ST,* January 1931, 18–21.

54. "Kenkō to Biyō kara Mita Suwarikata to Koshikakekata," *ST,* September 1936, 34–39.

55. "Odaidokoro Haiken," *ST* December 1933, 32–33.

56. See Sheldon Garon, *Molding Japanese Minds,* 132–33, and "Rethinking Modernization and Modernity in Japanese History: A Focus on State-Society Relations," *Journal of Asian Studies* 53, no. 2 (May 1994): 346–66. "Oshōgatsu no Risōtekina Okeshō to Kitsuke Gahō," *ST,* January 1936, 285–300; "Dansu Hōru wo Mitteisuru no Ki," *ST,* January 1936, 232–43; "Apaato Seikatsu no Taiken wo Kataru Zadankai," *ST,* October 1934, 146–55. As noted in Part 1, see Seidensticker, *Low City, High City,* 90–143, for the use of the term "double life." This term implies a hybrid culture, as opposed to a mosaic or a culture in montage.

57. "Apaato Seikatsu," 154. The discussants' class bias may be evident when they emphasize that they should not be confused with the unmarried residents of the newly built, suspicious-looking apartment buildings that have just gone up. One duplication of this modern phenomenon is the possibly apocryphal story (from more than a decade later) of the proud owner of one of the tract houses in Levittown, Long Island, walking into the wrong house.

58. "Otoko no Tachiba kara Ren'ai to Kekkon wo Kataru Zadankai," *ST,* January 1937, 102–13; "Sekai Taisen no Sanka wo Koetekita Doitsu, Furansu, Igirisu Taishi Fujin no Sokoku Ai," *ST,* October 1937, 88–93.

59. "Entatsu Achako Dai Tokyo Yaji Kita Manzai Tanbū," *ST,* November 1938, 90–97.

ASAKUSA EROTICISM

1. Nam-lin Hur, *Prayer and Play in Late Tokugawa Japan: Asakusa Sensōji and Edo Society* (Cambridge, MA: Harvard University Asia Center, distributed by Harvard University Press, 2000), 1–117 (for the list of *misemono,* see 60–61).

For a history of Asakusa during early-modern and modern times that includes key monuments, see Lippit, *Topographies of Japanese Modernism*, 140–44.

2. Kawabata Yasunari, *Asakusa Kurenaidan* (Senshinsha, 1930), facsimile ed. (Kindai Bungakukan, 1980); cited in text as KY. *Asakusa Kurenaidan* was originally serialized in the *Tokyo Asahi Shinbun* December 1929, January 1930, and February 1930. We are fortunate to have Alisa Freedman's careful and evocative English language translation of this complex text. Donald Ritchie's informed foreword is an important contribution. Kawabata Yasunari, *The Scarlet Gang of Asakusa*, trans. Alisa Freedman (Berkeley: University of California Press, 2005).

3. Gonda Yasunosuke, "Posutaa no Chimata: Asakusa no Minshū Goraku," *Minshū Goraku Mondai*, in Gonda, *GYS*, 1:268–78 (originally published in July 1921 by Dōjinsha Shoten). For a montage of groups, foods, and drinks, see p. 275.

4. Gonda, "Posutaa no Chimata," 271–75.

5. Gonda, "'Asakusa' o Chūshin toshite," *Minshū Goraku Mondai*, in Gonda, *GYS*, 1:279–86.

6. Gonda, "'Asakusa' o Chūshin toshite," 284–86.

7. Gonda, "Gorakuchi 'Asakusa' no Kenkyū," in Gonda, *GYS*, 4:174–230 (originally published in *Ōhara Shakai Mondai Kenkyūjo Zasshi*, March 1930). Gonda, "'Asakusa' o Chūshin toshite," 278, 282. The survey examined Asakusa with respect to several criteria: (1) population (numbers of males, females, and households); (2) "buildings" (Japanese versus Western, self-standing versus *nagaya*—the one-story row-house dwellings of Japanese workers—single versus multistory, business versus residential); (3) types of businesses (serving pleasure-seekers versus residents); (4) geographic subdivisions (buildings and facilities in the Temple section, the entertainment district, and the amusement area); (5) external analysis (entertainment facilities, amusement area, staffing of facilities, means of drawing in customers to separately listed theaters, including signs, photographs, flags, and lanterns, admission prices, total number and gender breakdown of employees in movie theaters and other sites [and types of amusements], types of eating and drinking places [Western, Chinese, tempura, etc.]); and (6) businesses catering to pleasure-seekers (restaurants, souvenir shops, toy stores, photography shops, etc.) versus Asakusa-specific businesses: religious icon shops, portrait businesses, fortune tellers, places to check belongings, and garages.

8. Gonda, "Shinsaiji ni Arawaretaru Goraku no Shokeisō," *Minshū Gorakuron*, in Gonda, *GYS*, 2:212–13. (*Minshū Gorakuron* was originally published in 1931, and the essay "Shinsaiji ni Arawaretaru Goraku no Shokeisō" originally appeared in 1924.) Gonda, *Minshū Gorakuron*, 225, 385–86, 240.

9. Gonda, "Iwayuru 'Modan Seikatsu' to Goraku," *Minshū Gorakuron*, 240–47. The quote is from p. 246. See Ōya Sōichi, "Modan Sō to Modan Sō."

10. Gonda, *Minshū Gorakuron*, 251–54.

11. Regarding class base, see Gonda, *Minshū Gorakuron*, 250. Gonda, "1930 nen no Kaiko: Eiga," in Gonda, *GYS*, 4:231–33 (originally published in *Nagoya Shinbun*, December 14, 1930.)

12. Soeda Azenbō's poem appears in Kawabata's *Asakusa Kurenaidan*, 40. Soeda Azenbō, *Asakusa Teiryūki*, vol. 2 of *Soeda Azenbō/Soeda Tomomichi Chosakushū* (Tosui Shobō, 1982). This work is cited hereafter in the text as SA. A part of this work, coauthored with his son Tomomichi, was originally published in *Kaizō* (May 1928), and the book was first published in 1930. (Although Tomomichi claimed to have written this guide to Asakusa, I am following the lead of Ozawa Shōichi who emphasizes the joint nature of their work. Kimura Seiya lists the books by father and by son separately and he has placed *Asakusa Teiryūki* with the works by Azenbō. At the time Soeda was given credit for carrying on and revitalizing the political, satirical ballads *(enka)* that had first emerged from within the People's Right Movement of the 1880s. See Ozawa Shōichi, "Kaisetsu," in Soeda, 267–68 and Kimura Seiya, *Soeda Azenbō. Tomomichi: Enka Nidai Fūkyōden* (Riburo Pōto, 1987), 12, 285.

13. Audre Lorde, "Uses of the Erotic: The Erotic as Power," in *Take Back the Night: Women on Pornography,* ed. Laura Lederer (New York: Morrow, 1980), 295–300.

14. For a sophisticated treatment of this issue, see Anne Allison, *Permitted and Prohibited Desires: Mothers, Comics, and Censorship in Japan* (Berkeley: University of California Press, 1996).

15. Ellen Willis points to the distinction made by Robin Morgan and Gloria Steinem between "erotica . . . based on mutual desire and affection" and "pornography" premised "on male domination and exploitation of women" ("Feminism, Moralism, and Pornography," in *Powers of Desire: The Politics of Sexuality,* ed. Ann Snitow, Christine Stansell, and Sharon Thompson [New York: Monthly Review Press, 1983], 463). This essay was originally written in 1979. Linda Williams, *Hard Core: Power, Pleasure, and the "Frenzy of the Visible"* (Berkeley: University of California Press, 1989), 30, 271.

16. Williams, *Hard Core,* 273.

17. Willis argues that pornography must "reflect a male outlaw mentality that rejects the conventions of romance" ("Feminism, Moralism, and Pornography," 461). I do not endorse that view here because all sex work in Asakusa was part of a romantically encoded sex culture. Nor do I side with Willis's rejection of relations, and a desire for self-abandon" or with Japanese feminist scholars who have referred to a "prostitution society" in Japan. Matsui Yayori, interviewed by Sandra Buckley in *Broken Silence: Voices of Japanese Feminism* (Berkeley: University of California Press, 1997), 140. Regarding the relativism, ambiguity, nuance, and overdetermination in eroticism, see Williams, *Hard Core,* 6, 9, 265, 277, 282n4.

18. Gonda, "Kibi Dango to Sukiyaki—Okayama to Kōbe no Minshū Goraku," *Minshū Goraku Mondai* in Gonda, GYS, 1:256. Gonda, "Gorakuchi 'Asakusa' no Kenkyū," 218–19.

19. Kon Wajirō, *Shinban Dai Tōkyō Annai,* 115–17. Gonda, "Posutaa no Chimata," 270–71.

20. Lippit captures the montage aspect of the novel in the following manner: "It is written in a fragmentary style, with the narrative moving from image

to image in rapid succession and frequently interrupted by anecdotes, myths, and reminiscences. Kawabata once described the style as akin to 'the succession of images in a newsreel film.'" Lippit, *Topographies*, 135–37. For a synopsis which is as cogent as his analysis of the form of *Asakusa Kurenaidan* (his translation is *Scarlet Gang of Asakusa*), see 125–26, 136. The novel was serialized in the evening edition of the *Tokyo Asahi Shinbun* from December 12, 1929, to February 16, 1930.

21. Maeda Ai, "Kawabata Yasunari 'Asakusa Kurenaidan'—Asakusa," *Genkei no Machi: Bungaku no Toshi o Aruku* (Shōgakkan, 1986), 146. Also see Maeda, *Toshi Kūkan no Naka no Bungaku* (Chikuma Shobō, 1982), 402–16.

22. Mary Russo makes the distinction between the "normal" (or prevailing standard) and the "ordinary" in her definition of "ordinary feminism" (*The Female Grotesque: Risk, Excess, and Modernity* [New York: Routledge, 1994], vii). Mary Ann Doane quotes Joan Riviere's discussion of masquerade as reaction-formation: "Womanliness therefore could be assumed and worn as a mask, both to hide the possession of masculinity and to avert the reprisals expected if she was found to possess it" ("Film and the Masquerade: Theorizing the Female Spectator," in *Issues in Feminist Film Criticism*, ed. Patricia Erens (Bloomington: Indiana University Press, 1990), 48–49.

23. Sue-Ellen Case, "Toward a Butch-Femme Aesthetic," in *Making a Spectacle: Feminist Essays on Contemporary Women's Theater* (Ann Arbor: University of Michigan Press, 1989), 292. Doane, "Masquerade Reconsidered: Further Thoughts on the Female Spectator," in *Femmes Fatales: Feminism, Film Theory, Psychoanalysis* (New York: Routledge, Chapman, and Hall, 1991), 38–39. Judith Butler cites varied feminist writings on masquerade, emphasizing that her concern "is whether masquerade conceals a femininity that might be understood as genuine or authentic, or whether masquerade is the means by which femininity and the contests over its 'authenticity' are produced" (*Gender Trouble: Feminism and the Subversion of Identity* [New York: Routledge, 1990], 48, 143). Russo says that "to put on femininity with a vengeance suggests the power of taking it off" (*The Female Grotesque*, 70).

24. For example, see Gonda "Asakusa wo Chūshin toshite," 269–86. *Shūkan Asahi*, ed., *Nedan no Fūzokushi* (*Shūkan Asahi*, 1987–1989), 1:23, 487, 601, 607.

25. Reception analysis is of course a very tricky business, and I am only attempting to glean the flavor of film culture from select sources from and about Asakusa during the modern era.

26. Iwasaki Akira, "Shihonshugi Eiga Hattatsushi," in *Eiga to Shihonshugi* (Ōraisha, 1931), 16. According to Hansen, the mobilized gaze of the spectator could subvert the disciplining by capitalism, along with the general hierarchy of capitalism that "radically excluded women from the agency of the look." Miriam Hansen, *Babel and Babylon: Spectatorship in American Silent Film* (Cambridge, MA: Harvard University Press, 1991), 86. Iwasaki, "Eiga Hihyō no Mondai," in *Eiga Geijutsushi* (Sekaisha, 1930), 131–34.

27. Iwasaki, "Hitostuno Keimōteki Zuihitsu," in *Eiga Geijutsushi*, 88–90, 92. It is not surprising that this leading figure in the proletarian film movement

would be writing about montage, for Soviet montage theory and film was then reaching Japan. Iwasaki himself included a translation of S. Timoschenko's *Film Art and Montage* in the 1930 anthology of his own writings. But Iwasaki saw the form as a world force; Pudovkin may have theorized about this "foundation of film art," but the method was invented in Hollywood before it moved to France. Iwasaki, "Montaaju no Hanashi," in *Eiga to Shihonshugi* (Ōraisha, 1931), 311–26 (originally published in *Shinkō Eiga*, March 1930).

28. "Eiga Ideorogii" and "Keikō Eiga no Mondai," in *Eiga to Shihonshugi*, 233, 235, 247.

29. Iwasaki, "Kyarifoorunian Rapusodii," in *Eiga Geijutsushi*, 2–12.

30. Iwasaki, "Kyarufoorunian Rapusodii," 10–12.

31. Iwasaki, "Amerika Higeki," in *Eiga Geijutsushi*, 61–74.

32. Iwasaki, "Amerika Higeki," 65, 72.

33. Iwasaki, "Ai no Ansorojii," in *Eiga Geijutsushi*, 43–50.

34. Iwasaki, "Tookii no Nendaiki," in *Eiga no Geijutsu* (Kyōwa Shoin, 1936), 204–94 (esp. 272, 278). The term *new* Babel first appeared in "Ōbei Eigakai no Zen'eiteki Shokeikō," in *Eiga Geijutsushi*, 140. "Amerika Eigaron," in *Eiga to Shihonshugi*, 36.

35. Iwasaki was arrested on January 24, 1940. See Iwasaki, *Nihon Eiga Shishi* (Tokyo Asahi Shinbunsha, 1977), 5. "Eiga to Ongaku no Mondai," in *Eiga no Geijutsu*, 122.

36. Iwasaki, "Shina Eiga Inshōki," in *Eiga no Geijutsu*, 163–64.

37. Iwasaki, "Voeeto ni okeru Mondaaju ron," *Eigaron* (Mikasa Shobō, 1936), 118–19, 121. Iwasaki, "Shina Eigaron," in *Eiga no Geijutsu*, 153. See Stefan Tanaka, *Japan's Orient: Rendering Pasts into History* (Berkeley: University of California Press, 1993), for an explanation of meanings attached to the term *Shina*.

38. Ozaki, "Eiga Mansō, II," 315–16, 320–21 in *Ozaki Midori Zenshū* (Sōjunsha, 1979, 1980). Ernaux quoted in Madeleine Blais, review of *A Frozen Woman, Four Walls, Eight Windows*, by Anne Ernaux, *Los Angeles Times*, 13 August 1995, book review section.

39. Ozaki, "Eiga Mansō, II," 318–19; "Tsue to Bōshi no Henshitsusha," 359–65; "Mokuzu," 157; "Eiga Mansō, III," 331; "Eiga Mansō, IV," 337, all in *Ozaki Midori Zenshū* (Sōjunsha, 1979). Ozaki uses the second half of the compound of *seikatsu* for the word *ikasu* (to make alive).

40. Ozaki, "Eiga Mansō, I," in *Ozaki Midori Zenshū* (Sōjunsha, 1979), 310–11.

41. Ozaki, "Eiga Mansō, IV," 345, 347–48.

42. See, for example, Iijima Tadashi, *Shinema no ABC* (Kōseikaku Shoten, 1929), and *Eiga no Mikata* (Bunshōsha, 1943), 1–3, 8, 10, and passim.

DOWN-AND-OUT GROTESQUERIE

1. Yoshimi Shun'ya notes that the factory zone built in Honjō and Fukagawa, whose denizens crossed the Sumida River to become Asakusa customers,

inspired Gonda to study people at play. Here *down-and-out* refers to those below this level of society, those who did not even have the money to pay for the Asakusa specialty of Electric brandy, to go to the movies, or to partake of the beef on rice mentioned by Yoshimi in *Toshi no Doramaturugii* (Kōbundō, 1987, 1992), 216–18.

2. See Mikhail Bakhtin, *Rabelais and His World*, trans. Helene Iswolsky (Bloomington: Indiana University Press, 1984), 21–22, 52, 91, 367. Susan Stewart, *On Longing: Narratives of the Miniature, the Gigantic, the Souvenir, the Collection* (Durham, NC: Duke University Press, 1984, 1993), 103–14. Russo, *The Female Grotesque.*

3. Russo, *The Female Grotesque,* 7, 63. Peter Stallybrass and Allon White, in *The Politics and Poetics of Transgression* (Ithaca, NY: Cornell University Press, 1986) expand on the notion of a folkloric carnivalesque grotesquerie in order to examine the politics of binary extremism in class society.

4. Articles appearing in *Gurotesuku* included Umehara Hokumei, "Sekai Benjo Hattenshi" (September 1929, 170–73); Ueda Kyosuke, "Shina Akushoku kō" (November 1929, 8–22); Matsuura Sensaburō, "Meiji Misemono kō" (April 1931, 2–24); Shibuya Okan, "Georugu Gurosu" (July 1929, 248–63); Miyakawa Mangyo, "Edo Jidai no Mobo to Moga" (March 1929, 134–45); Matsuura Sensaburō, "Onnazumo" (January 1930, 138–48); Sakai Kiyoshi, "Resubiennu" (December 1928, 16–20); "Neguro Buyō no Joo, Jyosefiinu Beekaa" (March 1929, no page number). Its republication commemorative issue featured a roundtable, "Kinsei Gendai Zenkoku Gokunai Ryūchijo Taiken Zadankai" (April 1931, 235–59). Umehara Hokumei, "Hinin Kojiki kō" (November 1928, 116–33; December, 1928, 95–135). For an account of the journal, see Umehara Masaki, "Zasshi 'Gurotesuku' no Shūhen: Shōwa Ero Guro Bunka ni tsuite" *Dentō to Gendai* 17 (September 1972): 140–50.

5. Stallybrass and White, *Politics and Poetics of Transgression,* 4, 23, 26, 44, 56.

6. Theodore M. Porter, *Trust in Numbers: The Pursuit of Objectivity in Science and Public Life* (Princeton, NJ: Princeton University Press, 1995), 33, 37.

7. Soeda also notes that there is a category of drinking establishment catering to the rickshaw men and to low-level factory workers, but the workers are not members of the down-and-out communities in the drifter heaven that is Asakusa.

8. Yoshimi, *Toshi,* 59.

9. Kawabata describes beggars enjoying movie billboards (KY, 22).

10. Ishizumi Harunosuke, "Kojiki Ritan," in *Ryūmin*, vol. 4 of *Kindai Minshū no Kiroku*, ed. Hayashi Hideo (Shin Jinbutsu Ōraisha, 1971), 328–95. For a biography of Ishizumi, see "Kaidai" in Hayashi, 599. Other works by Ishizumi include *Asakusa Keizaigaku, Asakusa Onna Ritan,* and *Gakuya Ritan.* Ishizumi, "Kojiki Ritan," 329–30. For a history of beggars and entertainers that recognizes both restrictions by the Tokugawa order and the importance of agency, see the recent works by Herman Ooms, including *Tokugawa Village Practice: Class, Status, Power, Law* (Berkeley: University of California Press,

1996). I find Ooms's term *micro-practice* useful in thinking about the agency expressed by the practices of the down-and out communities in Asakusa during the modern years.

11. Ishizumi, "Kojiki Ritan," 331–50. Ishizumi placed the last four occupations into the category of pseudo-beggar. These were the *takari*, or delinquent children; the *gase*, or prostitutes who served the beggars; the *takamono*, or travelling entertainers (sometimes called *tsubu*); and the *kadozuke* or "at-the-gate" women, low-level beggar-entertainers, who performed at the front gates of houses (351–76). Ishizumi compared the income of the *kenta* from the five sites for the summer of 1927 to that of March 1929: the average income for a ten-hour day had been twenty sen (336–37). Regarding *nawabari* and fights among *shiroi*, see 348–49.

12. Ishizumi, "Kojiki Ritan," 347, 348.

13. Ishizumi, "Kojiki Ritan," 329–30, 331, 333. Shiomi Sen'ichirō, *Danzaemon to Sono Jidai: Senmin Bunka no Doramatsurugii* (Hihyōsha, 1993), 29, 105, 107. Shiomi notes that traveling entertainers, considered to be beggars because, like the *hinin*, they took money, were also expelled from Tokyo after the Restoration (41–42). Of course, Soeda's work shows that this restriction did not hold.

14. Ishizumi, "Kojiki Ritan," 333, 335, 359–60. For references to the beggars' *kenpō*, see, for example, 335, 347. He used the term *gendairashii* (of the present) to refer to the modern. Also see Kawabata, KY, 130.

15. Ishizumi, *Kojiki Ritan* (Seibunsha, 1929), reprinted as *Kindai Nihon no Kojiki* (Akashi Shoten, 1996), 114–16 (94–96 of original edition). I cite this recent edition here because it includes Ishizumi's discussion of Korean and Chinese vendors, which was omitted from the original edition. Arai Sen'o's visual catalog of this Asakusa grotesquerie captures an aspect not mentioned by either Soeda or Ishizumi: it was impossible to distinguish between the clothing and the housing of the Asakusa *bohemian* beggars, for they wore all their acquisitions and possessions on their persons. Arai, "Kojiki no Fūzoku," in Kon and Yoshida, *Moderunologio*, 269–71.

16. The term *donzoko* was made popular by the production of *The Lower Depths* in 1913.

17. See Yoshimi, *Toshi*, 248. Soeda notes that this weapon is brought out by officials whenever the topic of vagrancy is raised. It includes under the heading of profession such jobs as *handbill* distributor, trash collector, candy vendor, porter, street laborer, scavenger, miner, carpenter, and plasterer. He lists different wages, and the official average daily wage for a vagrant is given as seventeen sen five rin (SA, 155).

18. Kawabata was probably writing from experience in *Asakusa Kurenaidan* when he also noted that vagrants tended to move away from the surveyors. Kawabata must have read the dialogue between two vagrants in Soeda's *Asakusa Teiryūki* about an alcoholic acquaintance who is prone to violence: "One wonders whether this man has escaped from a hospital." The response: "No way that's possible. He's poor, so they can't send him to the hospital, and

they didn't know what to do with him, so they discarded him here on this isle; there are indeed all sorts of mental hospitals" (SA, 41).

Elaborating on how the bureaucrat is constrained, Theodore Porter says, "This is power not in Stalin's sense, but Foucault's. Potentially, at least, it can constrain the administrators almost as much as it constrains the workers. Quantification provided authority, but this is authority as Barry Barnes defines it: not power plus legitimacy, but power minus discretion" (Porter, *Trust in Numbers*, 98). Regarding numbers turning people into objects, and the relationship between power and a quantitative approach, see 77, 98, 195.

19. Kusama Yasoo, *Furōsha to Baishunfu no Kenkyū* (Bunmei Kyōkai, 1927): 27–29. Isomura Eiichi, "Jobun," *Hinmingai*, vol. 1 of *Kindai Kasō Minshū Seikatsushi*, ed. Isomura Eiichi and Yasuoka Norihiko (Akashi Shoten, 1987; hereafter cited as *KKMS*), 6. Like Gonda during the early years of his career, Kusama had an ambiguous relationship to the bureaucracy.

20. Kusama Yasoo, "Tsuyu no Yo ni Mitaru Kyūmin," in *Kindai Toshi Kasō Shakai* (hereafter *KTKS*), ed. Isomura Eiichi and Yasuoka Norihiko (Akashi Shoten, 1990), 2:1092–93 (originally published in *Shakai Jigyō* 5, no. 4 [July 1921]). One illustration of Kusama's awareness of group cohesion is his discussion of how a simpatico group would choose to sleep together, form a mutual-aid group, and share the scavenged leftovers equally. See, for example, Kusama Yasoo, *Furōsha to Baishunfu no Kenkyū*, *KKMS*, 1:39–40. This practice is also described by Soeda (SA, 162).

21. Kusama Yasoo, "Antei wo Tadayou Furōsha no Baiin to Tobaku," in *Kindai Nihon no Donzoko Shakai* (hereafter *KNDS*), ed. Yasuoka Norihiko (Akashi Shoten, 1992), 309–12 (originally published in *Kindai Manzai Kagaku Geppō*, no. 2 [December 1929]). My discussion of prostitutes is limited to *onna furōsha* because I focus on the grotesque social order within Asakusa Park. Kusama, however, published extensively on women engaged in sex work, seeing social circumstances as largely to blame for their plight. See for example, *Akari no Onna Yami no Onna* (Genrinsha, 1937); reprinted in *KTKS*, 2:769–1184.

22. Kusama Yasoo, "Rumpen Monogatari," *KNDS*, 351–58 (originally published in *Shinchō*, February 1932).

23. "Kigekio ga Setsunaru Negai, Omatsuri Sawagi no Kangei Zettai ni Okotowari," *Tokyo Asahi Shinbun*, April 3, 1932. See also Sagara Koji, "Chappurin Sobyō," *Tokyo Asahi Shinbun*, April 16–19, 1932. Regarding Chaplin's "views on life," see the two-part article by Ishikawa Kin'ichi, "Chappurin no Jinseikan," *Tokyo Nichinichi Shinbun* (hereafter cited as *TNS*), April 5–6, 1932. Also see Kishi Matsuo, "Teiō Chappurin no Yokogao," and Ōguro Toyoji, "Chappurin Shusse no Ashiato," in the "Tokushu Chappurin Kangei" section of *ET*, June 1930, 59–72. For the comparison of Chaplin to René Claire, see Iijima Tadashi, "Chaarii Chappurin—Sakuhin wo Chūshin to shite," *Kinema Junpō* (hereafter cited as *KJ*), May 11, 1932, 34–35; and "Fuan no Taibō Hisashii 'Jiyu wo Warerani,'" *TNS*, May 5, 1932. For Chaplin's statement that he was a friend of the poor, see "Kigekio no Tetsugaku, Watashi wa Hinja no Tomo," *TNS*, May

15, 1932. The *Tokyo Asahi Shinbun* refers to his Dickensian boyhood and the role of Chaplin as *lumpen* in *The Kid*. See Mori Iwao, "Waratte Bakari Mirarenu Kare no Eiga," *Tokyo Asahi Shinbun*, March 27, 1932.

24. "The Best Pictures of 1926," *KJ*, April 11, 1927, 11. "Chappurin Tenrankai," *Tokyo Asahi Shinbun*, May 14, 1932. "Sekai Eigakai no Ijin Chappurin Tenrankai," *KJ*, May 1, 1931, 77. For an account of how "our Charlie" was greeted by a wild crowd of eighty thousand, see "Michikusa wo Kutta Kigekiō Kyō Jōriku Daiippo," *TNS*, evening edition, May 14, 1932. "Teito no Akari ni Arawareta Chaarii," *TNS*, May 15, 1932. Also see "Hitogoroshi Sawagi no Kangei ni Kigekiō Sakuya Nyūkyō," *Miyako Shinbun*, May 15, 1932. "Kigekio Kyo Rainichi; Naganen no Nengan Kanatte," *TNS*, evening edition, May 15, 1932; and "Kigekio Tsui ni Kuru; Mirukara ni Kōshinshi!" *Tokyo Asahi Shinbun*, evening edition, May 15, 1932. For the caramel and *bushidō*, see *Tokyo Asahi Shinbun*, May 15, 1932. *Miyako Shinbun*, May 15, 1932, and *Tokyo Asahi Shinbun*, May 15, 1932. For an advertisement for "Welcome Charlie Chaplin Morinaga Milk Chocolate," see *TNS* May 15, 1932, and *Mainichi Shinbun*, May 17, 1932, 2. See also an androgynous-looking Chaplin in an ad for Smile eye drops, accompanied by fine print promoting a *"modern* patented container" (*TNS*, May 16, 1932). For a full-page advertisement for such products as Meiji Caramels and Utena Vanishing Cream passing as a series of stories passing as screenplays starring Chaplin, see "Sayonara Chappurin," *TNS*, May 27, 1932. The "screenplay" titles were "Chappurin no Bokushingu," "Chappurin no Kodomo Kyōjidai," and "Chappurin to Nihon Musume." Jingle from "Chappurin Kangei," *KJ*, May 11, 1932, 6–7.

25. The tracking of Chaplin's food intake expressed the determination by the press to document the extent to which Chaplin ventured outside his hotel room. See "Chappurin-kun, Beddo no Ue de Udetamago [*sic*] wo Futatsu," *Miyako Shinbun*, May 16, 1932. References to tempura extended even past Chaplin's twenty-day stay, as when, on June 11, *Kinema Junpō* queried in a heading, "Did He Get Tired of Eating 'Tempura'?" ("'Tenpura' mo Tabeakitaka? Chaarii sumiyaka ni kikoku," 7). See also "Chaarii Waraezu, Kyō Tonde Kaeru," *TNS*, June 2, 1932, and "Chaarii Kyo Nihon ni 'Guddobai,'" *Tokyo Asahi Shinbun*, June 3, 1932. Regarding the hat purchase, see "Chaarii Chikaku Kyoto e Kankanbō wo Kabutte," *Tokyo Asahi Shinbun*, May 25, 1932. See also "Chappurin shi no sutekki wa," *Miyako Shinbun*, May 17, 1932. The day after Chaplin's arrival, one heading exclaimed, "I Want to See Kabuki!" ("Kabuki ga Mitai! Kon'ya to iu Kon'ya wa Odoroita," *Tokyo Asahi Shinbun*, May 15, 1932). The newspaper chronicled his attendance at kabuki two days later in "Chaarii no Mikkame: Ukiyoe wo Mite Tsū wo Hakkishi, Shukugan no Kabuki Kenbutsu," *Tokyo Asahi Shinbun*, May 17, 1932. Also see "Nihon no Kabuki wa Sekai Ichi no Geijutsu to Chaarii-kun no Origami," *Miyako Shinbun*, May 19, 1932, and "Chappurin Kabuki Bitari," *Tokyo Asahi Shinbun*, May 19, 1932. For Chaplin's seclusion in the hotel, see, for example, "Nihon wo Minai to Heso wo Mageta Tetsudō," *TNS*, June 3, 1932, and "Kyō no Topikku: Nani ga Chaarii wo Yuutsu ni Shitaka," *KJ*, June 11, 1932, 8. For a reproduction of Chaplin's Fujiyama, see

"Chappurin no Kaita Fujiyama," *Tokyo Asahi Shinbun,* May 25, 1932. For reference to gypsy blood, "Sugao no Chaarii Chapurin," *Osaka Asahi Shinbun* April 3, 1932. For Anglo-Saxon, see "Sabishiki Tetsugakusha no Ashiato," *Otaru Shinbun* June 9, 1932.

26. David Robinson, *Chaplin: His Life and Art* (New York: McGraw-Hill, 1985), 440. "Sayonara! Kigekiō, Kyō Funade wo Mae ni Osekkyō," *TNS,* June 3, 1932.

27. "Nanatsu ni Natta Mikkii-kun," *ET,* February 1936, 90. Futaba Jūzaburō, "Marukusu Ichibannori," *ET,* January 1938, 124–25. Minami Yoshiko, "Hariwuddo Nyuu Goshippu," *ET,* January 1939, 110–12.

28. Iijima Tadashi, "Chaari Chappurin: Sakuhin wo Chūshin to shite," *KJ,* May 11, 1932, 34–35; "Aikoku Eiga Hihyō," *KJ,* February 1938, 47; Okada Shinkichi, "Chappurin no Shinsaku," *ET,* March 1936, 50; Yodogawa Nagaharu, "Chappurin to Shin Sakuhin 'Modan Taimusu,'" *ET,* December 1935, 76–77.

29. Kusama Yasoo et al., "Rumpen Zadankai," in *KNDS,* 325–50 (originally published in *Bungei Shunju,* February 1931). Kusama's essays usually appeared in journals focused on social policy and social work such as *Shakai Jigyō* and professional journals related to law enforcement, such as *Hanzai.*

30. Kusama et al., "Rumpen Zadankai," 327, 346. Garon, *Molding Japanese Minds.*

31. Kusama et al., "Rumpen Zadankai," 341, 346–49. My reading of Kusama's writings shows a (non-Marxist) critique of an inequitable social and economic order.

32. Kusama Yasoo, "Hoshi mo Kōru Kantenka no Nōjukugun: Rumpen Seikatsu no Jitchi Chōsa," in *KNDS,* 59–375 (originally published in *Asahi* 4, no. 2 [February 1932]).

33. Kawabata, quoted in Tamagawa Shinmei, *Boku wa Asakusa no Furyō Shonen: Jitsuroku Satō Hachirō Den* (Sakuhinsha, 1991), 47.

34. Tamagawa, *Boku wa,* 46. In addition, *Asakusa Kurenaidan (zoku)* appeared in *Kaizō,* September 1930. See also Kawabata, "Asakusa Aka Obikai," *Shinchō,* September 1930.

35. Kusama, *Furyōji,* in *KKMS,* 3:1607–1910 (originally published by Genrinsha, 1936).

36. Kusama, *Furyōji,* 1827–42. Now as in the past, the *enko* (the inversion of *koen,* the word for park) is the destination for runaways. During the Edo period youth gangs called *choyatsu* had terrorized citizens. From the Meiji era through the Taishō years, he recalled, these girls and boys had been lured into delinquency, and gang leaders ruled over delinquent *lumpen* and boy *lumpen.*

37. Kusama, *Furyōji,* 1846–47.

38. Regarding contemporary assessments of Kusama as "unscientific," see Yasuoka Norihiko, "Kaisetsu," in Kusama, *KTKS* 2:1477. Kusama, *Furyōji,* 1867–73.

39. Kusama, "Dai Tokyo no Chimata ni Shutsubotsu suru Furyō Shōnen," in *KTKS,* 2:1401–18 (originally published in *Shakai to Kyusai* 4, no. 11 [February 1921]). Kusama, "Asakusa ni Nozomi Furyō Shōnen Shōjo wo Miru," in

KTKS, 2:1419–21 (originally published in *Shakai Jigyō* 11, no. 6 [September 1927]). Kusama, *Furyōji*, 1905–9. Kusama must have considered himself one of the responsible persons. In 1936 he also called poverty and crime a social disease and quoted from children's compositions to illustrate their "spiritual life." Among the chosen texts were the descriptions of several policemen arresting a *hinin*. A sixth-grader concludes that the man's fate could not be helped because he had not worked diligently in his youth, and a girl in the third grade sympathizes with "Mr. Soldier in Manchuria," who must be suffering from the cold. Kusama, "Donzoko no Hitotachi," *KKMS*, 1:592–616 (originally published by Genrinsha, 1936).

40. Wada Nobuyoshi, "Tekiya Ōgisho," in *Ryūmin*, 245–312 (originally published between 1926 and 1929 in *Bungei Shijo* and *Sandee Mainichi*). See the editor's notes on Wada, *Ryūmin*, 596–97.

41. Wada, "Tekiya Ōgisho," 246–47. As in vagrant and delinquent society, these are the fictive kin notions of *oyabun* (to whom the hawker is the *kobun* or follower) and the tie between older and younger brother.

42. The discussion of dishonesty is almost an afterthought for Wada, who notes that dishonesty among hawkers can result in provincial or nationwide sanctions (Wada, "Tekiya Ōgisho," 261–63).

43. Wada's list of over fifty-five stalls near the entrance to the Mitsukoshi department store in front of Shinjuku Station is instructive, as is his distinction between mere street vendors and hawkers and his listing of the fifteen categories of *tekiya* recognized by the hawkers themselves. Hawkers who appear in the same place nightly in specific sites, including Asakusa, are called *hirabi*. Wada, "Tekiya Ōgisho," 252–54, 266, 287.

44. Wada, "Tekiya Ōgisho," 302. For similar formulations, see Gordon, *Labor and Imperial Democracy*. For hawkers' "thought activities," see Wada, 301–12.

45. Wada, "Tekiya Ōgisho," 250. Usui Seizō, "Furōsha no Nikki," in *Kindai Minshū no Kiroku*, 4:212.

46. Wada, 266–68, 296–300. For an excellent overview of Cockney, see William Matthews, *Cockney Past and Present: A Short History of the Dialect of London* (New York: E. P. Dutton, 1938). See also Peter Wright, *Cockney Dialect and Slang* (London: Batsford, 1981).

47. Apparently back slang exists in all European languages and in Hindustani as a means of expressing contempt. See Julian Franklyn, *The Cockney: A Survey of London Life and Language* (London: Deutsch, 1953), 298. The British underclass seems much more preoccupied with the body, as reflected in the numerous terms for face (according to Wright, because of the need for violence to the face) and for eyes, nose, ears, mouth, and hands. Regarding Cockney terms for the body, see also Wright, *Cockney Dialect*, 36, and Matthews, *Cockney Past and Present*, 125. For Wada's glossary, which devotes a section to monetary denominations, see Wada, "Tekiya Ōgisho," 296–300.

48. Stewart, *On Longing*, 109.

49. Asakura Musei, *Misemono Kenkyū* (Shibunkaku Shuppan, 1977, 1988),

139, 285. This work first began appearing in the August 1916 issue of *Chūō Kōron* and first appeared in book form in 1928. The video title is *Oto to Eizo to Moji ni yoru Nihon Rekishi to Geinō* (Heibonsha, 1991); see vol. 4, *Chūsei no Sairei*, and vol. 10, *Toshi no Shukusai*. Stewart, *On Longing*, 110. Amino Yoshihiko, Ozawa Shōichi, Miyata Noboru, et al., eds., *Daidōgei to Misemono*, vol. 13 of *Nihon Rekishi to Geinō* (Heibonsha, 1991). Russo, *The Female Grotesque*, 83.

50. Sigmund Freud, "The 'Uncanny,'" in *The Standard Edition of the Complete Psychological Works of Sigmund Freud*, translated under the general editorship of James Strachey, assisted by Alix Strachey and Alan Tyson (London: Hogarth Press, 1955), 220, 222, 234–36. Regarding Yumiko's identification with her sister, see KY, 37. A recent discussion of the uncanny in postmodern Australia, by Ken Gelder and Jane Jacobs, applies equally well to Asakusa:

> Freud's primary concern is certainly with the psyche, but the essay is also about one's sense of place in a modern, changing environment, and it attends to anxieties which are symptomatic of an ongoing process of realignment in the post-war modern world. In brief, Freud elaborates the "uncanny" by way of two German words whose meanings, which at first seem diametrically opposed, in fact circulate through each other. These two words are: *heimlich*, which Freud glosses as "home," a familiar or accessible place; and *unheimlich*, which is unfamiliar, strange, inaccessible, unhomely. An "uncanny" experience may occur when one's home is rendered, somehow and in some sense, unfamiliar; one has the experience, in other words, of being in place and 'out of place' simultaneously. This simultaneity is important to stress since, in Freud's terms, it is not simply the unfamiliar in itself which generates the anxiety of the uncanny; it is specifically the combination of the familiar and the unfamiliar—the way the one seems always to inhabit the other. (Gelder and Jacobs, *Uncanny Australia: Sacredness and Identity in a Postcolonial Nation* [Carlton, Australia: Melbourne University Press, 1998], 23)

Although I focus on the doubled aspect of Asakusa in *Asakusa Kurenaidan*, the theme of *heimlich* "developing in the direction of ambivalence" could undoubtedly be explored in this novel and in the documentary contributions of others. Marilyn Ivy also refers to uncanny doubles in her Lacanian gloss on the modern (what I would call the modern and the high modern if not the postmodern, as she covers Yanagita Kunio's era and the era following high-speed economic growth). Her subtle interpretation of the way the past has been conjured up within a nation-culture and her conclusion that "the modern uncanny also arises as the double of the modern subject" encourage much further analysis of what I have termed Japanese modern culture, along these lines. See Ivy, *Discourses of the Vanishing*, 28, 84, 85, 140.

51. Regarding the sale of candy as a front, see Ishizumi, "Kojiki Ritan," 385–86.

52. Kawabata's narrator recalls a Chinese girl performer of a decade earlier and refers to such foreigners—here he uses *gaikokujin*—as the miserable-looking American head of the *"water circus"* (KY, 147, 162, 165).

53. See the work of Kawamura Minato for very interesting formulations regarding the three-way conceptualization of power and culture. Kawamura, "Taishū Orientarizumu to Ajia Ninshiki," in *Bunka no Naka no Nihon*, vol. 7 of *Iwanami Kōza Kindai Nihon to Shokuminchi* (Iwanami Shoten, 1993), 107–36.

MODERN NONSENSE

1. Itami Mansaku, "Shin Jidai Eiga ni Kansuru Kōsatsu," *Itami Mansaku Zenshū* (Chikuma Shobō, 1961), 1:5–16 (originally published in *Eiga Kagaku Kenkyū*, April 1931). "Considerations on the New Period Film"—Itami recognized that there was a complexity of syntax and that the title given to him by the editors of *Studies in the Science of Film* could also be read as "Film of the New Era."

2. Yamada Seizaburō, ed., *Marukusushugi Bungei Sen'eigo Jiten* (Haku-yōsha, 1932), 160–61.

3. Hayden White, *Metahistory: The Historical Imagination in Nineteenth-Century Europe* (Baltimore: Johns Hopkins, 1973). Linda Hutcheon, *Irony's Edge: The Theory and Politics of Irony* (New York: Routledge, 1995), 2, 12, 17, 89.

4. Satō Hachirō, "Asakusa Nansensu," and "Keishi Sōkan ni Ataru no Sho," *Asakusa* (hereafter cited in text as SH; Seikōkan Shoten, 1932), 49–79, 265–84. Satō claimed that even Kusama Yasoo of the Social Bureau was ignorant of the practices of the girl delinquent Mine, who had invented a way of waylaying men by standing outside movie theaters, umbrella in hand, ready to escort them (19).

5. Hutcheon, *Irony's Edge*, 61–63.

6. I have already used the term *code-switching* to refer to the visual practice required of the reader of the illustrated movie magazines. Here it refers to recent formulations by linguists. See Lesley Milroy and Pieter Muysken, "Introduction: Code-Switching and Bilingualism Research," citing John Gumperz, in *One Speaker, Two Languages: Cross-Disciplinary Perspectives on Code-Switching*, ed. Milroy and Muysken (Cambridge: Cambridge University Press, 1995), 9–10. From Pierre Bourdieu, Monica Heller borrows the terms *symbolic capital* and *symbolic marketplaces*. The terms *speech economies* and *verbal repertoires* are from Gumperz, *Discourse Strategies* (Cambridge: Cambridge University Press, 1982). For Heller's discussion of Bourdieu and Gumperz, see Heller, "Code-Switching and the Politics of Language," in *One Speaker, Two Languages*, ed. Milroy and Muysken, 158–74.

7. Linda Hutcheon, *A Theory of Parody: The Teaching of Twentieth-Century Art Forms* (New York: Methuen, 1985), 37. The citation refers to Gilles Deleuze's *Difference et Repetition* (Paris: Presses Universitaires de France, 1968). Hutcheon also cites Susan Stewart's definition: "Substituting elements

within a dimension of a given text in such a way that the resulting text stands in an inverse or incongruous relation to the borrowed text" (36).

8. For representative overviews, see Uchiyama Sōjūrō, *Asakusa Opera no Seikatsu: Meiji Taishō kara Shōwa e no Nihon Kageki no Ayumi* (Yūzankaku, 1967), 145–49. For an English-language overview that relies heavily on Kawabata, see Seidensticker, *Tokyo Rising*, 74–87. Regarding the establishment of the Casino Folies, see Zakō Jun, *Asakusa Rokku (Enko) wa Itsumo Modan Datta* (Asahi Shinbunsha, 1984), 132–41.

9. Tamagawa Shinmei, *Boku wa*, 227–28; Ushijima Hidehiko, *Asakusa no Tomoshibi Enoken*, vol. 4 of *Mō Hitotsu no Shōwashi* (Mainichi Shinbunsha, 1979), 97.

10. Enomoto Ken'ichi, *Kigeki Hōdan Enoken no Seishun* (Meigensha, 1956), 190. Enomoto belonged to a merchant family that sold rice crackers in one of the wealthier Tokyo neighborhoods.

11. The Denki *Revue* that opened half a year before the Casino Folies made use of similar humor and a similar combination of genres. Ushijima has said that the term *phony* expressed disdain for the audience (*Asakusa no Tomoshibi*, 97). The event recounted in *Chūshingura* involved early eighteenth-century heroes whose samurai moral code had superseded and challenged the dictates of the feudal order. It had been canonized in a variety of theatrical and literary forms within weeks of their actual sentencing. For a sophisticated, historicist reading of the legend, see Samuel Hideo Yamashita, "Reading, Contesting and Consuming 'Revenge' in the Debate on the Akō Rōnin Affair" (paper presented at "Cultural Constructs, Social Representations in Japan," conference held at the University of California, Los Angeles, May 1993).

12. The discussion is premised on the existence of censorship, as in the discussion of the use of bloomers (as kimono sleeve guards). Although an actress cannot remove them on stage, censorship rules do not preclude her from lending them to a hero (Yasubei); she can be on her way home from shopping for bloomers and thus hand over the unused apparel to our hero. Satō and Enomoto were joined by Yanagida Teiichi, music arranger and leader of the Poupée Dansant troupe.

13. Hara Kentarō also quotes the comedian Furukawa Roppa, who first used the word *acharaka* in a poster advertising his group Warai no Ōkoku in 1933 or 1934. Roppa makes clear that the term had been in circulation in Asakusa before 1933 and had originally referred to things or people that had come from or come back from abroad. At some point the term took on the meaning of slapstick and lost the connotation of foreign. My sense is that both were intertwined. My position comes closest to Hara's contention that "*acharaka* should not be seen as a characteristic or method of comedy but as a spirit of protest both against everyday things in front of one and against existing power" (Hara, *Tōkyō Kigeki: Acharaka no Rekishi* [NTT Shuppan, 1994], 211–14).

14. Futabatei Shimei, *Ukigumo of Futabatei Shimei*, trans. Marleigh Grayer Ryan (New York: Columbia University Press, 1967).

15. Regarding the story of Enoken slugging a police officer who called him

Eroken, see Ushijima, *Asakusa no Tomoshibi*, 164–65. Uchiyama, *Asakusa Opera no Seikatsu*, 139–40. Hara, *Tōkyō Kigeki: Acharaka*, 98–100. Chapter 3 offers an excellent history that places the Asakusa Revue in the context of theater before and after the earthquake.

16. For gags regarding a bride, speed, and history, see Hara, *Tōkyō Kigeki: Acharaka*, 126. Regarding kabuki parodies, see Ushijima, *Asakusa no Tomoshibi*, 116.

17. Hara, *Tōkyō Kigeki: Acharaka*, 128.

18. Shimamura Ryūzō, "Rumpen Shakaigaku," in *Kajino Foorii Rebyuu Kyakuhonshū*, ed. Kajino Foorii Bungeibu (Chūshō Naigaisha, 1931), 2. One *tsubo* is approximately thirty-six square feet.

19. Shimamura, "Rumpen Shakaigaku," 8, 9, 14, 15, 17, 19, 20–21.

20. Shimamura, "Rumpen Shakaigaku," 27–28.

21. Shimamura, "Rumpen Shakaigaku," 25, 31–35. Hashimoto Yaoji, "Rumpen ni Megumu Haru," *Shūkan Asahi*, April 26, 1931.

22. *Mezhrabpom* (Storm over Asia), directed by Vsevolod Pudovkin (USSR, 1928).

23. Nakazawa Seitarō, "Konsen 'Ajia no Arashi,'" (hereafter NS), *Kajino Foorii Rebyuu Kyakuhonshū*, 155–212. Like "Rumpen Shakaigaku," this script must have been written before July 1931, when the introduction to the anthology of Casino Folies scripts was written.

24. Takeda Rintarō, *San Mon Opera*, in *Takeda Rintarō Zenshū*, vol. 1 (Shinchōsha, 1977), 142–58 (originally published in *Chūō Kōron*, July 1932). Takami Jun, *Ikanaru Hoshi no Moto ni*, vol. 32 of Shinchō Nihon Bungaku (Shinchōsha, 1970), 5–118 (originally serialized in *Bungei*, January 1939–March 1940).

25. Takeda refers to a "kindaiteki na toshi fūkei" (modern urban landscape) at the opening of the story (*San Mon Opera*, 142, 145).

26. Gordon, *Labor and Imperial Democracy*. Takeda, *San Mon Opera*, 154–58. Takeda does not adopt the documentary montage approach of Tokunaga Sunao's *Taiyō no nai Machi* about the Kyōdō printers' strike in 1926, but this is clearly fiction documenting labor strife.

27. Takeda, *San Mon Opera*, 154. The Nanyō (South Pacific) islands would constitute a separate *seimeisen*. See Sakakibara Shōji, *Shōwago: Rokujūnen Sesōshi* (Asahi Shinbunsha, 1986), 28.

28. The two comedians identified the characters in the roman à clef during their dialogue about the fate of the neighborhood and of their business at an Asakusa coffee shop in September 1939. See Zakō Jun, *Asakusa Rokku wa Itsumo*, 180–84. For Takami's formulation of the relationship among reality, fiction, and comedy *(manzai)*, see Takami, *Ikanaru Hoshi no Moto ni*, 69. Takami, *Ikanaru Hoshi no Moto ni*, 100–104.

29. Takami, *Ikanaru Hoshi no Moto ni*, 19. This reference to the working-class fare provides an ironic contrast to the use of the term "*okonomiyaki* liberalism" in *Eiga no Tomo*.

30. Takami, *Ikanaru Hoshi no Moto ni*, 56.

31. Takami, *Ikanaru Hoshi no Moto ni*, 42, 25–26, 29.

32. Takami, *Ikanaru Hoshi no Moto ni*, 31, 69–70, 77, 80, 118. For Takami's further parody of the names, see p. 80.

33. Hara, *Tōkyō Kigeki: Acharaka*, 307–12. *Tokyo Asahi Shinbun*, November 11, 1937.

34. Nakayama Hiroshi, ed., *Nihon Bunka Eiga Nenkan: Shōwa Jūgonenban* (Bunka Nihonsha, 1941). The 1939 Film Law used the term *culture film* to refer to all films exclusive of dramatic and news films. State regulators worked in tandem with private producers and distributors, as is clear from the pages of ads for the "major production and distribution companies for culture films." The state may have thus appropriated the word *culture* and dictated its meaning, but it was still big business. See "Sumō Kihon Taisō" and "Yakyū o Toku," *Bunka Eiga Nenkan*, 235. *Bunka Eiga Nenkan*, 179, 220, 257, 268. The Yellowstone documentary was produced by a "Ford Culture Film Company." Regarding *Utsukushiki Doitsu* (Beautiful Germany), see *Bunka Eiga Nenkan*, 257. For *Shuurumu no Kekkon (Marriage in Schwalm)*, see *Bunka Eiga Nenkan*, 258.

35. "Ryūkyū no Mingei" and "Ryūkyū no Fūbutsu," *Bunka Eiga Nenkan*, 255, 278.

36. "Mantetsu Sanjūnen" and "Manshū no Fūbutsu," *Bunka Eiga Nenkan*, 259, 285. The term for the national entity, combining Japan and *Manshū*, implies inseparability in the phrase referring to a joint ideology: *nichiman ryōkoku fukabun no ideorogii*.

37. *Daaku Kongo, Bunka Eiga Nenkan*, 272. See *KJ*, June 1, 1929, 43–50, both for the visual representations of bare-breasted women and muscular men in ink sketches and photographs and for text on *"Jungle"* referring to the "sexual desire of the primitive native." Kondō Hidezō, "Chappurin-shi Afurika Hōmon," *Kingu*, January 1933, 450–51. John Russell contends that "Western literary and visual representations of blacks rely heavily on imaginary Western conventions" and that "the Japanese are familiar with the Western stereotype of the African primitive Noble Savage." It is clear that by the 1920s, in part because of the film industry, the black Other did indeed serve as "the repository for negatively sanctioned values such as 'impurity,' 'primitivism,' 'laziness,' 'underdevelopment,' 'backwardness.'" Russell, "Race and Reflexivity: The Black Other in Contemporary Japanese Mass Culture," *Cultural Anthropology* 6, no. 1 (February 1991): 4, 5, 8, 13.

38. Iijima, *Eiga no Mikata*, 253–61. *Bunka Eiga Nenkan*, 6, 285. For Iijima's definition of the film, see *Eiga no Mikata*, 14–37.

39. Awaya Noriko, *Waga Hōrōki*, 125–28.

40. Iijima, *Eiga no Mikata*, 145–46. The quote is from p. 145. Takeuchi Yoshimi, ed., *Kindai no Chōkoku* (Fuzanbō, 1994), 263. Yamamoto Kikuo quotes Takizawa Osamu's "Saitō Torajirō Shōron," *KJ*, January 1956, for the description of the pieces of sushi tumbling off the conveyor belt. See Yamamoto, *Nihon Eiga ni Okeru Gaikoku Eiga no Eikyō* (Waseda Daigaku Shuppanbu, 1983), 320.

FREEZE FRAMES

1. For an English-language version of Tokaidō, *Hizakurige*, see *Shank's Mare*, trans. Thomas Satchell (Rutland, VT: Charles E. Tuttle Company, 1960). For a review of *Utau Yaji Kita*, see *KJ*, August 11, 1937, 98. For ads for the three Paramount films, see *KJ*, back cover, October 11, 1927; December 1, 1927, 89; and April 21, 1928.

2. *Cardinal Principles of the National Entity of Japan*, trans. John Owen Guntlett, ed. Robert King Hall (Newton: Crofton Publishing Corp., 1974), 150, 159, 175, 178. Monbushō, *Kokutai no Hongi* (1937), 115, 126, 143, 148.

3. Anthony C. Yu, trans. and ed., "Introduction," *Journey to the West* (Chicago: University of Chicago Press, 1977), 35. Kawamura's *dojin* are Asian and Southeast Asian, but they clearly fall within the relationship of mediation set up by John Russell. According to Kawamura, by finding the primitive in the colonies, the Japanese colonial finds his "civilized nature." By the same token, Kawamura warns that to find the primitive is to find one's own barbarity. For Kawamura, the problem of the "modern" for Japan was the simultaneous need to make culture and civilization its own while at the same time modernizing, which is to say "Orientalizing," surrounding Asian and Pacific peoples. Kawamura, "Taishū Orientarizumu to Ajia Ninshiki."

For a rich, detailed analysis of *Songokū* in the context of Japanese expansion, see Michael Baskett, "The Attractive Empire: Colonial Asia in Japanese Imperial Film Culture, 1931–1953," (Ph.D. dissertation, UCLA, East Asian Languages and Cultures, 2000).

4. *KJ*, June 1, 1929, 43–50. *KJ*, October 11, 1930, 98–99. *Janguuru* was the 1929 German film *Samba*, directed by August Bruckner.

5. *KJ*, December 1, 1929, 83–85. *KJ*, August 21, 1929, for the quote. See also *KJ*, September 21, 1929. Fukuzawa Yukichi, "Datsuaron," *Jiji Shahō*, March 16, 1885.

6. The giant toad appeared in the silent film *Jiraiya*, starring Onoe Matsunosuke and directed by Makino Shōzō.

7. For reference to the *shitamachi buumu* following the oil shock of 1973–1974, see Kamiyama Keisuke, *Asakusa no Hyakunen: Kamiya Baa to Asakusa no Hitobito* (Tōseisha, 1989), 232. Fujita Shōzō, "Aru Sōshitsu no Keiken: Kakurenbō no Seishinshi" and "Shinpin Bunka: Josetsu ni Kaete," *Seishinshiteki Kōsatsu*, vol. 5 of *Fujita Shōzo Chosakushū* (Misuzu Shobō, 1997), 3, 6–8, 14, 17, 33, 38–42 (originally published in *Kodomo no Yakata*, September 1981, and *Misuzu*, February 1981).

8. Kamiyama, *Asakusa no Hyakunen*, 104–5.

9. Asahi Shinbun Tokyo Honsha Shakaibu, *Shitamachi* (Asahi Shinbunsha, 1984), 158, 213, 229. For another reference to Asakusa down-and-out society and the term *lumpen*, see Kamiyama, *Asakusa no Hyakunen*, 104.

10. Kobayashi Nobuhiko, *Bokutachi no Suki na Sensō* (Shinchōsha, 1986), esp. 17–24; Kamiyama, *Asakusa no Hyakunen*, 83–185.

11. "'Shōwa Retoro Modanshugi"; Kawaguchi Akiko, "Moga 1, Yoshiya Nobuko," "Moga 2, Iriye Takako," and "Moga 3, Tanaka Chiyo"; Okayama Yukiko, "Sanjū Nendai Ginza Moga no Shōzō: 'Kindai Mōdo no Niou Basho—'Shiseidō Gurafu' ni Tōjō suru 'Machi no Zolatachi," all in *Zola*, October 1998, 28–29, 38–39, 48–49, 94–95.

Bibliography

INTERVIEWS

Interview with Sata Ineko, at her home in Tokyo, October 1982
Interview with Sata Ineko, at her home in Karuizawa, August 1986
Interview with Sata Ineko, at her home in Tokyo, August 1990

JOURNALS CITED

Chūō Koron
Eiga Hyōron
Eiga Kagaku Kenkyū
Eiga no Tomo
Fujin Kōron
Ginza
Grotesque
Ie no Hikari
Kindai Seikatsu
Kindai Shisō
Kinema Junpō
Kingu
Kōga
Miyako Shinbun
Nyonin Geijutsu
Seikatsu
Shinchō
Shufu no Tomo
Shūkan Asahi
Tokyo Asahi Shinbun
Tokyo Nichinichi Shinbun

JAPANESE-LANGUAGE SOURCES

Place of publication is Tokyo unless otherwise noted.

Akazawa Shirō and Kitagawa Kenzō, eds. *Bunka to Fasshizumu*. Nihon Keizai Hyōronsha, 1993.

Amino Yoshihiko, Ozawa Shōichi, Miyata Noboru, eds. *Daidōgei to Misemono*. Vol. 13 of *Nihon Rekishi to Geinō*. Heibonsha, 1991.

Andō Kōsei. *Ginza Saiken*. Chūō Kōronsha, 1977.

Arahata Kanson. "Kankōsha to shite no Omoide." *Kindai Shisō Fukkokuban*. Chirokusha, 1960.

Arai Sen'o. "Kojiki no Fūzoku." In Kon and Yoshida, *Moderunologio*.

Asahi Shinbunsha, ed. *Asahi Gurafu ni Miru Shōwa no Sesō*. Asahi Shinbunsha, 1975.

Asakura Musei. *Misemono Kenkyū*. Shibunkaku Shuppan, 1977, 1988.

———. *Oto to Eizō no Moji ni yoru Nihon Rekishi to Geinō*. Heibonsha, 1991.

Awaya Noriko. *Waga Hōrōki*. Nihon Tosho Sentaa, 1997.

Awazu Kiyoshi, Ii Tarō, and Hosaka Kunio, eds. *Shōwa Jūichinen no Onna: Abe Sada*. Tabata Shoten, 1976.

Chiba Nobuo. *Chappurin wa Nihon wo Hashitta*. Seiabō, 1992.

Deguchi Takehito. "Nani ga Hakujin Konpurekkusu wo Umidashitaka." In *Nihon Eiga no Modanizumu, 1920–1930*, edited by Iwamoto Kenji. Riburopōtō, 1991.

Enomoto Ken'ichi. *Kigeki Hōdan Enoken no Seishun*. Meigensha, 1956.

Ezaki Kiyoshi. *Shajō Jinbutsu Satsuei Nyūmon*. Hikaridaisha, 1938.

Fujime Yuki. *Sei no Rekishigaku*. Fuji Shuppan, 1997.

Fujimori Seikichi. *Nani ga Kanojo wo sō Sasetaka*. Kaisōsha, 1927.

Fujimori Terunobu. "Kon Wajirō to Barakku Sōshokusha: Shinsai Fukkoku no Kenchiku." *Karamu* 88, April 1983.

———, Hatsuda Tōru, and Fujioka Hiroyasu, eds. *Ushinawareta Teito Tokyo: Taishō, Shōwa no Machi to Sumai*. Kashiwa Shobō, 1991.

Fujita Shōzō. *Seishinshiteki Kōsatsu, Fujita Shōzō Chosakushū*, vol. 5. Misuzu Shobō, 1997.

Fukasaku Yasubumi. *Kaitei Gendai Joshi Shūshin*. Okura Kobundō, 1931.

Gonda Yasunosuke. "1930 nen no Kaiko: Eiga." In Gonda, *Gonda Yasunosuke Chosakushū* (hereafter abbreviated as *GYS*), vol. 4. Bunwa Shobō, 1974–1975.

———. "'Asakusa' o Chūshin to shite." In *GYS*, 1:279–86.

———. "Eiga Setsumei no Shinka to Setsumei Geijutsu no Tanjō" (1923). In *GYS*, 4:119–29.

———. "Fukkō no Miyako o Nagamete" (1924). In *GYS*, 4:130–46.

———. "Gendai Goraku ni Arawaretaru Jidaisō" (1929). In *GYS*, 4:169–73.

———. "Ginbura to Dōbura: Santo Jōshu," (1922). In *GYS*, 4:68–71.

———. "Gorakuchi 'Asakusa' no Kenkyū" (1930). In *GYS*, 4:174–230.

———. *Gorakugyōsha no Mure*. Jitsugyō no Nihonsha, 1923.

———. "Iwayuru 'Modan Seikatsu' to Goraku." In *GYS*, 2: 240–246.

————. "Katei ni okeru Goraku" (1928). In *GYS*, 4:161–68.

————. "Kdf to sono Hoken Jigyō." *Onsen*, June 1942.

————. "Kibi Dango to Sukiyaki—Okayama to Kōbe no Minshū Goraku." In *GYS*, vol. 1.

————. *Kokumin Goraku no Mondai* (1941). In *GYS*, 3:5–225.

————. "Kokumin Kōsei Undō no Nachisuteki Seikaku." *Doitsu*, July 1942.

————. "Minshū Goraku" (1923). In *GYS*, 4:72–82.

————. *Minshū Goraku no Kichō*. Dōjinsha Shoten, 1922. Reprinted in *GYS*, 1:289–403.

————. *Minshū Gorakuron*. Ganshodō Shoten, 1931.

————. "Minshū no Goraku Seikatsu ni Arawaretaru Kokuminseijō" (1921). In *GYS*, 4:33–39.

————. *Nachisu Kōseidan*. Kurita Shoten, 1942.

————. "Postaa no Chimata: Asakusa no Minshū Goraku" (1921). In *GYS*, 1:268–78.

————. "Rōdōsha Gorakuron" (1933). In *GYS*, 4:255–80.

————. "Seinen Goraku no Suii to Gendai Seinen Goraku no Tokuchō" (1923). In *GYS*, 4:83–97.

————. "Shakai Seikatsu ni okeru Goraku no Ichikōsatsu" (1924). In *GYS*, 2:183–254.

————. "Shihonshugi Shakai to Ryūkō" (1922). In *GYS*, 4:57–67.

————. "Shinsaiji ni Arawaretaru Goraku no Shokeisō." In *GYS*, vol. 2.

Hamill, Barbara. "Josei: Modanizumu to Kenri Ishiki." In Minami, *Nihon Modanizumu no Kenkyū*.

————. "Nihon Modanizumu no Shisō: Hirabayashi Hatsunosuke o Chūshin to shite." In Minami, *Nihon Modanizumu no Kenkyū*.

Hara Kentarō. *Tōkyō Kigeki: Acharaka no Rekishi*. NTT Shuppan, 1994.

Hayashi Fumiko. *Hōrōki*. Shinchōsha, 1947, 1974.

Hiratsuka Raichō. *Hiratsuka Raichō Chosakushū*. Ōtsuki Shoten, 1983.

Hirotsu Kazuo. *Jokyū*. In *Hirotsu Kazuo Zenshū*, 5:7–242. Chūō Kōronsha, 1988.

Horino Hatsuko, ed. *Omoide no Merodii*. Seibidō, 1992.

Hoshino Tatsuo. "Modaan Shinbun Zasshi Eiga Mandan." *Kaizō*, June 1929.

Ichikawa Kōichi. "Ryukōka ni Miru Modanizumu to Ero Guro Nansensu." In Minami, *Nihon Modenizumu no Kenkyū*.

Ie no Hikari Kyōkai, ed. *Ie no Hikari no Shijūnen*. Ie no Hikari Kyōkai, 1968.

Igarashi Tomio. *Meshimori Onna*. Shinjinbutsu Ōraisha, 1981.

————. *Nihon Josei Bunkashi*. Agatsuma Shoten, 1984.

Iijima Tadashi. *Eiga no Mikata*. Bunshōsha, 1943.

————. *Shinema no ABC*. Kōseikaku Shoten, 1929.

Ikei Masaru. "Senkyūhyaku Nendai no Masu Meida." In *Saikō Taiheiyō Sensō Zen'ya: Nihon no Senkyūhyaku Sanjū Nendai Ron toshite*, edited by Miwa Kimitada. Sōseiki, 1981.

Imai Seiichi, ed. *Shinsai ni Yuragu*. Vol. 6 of *Nihon no Hyakunen*. Chikuma Shobō, 1962.

Ina Nobuo. "Shashin ni Kaere." *Kōga* 1, no. 1, 1932, 1–14.

Inagaki Yoshihiko and Yoshizawa Norio. *Shōwa Kotobashi 60 Nen*. Kōdansha, 1985.

Inoue Kiichirō, "Modan Kairaku Seikatsu no Saiginmi." *Chūō Kōron*, January 1932, 127–31

Ishii Ryōsuke. *Yoshiwara*. Chūō Kōronsha, 1967.

Ishikawa Hiroyoshi, ed. *Goraku no Senzenshi*. Shoseki Kabushikigaisha, 1981.

Ishizumi Harunosuke. "Kojiki Ritan." In *Ryūmin*, vol. 4 of *Kindai Minshū no Kiroku*, edited by Hayashi Hideo. Shin Jinbutsu Ōraisha, 1971. Reprinted as *Kindai Nihon no Kojiki*, Akashi Shoten, 1996.

Isomura Eiichi. "Jobun." In *Hinmingai*, vol. 1 of *Kindai Kasō Minshū Seikatsushi*, by Kusama Yasoo, edited by Isomura Eiichi and Yasuoka Norihiko. Akashi Shoten, 1987.

Isono Seiichi and Isono Fujiko. *Kazoku Seido*. Iwanami Shoten, 1958.

Itami Mansaku. "Shin Jidai Eiga ni Kansuru Kōsatsu." *Itami Mansaku Zenshū*. Vol. 1. Chikuma Shobō, 1961:5–16.

Itō Mikiharu. *Kazoku Kokkakan*. Mineruva Shobō, 1982.

Iwasaki Akira. *Eiga Geijutsushi* (Sekaisha, 1930).

———. *Eiga no Geijutsu*. Kyōwa Shoin, 1936.

———. *Eigaron*. Mikasa Shobō, 1936.

———. *Eiga to Shihonshugi*. Ōraisha, 1931.

———. *Nihon Eiga Shishi*. Tokyo Asahi Shinbunsha, 1977.

Kajino Foorii Bungeibu. *Kajino Foorii Rebyuu Kyakuhonshū* Chūshō Naigaisha, 1931.

Kamishima Jirō. "Atogaki ni Kaete." In Kuno and Kamishima, *"Tennōsei" Ronshū*.

Kamiyama Keisuke. *Asakusa no Hyakunen: Kamiya Baa to Asakusa no Hitobito*. Tōseisha, 1989.

Kano Masanao. *Fujin, Josei, Onna*. Iwanami Shoten, 1989.

———. *Senzen "Ie" no Shisō*. Sōbunsha, 1983.

———. *Taishō Demokurashii no Teiryū: Dozokuteki Seishin e no Kaiki*. NHK Books, 1974.

Kanō Mikiyo, ed. *Josei to Tennōsei*. Shisō no Kagakusha, 1979.

Kanō Mikiyo and Amano Yasukazu. *Han Tennōsei*. Shakai Hyōronsha, 1990.

Kataoka Teppei. "Modan Gaaru no Kenkyū." In Minami, *Kindai Shomin Seikatsushi*.

———. "Onna no Kyaku." In Minami, *Kindai Shomin Seikatsushi*.

Katō Akemi. " 'Mimpō Kaisei Yōkō' to Josei." In *Onnatachi no Kindai*, edited by Kindai Joseishi Kenkyūkai. Kashiwa Shobō, 1978.

Kawabata Yasunari. *Asakusa Kurenaidan*. Senshinsha, 1930. Facsimile ed. Kindai Bungakukan, 1980.

Kawada Shirō. "Kanchōsei Kazoku Soshiki no Hōkai: Kazoku Seido Hōkai no Kiun." In Yasuhiko Yuzawa, ed., *Kazoku seido*, vol. 5 of *Nihon Fujin Mondai Shiryō Shūsei*. Domesu Shuppan, 1980.

Kawamura Minato. "Taishū Orientarizumu to Ajia Ninshiki." In *Bunka no naka no Nihon*. Vol. 7 of *Iwanami Kōza Kindai Nihon to Shokuminchi*. Iwanami Shoten, 1993.

Kawazoe Noboru. *Kon Wajirō: Sono Genshōgaku*. Riburo Pooto, 1987.

Kim Il-myon [Kimu Irumyon]. *Tennō no Guntai to Chōsenjin Ianfu*. San'ichi Shobō, 1976.

Kimura Ryōko. "Fujin Zasshi no Jōhō Kūkan to Josei Taishū Dokushazō no Seiritsu." *Shisō*, February 1992, 229–52.

Kishida Ryūsei. *Kishida Ryūsei Zenshū*. Iwanami Shoten, 1979.

Kitamura Kaneko. "Kai Teisō." In Minami, *Kindai Shomin Seikatsushi*, vol. 1.

Kiyosawa Kiyoshi. "Modaan Gaaru no Kenkyū." In Minami, *Kindai Shomin Seikatsushi*.

Kobayashi Nobuhiko. *Bokutachi no Suki na Sensō* Shinchōsha, 1986.

Koike Tomihisa. "Marubiru Moga Sanpo Koosu." In Kon and Yoshida, *Moderunologio*.

Kon Wajirō. *Chōsen Buraku Chōsaka Hōkoku Dai 1-satsu Minka*. Seoul: Chōsen Sōtokufu, 1924.

———. "Depaato Fūzoku Shakaigaku" (1928). In Kon and Yoshida, *Moderunologio*, 206–16.

———. "Doma no Kenkyūzu." In *KWS*, vol. 9.

———. "Gendai Fūzoku." In Nagasaka Kaneo, ed., *Nihon Fuzokushi Kōza*, vol. 10. Yūzankaku, 1929.

———. "Honjo-Fukagawa Hinminkutsu Fukin Fūzoku Saishū" (1925). In Kon and Yoshida, *Moderunologio*, and in *KWS*, 1:109–33.

———. "Inokashira Kōen Haru no Pikunikku" (1927). In Kon and Yoshida, *Moderunologio*, and in *KWS*, 1:291–94.

———. "Inokashira Kōen Jisatsu Basho Bunpu Zu." In Kon and Yoshida, *Moderunologio*.

———. "Kōgengaku Sōron" (1931). In Kon and Yoshida , *Kōgengaku Saishū*, 11–34.

———. "Kōgengaku to wa Nanika?" (1930). In Kon and Yoshida, *Moderunologio*, and *KWS*, 1:13–23.

———. *Kon Wajirō Shu*. Domesu Shuppan, 1971–72.

———. "Otaru-shi Fūzoku Chōsa." In Kon and Yoshida, *Kōgengaku Saishū*, 267–321.

———. *Shinban Dai Tōkyō Annai*. Hihyōsha, 1986.

———. "Shinkatei no Shinamono Chōsa" (1926). In Kon and Yoshida, *Moderunologio*, and *KWS*, 1:345–66.

———. "Tokyo Ginzagai Fūzoku Kiroku" (1925). In Kon and Yoshida, *Moderunologio*, and *KWS*, 1:53–108.

Kon Wajirō and Yoshida Kenkichi. *Kōgengaku Saishū: Moderunologio*. Kensetsusha, 1931.

———. *Moderunologio (Kōgengaku)*. Gakuyō Shobō, 1930.

Koyama Shizuko. *Ryōsai Kenbo to iu Kihan*. Keisō Shobō, 1991.

Kuki Shūzō. *Iki no Kōzō*. Iwanami Shoten, 1979.

Kuno Osamu and Kamishima Jirō, eds. "Tennōsei" Ronshū. San'ichi Shobō, 1976.

Kusama Yasoo. Furōsha to Baishunfu no Kenkyū. Bummei Kyōkai, 1927.

———. Kindai Kasō Minshū Seikatsushi, 3 vols. Edited by Isomura Eiichi and Yasuoka Norihiko. Akashi Shoten, 1987.

———. Kindai Nihon no Donzoko Shakai. Edited by Yasuoka Norihiko. Akashi Shobō, 1992.

———. Kindai Toshi Kasō Shakai. Vol. 2., Hinmingai, Furōsha, Furyōji, Hinji, edited by Isomura Eiichi and Yasuoka Norihiko. Akashi Shoten, 1990.

Kuwabara Kineo. Tokyō Shōwa Jūichinen. Shōbunsha, 1974.

Maeda Ai. Genkei no Machi: Bungaku no Toshi o Aruku. Shōgakkan, 1986.

———. Kindai Dokusha no Seiritsu. Yūseidō, 1972. Reprinted by Iwanami Shoten, 1993.

———. Toshi Kūkan no Naka no Bungaku. Chikuma Shobō, 1982.

Maeda Ai and Shimizu Isao, eds. Taishō Kōki no Manga. Chikuma Shobō, 1986.

Maeda Hajime. Shokugyō Fujin Monogatari. Tōyō Keizai Shuppanbu, 1921.

Makino Mamoru, ed. Fukkokuban Eiga Ken'etsu Jihō Kaisetsu. Fuji Shuppan, 1985.

Makise Kikue. "Jinbunshi no Naka no Tennōsei." In Josei to Tennōsei, edited by Kanō Mikiyo. Shisō no Kagakusha, 1979.

Maruoka Hideko, ed. Kazoku Mondai. Vol. 8 of Nihon Fujin Mondai Shiryō Shūsei. Domesu Shuppan, 1976.

Maruoka Hideko and Yamaguchi Miyoko, eds. Kindai Nihon Fujin Mondai Nenpyō. Vol. 10 of Nihon Fujin Mondai Shiryō Shūsei.

Minakami Takitarō. "Teito Fukkōsai Yokyō." In Imai, Shinsai ni Yuragu.

Minami Hiroshi, ed. Kindai Shomin Seikatsushi. San'ichi Shobo, 1984–1998.

———. Nihon Modanizumu: Ero Guro Nansensu, vol. 188 of Gendai no Esupuri. Shibundō, 1983.

———. Nihon Modanizumu no "Hikari" to "Kage": Kindai Shomin Seikatsu. 20 vols. San'ichi Shobō, 1984.

———, ed. Nihon Modanizumu no Kenkyū: Shisō, Seikatsu, Bunka. Bureen Shuppan, 1982.

———. Taishō Bunka. Keisō Shobō, 1965.

Minami Hiroshi and Shakai Shinri Kenkyūjo, eds. Shōwa Bunka. Keisō Shobō, 1992.

Moroo Genzō. Shin Chōsen Fūdoki. Banrikaku Shobō, 1930.

Murakami Nobuhiko. Taishō Joseishi. Rironsha, 1982.

———. Taishōki no Shokugyō Fujin. Domesu Shuppan, 1983.

Murayama Tomoyoshi. Engekiteki Jijoden, 2:1922–1927. Tona Shuppansha, 1971.

———. Genzai no Geijutsu to Mirai no Geijutsu. Ōbundō, 1924.

———. Kōseiha Kenkyū. Chūō Bijutsusha, 1926.

———. Nihon Puroretaria Engekiron. Tenjinsha, 1930.

———. Puroretaria Bijutsu no Tameni. Atoriesha, 1930.

Nagae Michitarō. *Eiga Hyōgen Keishiki.* Kyoto: Kyōiku Tosho Kabushikigaisha, 1942.

Nakano Kaichi. *Modanizumu Shi no Jidai.* Hōbunkan, 1986.

Nakao Tatsurō. *Sui, Tsū, Iki.* Miyai Shoten, 1984.

Nakayama Hiroshi, ed. *Nihon Bunka Eiga Nenkan: Shōwa Jūgonenban.* Bunka Nihonsha, 1941.

Nakazawa Seitarō. "Konsen 'Ajia no Arashi.'" In *Kajino Foorii Rebyuu Kyakuhonshū,* edited by Kajino Foorii Bungeibu. Chūshō Naigaisha, 1931.

Nii Itaru. "Modan Gaaru no Rinkaku." *Fujin Kōron,* April 1925.

———. Kataoka Teppei, Miyake Yasuko, et al., "Modaan Seikatsu Mandankai," *Shinchō,* January 1928, 123–47.

Nishikawa Yūko. *Shakuya to Mochiie no Bungakushi: "Watashi" no Utsuwa no Monogatari.* Sanseidō, 1998.

———. "Sumai no Hensen to 'Katei' no Seiritsu." In *Nihon Josei Seikatsu-shi.* Vol. 4. Edited by Joseishi Sōgō Kenkyūkai. Tokyo Daigaku Shuppankai, 1990, 4:1–49.

Nishiyama Matsunosuke. *Edo Chōnin no Kenkyū.* Yoshikawa Kōbunkan, 1973.

———. *Edokko.* Yoshikawa Kōbunkan, 1980.

———. *Edo Kobota Hyakuwa.* Yoshikawa Kōbunkan, 1980.

———. *Edo no Seikatsu Bunka.* Yoshkawa Kōbunkan, 1983.

———. *Kinsei Bunka no Kenkyū.* Yoshikawa Kōbunkan, 1983.

Hon no Mori Henshūbu, ed. *Abe Sada: Jiken Chōsho Zenbun.* Kosumikku Intaanashonaru, 1997.

Ōbayashi Munetsugu. *Jokyū Seikatsu no Shinkenkyū.* Ōhara Shakai Mondai Kenkyūjo, 1931.

Ogata Akiko. *Nyonin Geijutsu no Sekai.* Domesu Shuppan, 1980.

Oguma, Eiji. *Nihonjin no Kyōkai: Okinawa, Ainu, Taiwan, Chōsen Shokuminchi Shihai kara Fukki Undō made.* Shin'yōsha, 1998.

Ōya Sōchi. "Hyaku Paasento Moga." In *Ōya Sōichi Zenshū.* 2:10–17.

———. "Modan Raifu Saiginmi." *Chūō Kōron,* February 1929, 177–82.

———. "Modan Sō to Modan Sō." *Chūō Kōron,* February 1929, reprinted in *Ōya Sōichi Zenshū.* Sōyōsha, 1981, 2:5–8.

Ozaki Midori. "Eiga Mansō, I–IV." In *Ozaki Midori Zenshū.* Sōjunsha, 1979, 314–42.

———. "Mokusei." In *Ozaki Midori Zenshū,* 154–59.

———. "Tsue to Bōshi no Henshitsusha." In *Ozaki Midori Zenshū,* 359–64.

Rōdō Undōshi Kenkyūkai and Rōdōsha Kyōiku Kyōkai, eds. *Nihon Rōdō Undō no Rekishi.* San'ichi Shobō, 1960.

Sakakibara Shōji. *Shōwago: Rokujūnen Sesōshi.* Asahi Shinbunsha, 1986.

Sakuramoto Tomio. *Dai Tōa Sensō to Nihon Eiga: Tachimi no Senchū Eigaron.* Aoki Shoten, 1993.

Sata Ineko. "Kanabu Jokō no Namida." In vol. 1 of *Sata Ineko Zenshū,* ed. Ōe Kenzaburō et al. Kōdansha, 1977.

———. "Kitō." In vol. 1 of *Sata Ineko Zenshū.* Kōdansha, 1977.

————. "Kyōsei Kikoku." In vol. 1 of *Sata Ineko Zenshū*, ed. Ōe Kenzaburō et al. Kōdansha, 1977.

————. "Shōkanbu." In vol. 1 of *Sata Ineko Zenshū*, ed. Ōe Kenzaburō et al. Kōdansha, 1977.

Satō Hachirō. *Asakusa*. Seikōkan Shoten, 1932.

Satō Takeshi. "Modanizumu to Amerikaka: 1920, Senkyūhyaku Nijūnen wo Chūshin to shite." In Minami, *Nihon Modanizumu no Kenkyū*.

Shimamura Ryūzō. "Rumpen Shakaigaku." In *Kajino Foorii Rebyuu Kyakuhonshū*, edited by Kajino Foorii Bungeibu. Chūshō Naigaisha, 1931.

Shimonaka Yasaburō, ed. *Dai Jiten*. Heibonsha, 1934.

Shiomi Sen'ichirō. *Danzaemon to Sono Jidai: Senmin Bunka no Doramatsurugii*. Hihyōsha, 1993.

Shisō no Kagaku Kenkyūkai, ed. *Kyōdō Kenkyū: Tenkō*. Heibonsha, 1959–1962; reprinted 1973.

Shūkan Asahi, ed. *Nedan no Fūzokushi*. Vol. 1. Shūkan Asahi, 1987–1989.

Soeda Azenbō. *Asakusa Teiryūki*. Vol. 2 of *Soeda Azenbō/Soeda Tomomichi Chosakushū*. Tosui Shobō, 1982.

Sone Hiromi. "Baitakō—kinsei no baishun." In Josei Shi Sōgō Kenkyōkai, ed. *Nihon josei shi seikatsu shi*, vol. 3: *Kinsei*. Tokyo Daigaku Shuppankai, 1991.

Takahashi Akira. "Toshika to Kikai Bunmei." *Jiga to Kankyō*. Vol. 6 of *Kindai Nihon Shisōshi Kōza*. Tokyo Daigaku Shuppankai, 1957.

Takahashi Shōji, ed. *Modan Tōkyō Hyakkei*. Special issue of *Taiyō: Nihon no kokoro*, no. 54. Series edited by Unno Hiroshi. Heibonsha, 1986.

Takami Jun. *Ikanaru Hoshi no Moto ni*. Shinchōsha, 1970.

Takeda Rintarō. *San Mon Opera*. In *Takeda Rintarō Zenshū*. Vol. 1. Shinchōsha, 1977.

Takemura Tamio. *Taishō Bunka*. Kōdansha, 1980.

Takeuchi Yoshimi, ed. *Kindai no Chōkoku*. Fuzanbō, 1994.

Takeyama Akiko. "Radio Bangumi ni Miru Modanizumu." In Minami, *Nihon Modanizumu no Kenkyū*.

Tamagawa Shinmei. *Boku wa Asakusa no Furyō Shōnen: Jitsuroku Satō Hachirō Den*. Sakuhinsha, 1991.

Tanaka Jun'ichirō. *Musei kara Tookii e: Nihon Eiga Hattatsushi 2*. Chūō Kōronsha, 1968.

Tanaka Sumiko, ed. *Josei Kaihō no Shisō to Kōdō*. Prewar vol. Jiji Tsūshinsha, 1975.

Tanizaki Jun'ichirō. *Chijin no Ai*. Vol. 10 of *Tanizaki Jun'ichirō Zenshū*. Chūō Kōronsha, 1967.

Tokunaga Sunao. *Taiyō no nai Machi*. Shinchō Bunko, 1953. Reprinted by Shinchōsha, 1983.

Tokyo Metropolitan Art Museum, ed. *The 1920s in Japan: 1920 Nendai Nihonten*. Asahi Shinbunsha, 1988.

Tomoeda Takahiko. *Chūgaku Shūshin*. Vol. 5. Tozanbō, 1922, 1928.

Tosaka Jun. "Ken'etsuka no Shisō to Fūzoku." In *Nihon Modanizumu: Ero Guro Nansensu*, vol. 188 of *Gendai no Esupuri*, edited by Minami Hiroshi, 44–47. Shibundō, 1983.

Tsuchida Mitsufumi, ed. *Meiji Taishō Fūzokugoten*. Kadokawa Shoten, 1979.

Tsurumi Shunsuke. "Minshū Goraku kara Kokumin Goraku e." *Shisō* 624, June 1976.

Uchiyama Sōjūrō. *Asakusa Opera no Seikatsu: Meiji Taishō kara Shōwa e no Nihon Kageki no Ayumi*. Yūzankaku, 1967.

Ueda Yasuo. "Josei Zasshi ga Mita Modanizumu." In Minami, *Nihon Modanizumu no Kenkyū*.

Ueno Chizuko. "Kaisetsu." In *Fūzoku Sei*. Vol. 23 of *Nihon Kindai Shisō Taikei*. Iwanami Shoten, 1990.

Umehara Masaki. "Zasshi 'Gurotesuku' no Shūten: Shōwa Ero Guro Bunka ni tsuite," *Dentō to Gendai* 17, September 1972, 140–50.

Ushijima Hidehiko. *Asakusa no Tomoshibi Enoken*. Vol. 4 of *Mō Hitotsu no Shōwashi*. Mainichi Shinbunsha, 1979.

Usui Seizō. "Furōsha no Nikki." In *Ryūmin*. Vol. 4 of *Kindai Minshū no Kiroku*, edited by Hayashi Hideo. Shinjinbutsu Ōraisha, 1971.

Wada Nobuyoshi. "Tekiya Ōgisho." In *Ryūmin*. Vol. 4 of *Kindai Minshū no Kiroku*, edited by Hayashi Hideo. Shinjinbutsu Ōraisha, 1971.

Wakakuwa Midori. *Sensō ga Tsukuru Joseizō*. Chikuma Shobō, 1995.

Watanabe Etsuji and Suzuki Yūko, eds. *Takaki ni Ikite: Senzen Fujin Rōdō Undō e no Shōgen*. Domusu Shuppan, 1980.

Yamada Seizaburō, ed. *Marukusushugi Bungei Sen'eigo Jiten*. Hakuyōsha, 1932.

Yamada Waka. *Watashi no Ren'aikan*. Asahi Shinbunsha, 1936.

Yamakawa Kikue. "Gendai Shokugyō Fujinron." In Yasuhiko Yuzawa, ed., *Nihon Fujin Mondai Shiryō Shūsei*. Domesu Shuppan, 1976.

———. *Yamakawa Kikueshū*. Edited by Tanaka Sumiko and Yamakawa Shinsaku. Iwanami Shoten, 1981–1982.

Yamamoto Kikuo. *Nihon Eiga ni okeru Gaikoku Eiga no Eikyō*. Waseda Daigaku Shuppanbu, 1983.

Yamamoto Tsuneo. *Kindai Nihon Toshi Kyōkashi Kenkyū*. Reimei Shobō, 1972.

Yasuoka Norihiko. "Kaisetsu." In *Kindai Toshi Kasō Shakai*, vol. 2.

Yoshimi Shun'ya. "Kindai Kūkan to shite no Hyakkaten." In *Toshi no Kūkan Toshi no Shintai*, edited by Yoshimi Shun'ya. Keisō Shobō, 1996.

———. *Toshi no Doramaturugii*. Kōbundō, 1987, 1992.

Yuzawa Yasuhiko, ed. *Kazoku Mondai*. Vol. 5 of *Nihon Fujin Mondai Shiryō Shūsei*. Domesu Shuppan, 1978.

Zakō Jun. *Asakusa Rokku (Enko) wa Itsumo Modan Datta*. Asahi Shinbunsha, 1984.

ENGLISH-LANGUAGE SOURCES

Agnew, Jean-Christophe. "Coming Up for Air: Consumer Culture in Historical Perspective." In *Consumption and the World of Goods*, edited by Jon Brewer and Roy Porter. New York: Routledge, 1993.

Allen, G. C. *A Short Economic History of Modern Japan, 1867–1937.* London: George Allen & Unwin, 1946.

Allison, Anne. *Permitted and Prohibited Desires: Mothers, Comics, and Censorship in Japan.* Berkeley: University of California Press, 1996.

Anderson, Joseph L., and Donald Richie, eds. *The Japanese Film: Art and Industry.* New York: Grove Press, 1959.

Anderson, Perry. "Modernity and Revolution." In *Marxism and the Interpretation of Culture,* edited by Cary Nelson and Lawrence Grossberg. Urbana: University of Illinois Press, 1988.

Appadurai, Arjun. *The Social Life of Things: Commodities in Cultural Perspective.* Cambridge: Cambridge University Press, 1986.

Aumont, Jacques. *Montage Eisenstein.* Bloomington: Indiana University Press, 1987.

Bailey, Peter. "Parasexuality and Glamour: The Victorian Barmaid as Cultural Prototype." *Gender and History* 2 (1990): 148–72.

Bakhtin, Mikhail. *Rabelais and His World.* Translated by Helene Iswolsky. Bloomington: Indiana University Press, 1984.

Bann, Stephen, ed. *The Tradition of Constructivism.* New York: Da Capo, 1974.

Banner, Lois. *American Beauty.* Chicago: University of Chicago Press, 1983.

Barron, Stephanie, and Maurice Tuchman, eds. *The Avant-Garde in Russia: 1910–1930.* Cambridge, MA: MIT Press, 1980.

Benjamin, Jessica. *The Bonds of Love: Psychoanalysis, Feminism, and the Problem of Domination.* New York: Pantheon Books, 1988.

Bennett, Tony. "A Thousand and One Troubles: Blackpool Pleasure Beach." In *Formations of Pleasure.* London: Routledge and Kegan Paul, 1983.

Bernheimer, Charles. *Figures of Ill Repute: Representing Prostitution in Nineteenth-Century France.* Durham, NC: Duke University Press, 1997.

Bhabha, Homi K. *The Location of Culture.* New York: Routledge, 1994.

Bordwell, David. *Ozu and the Poetics of Cinema.* Princeton: Princeton University Press, 1988.

Bourdieu, Pierre. *Distinction: A Social Critique of the Judgement of Taste.* Translated by Richard Nice. Cambridge: Cambridge University Press, 1977.

———. *Outline of a Theory of Practice.* Translated by Richard Nice. Cambridge, MA: Harvard University Press, 1977.

Bowlby, Rachel. *Just Looking: Consumer Culture in Dreiser, Gissing, and Zola.* New York: Methuen, 1985.

Bradbury, Malcolm, and James McFarlane, eds. *Modernism, 1890–1930.* New York: Penguin Books, 1976.

Bryant, Taimie Lee Tysan. "Mediation of Divorce Disputes in the Japanese Family Court System: With Emphasis on the Tokyo Family Court." Ph.D. diss., University of California, Los Angeles, 1984.

Buckley, Sandra. *Broken Silence: Voices of Japanese Feminism.* Berkeley: University of California Press, 1997.

Buck-Morss, Susan. *The Dialectics of Seeing: Walter Benjamin and the Arcades Project.* Cambridge, MA: MIT Press, 1991.

Butler, Judith. *Gender Trouble: Feminism and the Subversion of Identity*. New York: Routledge, 1990.

Calinescu, Matei. *Five Faces of Modernity*. Durham, NC: Duke University Press, 1987.

Carby, Hazel. "It Just Be's Dat . . . Way Sometime: The Sexual Politics of Women's Blues." In *Unequal Sisters: A Multicultural Reader in U.S. Women's History*, edited by Ellen Carol DuBois and Vicki L. Ruiz. New York: Routledge, 1990.

Case, Sue-Ellen. "Toward a Butch-Femme Aesthetic." In *Making a Spectacle*, edited by Lynda Hart. Ann Arbor: University of Michigan Press, 1989.

Chaplin, Charles. *My Autobiography*. London: Penguin Books, 1992.

Choi, Chungmoo, ed. "The Comfort Women: Colonialism, War, and Sex." Special issue, *positions* 5, no. 1 (Spring 1997).

Clarke, T. J. *The Painting of Modern Life: Paris in the Art of Manet and His Followers*. Princeton, NJ: Princeton University Press, 1984.

Clifford, James. *The Predicament of Culture: Twentieth-Century Ethnography, Literature, and Art*. Cambridge, MA: Harvard University Press, 1988.

Coward, Rosalind. *Female Desires: How They Are Sought, Bought, and Packaged*. New York: Grove Press, 1985.

Davis, Angela Y. *Blues Legacies and Black Feminism: Gertrude "Ma" Rainey, Bessie Smith, and Billie Holiday*. New York: Pantheon Books, 1998.

Davis, Natalie Zemon. *Fiction in the Archives: Pardon Tales and Their Tellers in Sixteenth-Century France*. Stanford, CA: Stanford University Press, 1987.

———. *Society and Culture in Early Modern France: Eight Essays*. Stanford, CA: Stanford University Press, 1975.

De Becker, Joseph Ernest. *The Nightless City: Or, the History of the Yoshiwara Yukwaku*. Yokohama: Z. P. Maruya, 1899.

de Certeau, Michel. *The Practice of Everyday Life*. Translated by Steven Rendall. Berkeley: University of California Press, 1984.

Doane, Mary Ann. *Femmes Fatales: Feminism, Film Theory, Psychoanalysis*. New York: Routledge, Chapman, and Hall, 1991.

———. "Film and the Masquerade: Theorizing the Female Spectator." In *Issues in Feminist Film Criticism*, edited by Patricia Erens. Bloomington: Indiana University Press, 1990.

Dower, John W. *Japan in War and Peace: Selected Essays*. New York: New Press, 1993.

———. *War without Mercy: Race and Power in the Pacific War*. New York: Pantheon, 1986.

Duus, Peter. *The Rise of Modern Japan*. Boston: Houghton Mifflin, 1976.

Eisenstein, Sergei. *Film Form: Essays in Film Theory and the Film Sense*. Edited and translated by Jay Leyda. Cleveland: World Publishing Company, 1957.

Elliott, David. *New Worlds: Russian Art and Society, 1900–1937*. New York: Rizzoli, 1986.

Fass, Paula. *The Damned and the Beautiful*. New York: Oxford University Press, 1977.

Foucault, Michel. *The History of Sexuality, Volume 1: An Introduction.* Translated by Robert Hurley. New York: Vintage Books, 1978.

Franklyn, Julian. *The Cockney: A Survey of London Life and Language.* London: Deutsch, 1953.

Freud, Sigmund. "The 'Uncanny.'" *The Standard Edition of the Complete Psychological Works of Sigmund Freud.* Translated under the general editorship of James Strachey and assisted by Alix Strachey and Alan Tyson. London: Hogarth Press, 1955.

Frow, John. "What Was Post-Modernism." In *Past the Last Post: Theorizing Post-Colonialism and Post-Modernism,* edited by Ian Adam and Helen Tiffin. New York: Harvester Wheatsheaf, 1991.

Fujitani, Takashi. *Splendid Monarchy: Power and Pageantry in Modern Japan.* Berkeley: University of California Press, 1998.

Garon, Sheldon. *Molding Japanese Minds: The State in Everyday Life.* Princeton, NJ: Princeton University Press, 1997.

―――. "Rethinking Modernization and Modernity in Japanese History: A Focus on State-Society Relations." *Journal of Asian Studies* 53 (1994): 346–66.

―――. "The World's Oldest Debate? Prostitution and the State in Imperial Japan, 1900–1945." *American Historical Review* 98 (1993): 710–33.

Gelder, Ken, and Jane M. Jacobs, *Uncanny Australia: Sacredness and Identity in a Postcolonial Nation.* Carlton, Australia: Melbourne University Press, 1998.

Gluck, Carol. *Japan's Modern Myths: Ideology in the Late Meiji Period.* Princeton: Princeton University Press, 1985.

Goffman, Erving. *Gender Advertisements.* New York: Harper Torchbooks, 1979.

Gordon, Andrew. *Labor and Imperial Democracy in Prewar Japan.* Berkeley: University of California Press, 1991.

Grossman, Atina. "Girlkultur or Thoroughly Rationalized Female: A New Woman in Weimar Germany." In *Woman in Culture and Politics: A Century of Change,* edited by Judith Friedlander, Blanche Wiesen Cook, Alice Kessler-Harris, and Carroll Smith-Rosenberg. Bloomington: Indiana University Press, 1986.

Gumperz, John J. *Discourse Strategies.* Cambridge: Cambridge University Press, 1982.

Hansen, Miriam. *Babel and Babylon: Spectatorship in American Silent Film.* Cambridge, MA: Harvard University Press, 1991.

Harootunian, Harry. *History's Disquiet: Modernity, Cultural Practice, and the Question of Everyday Life.* New York: Columbia University Press, 2000.

―――. *Overcome by Modernity: History, Culture, and Community in Interwar Japan.* Princeton: Princeton University Press, 2000.

Harrison, Daphne Duval. *Black Pearls: Blues Queens of the 1920s.* New Brunswick, NJ: Rutgers University Press, 1998.

Harvey, David. *The Condition of Postmodernity.* Cambridge: Blackwell, 1989.

Hershatter, Gail. *Dangerous Pleasures: Prostitution and Modernity in Twentieth-Century Shanghai.* Berkeley: University of California Press, 1997.

High, Peter B. "The Dawn of Cinema in Japan." *Journal of Contemporary History* 1, no. 19 (January 1984): 23–57.

Hobsbawn, Eric. *The Age of Capital, 1848–1875.* London: Weidenfeld and Nicolson, 1975.

Hoston, Germaine. *Marxism and the Crisis of Development in Prewar Japan.* Princeton: Princeton University Press, 1986.

Hutcheon, Linda. *Irony's Edge: The Theory and Politics of Irony.* New York: Routledge, 1995.

———. *A Theory of Parody: The Teaching of Twentieth-Century Art Forms.* New York: Methuen, 1985.

Huyssen, Andreas. *After the Great Divide: Modernism, Mass Culture, Postmodernism.* Bloomington: Indiana University Press, 1986.

Ivy, Marilyn. *Discourses of the Vanishing: Modernity/Phantasm/Japan.* Chicago: University of Chicago Press, 1995.

Jackson, Earl, Jr. "Kabuki Narratives of Male Homoerotic Desire in Saikaku and Mishima." *Theater Journal* (December 1989): 459–77.

Kasza, Gregory. *The State and the Mass Media in Japan, 1918–1945.* Berkeley: University of California Press, 1988.

Katō Shūichi. "Taishō Democracy as the Pre-Stage for Japanese Militarism." In *Japan in Crisis: Essays on Taishō Democracy,* edited by Bernard S. Silberman and H. D. Harootunian. Princeton, NJ: Princeton University Press, 1974.

Kenritsu Kindai Bijutsukan, ed. *Modern Boy Modern Girl: Modernity in Japanese Art, 1910–1935.* Kanagawa: Kenritsu Kindai Bijutsukan, 1998.

Laqueur, Thomas. *Making Sex: Body and Gender from the Greeks to Freud.* Cambridge, MA: Harvard University Press, 1990.

Lavin, Maud. *Cut with the Kitchen Knife: The Weimar Photomontages of Hannah Hoch.* New Haven, CT: Yale University Press, 1993.

Lears, T. J. Jackson. "From Salvation to Self-Realization: Advertising and the Therapeutic Roots of the Consumer Culture, 1880–1930." In *The Culture of Consumption,* edited by Richard Wightman Fox and T. J. Jackson Lears. New York: Pantheon, 1983.

Lévi-Strauss, Claude. *The Savage Mind.* Chicago: University of Chicago Press, 1966.

Lippit, Seiji. *Topographies of Japanese Modernism.* New York, Columbia University Press, 2002.

Lorde, Audre. "Uses of the Erotic: The Erotic as Power." In *Take Back the Night: Women on Pornography,* edited by Laura Lederer. New York: Morrow, 1980.

Maravall, Jose Antonio. *Culture of the Baroque: Analysis of a Historical Structure.* Minneapolis: University of Minnesota Press, 1986.

Marchand, Roland. *Advertising the American Dream: Making War for Modernity, 1920–1940.* Berkeley: University of California Press, 1985.

Marcus, George, and M. J. Fischer, eds. *Anthropology as Cultural Critique: An Experimental Moment in the Human Sciences.* Chicago: University of Chicago Press, 1986.

Maruyama Masao. "Patterns of Individuation and the Case of Japan: A Conceptual Scheme." In *Changing Japanese Attitudes toward Modernization,* edited by Marius Jansen. Princeton, NJ: Princeton University Press, 1965.

Matthews, William. *Cockney Past and Present: A Short History of the Dialect of London.* New York: E. P. Dutton, 1938.

Mayne, Judith. *Cinema and Spectatorship.* New York: Routledge, 1993.

Milroy, Lesley, and Pieter Muysken, eds. *One Speaker, Two Languages: Cross-Disciplinary Perspectives on Code-Switching.* Cambridge: Cambridge University Press, 1995.

Mitchell, Timothy. "Everyday Metaphors of Power." *Theory and Society* 19, no. 5 (1990).

Miyake, Yoshiko. "Women, Work, Family, and the State in Japan, 1868–1990: Rewriting Modern Japanese Social History from a Feminist Perspective." Ph.D. diss., University of California, Santa Cruz, 1991.

Morris-Suzuki, Tessa. *Re-Inventing Japan: Time, Space, Nation.* Armonk, NY: M. E. Sharpe, 1998.

Nagy, Margit. "'How Shall We Live?' Social Change, the Family Institution, and Feminism in Prewar Japan." Ph.D. diss., University of Washington, 1981.

———. "Middle-Class Working Women during the Interwar Years." In *Recreating Japanese Women, 1600–1945,* edited by Gail Lee Bernstein. Berkeley: University of California Press, 1991.

Naruse, Tatsuo. "Taylorism and Fordism in Japan." *International Journal of Political Economy* 21, no. 3 (Fall 1991): 32–48.

Nishikawa, Yūko. "The Changing Form of Dwellings and the Establishment of the Katei (Home) in Modern Japan." *U.S.-Japan Women's Journal,* English supplement, no. 8 (1995).

Nolte, Sharon. *Liberalism in Modern Japan.* Berkeley: University of California Press, 1987.

———. "Women's Rights and Society's Needs: Japan's 1931 Suffrage Bill." *Comparative Studies in Society and History* 28 (October 1986), 690.

Ooms, Herman. *Tokugawa Village Practice: Class Status, Power, Law.* Berkeley: University of California Press, 1996.

Orlove, Benjamin and Henry Rutz. *The Social Economy of Consumption.* Lanham, MD: University Press of America, 1989.

Peiss, Kathy. *Cheap Amusements: Working Women and Leisure in Turn-of-the-Century New York, 1880–1920.* Philadelphia: Temple University Press, 1985.

Perrot, Michelle, ed. *From the Fires of Revolution to the Great War.* Vol. 4 of *A History of Private Life.* Translated by Arthur Goldhammer. Cambridge, MA: Harvard University Press, 1990.

Pincus, Leslie. *Authenticating Culture in Imperial Japan.* Berkeley: University of California, 1996.

Porter, Theodore. *Trust in Numbers: The Pursuit of Objectivity in Science and Public Life.* Princeton, NJ: Princeton University Press, 1995.

Powers, Richard Gid, and Hidetoshi Katō. *Handbook of Japanese Popular Culture.* New York: Greenwood Press, 1989.

Prost, Antoine, and Gerard Vincent, eds. *Riddles of Identity in Modern Times.* Vol. 5 of *A History of Private Life.* Translated by Arthur Goldhammer. Cambridge, MA: Harvard University Press, 1991.

Rapp, Rayna, and Ellen Ross. "The 1920s: Feminism, Consumerism, and Political Backlash in the United States." In *Woman in Culture and Politics: A Century of Change,* edited by Judith Friedlander, Blanche Wiesen Cook, Alice Kessler-Harris, and Carroll Smith-Rosenberg. Bloomington: Indiana University Press, 1986.

Riley, Denise. *"Am I That Name?" Feminism and the Category of "Women" in History.* Minneapolis: University of Minnesota Press, 1988.

Robertson, Jennifer. *Takarazuka: Sexual Politics and Popular Culture in Modern Japan.* Berkeley: University of California Press, 1998.

Robinson, David. *Chaplin: His Life and Art.* New York: McGraw-Hill, 1985.

Roden, Donald. "Taishō Culture and the Problem of Gender Ambivalence." In *Culture and Identity: Japanese Intellectuals during the Interwar Years,* edited by J. Thomas Rimer. Princeton, NJ: Princeton University Press, 1990.

Rosen, Ruth. *The Lost Sisterhood: Prostitution in America, 1990–1918.* Baltimore: Johns Hopkins University Press, 1982.

Rubin, Gayle. "Thinking Sex." In *Pleasure and Danger: Exploring Female Sexuality,* edited by Carole Vance. Boston: Routledge & Kegan Paul, 1990.

Russell, John. "Race and Reflexivity: The Black Other in Contemporary Japanese Mass Culture." *Cultural Anthropology* 6 (February 1991): 3–25.

Russo, Mary J. *The Female Grotesque: Risk, Excess, and Modernity.* New York: Routledge, 1995.

Ryan, Mary. *Womanhood in America: From Colonial Times to the Present.* New York: Franklin Watts, 1983.

Sand, Jordan. "At Home in the Meiji Period: Inventing Japanese Domesticity." In Vlastos, *Mirror of Modernity.*

———. *House and Home in Modern Japan: Architecture, Domestic Space, and Bourgeois Culture, 1880–1930.* Cambridge, MA: Harvard University Press, 2003.

Sato, Barbara. *The New Japanese Woman: Modernity, Media, and Women in Interwar Japan.* Durham and London: Duke University Press, 2003.

Scott, Joan. *Gender and the Politics of History.* New York: Columbia University Press, 1988.

Scott, James C. *Domination and the Arts of Resistance: Hidden Transcripts.* New Haven, CT: Yale University Press, 1990.

Sedgwick, Eve Kosofsky. *Epistemology of the Closet.* Berkeley: University of California Press, 1990.

Seidensticker, Edward. *High City, Low City: Tokyo from Edo to the Earthquake.* Tokyo: Tuttle Books, 1983.

———. *Tokyo Rising: The City Since the Great Earthquake*. New York: Knopf, 1990.

Sievers, Sharon. *Flowers in Salt: The Beginnings of Feminist Consciousness in Modern Japan*. Stanford: Stanford University Press, 1983.

Silverberg, Miriam. "Advertising Every Body." In *Choreographing History*, edited by Susan Leigh Foster. Bloomington: Indiana University Press, 1995.

———. "The Café Waitress Serving Modern Japan." In Vlastos, *Mirror of Modernity*.

———. *Changing Song: The Marxist Manifestos of Nakano Shigeharu*. Princeton, NJ: Princeton University Press, 1990.

———. "Constructing a New Cultural History of Prewar Japan." *boundary 2* (1991): 61–89. Reprinted in *Japan in the World*, edited by Masao Miyoshi and H. D. Harootunian. Durham, NC: Duke University Press, 1991.

———. "Forgetting Pearl Harbor, Remembering Charlie Chaplin, and the Case of the Disappearing Westerner." *positions* 1 (Spring 1993): 23–76. Reprinted in *Formations of Colonial Modernity in East Asia*, edited by Tani E. Barlow. Durham, NC: Duke University Press, 1997.

———. "The Massacre of Koreans after the Great Kantō Earthquake." MA thesis, Georgetown University, 1979.

———. "Osmanthus." *Manoa* 3 (Fall 1991): 187–90.

Song, Youn-ok. "Japanese Colonial Rule and State-Managed Prostitution: Korea's Licensed Prostitutes." *positions* 5, no. 1 (Spring 1997): 171–217.

Spivak, Gayatri. *In Other Worlds: Essays in Cultural Politics*. New York: Methuen, 1987.

Stallybrass, Peter, and Allon White. *The Politics and Poetics of "Transgression."* Ithaca, NY: Cornell University Press, 1986.

Stewart, Susan. *On Longing: Narratives of the Miniature, the Gigantic, the Souvenir, the Collection*. Durham, NC: Duke University Press, 1984, 1993.

Stott, William. *Documentary Expression and Thirties America*. London: Oxford University Press, 1973.

Tada, Michitarō. "Japanese Sensibility: An 'Imitation' of Yanagita." In *International Perspectives on Yanagita Kunio and Japanese Folklore Studies*, edited by J. Victor Koschmann, Oiwa Keibō, and Yamashita Shinji. Ithaca, NY: Cornell University Press, 1985.

Tamanoi, Mariko Asano. *Under the Shadow of Nationalism: Politics and Poetics of Rural Japanese Women*. Honolulu: University of Hawaii Press, 1998.

———. "Women's Voices: Their Critique of the Anthropology of Japan." *Annual Review of Anthropology* 19 (1990): 17–37.

Teitelbaum, Matthew, ed. *Montage and Modern Life*. Cambridge, MA: MIT Press, 1992.

Todorov, Tzvetan. *The Morals of History*. Trans. Alyson Waters. Minneapolis: University of Minnesota Press, 1995.

Tsivian, Yuri. *Early Cinema in Russia and Its Cultural Reception*. Edited by Richard Taylor and translated by Alan Bodger. New York: Routledge, 1994.

Tsurumi, E. Patricia. "Female Textile Workers and the Failure of Early Trade Unionism in Japan." *History Workshop* 18 (Fall 1984): 3–27.

Tsurumi, Shunsuke. *An Intellectual History of Wartime Japan.* London: KPI, distributed by Routledge & Kegan Paul, 1986.

Tsutsui, William M. *Manufacturing Ideology: Scientific Management in Twentieth-Century Japan.* Princeton, NJ: Princeton University Press, 1998.

Vlastos, Stephen, ed. *Mirror of Modernity: Invented Traditions of Modern Japan.* Berkeley: University of California Press, 1998.

White, Hayden. *The Content of the Form: Narrative Discourse and Historical Representation.* Baltimore: Johns Hopkins University Press, 1987.

———. *Metahistory: The Historical Imagination in Nineteenth-Century Europe.* Baltimore: Johns Hopkins University Press, 1973.

Williams, Linda. *Hard Core: Power, Pleasure, and the "Frenzy of the Visible."* Berkeley: University of California Press, 1989.

Williams, Raymond. *The Politics of Modernism.* London: Verso, 1989.

Willis, Ellen. "Feminism, Moralism, and Pornography." In *Powers of Desire: The Politics of Sexuality,* edited by Ann Snitow, Christine Stansell, and Sharon Thompson. New York: Monthly Review Press, 1983.

Wright, Peter. *Cockney Dialect and Slang.* London: Batsford, 1981.

Yoshimi, Yoshiaki. *Comfort Women: Sexual Slavery in the Japanese Military during World War II.* Translated by Suzanne O'Brien. New York: Columbia University Press, 2000.

Young, Louise. *Japan's Total Empire: Manchuria and the Culture of Imperialism.* Berkeley: University of California Press, 1998.

Young, Robert. *White Mythologies: Writing History and the West.* New York: Routledge, 1990.

Index

Compositor:	Binghamton Valley Composition, LLC
Indexer:	Kevin Millham
Text:	10/13 Aldus
Display:	Aldus